Tulsian's Company and Compensation Laws

A Self-Study Textbook

For B.Com.

(Delhi University)

Dr. P. C. TULSIAN
M.Com.(Delhi), Ph.D., F.C.A., P.G.D.F.M
Chartered Accountant

Head
Department of Commerce,
Ramjas College,
University of Delhi

S. CHAND & COMPANY LTD.
(AN ISO 9001 : 2000 COMPANY)
RAM NAGAR, NEW DELHI – 110055

S. CHAND & COMPANY LTD.
(An ISO 9001 : 2000 Company)
Head Office : 7361, RAM NAGAR, NEW DELHI - 110 055
Phones : 23672080-81-82, 9899107446, 9911310888;
Fax : 91-11-23677446
Shop at: **schandgroup.com;** E-mail: **schand@vsnl.com**

Branches :

- 1st Floor, Heritage, Near Gujarat Vidhyapeeth, Ashram Road, **Ahmedabad**-380 014. Ph. 27541965, 27542369, ahmedabad@schandgroup.com
- No. 6, Ahuja Chambers, 1st Cross, Kumara Krupa Road, **Bangalore**-560 001. Ph : 22268048, 22354008, bangalore@schandgroup.com
- 238-A M.P. Nagar, Zone 1, **Bhopal** - 462 011. Ph : 4274723. bhopal@schandgroup.com
- 152, Anna Salai, **Chennai**-600 002. Ph : 28460026, chennai@schandgroup.com
- S.C.O. 2419-20, First Floor, Sector- 22-C (Near Aroma Hotel), **Chandigarh**-160022, Ph-2725443, 2725446, chandigarh@schandgroup.com
- 1st Floor, Bhartia Tower, Badambadi, **Cuttack**-753 009, Ph-2332580; 2332581, cuttack@schandgroup.com
- 1st Floor, 52-A, Rajpur Road, **Dehradun**-248 001. Ph : 2740889, 2740861, dehradun@schandgroup.com
- Pan Bazar, **Guwahati**-781 001. Ph : 2514155, guwahati@schandgroup.com
- Sultan Bazar, **Hyderabad**-500 195. Ph : 24651135, 24744815, hyderabad@schandgroup.com
- Mai Hiran Gate, **Jalandhar** - 144008 . Ph. 2401630, 5000630, jalandhar@schandgroup.com
- A-14 Janta Store Shopping Complex, University Marg, Bapu Nagar, **Jaipur** - 302 015, **Phone : 2719126**, jaipur@schandgroup.com
- 613-7, M.G. Road, Ernakulam, **Kochi**-682 035. Ph : 2381740, cochin@schandgroup.com
- 285/J, Bipin Bihari Ganguli Street, **Kolkata**-700 012. Ph : 22367459, 22373914, kolkata@schandgroup.com
- Mahabeer Market, 25 Gwynne Road, Aminabad, **Lucknow**-226 018. Ph : 2626801, 2284815, lucknow@schandgroup.com
- Blackie House, 103/5, Walchand Hirachand Marg , Opp. G.P.O., **Mumbai**-400 001. Ph : 22690881, 22610885, mumbai@schandgroup.com
- Karnal Bag, Model Mill Chowk, Umrer Road, **Nagpur**-440 032 Ph : 2723901, 2777666 nagpur@schandgroup.com
- 104, Citicentre Ashok, Govind Mitra Road, **Patna**-800 004. Ph : 2300489, 2302100, patna@schandgroup.com

First Edition 2008

ISBN : 81-219-2947-4
Code : 07 457

PRINTED IN INDIA

By Rajendra Ravindra Printers (Pvt.) Ltd., 7361, Ram Nagar, New Delhi-110 055 and published by S. Chand & Company Ltd., 7361, Ram Nagar, New Delhi-110 055.

Preface

This book adopts a fresh and novel approach to the study of Company and Compensation Laws for the students of B.Com (Programme) University of Delhi.

It has been written in a "Teach Yourself Style", strictly following a student friendly approach and is essential meant to serve as a tutor at home.

Pedagogical Features

- **Simple Language:** The Text is presented in the simplest language, meant to serve beginners".
- **Heading for each Paragraph:** Each paragraph has been arranged under a suitable heading for easy retention of concepts.
- **Tabular Form:** Wherever possible the text matter relating to a particular topic/sub-topic has been presented in a Tabular Form.
- **Eye-catching Screens:** All important equations, formulae, figures and practical steps have been presented in screen format to catch the eye.
- **Uniform Format of Chapter:** Each chapter has been uniformly organised under five headings, viz., Text supported by suitable Illustrations, Very Short Answer Type Questions, Short Answer Type Questions, Long Answer Type Questions and Practical Problems

Distinctive Features

- **50 Exhibits:** To acquaint students with various provisions
- **200 Very Short Answer Type Questions:** To enable students to test their understanding of the subject.
- **150 Short Answer Type Questions**:
- **100 Long Answer Type Questions:**
- **Appendix–I: Important Distinctions**
- **Appendix–II: Important Short Notes**
- **Appendix–III: Special Revisional Test Paper**

I am confident that all these features would make this book an invaluable asset to students learning *Company and Compensation Laws.*

I wish to express my Sincere thanks to several individuals who have been a source of inspiration and support both personally and professionally including Shri R. P. Tulsian, Shri S.C. Gupta, Shri Naresh Gupta, Shri N.K. Kakkar, Shri N.D.Vohra, Shri S.C. Garg, Shri N.K. Aggarwal, Shri K.B. Gupta, Shri M.M. Goyal, Shri Sandeep Aggarwal, Mrs. Renu Gupta, Mrs. Sushma Aggarwal, Mrs. Himanshu Garg, Mrs. Poonam, Mrs. Indu Jain, Shri P.V. Khatri, Mrs. Madhu Gupta, Mrs. Kusum Gupta, Shri S.K. Grover, Shri V.K.. Jain, Shri Harpal Singh, Shri Pradeep Aggarwal, Shri J.M. Gupta, Shri N.K. Puri, Shri Y.P. Tyagi, Shri R.D. Arora, Shri S.L. Gupta, Shri S.K. Gupta, Shri Rajeev Goel, Dr. G.C. Kasturi, Dr. P.P. Joshi, Dr. Venkat Kumar, Dr. Ravinder Gupta.

I must conclude that this book would never have been written without the support, encouragement and prodding of our family members. Many thanks to all of them.

Any suggestion for improvement will be gratefully acknowledged and appreciated.

Dr. P.C. TULSIAN

SYLLABUS

COMPANY AND COMPENSATION LAWS

[B.Com. — Part II — Paper VIII]

Duration : 3 hrs. **Max. Marks: 75**

Lectures : 75

Objective: To make the students familiar with company and compensation laws.

Unit	*Topics*	*Relevant Chapter of the Book*
I	**(20 Lectures)** Company: Definition, Characteristics, Lifting of Corporate Veil. Types of Companies. Formation of a Company: Promoters, Pre-incorporation Contracts, Provisional Contracts, Memorandum of Association, Articles of Association.	**1, 2, 3, 4, 5**
II	**(10 Lectures)** Prospectus: Contents, Abridged Prospectus, Red-herring Prospectus, Shelf Prospectus, Statement in lieu of Prospectus. Misrepresentation of Prospectus, Share Capital: Issue and allotment of shares, SEBI guidelines on allotment, Issue of Shares at premium and at discount, buy back of shares, rights issue. Book Building, Concept of Bonus Shares, Share Certificate, Demat System.	**6, 7, 8, 9**
III	**(10 Lectures)** Calls on shares, Forfeiture and Surrender of Shares, Transfer & Transmission of shares, Provisions relating to payment of dividend, Investor's Education and Protection Fund.	**10**
IV	**(15 Lectures)** Directors: appointment, share qualification and legal position.	**11**
	Meetings: Meeting of Board of Directors, Meeting of Shareholders, Requisites of a valid meeting: Notice, Agenda, Quorum, Chairman, Resolution and Minutes. Proxy.	**12**
	Compulsory Winding up (Sec. 433).	**13**
	Emerging Issues in Company Law.	**14, 15**

Unit	*Topics*	*Relevant Chapter of the Book*
V	**(10 Lectures)** **Employees' State Insurance Act, 1948** Definitions: Personal Injury, Factory, Manufacturing Process, Wages, Partial and Permanent Disablement. ESI Corporation, Standing Committee and Medical Benefit Council Contributions, Adjudication of Dispute and Claims, Benefits	**16**
VI	**(10 Lectures)** **Workmen's Compensation Act, 1923** Definitions: Dependent, Employer, Partial and Total Disablement, Workmen, Injury, Accident, Payment of Compensation, Contracting, Commissioner	**17**

Contents

Emerging Issues in Company Law

Section B
Compensation Laws

APPENDICES

SECTION A

The Companies Act, 1956

1. Definition and Nature of Company
2. Types of Companies
3. Formation of a Company
4. Memorandum of Association
5. Articles of Association
6. Prospectus
7. Shares
8. Share Capital
9. Membership
10. Dividend, Interest and Bonus Shares
11. Directors
12. Meetings and Procedures
13. Winding Up
14. Producer Companies
15. Corporate Governance

CHAPTER 1

Definition and Nature of Company

1.0 MEANING OF COMPANY

The company is one of the form of organisation. It has its distinctive characteristics and advantages which make it suitable for different purposes.

1.1 Literary Meaning

The term 'Company' implies an association of a number of persons formed for some common object or objects.

1.2 Legal Meaning

According to Section 3(1)(i) of The Companies Act, 1956, "Company means a company formed and registered under this Act or an existing company. An existing Company means a company formed and registered under any of the previous Companies laws."

The above definition is not exhaustive because it does not reveal the characteristics of the company.

Let us analyse some other definitions given in various judicial decisions to ascertain the characteristics of the company.

1.3 Meaning as per Judicial Pronouncements

1. According to Lord Justice Lindley *"By a company is meant an association of many persons who contribute money or money's worth to a common stock and employ it in some trade or business and who share the profit and loss (as the case may be) arising therefrom. The common stock so contributed is denoted in money and is the capital of the company. The persons who contribute it, or to who it belongs, are called members. The proportion of capital to which each member is entitled is his share. Shares are always transferable although the right to transfer them is often more or less restricted."*

2. According to Chief Justice Marshall *"A company is person, artificial, invisible, intangible and existing only in the eyes of law. Being a mere creature of law, it possesses only those properties which the charter of its creation confers upon it, either expressly or as incidental to its very existence."*

3. According to Lord Haney *"A company is an incorporated association which is an artifical person created by law, having a separate entity, with a perpetual succession and a common seal."*

From the above definitions, it is clear that a company has a corporate and legal personality. It is an artificial person and exists only in the eyes of law. It has an independent legal entity, a common seal and perpetual succession.

2.0 MEANING OF CORPORATION SOLE, CORPORATION AGGREGATE AND BODY CORPORATE

2.1 Meaning of Corporation Sole

Corporation Sole refers to a single person constituted as a Corporation in respect of some function or office enjoying perpetual succession and separate legal entity. *For example*, The President of India, Governor of a State, The Prime Minister of India,

2.2 Meaning of Corporation Aggregate

Corporation Aggregate refers to an association of persons constituted as a corporation enjoying perpetual succession and separate legal entity.
It includes:

(a) companies incorporated under The Companies Act, 1956

(b) companies incorporated under The Special Act of Parliament

(c) companies incorporated Outside India

2.5 Body Corporate

(a) Body Corporate refers to an association of persons which has:

(i) been incorporated under any law

(ii) a separate legal entity

(iii) perpetual succession, and

(iv) a common seal.

(b) The term 'Body Corporate' includes:

(i) companies incorporated under The Companies Act, 1956

(ii) companies incorporated under The Special Act of Parliament

(iii) companies incorporated Outside India

(iv) Public Financial Institutions u/s 4A [*for example*, LIC, UTI, RBI, ICICI, IDBI]

(c) The term 'Body Corporate' does not include:

(i) a Corporation Sole

(ii) a Co-operative Society registered under any law relating to Co-operative Societies.

(iii) Any other body corporate (not being a company as defined in this Act) which the Central Government may specify in this behalf.

(iv) a Society registered under the Societies Registration Act 1860 [*Board of Trustees Ayurvedic and Unani Tibbia College Delhi vs State of Delhi*]

Thus, the term body corporate is much wider in concept than the word 'company'.

3.0 CHARACTERISTICS OF A COMPANY

On analysing the aforesaid definitions the following characteristics of a company are revealed:

1. An Artificial Person Created by Law A company is called an artifical person because it does not take birth like a natural person but comes into existence through law. Being the creation of law, the company possesses only those properties which are conferred upon it by its charter (i.e., Memorandum of Association). Within the limits of powers conferred by its charter, it can do all acts as a natural person can do.

Like a natural person—

(a) The company can enter into contracts.
(b) The company can enforce the contractual rights against others.
(c) The company can sue in its own name.
(d) The company can be sued in its own name.
(e) The company can own and hold property in its own name.
(f) The company has nationality. The registration of a company in a country determines the nationality of that company to that country.

Unlike a natural person—

(a) The company has no physical shape or form.
(b) The company can not shake by hand.
(c) The company can not marry.
(d) The company can not smile or weep.
(e) The company can not take oath.
(f) The company can not commit a crime like murder.
(g) The company has no citizenship because a citizen of a country is a personal right peculiar to human beings only.

2. Separate Legal Entity The case of *Salomon* v. *Saloman & Co. Ltd.* (1897) (AC) (22) clearly established the concept of corporate personality as distinct and different from that of its members individually and collectively (known as the Doctrine of Corporate veil).

In case of *Saloman* v. *Salomon and Company Ltd.* Mr. Saloman was running a shoe business in England. He formed a company known as 'Saloman and Co. Ltd.' It consisted of Saloman himself, his wife, his four sons and a daughter. The shoes business of Mr. Saloman was sold to the company for £30,000. Mr. Saloman received from the company purchase price in the form of £20,000 fully paid shares of £1 each and £10,000 in debentures which carried a floating charge over the assets of the company. One share of £1 each was subscribed for in cash by each member of Saloman's family. Saloman was the managing director of the company. During the course of business, the company became liable for some unsecrued loan. The company ran into financial difficulties after some time and went into liquidation within a year. On winding up, the assets realised £6,000. The company owed £10,000 to Mr. Saloman and £7,000 to unsecured creditors. Thus, after paying off the debenture- holder. (Mr. Saloman), nothing was left for unsecured creditors. The creditors claimed priority over the debentures contending that Mr. Saloman and Saloman and Co. Ltd. were one and the same person, the company was only a facade to defraud the innocent creditors. Mr. Saloman should not therefore, be treated as a secured creditor. *The House of Lords held* that the company had been validly constituted and it had an independent existence distinct from its members. Therefore, Mr. Saloman was entitled to be paid his dues first as a secured creditor. It was observed that the business belonged to the company and not to Mr. Saloman. The company and Mr. Saloman enjoyed separate legal entities. The fact that the members were from one single family had no bearing upon the validity of the company.

The legal status of a company has been aptly described by the Supreme Court of India in *Tata Engineering & Locomotive Co. Ltd.* v. *State of Bihar*, as follows:

"The corporation in law is equal to natural person and has a legal entity of its own. The entity of the corporation is entirely separate from that of its shareholder; it bears its own name and has seal of its own; its assets are separate and distinct from those of its members; it can sue and be sued exclusively for its own purpose".

Effects As a consequence of separate legal entity—

(a) The company may enter into contracts with its members and *vice versa.* Thus, a member can be both a debtor and creditor of the company at the same time.
(b) Its members can not be held liable for the acts of the company even if he holds virtually the entire share capital.
(c) Its members cannot claim ownership right in company's assets.
(d) Its members can not have any insurable interest in the company's properties.
(e) Its creditors' remedy for the recovery of their debts lie only against the company and not against its members or directors.

3. Perpetual Succession The term '*perpetual succession*' means the continued existence. The death, insolvency or unsoundness of mind of its members or transfer of shares by its members does not in any way affect the existence of the company. Members may come and members may go but the company goes on forever. The company can be compared with flowing river where water (members) keeps on changing continuously, still the identity of the river (company) remains the same. The company continues to exist even if all its human members die. According to Gower, 'even a hydrogen bomb cannot destory a company'. Since it is created by law, it can be brought to an end by the process of law.

Thus, a company still continue to exist for an indefinite period till it is wound up in accordance with the provisions of the Companies Act.

4. Common Seal The term '*Common Seal*' means the official signature of the company. Since the company being an artificial person can not sign its name on a document, every company is required to have its common seal with its name engraved on the same. This seal acts as the official signature of the company. Any document bearing the common seal of the company and duly witnessed by at least two directors will be binding on the company.

5. Limited Liability This specific characteristics of '*Limited Liability*' is possessed by limited companies and not by unlimited companies. In case of a *company limited by shares,* the liability of a member is limited upto the amount remaining unpaid (if any) on the shares held by a member. In case of *a company limited by guarantee,* the liability of a member is limited upto the amount guaranteed by a member.

6. Free Transferability of Shares This specific characteristic of 'Free Transferability of Shares' is possessed by public companies and not by private companies.

The shares of a public company are freely transferable. A shareholder can transfer his shares to any person without the consent of other members. Under the articles of association, even a public limited company can put certain restrictions on the transfer of shares but it cannot altogether stop it. A shareholder of public company possessing fully paid up shares is at liberty to transfer his shares to anyone he likes in accordance with the manner provided for in the articles of association of the company.

It may be noted that although restriction on the right to transfer may be placed in certain cases (e.g. in case of partly paid up shares) but absolute right of members to transfer shares cannot be restricted and any provision in the Articles to that affect shall be void.

Section 3(1)(iii) requires a private company to put restriction on transferability of its shares.

4.0 LIFTING THE CORPORATE VEIL

4.1 Meaning of Lifting the Corporate Veil

Lifting the corporate veil means 'disregarding the corporate entity and paying regard to the individual members behind the legal facade'.

When the company starts using the corporate veil for improper conduct, or to protect fraud or to justify wrongs, the law disregards the corporate veil and looks at the persons behind and treat the company and its members as same persons.

4.2 Circumstances when the Corporate Veil can be Pierced/Lifted

The circumstances and cases in which the corporate veil can be lifted may broadly be classified as follows:

Let us discuss the aforesaid cases one by one as follows:

Circumstances when Corporate Veil can be Lifted

Under Express Statutory Provisions	Under Judicial Interpretations
(a) When the no. of members falls below the statutory minimum [Section 45]	(a) For determination of the character of the company
(b) Non-disclosure of Representative capacity [Section 147]	(b) For prevention of fraud or improper conduct
(c) To examine the relationship of holding and subsidiary [Section 212]	(c) For the protection of revenue
(d) To investigate into the affairs of related companies [Section. 239]	(d) When company is formed to act as an agent of its members
(e) To investigate ownership of a company [Section 247]	(e) When company is formed to avoid the welfare laws
(f) When business is carried on to defraud the creditors [Section 542]	

4.3 Cases under Express Statutory Provisions

(a) When the Number of Members Falls Below Statutory Minimum [Section 45]

According to Section 45 of the Act if at any time the number of members of a company is reduced below the statutory requirement and the company carries on business for more than six months while the number is so reduced, every person who was member of the company during the time when it carried on business after those six months and who was aware of this fact, shall be severally liable for all debts of the company contracted during that time. It should be noted that the personal liability of the members commences only after six months of carrying on business with reduced members and this liability is only for the debts contracted after those six months.

Although the company continues to enjoy its distinct personality but loses the important feature of limited liability of the members of the company. Such a situation entitles the creditors to disregard the separate entity of the company, and the creditors can take action against the members directly.

(b) Misrepresentation in Prospectus [Sections 62 and 63]

(c) Failure to Return Application Money [Section 69 and SEBI Guidelines]

(d) Non-disclosure of Representative Capacity [Section 147(4)]

As a rule when an officer of a company or any person on its behalf signs or authorizes to be signed, on behalf of the company, any bill of exchange, hundi, promissory note, endorsement, cheque or order for money or goods without disclosing the name of the company on whose behalf he is acting. Such officer or person shall be personally liable for the amount due if the company refuses to pay it. For example, a bill of exchange drawn upon a company is accepted by a director in his personal capacity i.e., without disclosing that he is accepting the bill on behalf of the company, such a director shall be personally liable for the bill.

(e) To examine the Relationship of Holding and Subsidiary Company [Section 212]

When one company controls the composition of the board of directors of another company or holds majority of its shares, the former is called the holding company and the latter as subsidiary company. In general, a subsidiary company is altogether treated as a separate entity and the holding company is not liable for its acts. But, under Section 212 of the Act, every holding company is required to disclose to its shareholders the accounts of its subsidiaries. It requires that the copies of balance sheet, profit and loss account, directors' report and auditor's report of each subsidiary company be attached to the balance sheet of the holding company. Thus, companies under the same group are treated as one entity disregarding the rule that each subsidiary company has a separate legal entity.

(f) To Investigate into Affairs of Related Companies [Section 239(7)]

According to Section 239(7) of the Act, if an inspector is appointed by the Central Government to investigate the affairs of a company, he shall also have the power to investigate into the affairs of related (subsidiary) companies in the same management. The power to do so may thus lift the corporate veil.

(g) To Investigate Ownership of a Company [Section 247]

When the Central Government feels it necessary to know about the membership of any company and also some other matters relating to the company with the object of determining true persons who are (or have been) financially interested in the success or failure of the company or who are (or have been) able to control the policy of the company, may appoint one or more inspectors to investigate and report on these matters. This will be done by lifting the corporate veil so as to find out the true persons controlling it.

(h) When Business is Carried on to Defraud the Creditors [Section 542]

According to Section 542 of the Act, if in the course of the winding up of a company, it appears that any business of the company has been carried on with the intention to defraud its creditors or any other persons, in such a case the persons who were knowingly parties to such acts may be held personally liable for any debts and other liabilities of the company. In such a situation, the court may disregard the legal entity of a company and make the fraudulent persons personally liable for the debts of the company.

4.4 Cases under Judicial Interpretations

Besides the above-mentioned circumstances, the courts have allowed the lifting of corporate veil for proper administration of taxation laws, wealth tax law, etc. and also in some other circumstances. Let us now study some of the cases where the corporate veil was lifted.

(a) For Determination of the Character of the Company

Sometimes, particularly during the war between countries, it becomes necessary to ascertain the character of certain companies. At such times the courts are justified in lifting the corporate veil of a company which is controlled by alien enemy. In this way a company registered in India may be declared alien enemy if it is found that the persons controlling such a company are citizens of an enemy country. For example in case of *Daimler Co. Ltd.* v. *Continental Tyre and Rubber Co. Ltd.*, [(1916) 2 A.C. 207]. A company with the name Continental Tyre and Rubber Co. Ltd. was registered in England. The object of this company was to sell tyres in United Kingdom, which were manufactured in Germany by a German company. Majority of the shares of this company were held by Germans. Besides this, all the directors of the company were German residents. When the First World War broke out, the company filed a suit to recover a trade debt. The court came to the conclusion that the company was an enemy company because the effective control of the company was in the hands of Germans who were alien enemy. Hence, the claim of the company was disallowed on the ground that it was against public policy to allow alien enemies to trade by using the corporate veil.

Similarly in case of *Connors Bros.* v. *Connors,* [(1940) 4 All E.R. 197] the principle was applied against the managing director who made use of his position contrary to public policy. In this case the House of Lord determined the character of the company as "enemy" company, since the persons who were *de facto* in control of its affairs, were residents of Germany, which was at war with England. The alien company was not allowed to proceed with the action, as that would have meant giving money to the enemy, which was considered as monstrous and against "public policy".

(b) For the prevention of fraud or improper conduct

The courts will allow lifting of the corporate veil if the purpose of the company is to avoid legal obligations or to defraud the creditors. In the case of *Gilford Motor Co. Ltd.* v. *Horne* [(1933) 1 Ch. 435], Horne was appointed as a managing director of Gilford Motor Co. with the condition that he would not solicit or entice away the customers of the company, so long as he was in the employment of the company and afterwards. After leaving the company, Horne formed another company which was to carry on the same business. This new company of Horne solicited the customers of Gilford Motor Co. Ltd. In a suit filed by Gilford Motor Co. Ltd. against Horne to restrain him from soliciting the business, the court came to the conclusion that Horne had created the company for his own benefit and to solicit the customers of his employer's company. The court issued an injunction against Horne and his new company and held that the new company was a mere cloak for the purpose of enabling the defendant to commit a breach of his contract that he would not solicit the business of his employer's company.

Similarly, in case of *Jones* v. *Lipman*, (1962), I.W.L.R. 832, *A* agreed to sell certain land to *B*. Pending completion of formalities of the said deal, *A* sold and transferred the land to a company which he had incorporated with a nominal capital of $100 and of which he and a clerk were the only shareholders and directors. This was done in order to escape a decree for specific performance in a suit brought by *B*. The court held that the company was the creature of A and a mask to avoid recognition and that in the eyes of equity A must complete the contract, since he had the full control of the limited company in which the property was vested, and was in a position to cause the contract in question to be completed.

(c) For the Protection of Revenue

The court will allow lifting of corporate veil if it is of the opinion that the company has been formed for evading the tax or to circumvent tax obligations. If such is the case, the court will disregard the corporate entity and would instead hold individual members liable to fulfil the revenue obligations. In case of *Re Sir Dinshaw Manekjee Petit,* AIR 1927 Bombay 371, the assessee, Sir Dinshaw who was a very rich man, was earning huge dividend and interest income. He formed four private companies and entered into an agreement with each company to hold a block of investment as his agent. Under the arrangement the income received was credited in company's account and the company handed the amount back to him as a loan (which was never repaid). In this way he divided his income in four parts in order to reduce his tax liability. The court ignored the corporate facade of these companies and held that the company was nothing more than the assessee himself. Sir Dinshaw was held the owner of total income and liable to pay tax.

(d) Where Company is Formed to Act as an Agent of its Members

Where a company is regarded as an agent or trustee of its members or of another company, for the acts done by the company, it will be the members who would be responsible and not the company. *Re F.G. Films Ltd.*, case, an American company financed and produced a film 'Mansoon' in India. But, technically, the film was made in the name of a company incorporated in England. This British company had only a capital of $100 divided into 100 shares of $1 each, of this, 90 shares were held by President of the American company. The Board of trade declined to register the film as a British film. The view of the Board of Trade was upheld by the court. The court held that the British company acted only as an agent of the American company which was the true maker of the film.

(e) When a Company is Formed to Avoid Welfare Laws

The courts have disregarded the separate legal personality of the company when the company's independent status was being used as a device to reduce the amount payable by the company to defect the provisions of welfare laws, such as payment of bonus to its workmen. In the case of *Workmen Employed in Associated Rubber Industries Ltd., Bhavnagar* v. *The Associated Rubber Industries Ltd., Bhavnagar and Others*, a new company was formed with no assets of its own except those transferred to it by the principal company. The new company had no business of its own, it received dividend on shares transferred to it by the principal company. Thus, the principal company was able to reduce its gross profits and consequently the amount of bonus payable to workman was also reduced. The Supreme Court rejected the independent status of the new company and directed that the amounts paid to the new company as dividend shall also be taken into account while determining the gross profits of the principal company.

The court held that "in every case where ingenuity is expected to avoid taking and welfare legislations, the court will go behind the smoke-screen and discover the true state of affairs.

Thus, in all circumstances, 'honest enterprises by means of companies are allowed but the public are protected against kiting and humbuggary.

5.0 DISTINCTION BETWEEN A PARTNERSHIP AND A COMPANY

A partnership differs from a company in the following respects:

Basis of Distinction	*Partnership*	*Company*
1. ***Legal entity***	A firm doesn't enjoy separate legal existence. Partners are collectively termed as a firm and individually as partners.	It has a separate legal existence. A company is separate from the members.

(Contd.)

(*Contd.*)

2. ***Liability***	The liability of partners is unlimited.	Liability of its members is limited to the extent of unpaid amount on shares held by them.
3. ***Tenure/Existence***	It does not enjoy a long lease of life. Death, sickness, retirement of partners may affect its existence so as to dissolve it. Dissolution may taken place on flimsy grounds.	It enjoys perpetual existence. Even an atom bomb cannot destroy a company unless it is wound up under the due process of law. Winding up may take years.
4. ***Number of members***	Minimum number of partners is two. Maximum may be ten (in case of banking business) or twenty (in case of non-banking business).	A public company must have a minimum 7 members to start with. However, there is no limit on the maximum number of members of a company.
5. ***Transfer of interest***	A partner cannot transfer his share without the consent of other partners.	A member of a public company may transfer his shares as and when he likes. There is no restriction on transfer of shares.
6. ***Agency***	Each partner represents the other partners so as to bind and be bound to others.	There is no agency relation-ship among members of a company as they do not bind each other with their actions.
7. ***Distribution of profit***	Profits are distributable among partners as per the partnership deed.	There is no such compulsion that profits must be distributed. Only when the dividends are declared that the members get a share of profits.
8. ***Management***	The entire management lies with all the partners.	Members cannot participate in management unless appointed as directors. However, members may attempt and vote at meetings while making the appointment of Directors, Auditors, etc.
9. ***Property***	Property of the firm is the joint property of all its partners.	Property of the company is not the property of its members as the company and members have separate legal existence.
10. ***Remedy of creditors***	The creditors of a firm can proceed against the partners jointly and severally.	The creditors of a company can proceed only against the company and not against its members.
11. ***Restriction on authority***	Restriction on a partner's authority contained in partnership contracted do not bind outsiders.	Restriction on authority of directors contained in Articles bind the outsiders because they are deemed to have the knowledge of Articles.
12. ***Compulsory audit***	Audit of a firm is not compulsory under The Indian Partnership Act.	Audit of a company is compulsory under The Companies Act.
13. ***Dissolution***	Firm can be dissolved at any time by mutual agreement.	A company, being the creature of law, can only be dissolved by law.

EXERCISES

VERY SHORT ANSWER TYPE QUESTIONS

1. Define Company.
2. Define Corporation Sole.
3. Define Corporation Aggregate.
4. Define Body Corporate.
5. What is a Corporate Veil?
6. What is meant by 'Perpetual Succession'?
7. What is Common Seal?
8. What is meant by 'Limited Liability'?
9. What is meant by 'Free transferability of shares'?

SHORT ANSWER TYPE QUESTIONS

1. Why is a company called an 'Artificial person'?
2. What are the acts which a company can do like a natural person?
3. What are the acts which a company cannot do like a natural person?
4. The term 'Body Corporate' is much wider concept than the term 'Company'. Explain.
5. Distinguish between the following:
   (a) Body Corporate and Company
   (b) Corporation Sole and Corporation Aggregate
   (c) Partnership and Company

LONG ANSWER TYPE QUESTIONS

1. Define a company. Explain its characteristics.
2. "A company is an artificial person created by law with a perpetual succession and a common seal." Explain.
3. "A company is a legal entity quite distinct from its members." Explain.
4. What do you understand by the concept of corporate personality? Under what circumstances is a lifting of corporate veil possible?
5. Distinguish between the partnership and a limited company.
6. Comment on the following:
   (a) "Member of a limited company may nevertheless have unlimited liability".
   (b) A limited liability company can become a partner in a firm.
7. Write short notes on the following:
   (a) Illegal Association
   (b) Common Seal
   (c) Perpetual Succession
   (d) One man company
   (e) Lifting of corperate veil

PRATICAL PROBLEMS

1. An English company was formed for selling in England tyres produced by a German company in Germany. The bulk of English company's shares were held by the Germen company. The overwhelming majority of the shareholders and all the directors were Germen nationals residing in Germany. The English company filed a suit during the World War I to recover a trade

debt. Could the company be allowed to proceed with the action? [No]

2. H was appointed the managing director of A&Co. on the term that he must not, at any time during the tenure of his office as such, or afterwards, entice away the customers of A&Co. Subsequent to the cessation of H's employment under an agreement he set up a business in the name of H&Co. which solicited the customers of A&Co. Evidence showed that H&Co. was formed to enable H to commit a breach of his covenant against solicitation. Could H&Co. and H be restrained from doing so? [Yes]
3. *X*, having huge dividend and interest income, formed four private companies. He agreed with each of such companies to hold a block of investment as an agent for the company. The income received was credited to the accounts of the company but the company gave it back to *X* as a pretended loan. In this way, *X* divided his income with a view to reduce his tax-burden. In a legal proceeding against *X*, the court ignored the company and concerned itself directly with *X*. Could the court do so? [Yes]
4. A Hindu undivided family consisting of 11 persons carries on banking with a view to acquiring profit for itself or its members without itself being registered under the Banking Regulation Act, 1949 (a) Will it be a legal association? (b) Will your answer be the same, if two undivided families would have carried on the said business? [(a) Yes (b) No]
5. At the inception the association was not registrable under the Act as its membership number did not exceed the statutory limit. But long thereafter the number of its members exceeded that statutory limit. Could the association continue with the business for gain without registration? [No]

CHAPTER 2

Types of Companies

1.0 TYPES OF COMPANIES

The companies can be classified under the three categories as follows:

1. On the basis of incorporation
2. On the basis of liability
3. On the basis of control

The various types of companies on the aforesaid basis are shown below:

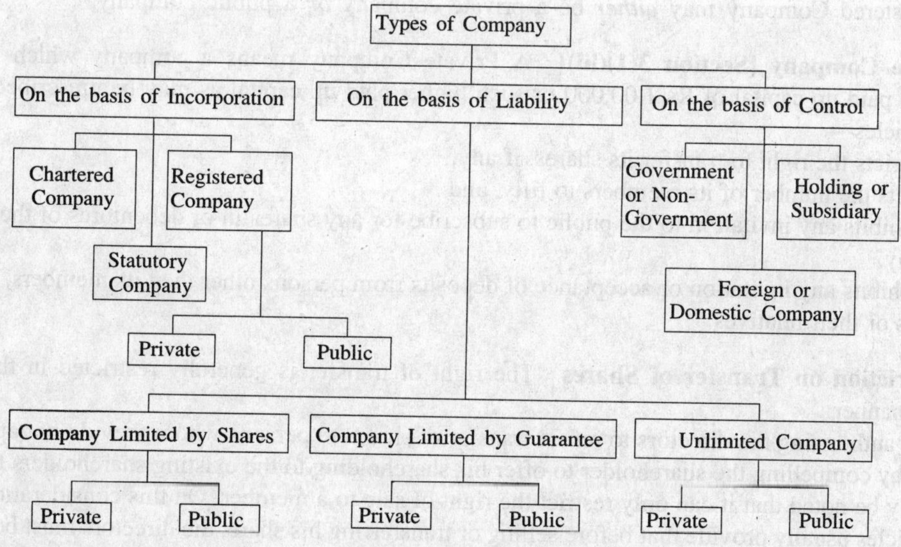

Let us discuss the various types of companies one by one.

2.0 COMPANIES ON THE BASIS OF INCORPORATION

On the basis of incorporation, companies may be divided into the following three categories:

2.1 Chartered company A company incorporated under a special charter granted by the King or Queen of England is called '**Chartered Company**'. A chartered company is regulated by its charter and the Companies Act does not apply to it. The charter also prescribes the nature of business and the powers of the company. The familiar examples of chartered company are the *East India Company* and the *Bank of England*. This type of company cannot now be formed in India.

2.2 Statutory company A statutory company is one which is created by a Special Act of Parliament or a State Legislature. Such companies are usually formed for achieving a purpose related with public utilities. The nature and powers of such companies are laid down in the Special Act under which they are created. However, the provisions of the Companies Act are also applicable to them insofar as they are consistent with the provisions of the Special Act. Such companies need not have a Memorandum of Association. A statutory company has also a separate legal entity and it is not required to use the word 'limited' after its name. The audit of such companies is conducted under the control and supervision of the Auditor General of India and the annual report of working is required to be placed before the Parliament or State legislature, as the case may be. Familiar examples of such companies are Reserve Bank of India, Unit Trust of India. The Life Insurance Corporation of India, State Trading Corporation, The Food Corporation of India, State Bank of India, etc.

2.3 Registered or Incorporated Company A registered company is one which is registered in accordance with the provisions of the Companies Act of 1956 and also includes the existing companies. By existing company we mean a company formed and registered under any of the previous laws. A registered company comes into existence only when it receives the certificate of incorporation. Registered companies are governed by the provisions of The Companies Act.

A registered Company may *either* be a private company *or* a public company.

I. Private Company [Section 3(1)(iii)] A Private Company means a company which has a minimum paid up capital of Rs 1,00,000 or such higher paid up capital as may be prescribed, and by its articles—

(a) restricts the right to transfer its shares, if any,
(b) limits the number of its members to fifty, and
(c) prohibits any invitation to the public to subscribe for any shares in or debentures of the company.
(d) prohibits any invitation or acceptance of deposits from persons other then its members, directors or their relatives.

(a) Restriction on Transfer of Shares The right of transfer is generally restricted in the following manner:

(i) By authorising the directors to refuse transfer of shares to persons whom they do not approve or by compelling the shareholder to offer his shareholding to the existing shareholders first. It may be noted that it can only restrict the right of sale to a member. On this consideration, the articles usually provide that before selling or transferring his share, the directors must be communicated in writing of such intention of the shareholder.
(ii) By specifying the method for calculating the price at which the shares may be sold by one member to another. Generally, it is left to be determined either by the auditor of the company or by the company at a general meeting.
(iii) By providing that the shareholders who are employees of the company shall offeer the shares to specified persons or class of persons when they leave the company's service.

(b) Limitation of Membership The articles must contain a provision whereby the company limits the number of its members to 50.

Note: For the purposes of limit of 50, present employees who are members and ex-employees who were members while in that employment and have continued to be members after the employment ceased, are excluded and the joint shareholders are counted as a single member.

(c) Prohibition on Making an Invitation to Public The articles must prohibit any invitation to the public to subscribe for any of its shares or debentures. Such a prohibition is necessary for the substance of the private character of the company. One should note that under Section 67, an offer or invitation to a section of the public selected as members of the company is an offer or invitation to the public or debentureholders of the company. Such an invitation to the public shall be excluded from the category of 'invitation to the public' if such offer or investigation can be properly regarded in all circumstances:

(i) as not being calculated to result directly or indirectly in the shares or debentures becoming available for subscription or purchase by person other than those receiving the offer or invitation; or

(ii) otherwise as being a domestic concern of the persons making and receiving the offer or invitation.

An offer of shares by the directors to their friends by a document marked "private and confidential not for publication" is not an invitation to the public. [*Sharewell* vs. *Combined Incandescent Metals Syndicate,* [1907] 23 *T.L.R.* 482]

(d) Prohibition on Invitation/Acceptance of Deposit It is desirable and advisable as a good secretarial practice to alter the articles.

Therefore, immediately by passing Special Resolution under Section 31 to provide for restriction, in particular item (d) above. If these restrictions are not there, the company will be treated as public company.

Notes:

(i) Since the above-mentioned four restrictions must be contained in the articles of a private limited company, it is necessary for a private company to frame its own articles. However, the articles of a private company not having share capital is not required to contain the restriction regarding the transfer of shares.

(ii) A private company may be (a) a company limited by shares, or (b) a company limited by guarantee, or (c) an unlimited company.

(iii) In case a private company is a limited company, then it must add the words '*Private Limited*' at the end of its name.

(iv) If a private company does not comply with any of the restrictions contained in the articles, it ceases to enjoy some of the privileges granted to a private company.

(v) A private company must have at least 2 directors.

II. Public Company [Section 3(1)(iv)] Public company means a company which is Either

(a) not a private company and has a minimum paid-up capital of Rs 5,00,000 or such higher paid-up capital as may be prescribed; or

(b) is a private company which is subsidiary of public company.

Notes:

(i) There is no restriction on the maximum number of members. However, the maximum number of members depends upon the number of shares allotted.

(ii) A public company may be (a) a company limited by shares, or (b) a company limited by guarantee, or (c) an unlimited company.

(iii) In case a public company is a limited company, then it must add the words '*Limited*' at the end of its name.

(iv) A public company must have at least 7 members. [Section 12(1)]

(v) A public company must have at least 3 directors.

2.4 Licensed Company or Association not for Profit [Section 25]

According to Section 25, the Central Government may by license grant that an association may be registered as a company with limited liability, without using the words 'limited' or 'private limited' as part of its name. The license will be granted only in the case of 'association not for profit'. In other words, the Central Government will grant the license only if it is satisfied that:

(a) the association about to be formed as a limited company aims at the promotion of commerce, art, science, religion, charity or any other useful object;

(b) it intends to apply its profits, if any, for promoting its objects; and

(c) it prohibits the payment of dividend to its members.

Such companies may be public or private companies and may or may not have share capital.

The Central Government may impose any terms and conditions that it deems fit for the grant of the license which shall be binding on the association.

On registration (subject to the provisions of Section 25), it will have the same privileges and obligations as a limited company has. This licence is revocable by the Central Government, and on revocation the Registrar shall put 'Limited' or 'Private Limited' against the company's name in the register. But before such revocation, the Central Government must give it a written notice of its intention to revoke the licence and opportunity to be heard in the matter.

3.0 COMPANIES ON THE BASIS OF LIABILITY

On the basis of liability, an incorporated company may either be (i) a company limited by shares, or (ii) a company limited by guarantee, or (iii) an unlimited company.

3.1 Company Limited by Shares [Section 12(2)(a)] A company limited by shares is a company in which the liability of its members is limited by its Memorandum to the amount (if any) unpaid on the shares respectively held by them. The companies limited by shares may be *either* public companies *or* private companies. If a member has paid the full amount of shares, then his liability shall be nil. For example, suppose Mr. *X* buys 1000 shares of a company of the face value of Rs 10 each. In this company his liability is fixed to the tune of Rs 10,000 only. If he paid (when called by the company) Rs 6,000 to the company. He is now liable to pay the only Rs 4,000, this being the amount unpaid on his shares. When he has paid the entire amount of Rs 10,000 (which means when his shares have been fully paid up) his liability shall be nil. The liability can be enforced against the members of the company.

Thus, the two main features of a company limited by shares are as follows:

(a) The liability of its members is limited to the amount (if any) remaining unpaid on the shares held by them.

(b) Such liability can be enforced *either* during the life time of the company *or* during the winding up of the company.

3.2 Company Limited by Guarantee [Section 12(2)(b)] A company limited by guarantee is a company in which the liability of its members is limited by its Memorandum to such an amount as the members may respectively undertake to contribute to the assets of the company in the event of its being wound up. Such companies are generally formed for the promotion of commerce, art, science, religion, charity or any other useful object. The companies limited by guarantee may be *either* private companies *or* public companies. Such a company may or may not have share capital.

The main features of such company are as follows:

Types of Company Limited by Guarantee	*Liability*
(i) ***Company Limited by Guarantee not having share capital***	(a) The liability of its members is limited to the amount guaranteed by them. (b) Such liability can be enforced only after the commencement of winding up of the company and not during the life time of the company.
(ii) ***Company limited by guarantee having share capital***	(a) The liability or its members is limited to following two amounts: (i) The amount (if any) remaining unpaid on the shares held by them. (ii) The amount guaranteed by them. (b) The liability in respect of guaranteed amount can be enforced only at the time of winding up of the company and not during the life time of the company.

Note: The Articles of a company limited by guarantee must state the number of members with which the company is to be registered. [Section 27(2)]

3.3 Similarity between Company Limited by Share and Company Limited by Guarantee

Both the companies are required to state in the memorandum that the members' liabilitiy is limited.

3.4 Distinction between Company Limited by Share and Company Limited by Guarantee

Members of company limited by share may be called upon to discharge their liability either during the company's life time or during its winding up.

Members of company limited by guarantee may be called upon to discharge their liability only after the commencemant of the winding up.

3.5 Unlimited Company [Section 12(2)(c)]

An unlimited company is a company in which the liability of its members is not limited by its mermorandum. In other words, the liability of members is unlimited i.e., there is no limit on the liability of members. The members of such companies may be required to pay company's losses from their personal property. Because such companies have separate legal entity, its creditors cannot file a suit against the members directly. The creditors will have to apply to the court for the winding up of the company and then the liquidator will direct the members to contribute to the assets of the company to pay-off its liabilities.

Such company may also be *either* public company *or* private company. Such company may or may not have a share capital.

Notes:

(i) Such a company must have its own Memorandum and Articles of Association.

(ii) The Articles of an unlimited company must state the number of members with which the company is to be registered. [Section 27(2)]

(iii) The Articles of an unlimited company having a share capital must also state the amount of share capital with which the company is to be registered. [Section 27(2)]

(iv) An unlimited company need not hold statutory meeting. [Section 165(1)]
(v) An unlimited company having share capital may alter its share capital without any restriction. [Section 94(1)]
(vi) An unlimited company having share capital may reduce its share capital without any restriction. [Section 100(1)]
(vii) Liability of a member of an unlimited company when he ceases to be a member.
(viii) The liability of each member extends to the whole amount of the company's debts and liabilities but he will be entitled to claim contribution from other members.
(ix) So long as the company is a going concern the liability on the shares is the only liability which can be enforced by the company, though the liability of the members is unlimited so far as creditors are concerned. [*Re Mayfair Property Co. Bartlett* v. *Mayfair Property* Co. [1898] 2 Ch. 28].
(x) An unlimited company can register it as a limited company if a resolution is passed to that effect [Section 98]. If the unlimited company has share capital, (a) it may increase the nominal value of its shares provided that no part of such increase shall be capable of being called up except in the event and for the purpose of the company being wound-up, or (b) to provide that a specified portion of its uncalled share capital shall not be capable of being called up except in the event and for the pureposes of the company being wound-up [Section 98].

4.0 COMPANIES ON THE BASIS OF CONTROL

On the basis of control i.e., who effectively control the affairs of the company, the companies may be grouped as follows:

4.1 Government Company

4.2 Non-Government Company

4.3 Foreign Company

4.4 Domestic Company

4.5 Holding Company

4.6 Subsidiary Company

Let us discuss these companies one by one:

4.1 Government Company According to Section 617 of the Companies Act, a government company means **"any company in which at least 51% of the paid-up share capital is held by the Central Government or by any State Government or Governments or partly by the Central Government and partly by one or more State Governments and includes a company which is a subsidiary of a government company as thus defined"**. For example, Indian Telephone Industry, Hindustan Aeronautics Ltd. Even a subsidiary company of a government company is regarded as a Government company. A government company registered under this Act is a non-statutory company and is not an agent of the government. Further, like any other company, it is governed by the provisions of the Companies Act. Section 620 of the Act, however, provides that the Central Government may by notification in the Official Gazette direct that any of the provisions of this Act specified in the notification—

(a) shall not apply to any government company, or

(b) shall apply to any government company, only with such exceptions, modifications and adaptations, as may be specified in the notification. A copy of such notification shall be laid before the Parliament.

Notes: Sections 618, 619 and 619(A) of the Act cannot be exempted as these sections specially deal with Government companies.

4.2 Non-government Company A company which may not be termed as a government company as defined in Section 617 is regarded as a non-government company.

4.3 Foreign Company A foreign company means **a company which is incorporated in a country outside India under the law of that country.** After the establishment of business in India, the following documents must be filed with the Registrar of companies within 30 days from the date of establishment:

(a) A certified copy of the charter or statutes under which the company is incorporated, or the memorandum and articles of the company translated into English,
(b) The full address of the registered office of the company,
(c) A list of directors and secretary of the company,
(d) The names and address of any person resident in India who is authorised to accept, on behalf of the company, service of legal process and any notice served on the company, and
(e) The full address of the company's principal place of business in India.

4.4 Domestic Company A company which cannot be termed as foreign company under the provisions of the Companies Act should be regarded as a domestic company.

4.5 Holding and Subsidiary Company Generally speaking, if one company controls another company, the controlling company may be termed as the 'Holding company' and company so controlled may be termed as a 'subsidiary company'.

Section 4(4) of the Act defines a holding company as "a company shall be deemed to be the holding company of another, if that other is its subsidiary".

A company (let us call it Company *S*) is deemed to be a subsidiary of another company (let us call it Company *H*) only in the following cases:

(i) When the company (Company *H*) controls the composition of Board of Directors of other Company (Company *S*).

The composition of the Board of directors of *S* shall be demeed to be controlled by *H* if *H* can appoint or remove all or majority of directors of *S* without the consent or approval of any other person. *H* will be demeed to possess the power to appoint majority of persons as directors of *S*: (i) when these persons cannot be appointed in that capacity without *H*'s consent, or (ii) when their appointments follow necessarily from their appointment as directors, manager or the holder of any office in *H* company, or (iii) when the holding company (*i.e.*, *H*) itself or its another subsidiary holds the directorship in 'S' company [Section 4(1)(a) and (2)].

(ii) When the Company *H* holds more than half in the nominal value of equity share capital of Company *S*.

For the purposes of this clause,

(a) Shares held by another person as a nominee for the company or any of its subsidiaries are regarded or being held by the company.
(b) Following shares are not regarded as being held by the company:
   (i) Shares held in a fiduciary capacity (e.g. shares held in trust for an individual)
   (ii) Shares held under the provisions of any debentures

(iii) Shares held as security in the ordinary course of business (which includes the lending of money)

(iii) When Company *S* is a subsidiary of a Company *T*, which in turn is the subsidiary of Company *H*.

Note: An Indian private company which is a subsidiary of a foreign company is treated as a subsidiary of a public company if its entire share capital is not held by that foreign company either alone or together with other foreign companies. [Section 4(7)]

4.6 Can a Subsidiary Company become a Member of Holding Company?

According to Section 42, a body corporate cannot be a member of its holding company and any allotment and transfer of shares in a company to its subsidiary shall be void. This section shall not apply:

1. where the subsidiary company is a legal representative of a deceased member of the holding company [Section 42(2)(a)].
2. where the subsidiary is concerned as a trustee, unless the holding company or its subsidiary is beneficially interested under the trust and its not so interested only by way of security for the purposes of a trasaction entered into by it in the ordinary course of a business which includes the lending of money [Section 42(2)(b)].

However, a subsidiary company may continue to be a member of its holding company if it was a member thereof either at the commencement of this Act or before becoming a subsidiary of the holding company [Section 42(3)]. But it would not except for two cases mentioned above in Section 42(2) enjoy any voting right at the holding company's meeting though it may exercise other rights of members.

Note: A subsidiary company may buy shares in its holding company under a scheme of amalgamation sanctioned by the Court. (*Himachal Telematics* v. *Himachal Futuristic Communication Ltd.*, (1996) 86 Comp. 325 Delhi).

5.0 PUBLIC FINACIAL INSTITUTIONS (SECTION 4A)

Under Section 4A of the Act, the following institutions are deemed to be public financial institutions:

1. The Industrial Credit and Investment Corporation of India Limited.
2. The Industrial Finance Corporation of India.
3. The Industrial Development Bank of India.
4. The Life Insurance Corporation of India.
5. The Unit Trust of India,
6. The Infrastructure Development Finance Company Limited (Included w.e.f. 31.10.1998 vide the Companies Amendment Act, 1999).

The Central Government by notification in the Official Gazette is empowered to specify any other institution as Public Finacial Institution if:

(a) It is constituted under any Central Act or is held or controlled by the Central Government.
(b) Not less than 51 per cent of its paid up capital is controlled or held by the Central Government.

In exercise of the powers conferred under Section 4A, the Central Government has included the following institutions in the category of Public Finacial Institutions; namely:

(a) The Industrial Reconstruction Corporation of India Ltd. (IRC)
(b) The General Insurance Corporation of India (GIC)
(c) The National Insurance Company Ltd. (NIC)
(d) The New India Assurance Company Ltd. (NIAC)
(e) The Oriental Fire and General Insurance Company Ltd. (OFGIC)

(f) The Tourism Finance Corporation of India Ltd. (TFCI)
(g) The Risk Capital and Technology Finance Corporation Ltd. (RCTFC)
(h) Technology Development and Information Company of India Ltd. (TDIC)
(i) Power Finance Corporation Limited. (PFC)
(j) National Housing Bank.
(k) Small Industries Development Bank of India. (SIDBI)
(l) Rural Electrification Corporation Ltd. (REC)
(m) The Shipping Credit and Investment Company of India Ltd. (SCICI)

6.0 DISTINCTION BETWEEN PRIVATE COMPANY AND PUBLIC COMPANY

A private company differs from a public company in the following respects:

Basis of Distinction	*Public company*	*Private company*
1. *Use of the word 'Private'*	The name of the public company is ***not required*** to use the word 'Private'.	The name of the private company ***must use*** the word 'Private'.
2. *Minimum no. of members*	The minimum number of members required to form a public company is *7*.	The minimum number of mem-bers required to form a private company is *2*.
3. *Maximum no. of members*	There is ***no restriction*** on the maximum number of members.	The maximum limit of member ***is 50.***
4. *Minimum paid up capital*	It must have a minimum paid up capital of ***Rs 5 lakh or higher paid up capital*** as may be prescribed.	It must have a minimum paid up capital of ***Rs 1 lakh or higher paid up*** capital as may be prescribed.
5. *Transferability of shares*	The right to transfer the shares is ***not restricted*** by the Articles of Association.	The right to transfer the shares is ***restricted*** by the Articles of Association.
6. *Invitation to the public to subscribe shares/ debentures*	It ***can invite*** public to sub-scribe for its shares or debentures.	It ***cannot invite*** public to subscribe for its shares or debentures.
7. *Invitation or Acceptance of Deposits*	It ***can invite or accept*** deposits from any person.	It ***cannot invite or accept*** deposits from persons other than its members, directors or their relatives.
8. *Articles of association*	It ***can either frame*** its own Articles of Association *or* adopt Table 'A' as its Articles of Association.	It *has to* ***compulsorily*** frame its own articles of associations so as to include four statutory restrictions.
9. *Delivery of prospectus/ Statement in lieu of Prospectus [Section 70]*	Prosecutes/Statement in lieu of Prospectus is ***required*** to be delivered to the Registrar before allotting shares.	Prospectus/Statement in lieu of Prospectus is ***not required*** to be delivered to the Registrar.
10. *Offer of further shares [Section 61]*	It is ***required*** to *offer* further shares first to the existing share holders unless a special resolution is passed or approval of Central Govt. is obtained.	It ***need not offer*** further shares to the existing shareholders.
11. *Commencement of Business [Section 149]*	It can commence its business only ***after*** obtaining the ***certificate of incorporation as well as the certificate to commence business***.	It can commence its business immediately ***after*** obtaining the ***certificate of incorporation.***

(Contd.)

(*Contd.*)

12. *Holding of Statutory Meeting [Section 165]*	It is ***required*** to *hold* statutory meeting and to send statutory report to shareholders and file the same with Registrar.	It is ***not required*** *to hold* statutory meeting and to send statutory report to share-holders and file the same with Registrar.
13. *Place of holding AGM [Section 166]*	It is required to hold its AGM *at* its ***registered office*** or at some other place within the city, town or village in which the registered office of the company is situated.	It can hold its AGM ***anywhere***.
14. *Quorum [Section 174]*	There must be **at *least 5*** members personally present to constitute a valid general meeting of a public company.	There must be at ***least 2*** members personally present to constitute a valid general meeting of a private company.
15. *Demand for poll [Sec. 179]*	In case of a public company, ***any member*** present in person ***or any proxy*** holding shares ***having*** at least ***1/10 of total voting power or at least Rs 50,000 paid up*** can demand for a poll.	In case of a private company **1** member present in person or by proxy (if not more than 7 such members are personally present) or **2** members (if more than 7 such members are personally present) can demand for a poll.
16. *Appointment of Firm or Body Corporate [Sec-tion 204]*	It ***cannot*** *appoint* a firm or body corporate to an office or place of profit under the company.	It ***can appoint*** a firm a body corporate to an office or place of profit under the company.
17. *Minimum No. of Directors [Section 252(2)]*	It must have at least ***3*** directors.	It must have at least **2** directors.
18. *Retirement of Directors by Rotation [Section 255(1)]*	***Two-thirds*** of the total no. of directors of a public company *must retire* by rotation.	Its directors ***need not retire*** by rotation. There can be perm-anent life directors.
19. *Statutory Notice to stand for election as director [Section 257(2)]*	Statutory notice etc. is ***required*** for a person to stand for election as a director.	Statutory notice is ***not required*** for a person to stand for election as a director.
20. *Approval of Central Government to effect increase in no. of Directors [Section 259]*	Approval of Central Govt. is ***required*** for increase in number of directors beyond 12 or the number fixed by Articles.	Approval of Central Govt. is ***not required*** for increase in no. of directors beyond 12 or the number fixed by Article.
21. *Appointment of Directors by single resolution [Section 263(1)]*	Two or more directors ***cannot*** be appointed by a single resolution.	Two or more directors ***can*** be appointment by a single regulation.
22. *Filing of consent to act as director [Section 264]*	Its directors are ***required to file*** the consent to act as director within 30 days of his appointment with the Registrar.	Its directors ***need not file*** the consent to act as directors and as a result minor can also be appointed as director.
23. *Restrictions on appointment or advertisment of directors [Section 266]*	Restrictions on appointment or advertisement of director contained in Section 266 ***apply*** to a public company.	Restrictions on appointment or advertisement of a director contained in Section 266 ***does not apply*** to a private company.

(*Contd.*)

(Contd.)

24. ***Approval of Central Govt. to modify the provisions relating to appointment [Section 268]***	Approval of Central Govt. is ***required*** to modify any provision relating to appointment of managing, whole time or non-rotational directions.	Such approval of Central Govt. is ***not required*** in case of private company.
25. ***Can Articles require to hold qualification shares [Section 273]***	The Articles of a public company can ***require*** the director to hold a qualification	The Articles of a private com-pany ***cannot require*** a director to hold qualification shares as this provision being contrary to Sectio 273 shall be void.
26. ***Restrictions on powers of B.O.D. [Section 293]***	There ***are*** certain restrictions on powers of Board of Direc-tors of a public company.	Restriction on Powers of Board of Directors ***do not apply*** to private company.
27. ***Prohibition against loan to directors [Section 295]***	There is ***prohibition*** against loan to directors of a public company.	There is ***no prohibition*** against loan to directors of a private company.
28. ***Prohibition against participation of Interested Directors [Sec. 300]***	Interested directors ***cannot*** participate in board meeting.	Interested directors ***can*** participate in board meeting.
29. ***Entry of date of birth of directors [Section 303]***	Date of birth of a director of a public company is ***required*** to be entered in the Register of Directors.	Date of Birth of a director of private company ***need not*** be entered in the register of directors.
30. ***Restrictions on remuneration of directors [Section 309]***	There are ***restrictions*** on remuneration payable to directors.	There is ***no restriction*** on remuneration payable to directors.
31. ***Approval of Central Govt. to change the remuneration of directors [Section 310]***	Approval of Central Govt. is ***required*** to change the remuneration of directors.	Such *approval* of Central Govt. is ***not required*** to change the remuneration of directors.
32. ***Restrictions on appointment of M.D./WTD [Sec-tion 316]***	There are ***restrictions*** on appointment of Managing Director or whole time director of a public company.	There is ***no restriction*** on appointment of Managing Director or while time Director of a private company.
33. ***Provisions relating to ascertainment of net profit and depreciation [Section 355]***	Provision relating to method of determination of net profits and ascertainment of depreciation ***apply*** to a public company.	Provision relating to method of determination of net profits and ascertainment of depreciation ***do not apply*** to a private company.
34. ***Restriction on Inter- Company loans and inter corporate invest-ment [Section 372A]***	There are ***restrictions*** on making loans/investments by a public company to other companies.	There is ***no restriction*** as mak-ing loan investments by a private company to other companies.
35. ***Power of Central Govt. to prevent change in BOD [Section 409]***	Central Govt. ***can exercise*** its power to prevent change in board of director which is likely to affect the company prejudicially.	Central Govt. ***cannot exercise*** its power to prevent change in Board of directors which is likely to affect the company prejudicially.
36. ***Undisclosed Principal on company's behalf [Section 416]***	***No person can enter*** into contract on behalf of public company as undisclosed principal.	***A person can*** enter into con-tract on behalf of private company as undisclosed company and need not give intimation to other directors.

7.0 PRIVILEGES OF AN INDEPENDENT PRIVATE COMPANY

Privileges available only to an independent private company (i.e. a private company which is *not* a subsidiary of a public company) are as follows:

1. **Minimum No. of Members [Section 12(1)]** A private company can be formed with only two members.
2. **Minimum Subscription [Section 69]** A private company can allot shares without waiting for the minimum subscription to be received, since it is prohibited from offering its shares or debentures to the public.
3. **Delivery of Prospectus/Statement in Lieu of Prospectus [Section 70]** A private company need not issue and deliver prospectus/statement in lieu of prospectus to the Registrar, since it is prohibited from offering its shares/debentures to the public.
4. **Financial Assistance for Purchase of shares [Section 77]** A private company can provide financial assistance for the purchase of its own shares.
5. **Issue of Further Shares [Section 81(3)]** A private company need not offer further shares to the existing shareholders.
6. **Commencement of Business [Section 149(7)]** A private company can commence its business immediately after obtaining the certificate of incorporation.
7. **Holding of Statutory Meeting [Section 165(1)]** A private company need not hold a statutory meeting or file a statutory report with the Registrar of companies.
8. **Any Place of Annual General Meeting [Section 166]** A private company can hold its annual general meetings anywhere. It is not necessary for it to hold annual general meeting at the registered office or at some other place within the city, town or village in which the registered office of the company is situated.
9. **Provision of Section 170 to 186 to apply to General meetings [Section 170]** An independent private company can exclude the provisions of Section 170 to 186 by formulating its own provisions in its Articles to regulate its general meetings.
10. **Quorum [Section 174]** Unless otherwise provided in the Articles of a private company, only two members personally present shall form the quorum of its general meeting.
11. **Demand for Poll [Section 179]** In case of a private company one member present in person or by proxy (if not more than seven such members are personally present) or two members (if more than seven such members are personally resent) can demand for a poll.
12. **Overall Managerial Remuneration limit [Section 198]** The restrictions regarding overall managerial remuneration do not apply to an independent private company.
13. **Appointment of Firm or Body Corporate [Section 204]** The restrictions regarding the appointment of a firm or body corporate to a place of profit do not apply to an independent private company.
14. **Retirement of Directors by Rotation [Section 255(1)]** The directors of an independent company need not retire by rotation. In other words, it can have permanent life directors.
15. **No Statutory Notice to Stand for Elections as Director [Section 257(2)]** No statutory notice is required for a person to stand for elections as a director of an independent private company.
16. **No approval of Central Govt. to Effect Increase in Number of Directors [Section 259]** In case of an independent company an approval of central government is not required for increase in number of directors beyond 12 or the number fixed by the Articles.
17. **Filing of Casual Vacancies Among Directors [Section 262]** The provisions relating to filling of casual vacancies among directors do not apply to an independent private company.
18. **Appointment of Directors by Single Resolution [Section 263 (1)]** In case of an independent private company, two or more directors can be appointed by a single resolution.

19. **Filing of Consent to Act as Director [Section 264]** The directors of an independent company need not file the consent to act as directors.
20. **Restriction on Appointment or Advertisement of Directors [Section 266]** Restriction on appointment or advertisement of a director contained in Section 266 does not apply to an independent private company.
21. **No Approval of Central Govt. to modify the Provision Relating to Appointment [Section 268]** No such approval of Central Govt. is required in case of an independent company.
22. **No Approval of Central Govt. to Appoint M.D./WTD or Manager [Section 269(2)]** No such approval of Central Govt. is required in case of an independent company.
23. **Qualification Shares [Section 273]** The articles of an independent private company can not require a director to hold qualification shares as this provision being contrary to Section 273 would be void.
24. **Grounds for Disqualification of Shares [Section 274(3)]** An independent private company may by its articles provide any grounds in addition to those specified in Section 274(1), for disqualification for appointment of directors.
25. **Max No. of Directorships [Section 278]** The directorship of a private company is not includible in the maximum number of directorships that a person may hold.
26. **No Restrictions on Powers of B.O.D. [Section 293]** The restrictions on powers of B.O.D. do not apply to an independent private company.
27. **No Prohibition against Loan to Director etc. [Section 295]** There is no prohibition against loan to directors etc. in case of an independent private company.
28. **No Prohibition against Participation of Interested Director [Section 300]** An interested director of an independent private company can participate in Board meeting.
29. **No Entry of Date of Birth of Director [Section 303]** Date of Birth of a director of an independent company need not be entered in the Register of Directors.
30. **No Restriction on Remuneration of Directors [Section 309]** The restriction on remuneration of directors does not apply to an independent private company.
31. **No Approval of Central Govt. to Change the Remuneration of Directors [Section 310]** No such approval of Cental Govt. is required to change the remuneration of directors in case of an independent company.
32. **No Limit on Number of Companies of which one Person may be Appointed Managing Director [Section 316]** The provision of the Act limiting the number of companies of which one person may be appointed managing director does not apply to an independent private company.
33. **Provisions Relating to Ascertainment of Net Profits and Depreciations [Section 355]** The provisions relating to ascertainment of net profits an depreciations do not apply to an independent private company.
34. **No Restriction on Inter-company Loan and Inter-corporate Investments [Section 372A]** The restrictions on Inter-company Loan and Inter-corporate Investments do not apply to an independent private company.
35. **No Power of Central Govt. to Prevent Change in B.O.D. [Section 409]** In case of an independent private company, Central Govt. cannot exercise its power to prevent change in Board of directors which is likely to affect the company prejudicially.
36. **Undisclosed Principal on Company's Behalf [Section 416]** A person can enter into contract on behalf of an independent private company as undisclosed principal and need not give notice to the other directors.

It may be noted that the moment a private company fails to comply with any of the statutory restrictions to be contained in its articles or it becomes a subsidiary of a public company, it shall lose these special privileges.

8.0 RESTRICTIONS ON A PRIVATE COMPANY

The restrictions placed on a private company are as follows:

Restrictions to be Placed in Articles

1. Restriction on the right to transfer shares,
2. Restriction on the maximum number of the members exceeding 5, and
3. Prohibition on invitation to the public for investment in its shares or debentures.
4. Prohibition or acceptance of deposits from persons other than its members, directors and their relatives.

Other Restrictions

5. **Restriction on Issue of Share Warrants [Section 114]**—A private company cannot issue share warrants payable to bearer.
6. **Annual List of Members [Section 159 and 161]**—Public companies are required to send an annual list of their members and a summary of certain particulars to the registrar of companies. A private company is also required to send with this return, a certificate, certifying that the company has not, since the last return, made any public invitation inviting the public to subscribe for its shares or debentures. It is also required to certify that where the annual return shows the number of members of the company exceeds fifty, the excess consists of those persons who are not to be included in counting the number of fifty.
7. The member of a private company is not allowed to appoint more than one proxy to attend and vote at a meeting of the company.

9.0 CONVERSION OF A PRIVATE COMPANY INTO A PUBLIC COMPANY [SECTION 3(1)(III), SECTION 44, SECTION 43B]

Conversion of a private company into a public company can take place in the following three ways:

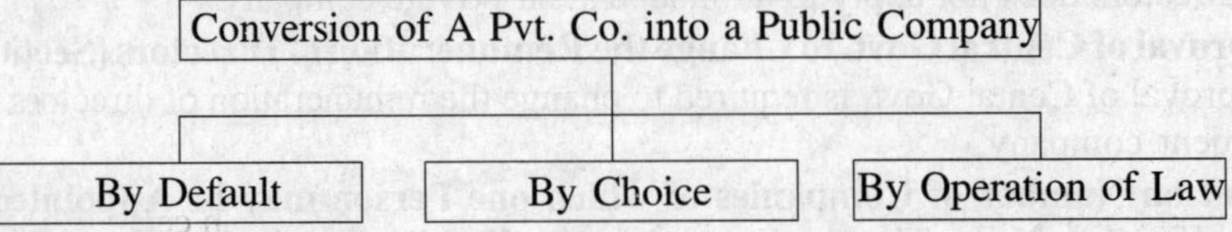

Let us discuss them one by one.

9.1 Conversion by Default [Section 43]

(a) If a private company makes a default in complying with the provisions of Section 3(1)(iii), or a private company becomes a subsidiary of public company then it ceases to be a private company and is treated as a public company.

(b) Then the special privileges are not available to the company.

(c) All the provisions of a public company shall become applicable to it as if it was a public company.

(d) It must however, be remembered that the Company Law Board has been given the power to grant relief in cases where it is satisfied that the default in respect of the provisions of Section 3(1)(iii) was purely accidental and not intentional.

The Company Law Board shall grant relief on such terms and conditions as it may think just and expedient.

The application for relief may be made by the company or any other person interested.

9.2 Conversion by Choice [Section 44]

Procedure for Conversion by Choice

In order to convert a private company into a public company, the following procedure is adopted:

1. **Convene Board Meeting** Board meeting must be convened to fix up the time, place and agenda for convening a general meeting to alter the articles of association and the "name clause" of the memorandom.
2. **Notice for General Meeting** It must issue notices for the general meeting together with the explanatory statements for the alteration of the articles and the memorandum.
3. **Passing of Special Resolution** The general meeting must be covened to pass special resolution to alter the memorandum and articles of association.
4. **Alteration of Articles of Association** It shall pass a special resolution to alter its Articles so as to exclude—
   (a) the four restrictions of Section 3(1)(iii), and
   (b) the provisions which may be inconsistent with the requirements of public company.
5. **Filing of Documents** Within 30 days of passing the special resolution, the following documents must be filed with the Registrar of companies.
   (a) a copy of the special resolution regarding alteration of the articles,
   (b) a copy of the altered articles, and
   (c) a copy of the prospectus containing the information required in accordance with Parts I and II of Schedule II of The Companies Act or a Statement in lieu of Prospectus in the prescribed form.
6. **Increase in No. of Members** The number of members must be increased to 7 if the existing number of members is less than 7.
7. **Increase in No. of Directors** The number of directors must be increased to 3 if the existing number of directors is less than 3.
8. **Increase in Paid-up Capital** The paid up capital must be increased to Rs 5,00,000 if the existing paid-up capital is less than Rs 5,00,000.
9. **Obtaining Fresh Certificate of Incorporation** It shall obtain fresh certificate of incorporation from the Registrar of Companies after filing the required documents.

Effects of Conversion by Choice

(a) The company becomes a public company from the date of passing the special resolution.

(b) It will have to delete the word 'private' from the name of the company.

(c) The change in its name becomes effective only on the issue of fresh certificate of incorporation.

(d) The conversion does not affect the legal personality of the company which continues to remain the same.

(e) Such conversion does not, in any way extinguishes the liability of the company, i.e. its liability remains the same as it was before conversion.

(f) Such conversion and consequent change of name would not effect the identity of the company. [*All India Reporter Ltd.* v. *Ramchandra Datar,* AIR (1962) Bom. 292]

Note: Conversion by Operation of Law [Sec 43 B] has already been deleted.

10.0 CONVERSION OF PUBLIC COMPANY INTO A PRIVATE COMPANY

10.1 Procedure

In order to convert a public company into a private company, the following procedure is adopted:

1. **Alteration of Articles of Association [Section 31]** It shall pass a special resolution to alter its Articles so as to:
   (a) Include the four restrictions of Section 3(1)(iii).
   (b) Exclude the provision which may be inconsistent with the requirements of private company. (e.g. Power to issue share warrants)
2. **Approval of Central Govt. [Section 31]** The approval of the Central Government must be obtained within 3 months of the date of passing the special resolution.
3. **Filling of Special Resolution within 30 days** A copy of the special resolution regarding alteration of articles alongwith explanatory statement annexed u/s 173 to the notice of meeting must be filed with the Registrar within 30 days from the date of passing the resolution.
4. **Filing of the Documents** Within 1 month of the date of receipt of the order of approval, the following documents must be filed with the Registrar:
   (a) A printed copy of the altered articles.
   (b) A certified copy of order of the Central Government.

10.2 Effects of Conversion

(a) The company becomes a private company from the date of obtaining the approval of central government.
(b) It will have to reduce the number of its members to 50 if number of members is more than 50.
(c) It will have to add the word 'Private' as part the name of the company.
(d) It shall enjoy all the privileges of a private company after the conversion takes effect.
(e) Legal personality of the company continues to remain the same inspite of the conversion since the conversion of public company into private company or *vice versa* does not bring into existence a new company [*Hindustan Lever Ltd.* v. *Bombay Soda Factory*].
(f) A special resolution passed to convert a public company into private company is binding on dissenting shareholders provided it is—
   (i) bona fide,
   (ii) in the interest of company as a whole, and
   (iii) consistent with the object in the Memorandum of Association, [*Bai Rampa* v. *Master Silk Mills,* 1955].

11.0 ILLEGAL ASSOCIATION [SECTION 11]

11.1 Meaning of Illegal Association [Section 11(1) and (2)]

According to Section 11, "No company, association or partnership consisting of more than 10 persons for the purpose of carrying on the business of banking and more than 20 persons for the purpose of carrying on another business shall be formed unless it is registered as a company under this Act, or is formed in pursuance of some other Indian law."

Example I Where an unregistered association is formed for carrying on the business of banking with 8 members. Subsequently 3 more persons join the association as members. The association would become an illegal association from the moment the number of its members exceed 10.

Example II Where an unregistered association is formed for carrying on the business of non-banking with 18 members. Subsequently 3 more persons join the association as members. The association would become an illegal association from the moment the number of its members exceed 20.

Example III Where an unregistered association is formed for non-commercial purposes such as promotion of religion, art, science, charity or any other useful object, with 18 members. Subsequently 3 more persons join the association as members. The association would not become an illegal association because the limit on maximum number of members is not applicable to such associations.

Example IV Where an association is formed between three partnership firms X (having 6 persons), Y (having 7 persons), and Z (having 8 persons). Such association would be an illegal association because the limit on maximum numbers of members exceed 20.

Notes:

(i) Every person (natural or otherwise) who holds an independent position in law and in capable of entering into contract shall be counted as one person.

(ii) Two or more persons holding a share jointly are treated as a single member.

11.2 Non-Applicability of Section 11

Section 11 does not apply in the following cases:

(a) Joint Hindu Family A Joint Hindu Family may carry on any business, even for earning profits and with any number of members without being registered in pursuance of any Indian Law as required by Section 11 of the Companies Act, 1956 and yet it will not be an illegal association. But, where two joint Hindu families join hands to carry on business, the provisions of Section 11 become applicable.

However, for computing the number of members of such an association, the minor members of such families shall not be included.

Accordingly, the No. of members of the purposes of Section 11(1) & (2), would consist of not only the Kartas but also other adult members of the joint families. [*Shayam Lal* v. *Madhusudan Ray* 1959 Cal.]

(b) Stock Exchange A stock exchange is not covered by Section 11 as it is not formed for the purpose of carrying on any business.

(c) Non-profit Earning Associations All religions, charitable, literary, social, sports and other associations whose object is not to make profit are also not covered by Section 11.

11.3 Consequences of An Illegal Association [Section 11(4)]

The consequences of an illegal association are as follows:

1. **Personal Liability** Every member shall be personally liable for all the liabilities incurred in carrying on the business.
2. **Punishable with Fine** Every member shall be punishable with fine not exceeding Rs. 10,000.
3. *Neither* such an association *nor* its members in their individual capacity can sue any outsider who has dealt with it.
4. *Neither* members *nor* outsiders can sue such association.
5. No member can sue another member in respect of any matter connected with such association.
6. Outside can sue the members but not such association.
7. Such an association can not enter into any contracts since it has no legal existence.
8. Such an association can not be wound up under the provisions of Companies Act relating to winding up of unregulated companies as well as through court because there is nothing to dissolve at all. [*Mewa Ram* v. *Ram Gopal*]
9. Once the association contravened the provision of Section 11, it remains illegal even if there is subsequent reduction in the number of its members. In other words, the illegality of an illegal association can not be cured by subsequent reduction in the number of its members. [*Madanlal* v. *Janki Parshad*]

10. Contracts made before the registration can not be validated and issued upon by subsequent registration. [*Gujarat Trading Co.* v. *Tricumji*]
11. Illegality or invalidity in the constitution of an association does not effect its liability to tax or its chargeability as a unit of assessment. [*Kumaraswamy Chettiar* v. *I.T.O.*, 1957]
12. No suit either for administration or partition of assets of an illegal association can be filed by any member of such an association.

    In *Mewa Ram* v. *Ram Gopal*, High Court of Allahabad held that such partition of assets of an illegal association is not possible at all because a decree for partition would amount to be in substance a direction for winding up or a decree for dissolution and accounts.
13. A member of an illegal association who has paid any money to such association would be able to recover it form the director or agents or association before the money so paid has been applied to an illegal purpose. [*Greenpur* v. *Co-operatives* (1926)]
14. Members of an illegal association have a beneficial interest in the property belonging to such association. [*Queen* v. *Tankard*, (1894)]

EXERCISES

VERY SHORT ANSWER TYPE QUESTIONS

1. What is a Private Company?
2. What is a Public Company?
3. What is meant by: 'Company limited by shares'?
4. What is meant by 'Company limited by Guarantee'?
5. What is an 'Unlimited Company'?
6. What is an 'Association not for profit'?
7. What is a 'Licensed Company'?
8. Define a Government Company.
9. Define a Foreign Company.
10. Define Holding and a Subsidiary Company.
11. What is an illegal association?
12. State the consequences of a default by a private company in complying with the provisions of Section 3(1)(iii) of the Company Act, 1956.

SHORT ANSWER TYPE QUESTIONS

1. Write a short note on 'one-may Company'.
2. List any five points of distribution between a private company and public company.
3. List any five privileges available to an independent private company only.
4. What is an illegal association? What are its consequences?

LONG ANSWER TYPE QUESTIONS

1. Distinguish between private company and a public company.
2. Enumerate the privileges available to any private company.
3. Enumerate the privileges available to an independent private company only.
4. How can a private company be converted into a public company?
5. How can a public company be converted into a private company?

6. Comment on the following:
   (a) The law not only recognises a private company but also perform its benedictions on the same.
   (b) A limited company can be formed without the word 'limited' as the last word of its name'.
   (c) A subsidiary company can be the member of its holding company.
7. State the restrictions under the Companies Act, 1956 on a company becoming a member of its holding company.

PRACTICAL PROBLEMS

8. An association of 12 persons starts a banking business without being registered. Four members retire and thereafter a suit is instituted by one of the continuing members for the partition of the assets of the business. Is the suit competent?
9. Two joint Hindu families carry on together a business as joint owners. The first family consists of 5 brothers and their respective sons, being 10 (including 2 minors) in number. The second family consists of the father, 6 major sons and 6 minor sons. Is the business illegal.
10. The paid up share capital of *XYZ* (Pvt.) Co. Ltd. is Rs 20 lakh consisting of 2 Lakh equity shares of Rs 10 each fully paid up. ABC (Pvt.) Co. Ltd. and its subsidiary *DEF* (Pvt.) Co. Ltd. are holding 60,000 and 50,000 shares respectively in *XYZ* (Pvt.) Co. Ltd.

    Examine with reference to the provisions of the Companies Act, 1956, whether *XYZ* (Pvt.) Co. Ltd. is holding 1,10,000 shares in *XYZ* (Pvt.) Co. Ltd. and no shares are held by *ABC* (Pvt.) Co. Ltd. in *XYZ* (Pvt.) Co. Ltd.?

CHAPTER

3

Formation of a Company

1.0 PROMOTION

1.1 Meaning of Promotion

Promotion is the first stage in the formation of a company. Promotion involves identification of a business opportunity or idea, analysis of its prospects and taking steps to implement it through the formation of a Company. *C.W. Gerstenberg* has defined promotion as the discovery of business opportunities and the subsequent organization of funds, property and managerial ability into a business concern for the purpose of making profit therefrom. Promotion stage comprises the following activities to be undertaken:

(a) Discovery of business idea or identification of business opportunity.
(b) Detailed investigation to find out the strong and weak points of the idea.
(c) Organisation of resources.
(d) Securing the cooperation of the required number of persons willing to associate themselves with the project.
(e) Obtaining the consent of persons willing to act as first directors.
(f) Appointing Legal Advisors.
(g) Application for proposed name of the company.
(h) Preparation of necessary documents like memorandum of association, articles of association.
(i) Entering into preliminary contracts.
(j) Filing of the necessary documents with the Registrars.

1.2 Meaning of Promoters

The Companies Act does not define the term promoters anywhere, it only refers to the liabilities of the promoters. A number of judicial decisions have defined the term 'promoter'.

1. *According to L.J. Bowen*, the term promoter is a term not of law but of business, usefully summing up in a single word, a number of business operations familiar to the commercial word by which a company is generally brought into existence.
2. *Lord Blackburn* states that "the term 'promoter' is a short and convenient way of designating those who set in motion the machinery by which the Act enables them to create an incorporated company."
3. *Justice C. Cockburn* described a promoter as "one who undertakes to form a company with reference to a given project and to set it going, and who takes the necessary steps to accomplish that purpose."

Thus, a **promoter is one who identifies a business opportunity or idea, analyses its prospects and takes steps to implements it through the formation of a company.**

A company may have more than one promoter. The promoter may be an individual, firm, an association of persons or a body corporate. For example, J.R.D. Tata was promoter of Tata Group, G.D. Birla was promoter of Birla Group, Dhirubhai Ambani was the promoter of Reliance Group.

1.3 Who are not Promoters?

Everyone who is associated with the process of the formation of a company cannot be called a promoter. The following persons cannot called promoters:

(a) **Persons acting only in a professional capacity.** [Section 62(6)]
For Example A solicitor who draws up the documents of the proposed company in his professional capacity is not a promoter in the eyes of law. Similarly, an engineer who advises on the selection of site or a valuer who helps with drawing the estimates would not be regarded as a promoter.

(b) **Merely Signatories to the Memorandum/Financier for formation expenses.** A person cannot be held as promoter merely because he has signed at the foot of the memorandum or that he has provided money for the payment of formation expense. [*G. Tiruvengadacharir* v. *Value Muaoliar,* (1838) I.L.R. Mad. 192]

(c) **Merely Vendors of Property** Individuals do not become promoters because they buy property, subsequently sold by them to a company at a profit even though the consideration consists of shares in the same company. But where certain persons buy property with a view to selling it later to a company to be formed by them, such persons will be regarded as promoters from the moment they took first step to carry out that object. [*Gluckstein* v. *Barnes,* (1900) A.C. 240]

From the above it should be clear to you that a promoter is one who performs the preliminary duties necessary to bring a company into existence. Thus, the true test to describe a person as a promoter lies in finding out whether he is keen to form a company and take steps to give it a concrete shape. Thus, whether a person is a promoter, in any particular case depends on the facts having regard to the nature of person's role and his relationship to the company that is formed.

1.4 Functions of a Promoter

The various functions performed by the promoters include the following:

1. **To Conceive Business Idea** First of all the promoters conceive the idea of business.
2. **To make Detailed Investigation** After conceiving the idea of business, they make detailed investigations to find out the weakness and strong points of the idea.
3. **To Organize the Resources** After satisfying about the profitability and feasibility of the idea, they organize the resources to convert the idea into a reality by forming a company. The steps to be taken in this regard include the following:
   (i) Securing the co-operation of a the required number of persons willing to associate themselves with the project (Note: 7 persons are required to form public company and 2 persons are required to form a private company)
   (ii) Appointing Legal Advisors and other experts.
   (iii) Entering into preliminary contracts.
   (iv) Preparing detailed financial plan.
4. **To Obtain the Consent of Persons Willing to Act as First Directors** The first directors are generally appointed by the promoters. The promoters seek the consent of some individuals whom they deem appropriate so that they agree to be the first directors.
5. **To Decide about the Name of the Company** The promoters have to seek the permission of the Registrar of companies for selecting the name of the company. The promoters usually give

three names in order of preference. The promoters should ensure that the name of the company should not be identical with or should not too closely resemble the name of another existing company.

6. **To Get the Necessary Documents Prepared** The promoters on the advise of legal experts get the memorandum of association and articles of association prepared and printed.
7. **To Arrange for Filing of the Necessary Documents with the Registrar** The promoters are required to pay the stamp duty, filing fee and other charges for registration of the company. The promoters are to see that the various legal formalities for incorporating the company are complied with.

1.5 Legal Position of Promoters

The legal position of a promoter is somewhat peculiar. The promoter's legal position is that he is *neither* an agent *nor* a trustee of the company he promotes. He is not an agent because there is no principal in existence. You will recall from your exposure to the Contract of Agency that in order to be a valid contract of agency both the principal and the agent must be in existence. For the same reason, he also cannot be called the trustee of the company.

However, it does not mean that the promoters do not have any legal relationship with the proposed company. The legal position of a promoter can be correctly described by saying that **he stands in a fiduciary position (relationship of trust and confidence) in relation to the company he promotes. The fiduciary relation of a promoter really begins when the company is formed.**

Lord Cairns has rightly stated the position of promoter in *Erlanger* v. *New Sambrero Phosphate Co.,* "The promoters of company stand undoubtedly in a fiduciary position. They have in their hands the creation and moulding of the company. They have the power of defining how and when and in what shape, and under whose supervision, it shall come into existence and begin to act as a trading corporation." In fact, the promoters occupy a fiduciary position in regard to the company they promote and also the original allottees whom they induce to buy shares of the company.

1.6 Duties of Promoters

The fiduciary obligation of a promoter begins as soon as he sets out to act for or promote the company. **The fiduciary obligation of promoters means an obligation of promoters to disclose fully all material facts relating to the nature and extent of contract and profit made by them either directly or indirectly**. Such disclosure must be express and actual and not merely constructive. The promoters in their fiduciary capacity has the following important duties:

1 **Not to make Secret Profit** A promoter cannot make any direct or indirect profits out of the promotion of the company. Since he occupies a position of a trust, it is his duty to be honest and uphold the trust of his position. The law prohibits only the making of secret profits i.e. the profits which the promoter has not disclosed to the company. The promoters of a company are perfectly free to make a profit provided they disclose this fact to an independent Board of Directors. If there is no independent Board of Directors, then he must disclose the profits to the intended shareholders. When a promoter makes a secret profit, the company has the following **remedies against him:**

   (a) **Recession of the Contract** The company may on learning of the secret profit, rescind the contract entered into by the promoter to make the said profit.

   (b) **Order for Refund** The company may require the promoter to refund the amount of secret profit.

(c) **Suit for Breach of Duty** The company may sue the promoter for misfeasance, as the promoter, by making the secret profit, has defaulted in his duty towards the company.

2. **To make full Disclosure to the Company of all Relevant Facts** In keeping with his fiduciary capacity, a promoter is bound to disclose to the company all relevant facts including any profit made from the sale of his own property to the company and his personal interest in a transaction with company. While making a disclourse the promoter must make the full and complete disclosure. If he contracts to sell his own property to the company without making a full disclosure, the company may *either* repudiate the contract *or* affirm the contract and recover the profits made by the promoter. Such disclosure is ineffective if made merely to directors who are nominees of the promoters. Disclosure may be made either to an independent board, or by means of a prospectus to the prospective shareholders. If the promoter makes a secret profit the company can rescind the contract of compel him to account for it. Where all the members of a private company are cognisant of the facts, the rule would not apply.

   Let us explain these fiduciary duties of the promoter with the help of case of *Erdanger* v. *New Sombrero Phosphate Co.,* (1878) 3 A.C. 1218.

   '*A*' was the owner of some land. He and some of his friends, decided to form a company to manufacture microchips. They appointed the first directors of the company and '*A*' sold his own land to the company at a price higher than the actual valuation of the land. When the company was formed, the purchase agreement of land was approved at the meeting of the shareholders but the fact of *A*'s ownership and the profit made by him were not disclosed at the meeting. Subsequently when the company went into liquidation, the liquidator filed a suit against '*A*' to recover the profits made by him in the sale of land. You would observe that in this case '*A*' had defaulted in his duty to make full disclosure of all material facts and had made a secret profit out of promotion. As there was no disclosure by the promoters of the profits they were making, the company is entiled to rescind the contract. '*A*' could have retained the profit made by him if he had made a full disclosure to the directors of the company or to the shareholders of the company, all the relevant facts of the transaction including his personal interest and the profits made.

3. **To give the Benefit of Negotiations to the Company** The promoter must pass on to the company, the benefit of any negotiation or agreement that he has carried on in his capacity of a promoter. *For example*, when he has negotiated a certain price for some land for the company, he must sell the property to the company at the negotiated price. If he charges a price higher than the negotiated price, the company may rescind the contract on discovering the truth of the matter. If, due to some reason, the contract could not be rescinded, the company is entitled to claim damages from the promoters and the amount of damages shall be equal to the amount of profits made by promoters. However, it should be remembered that secret profits on the sale of property can be recovered from the promoter only when the property was bought and sold to the company while he was acting as a promoter. The promoter must act honestly and diligently to escape liability with respect to dealing with the future company and the outsiders.

4. **Duty of Promoters Towards Future Allottees** The promoters stand in a fiduciary position towards the company. It does not mean that they stand in such relation only to the company but they also stand in this position to the future allottees of shares. The promoters must ensure that the prospectus issued at their instance contains all materials facts and particulars and does not contain any mis-statements.

1.7 Liabilities or Promoters

The liabilities of the promoters under the various provisions of The Companies Act are discussed below:

1. **Liability for not Complying with the Provisions of Section 56** Section 56 explains the matters that should be stated and the reports that should be set out in the prospectus. If this provision is not complied with, the promoter may be held liable by the shareholders.
2. **Civil Liabilities for Any Untrue Statements made in the Prospectus [Section 62]** The promoter may be held liable to pay compensation to every person who subscribes for shares or debentures for any loss or damage sustained by him on account of the untrue statement made in the prospectus. Under Section 62 specific provisions have also been made of the grounds on which the promoter can avoid his liability.
3. **Criminal Liabilities for Issuing a Prospectus which Contains Untrue Statements [Section 63]** The promoter can be held criminally liable if the prospectus issued by them contained mis-statements. The punishment prescribed is imprisonment extending upto two years or a fine upto Rs 50,000 or both. The promoters may have to bear this criminal liability for misstatements unless he can prove that the untrue statement was immaterial or that he was justified in believing, because of reasonable grounds, that the statement was true at the time of issue of prospectus.
4. **Liabilities for Public Examination [Section 478]** If in the event of winding up of the company the liquidator's report alleges a fraud in the promotion or formation of the company, the promoter can also be held liable for public examination by the Court like any other director or officer of the company.
5. **Liability for Misfeasance or Breach of Trust by Misapplication of Funds [Section 543]** Like any other director or officer of the company, a promoter can also be held liable if he had misapplied or retained any of the property of the company or is found guilty of breach of trust or misfeasance in relation to the company.
6. **Liable to be Suspended from Taking Part in the Management of the Company [Section 203]** The court may suspend a promoter from taking part in the management of the company for a period of five years if he is convicted of any offence in connection with the promotion, formation or management of a company.
7. **Personally Liability for Pre-incorporation Contracts** Even the death of the promoter does not relieve him from this liability.

1.8 Remuneration of Promoters

(a) No Right to claim Remuneration

A promoter has no right to demand any remuneration from the company, for his promotional services in the absence of an express contract with the company. In the absence of a contract, he cannot even recover from the company payments he has made towards legal fees, stamp duties, registration fees, or other expenses in connection with the formation of the company.

He, therefore, is not entitled to recover any remuneration for his services unless the company after getting formed enters into a specific contract with the promoter for this purpose. Even if the promoter has entered into a contract with the prospective directors before the incorporation, he has no valid claim against the company for remuneration. This is so because the directors cannot enter into any contract on behalf of a company that is not yet in existence. There are also cases where the articles of a company may specifically provide that a specified sum may be paid to the promoters as remuneration for their services. While this provision gives the director an authority to make such payment, it does not give the promoters a right to claim remuneration or to sue the company, for the same.

(b) Modes of Giving Remuneration

The remuneration may be paid to the promoters in any of the following ways:

(i) He may be allowed to sell his own property to the company for cash at a price higher than the valuation, after he has made a full disclosure about the valuation and the profit earned to an independent Board of Directors.

(ii) If the promoter has purchased some business or some other property to be sold to the company, he may sell the same to the company at a higher price after making a full disclosure of the price paid and the profit earned.

(iii) The company may allot to the promoters fully paid up shares of the company.

(iv) He may be paid a certain lump-sum by the company as a remuneration of services rendered.

(v) He may be given a commission at fixed rate on the shares sold.

(vi) The company may give him an option to subscribe for a certain number of the company's unissued shares at par. This option is generally limited to a certain period which means that the promoter must subscribe to the shares within a certain time.

(c) Disclosure of Promoters' Remuneration in Prospectus

Whatever is the manner in which the company chooses to compensate for the services of the promoter, **the amount of remuneration and the manner of payment must be disclosed in the prospectus, if the remuneration is paid within two years preceding the date of the prospectus.**

2.0 PRELIMINARY CONTRACTS OR PRE-INCORPORATION CONTRACTS

2.1 Meaning of Preliminary Contracts

Preliminary contracts are those contracts which are entered into by the promoters for and on behalf of the proposed company before its incorporation. These contracts are generally entered into by the promoters to acquire some property or some rights for the proposed company. For example, contract with the vendor to sell his running business to the proposed company, contract for the purchase of property for the proposed company, contract for the grant of a lease for the proposed company.

2.2 Legal Position of Preliminary Contracts

The legal position of preliminary contracts can be explained as follows:

1. **The Company is not bound by the Preliminary Contracts** The company cannot be held liable for the preliminary contracts. A company is not bound by the preliminary contracts even if the company has taken the benefit of the work on its behalf under the contract. In case of *Re English* and *Colonial Produce Ltd.*, (1906) 2 Ch. 435, a solicitor was appointed by the promoters of the company and was instructed by them to prepare the articles and the memorandum of the company. The solicitor also paid the necessary registration fee of the company. These promoters later became the directors of the company. The solicitor sued for his expenses and the fees paid by him. It was held that since the company was not in existence when these expenses were incurred, the company is not bound to pay.
2. **The Company cannot enforce Preliminary Contracts** The company cannot enforce such contracts made before incorporation, by the promoters. This means that on account of a preliminary contract the company does not get a right to sue the third party for fulfilment of the contract. In case of *Natal Land Co.* v. *Pauline Colliery Syndicate* (1904) A.S. 120, the owner of a piece of land agreed to lease it to a company to be formed by promoters. The promoters

later on formed a company. On some prospecting of the land, it was discovered that there was a definite possibility of striking of in that land. Subsequently 'owner' refused to grant the lease to the company. It was held that the company cannot sue 'owner' and cannot claim specific performance as it was not even in existence when the lease was signed.

Thus, preliminary contracts can not be enforced by or against the company.

Exception to above principles The provisions of Sections 15(h) and 19(e) of The Specific Relief Act, 1963 provide an important exception to the general principle 'preliminary contracts can not be enforced by or against the company'.

According to Sections 15(h) and 19(e) of the Specific Relief Act, 1963, where the promoters of the company have entered into contracts before its incorporation, specific performance may be obtained by or against the company if—

(a) Such contracts are for the purposes of the company.

The term *"contracts for the purposes of the company"* means contracts which are necessary for the incorporation and working of the company. For example, contracts for the preparation and printing of the memorandum and articles or contracts for the supply of necessary raw material for the production work in the company are contracts for the purposes of the company.

(b) Such contracts are warranted by terms of incorporation.

(c) Such contracts are accepted by the company after its incorporation.

(d) The acceptance of such contracts is communicated by the company to the other party to the contract.

However the above provisions are not applicable for:

(a) Contract to take shares

(b) Contract to render personal services.

3. **The Company cannot ratify the Preliminary Contracts** The company cannot ratify the preliminary contracts after incorporation because for valid ratification of a contract, the principal must have been in existence on the date when the contract is originally entered into. In case of *Kelner* v. *Baxter*, it was held as the company was not in existence when the preliminary contracts were made, it could not be bound by a purported ratification. What the company can do is to enter into a new contract with the vendors after incorporation to give effect to the terms of the contract made before incorporation.

4. **The Company cannot adopt Preliminary Contracts** The company cannot adopt preliminary contracts after its incorporation either by passing a special resolution or by making adoption of such contract as one of the objects of company in its memorandum of association. *[North Sydney Investment Company* v. *Higgins* (1999) A.C. 263]

5. **Personal Liability of the Promoter for Preliminary Contracts** The promoters are personally liable for the preliminary contracts. The reason for this is that the preliminary contract is made for a company which, as known to both the contracting parties, is as yet non-existent. The contract, therefore, is deemed to be personally entered into by the promoters and they will be held personally liable for the performance of these contracts. The promoters will continue to be personally liable until the company after its incorporation adopt preliminary contracts by entering into new contracts with the third parties on the same terms as were embodied in the original contracts.

The preliminary contracts made by the promoters generally contain a provision that if the company adopts the agreements on incorporation, the liability of the promoters shall come to an end and if the company does not adopt the preliminary contract within a specified period *either* party may rescind the contract. In such a case liability of the promoter will cease on the expiry of the specified period.

3.0 HOW TO FORM A COMPANY

The various steps involved in the formation of a company are given below:

I. Approval of Name

Step No. 1 Consult—

(a) the latest edition of Directory of Companies together supplements updating it,
(b) the Guidelines issued by the Department of Company affairs, and
(c) the Emblems and Names (Prevention of Improper Uses) Act, 1950

Step No. 2 Select in order of preference at least three names which—

(a) are not identical with or too similar to the name of another registered company,
(b) are not prohibited under the Emblem and Names (Prevention of Improper Uses) Act, 1950, and
(c) are not in contravention of the Guidelines issued by the Department of Company affairs.

Step No. 3 Apply to the Registrar of Companies of the State in which registered office is to be situate to ascertain the availability of names in the prescribed Form No. 1A along with a fee of Rs 500.

Step No. 4 Get ensured about the availability of names within 14 days from date of submission of application since the Registrar is required to inform the status of the application within 14 days.

(a) If available—Complete all the formalities within a period of 3 months.
(b) If not available—Apply again (if satisfied with the reason for refusal given) or, Make an appeal against refusal.

II. Memorandum and Articles of Association

Step No. 5 Get the Drafts of Memorandum of Association and Articles of Association **prepared.** However a public company limited by shares need not prepare its own articles. It may adopt Table A as given in Schedule I of the Act.

Step No. 6 Get the Draft of Memorandum of Association and the Articles of Association **vetted** by the Registrar.

Step No. 7 Get the Memorandum Association and Articles of Association **printed**.

Step No. 8 Get the Memorandum of Association and Articles of Association **stamped.**

Step No. 9 Get the Memorandum of Association and Articles of Association **signed** by at least 2 subscribers in case of a private company and 7 subscribers in case of a public company. Each subscriber shall also write in his own hand his address, description, occupation and number of shares subscribed for in presence of at least one witness who shall attest the signature and shall write in his own hand his address, description and occupation (if any). These documents may be signed by an agent if he is authorized to do so by a power of attorney.

Step No. 10 Ensure that Memorandum and Articles of Association are **dated** on a date after the date of stamping.

III. Consent to Act as Director in Form No. 29

Step No. 11 Get Form No. 29 (in duplicate) duly filled up and signed to accord to **consent** of a person willing to act as director if he is so appointed by the Articles of Association of a public company having share capital [Section 266].

IV. Notice of Situation in Form No. 18 (May be given within 30 days of Incorporation)

Step No. 12 Get Form No. 18 (in duplicate) duly filled up and signed to give the notice of the situation of the registered office of the company if the subscribers have already chosen a registered office and they wish to give notice to the Registrar at the time of registration. *Alternatively* such notice may be given within 30 days of the incorporation of the company. [Section 146]

V. Particulars of Directors, Manager or Secretary in Form No. 32 (May be given within 30 days of Incorporation)

Step No. 13 Get Form No. 32 (in duplicate) duly filled up and signed to provide particulars of directors, manager or secretary if they are appointed by Articles of Association and the subscribers wish to give notice to the Registrar at the time of registration. *Alternatively,* such form may be sent within 30 days of appointment of first directors.

VI. Statutory Declaration in Form No. 1

Step No. 14 Get the Statutory Declaration prepared in Form No. 1. Statutory declaration is a declaration to the effect that all the requirements of the act and rules thereunder relating to the registration of the company have been complied with. Such declaration can be signed by any one of the following persons:

(a) an advocate of the Supreme Court or of a High Court; or

(b) an attorney or a pleader entitled to appear before a High Court; or

(c) a secretary, or a chartered accountant practicing in India and who has been engaged in the formation of the company; or

(d) by a person named in the articles as a director, manager or secretary of the company.

VII. Filing of Documents with Fees

Step No. 15 File the following documents with the Registrar of companies along with the forwarding application with necessary registration and filing fees:

(a) The Memorandum of Association, duly signed by the prescribed minimum number of subscribers, and duly stamped and signed by witness. [Section 33(1)(a)]

(b) The Articles of Association similarly signed, stamped and witnessed. [Section 33(1)(b)]

(c) A copy of agreement, if any, which the company purposes to enter into with any individual for appointment as its Managing Director or Whole-time Director or Manager. [Section 33(1)(c)]

(d) A copy of any other agreement, if referred to in the Memorandum and Articles of Association in that case, it will form a part of the Memorandum and Articles of Association.

(e) Power of Attorney duly stamped and signed by the subscribers authorizing a representative to make amendments and/or alterations in the Memorandum and Articles of Association at the time of registration.

(f) A Certified copy of letter of the Registrar of Companies, intimating the availability of the proposed name.

(g) Consent of director to act in Form No. 29 (in duplicate) wherever necessary).

(h) Notice of the situation of the registered office in Form No. 18 (in duplicate) wherever necessary.

(i) Particulars of Directors, Managing Director, Manager and Secretary in Form No. 32 (in duplicate) wherever necessary.

(j) Statutory Declaration in Form No. 1.

VIII. Certificate of Incorporation

Step No. 16 Get the Certificate of incorporation.

4.0 CERTIFICATE OF INCORPORATION

4.1 Meaning of Certificate of Incorporation

When the necessary documents have been filed with the Registrar along with the payment of requisite fee, the Registrar shall scrutinize these documents and if he is satisfied that (a) all the documents are in order, and (b) the requirements of the Act in respect of registration have been duly complied with, he shall enter the name of the company in the Register of Companies and shall issue a certificate which is termed as 'Certificate of Incorporation.'

Note: If the Registrar is of the view that there are some minor defects in any document, he may require that the defects be rectified. But, if there are some material and substantial defects, the Registrar may refuse to register the company.

4.2 Contents of Certificate of Incorporation

The certificate of incorporation contains:

(a) the name of the company,
(b) the date of its issue, and
(c) the signature of the Registrar with his seal.

This certificate is literally the birth certificate of the company evidencing that the company is born with its name on the date mentioned in the certificate.

Note: A print of this certificate is to be a part of all copies of Memorandum and Articles of association.

4.3 Conclusiveness of Certificate of Incorporation

1. According to Section 35 of the Companies Act
   Certificate of incorporation given by the Registrar of Companies in respect of any association shall be conclusive evidence that all the requirements of Companies Act have been complied with in respect of its registration as well as matters precedent and incidental thereto, and the association is a company authorized to be registered and duly registered under the Act.
2. Certificate cannot be disputed on any ground whatsoever and nothing is required to be inquired into as to the regularity of the prior proceedings.
3. In view of the exclusiveness of its Certificate of Incorporation, irregularities relating to procedural matters pertaining to registration such as defects in the signatures of the subscribers, or other prescribed particulars will not affect the legal status or personality of the company though it does not prevent an aggrieved person presenting a claim against persons responsible for getting the company incorporated.
4. In *Peer's* case, the memorandum was found materially altered after the signatories had signed but before registration. It was held that the corporate status remained unaffected and the certificate of incorporation was valid. Highlighting the necessity of this rule, Lord Cairns observed as follows:

   "When once the memorandum is registered and the company holds out to the world as a company undertaking business, willing to receive shareholders and ready to contract engagement, then, it would be of the most disastrous consequence if after all that has been done, any person was allowed to go back and enter into an examination of the circumstances attending the original registration and the regularity of the execution of the documents."

5. In *Moosa Goolam Arif* v. *Ebrahim Goolam Arif,* the memorandum of association of a public limited company was signed by two adult persons. Other five members of the company were minors. Their guardian made separate signatures for each of the minors. The Registrar registered the company and issued the certificate of incorporation. The incorporation of the company was challenged and the plaintiff prayed that the certificate of incorporation should be declared void. The Privy Council rejected the plea of the plaintiff and held that the certificate of incorporation was valid.
6. The certificate of incorporation is also a conclusive proof of the fact that the company came into existence on the date mentioned in the certificate.

   In the case of *Jubilee Cotton Mills Ltd.* v. *Lewis,* the company delivered to the Registrar of Companies documents required for the registration of the company on 6th January. On 8th January, the Registrar registered the company and issued the certificate of incorporation but dated it January 6. The company allotted few shares to Mr. Lewis of 6th January. The allotment was challenged and the court was requested to declare the allotment as void. The court held that the certificate of incorporation is conclusive evidence of all that it contains. Hence, the company shall be deemed to have been formed on 6th January and allotment of shares was valid.
7. Certificate of incorporation is not the conclusive proof with respect to the legality of the objective of the company, mentioned in the objects clause of the Memorandum of Association. As such, if a company has been registered whose objects are illegal, the incorporation does not validate the illegal objects. In such a case the only remedy available is to wind up the company.

4.4 Effects of Registration

1. From the date of incorporation, the original subscribers to the memorandum as well as the other persons who may, from time to time, become members of the company, shall constitute a body corporate by the name contained in the Memorandum of Association. [Section 34(2)]
2. The body corporate shall be capable of exercising all the functions of an incorporated company. [Section 34(2)]
3. The company shall have perpetual succession. [Section 34(2)]
   Perpetual existence shows the properties of immortality. In other words, it means that a company's existence persists irrespective of the change in the composition of its membership. It continues to exist even if all its human members are dead. The company may be compared with a flowing river where water (members) keeps as changing continuously still the identity of the river (company) remain the same. Since it is created by law, it can be put to an end only by the process of law. Thus, a company shall continue to exist indefinitely till it is wound up in accordance with the provision of the Companies Act.
4. The company shall have a Common Seal. [Section 34(2)]

   Common Seal means the official signatures of the company. Any document bearing the common seal of the company and duly witnessed by at least two directors will be legally binding on the company.
5. Members are liable to contribute to the assets of the company in the events of its being wound up to the extent of their contract or guarantee as the case may be. [Section 34(2)]

6. The memorandum and articles when registered shall bind the company and members. [Sec 36(1)]
7. All money payable by any member to the company under Memorandum or Articles shall be a debt due from him to the company. [Section 36(2)]
8. The subscribers of the memorandum of a company shall be deemed to have agreed to become members of the company and on its registration, shall be entered as members in its Register of Members. [Section 41(1)]
9. A private company can commence its business immediately after obtaining the certficate of incorporation.

Judicial Rulings

1. A company on registration acquires a separate existence and the law recognises it as a legal person separate and distinct from its members [*State Trading Corporation of India* v. *Commercial Tax Officer*, AIR 1963 SC 1811].
2. Merely because a company purchases all shares of another company it will not serve as a means of putting an end to the corporate character of another company because each company is a separate juristic entity [*Spencer & Co. Ltd. Madras* v. *CWT Madras*, [1969] 39 Comp. Case 212].
3. Even if the entire share capital is held by the President of India it does not make a company an agent either of the President [*Heavy Electrical Union* v. *State of Bihar*, AIR 1970 SC 82].

5.0 CERTIFICATE OF COMMENCEMENT OF BUSINESS

5.1 Meaning of Certificate of Commencement of Business

The certificate of commencement of business is a certificate **which entitles a company to** commence business or to exercise borrowing powers.

5.2 Companies not Required to Obtain Certificate of Commencement of Business

Since a private company (whether or not having share capital) and **a public company having no share capital** can commence business immediately after its incorporation, such companies are not required to obtain certificate of commencement of business.

5.3 Company which is Required to Obtain Certificate of Commencement of Business

A public company having share capital is required to obtain certificate of commencement of business from the Registrar before it can commence its business or exercise borrowing powers.

5.4 Procedure for Obtaining the Certificate of Commencement of Business

I. If a public company, having share capital, has issued a prospectus, inviting the public to subscribe for its shares or debentures, it cannot commence any business or exercise borrowing power unless—
   (a) **Allotment of Shares upto minimum subscription.** The company has allotted the shares upto the amount of minimum subscription.
   (b) **Payment of Application & Allotment Money by every Director**. Every director has paid to the company, in cash, the application and allotment money on the shares taken or contracted to be taken by him in the same proportion as public.

(c) **No money is repayable**. No money is liable to be repaid to the applicants for failure to apply for or to obtain permission for the shares or debentures to be listed on any recognized stock exchange.

(d) **Filing of Declaration**. Duly verified declaration in the prescribed Form No. 19 has been filed with the Registrar. The declaration must specify that Clauses (a), (b), and (c), as above have been complied with. The declaration must be verified by one of the directors or the Secretary of the Company. Where the Company has not appointed a Secretary, the declaration may be verified by a Secretary in whole-time practice.

II. If the company has a share capital but does not issue a prospectus inviting the public to subscribe for its shares, the company cannot commence any business unless—

(a) **Filing of Statement in lieu of Prospectus.** The company files with the Registrar, a statement in lieu of prospectus, alongwith the report specified in Part II of Schedule III. The statement should be filed with the Registrar at least three days before the first allotment.

(b) **Payment of Application & Allotment Noney by every Director.** Every director of the company has paid to the company, in cash, the application and allotment money on the shares taken or contracted to be taken by him.

(c) **Filing of Declaration.** A duly verified declaration in the prescribed form has been filed with the Registrar at least three days before the first allotment is made. The declaration must specify that the above conditions have been complied with and must be verified by one of the directors or the Secretary of the Company. In case the company has not appointed a Secretary, the declaration may be verified by a Secretary in whole time practice. [Section 149(2)]

When the above requirements are duly fulfilled, the Registrar shall issue a certificate known as 'certificate of commencement of business'. This document certifies that the company is entitled to commence business and is also a conclusive evidence of the fact that the company is so entitled. Any contract entered into will be binding on the company.

5.5 Consequences of Default [Section 149(6)]

If any company commences business in contravention of these provisions, **every persons** who is responsible for the default shall be punishable with fine upto **Rs 50,000 for every day** during which the default continues.

5.6 Consequences of not Commencing Business within 1 year [Section 433(c)]

If any company does not commence its business within one year of its incorporation, **it is liable to be wound up by the Court under Section 433.**

6.0 PROVISIONAL CONTRACTS

6.1 Meaning of Provisional Contracts

Provisional Contracts are those contracts which are entered into by the company after obtaining the certificate of incorporation but before obtaining the certificate of commencement of business.

6.2 Legal Position of Provisional Contracts

According to Section 149(4) such contracts are purely provisional in nature and shall not be binding on the company until the date on which it becomes entitled to commence business. Therefore, if a company enters into contract after its incorporation but never gets the certificate to commence business, contracts so entered shall not be binding upon the company. However, **on the issue of the commencement certificate, such contracts become automatically binding on the company and need no ratification.** *For example*, Mr. *X*, a machinery dealer entered into a contract with the company for supplying some machinery to the company. The company went into liquidation before it could obtain the certificate of commencement of business. Mr. X will not succeed in recovering the amount from the company because the company never became entitled to commence business. [*Re Otto Electrical Co.*, (1906)]

7.0 DISTINCTION BETWEEN PRELIMINARY CONTRACTS AND PROVISIONAL CONTRACTS

Preliminary Contracts differ from Provisional Contracts in the follwing respects:

Basis of Distinction	*Preliminary Contracts*	*Provisional Contracts*
1. Time when entered into	Preliminary contracts are entered into **before the incorporation** of company.	Provisional contracts are entered into **after the incorporation** of the company but before obtaining the certificate to commence business
2. Contracting Parties	These are entered into between the **promoters and outsiders.**	These are entered into between the **company and outsiders.**
3. Companies to which apply	These apply to **both private and public** companies.	These apply **only to public** companies.
4. Ratification	The company can **neither ratify nor adopt** such contracts.	Such contracts become automatically binding on the company and need **no ratification** on issue of certificate to commence business.

EXERCISES

VERY SHORT ANSWER QUESTIONS

1. What is meant by 'Promotion of a Company'?
2. Who are called 'Promoters'?
3. What is meant by 'Preliminary Contracts'?
4. What is meant by 'Provisional Contracts'?
5. What is meant by 'Certificate of Incorporation'?
6. What is meant by 'Certificate of Commencement of Business'?
7. From which date is a company said to be incorporated?

SHORT ANSWER TYPE QUESTIONS

1. Everyone who is associated with the process of the formation of a company is called 'promoter.' comment.
2. Enumerate the functions performed by the promoters.
3. State the legal position of promoters.
4. Enumerate the duties of promoters.
5. Enumerate the liabilities of promoters.
6. (a) can the promoters claim as a matter of right any remuneration from the company?
   (b) can the promoters claim remuneration if they have already entered into a contract with the prospective directors before the incorporation?
   (c) can the promoters claim remuneration of the Articles provide that a specified sum may be paid to the promoters or remuneration?
   (d) state the various modes of giving remuneration to the promoters.
   (e) what are the disclosure requirements in respect of remuneration to promoters in prospectus?
7. Mention the documents which are filed with the registrar for incorporation.
8. (a) State the meaning and contents of certificate of incorporation.
   (b) What is meant by 'conclusiveness of certificate of Incorporation'?
9. State the effects of Registration.
10. Comment on the following:
    (a) A promoter is not a trustee or an agent of the company but he stands in a fiduciary position towards it.
    (b) The validity of a certificate of incorporation cannot be disputed on any ground whatsoever.
    (c) The services of a promoter are very peculiar.
    (d) Promoters can demand remuneration if the Articles provide for the payment thereof.
11. Distinguish between Preliminary Contracts and Provisional Contracts.

LONG ANSWER TYPE QUESTIONS

1. Explain the various functions performed by the promoters.
2. (a) Explain the duties and liabilities of promoters?
   (b) How can promoters be remunerated by the company for his work?
3. (a) What is meant by preliminary contracts?
   (b) Discuss the legal position of preliminary contracts?
   (c) Can a company rectify such contracts?
4. Enumerate the practical steps involved in the incorporation of a company.
5. (a) What is meant by 'Certificate of Commencement of Business'?
   (b) State the company which is required to obtain such certificate.
   (c) State the companies which are not required to obtain such certificate.
   (d) State the procedure for obtaining such certificate.
   (e) State the consequence of default.
   (f) State the consequence of not commencing business.
6. State the meaning and legal position of provisional contracts. Is the company required to ratify such contracts?

CHAPTER 4

Memorandum of Association

1.0 MEANING OF MEMORANDUM OF ASSOCIATION

According to Section 2(28) of The Companies Act, Memorandum means **"the memorandum of association of a company as originally framed or as altered from time to time in pursuance of any previous company laws or of this Act"**. But this definition is not an exhaustive one.

The status and importance of Memorandum of Association has been clearly brought out in many decided cases as follows:

1. "Memorandum of Association of a company contains the fundamental conditions upon which alone the company is allowed to be incorporated. They are conditions introduced for the benefit of the creditors and the outside public as well of the shareholders". [*Guinness* v. *Land Corporation of Ireland,* (1882) 22 Ch. D. 359]
2. "In the case of *Ashbury Rly. Carriage and Iron Co.* v. *Riche,* (1875) LR 7HL 653, *Lord Cairns* observed Memorandum of association of a company is its charter and defines the limitations on the powers of the company established under the Act, that it contains in it, both that which is affirmative and that which is negative and that it states affirmatively, the ambit and extent of vitality and power which by law are given to the corporation and it states negatively that nothing shall be done beyond that ambit".
3. Memorandum of Association defines its relations with the outside world and the scope of its activities. Its purpose is to enable the shareholders, creditors and those who deal with the company to know that is its permitted range of activities [*Egyptian Salt and Soda Co. Ltd.* v. *Portsaid Salt Association*, 1931 A.C. 677].

To sum up **Memorandum of Association is the constitution of the company which lays down the fundamental conditions upon which alone the company is allowed to be formed. It defines as well as confines the powers of the company.** It not only shows the objects of formation but also determines the utmost possible scope of its operations beyond which its action cannot go. If it enters into a contract which is beyond the powers conferred on it by the memorandum, such contract will be *ultra vires* the company and hence void. Even the unanimous consent of the entire body of its members cannot ratify such contract.

Thus, in this respect it is the company's charter defining its constitution and scope of the powers with which it has been established under the Act.

2.0 PURPOSE OF MEMORANDUM OF ASSOCIATION

The Memorandum of Association is a public document which is open for inspection by any member of the public on payment of prescribed fees [Section 610]. Therefore, every person who deals with the company is presumed to have the knowledge of its contents.

The purpose of Memorandum is two-fold.

(a) First, **to enable the intending shareholders** to know the purpose for which their money is going to be used and within what field they are taking risk in making the investment.

(b) Second, **to enable the persons intending to deal** with the company to know with certainty as to whether the contractual relationship which they intend to enter into with the company is within its corporate objects or not [*Cotman* v. *Broughman,* (1918) A.C. 514].

Thus, Memorandum gives protection not only to the shareholders but also to persons who intend to deal with the company.

3.0 FORM OF MEMORANDUM OF ASSOCIATION [SECTION 14]

According to Section 14, the Memorandum of Association of a company must be in one of the forms given in Schedule I as may be applicable to the case of the company or in a form as near thereto as circumstances admit.

The Tables in Schedule I to the Act specify the following forms applicable to different types of companies as under:

Table B: Memorandum of Association of a Company Limited by Shares.

Table C: Memorandum of Association of a Company Limited by Guarantee and not having a share capital.

Table D: Memorandum of Association of a Company Limited by Guarantee and having a share capital.

Table E: Memorandum of Association of an Unlimited Company.

4.0 PRINTING AND SIGNATURE OF MEMORANDUM [SECTION 15]

The memorandum must be—

(a) printed,

(b) divided into paragraphs numbered consecutively, and

(c) signed by at least 7 persons in case of a public company and by at least 2 persons in case of a private company. The persons signing the Memorandum are known as subscribers to the Memorandum.

— Each subscriber must give his address, description and occupation (if any).

— The signature of each subscriber must be attested in the presence of at least one witness.

— The witness must attest the signature and add his address, description and occupation (if any).

5.0 CONTENTS OF MEMORANDUM [SECTION 13]

The memorandum of association of a company must state the following clauses:

1. The Name Clause;
2. The Registered Office Clause;
3. The Objects Clause;
4. The Territorial Limit Clause;
5. The Liability Clause;
6. The Capital Clause; and
7. The Subscription Clause.

Let us know about each of the aforesaid clauses in detail.

6.0 NAME CLAUSE

1. Legal Requirements

(a) Last Word [Section 13(1)(a)] The Memorandum of every company must state the name of the company with the word "**Limited**" as the last word of the name in the case of a Public Limited Company and with "**Private Limited**" as the last words of the name in the case of a private limited company.

Exception in Case of Licensed (Associations Not for Profit) Companies [Section 25] The Central Government may by licence direct that a non-profit making association be registered as a company with limited liability without the addition of the word 'Limited' or the words 'Private limited'. A non-profit making association is an association which—

(i) is formed for promoting commerce, art, science, religion, charity or any other useful object,

(ii) intends to apply its profits/income in promoting its objects, and

(iii) prohibits the payment of any dividend to its members.

(b) Undesirable Name to be avoided [Section 20(1)] The name must not be undesriable in the opinion of Central Government. The name shall be considered as undesirable if—

(i) It is identical with or too nearly resembles the name of an existing company [Section 20(2)(i)] or a registered trademark, or a trade mark which is subject of an application for registration of any other person under the Trade Marks Act 1999 [Section 20(2)(ii)]. However the Central government before deeming a name as undesirable under Section 20(2)(ii) consult the Registrar of Trade Mark [Section 20(3)].

In *Society of Motor Manufacturers and Traders Ltd.* v. *Motor Manufacturers and Traders Mutual Assurance Co. Ltd.*, (1925) 1 Ch. 675, where a company was incorporated to conduct the business of motor vehicle assurance under a name somewhat similar to that of a motor dealer's trade protection association, the court refused an injunction to the association because the difference between the activities of the company and the association precluded any possibility of confusion.

In *Ewing* v. *Buttercup Margarine Co.*, (1917) 2 Ch. 1, Ewing was carrying on business under the name of Buttercup Dairy Company as a wholesale and retail provision merchant. A new company, Buttercup Margarine Co., was formed with the object of manufacturing and selling margarine in wholesale. Ewing applied to the court for restraining the new company from using the name, contending that it was calculated to deceive and that people were likely to be confused into thinking of both companies as one or closely related. The court granted an injunction.

The court, however, will not grant an injunction to prevent the use of a purely descriptive word with a definite meaning and in common use. In *Aerators Ltd.* v. *Tollit*, (1902) 2 Ch. 319, the business of the plaintiff was the sale of apparatus by which small quantities of liquids could be aerated. The defendant proposed to register a company to be called Automatic Aerators Limited, the object of which was to work under patents in respect of aeration of liquids in large quantities. The court did not grant the injunction as both companies had different patents and apparatus although the main object of both was to manufacture apparatus for the instantaneous, automatic aeration of liquids.

(ii) It is prohibited by the Emblems and Names (Prevention of Improper Use) Act, 1950. This Act prohibits the use of the name and emblems of the United Nations and the World Health Organisation, the official seal and emblems of the Central and State Governments, the Indian National Flag, the name and pictorial representation of Mahatma Gandhi and the Prime Minister of India.

(iii) It is in the contravention of the guidelines issued by the Department of Company Affairs (Govt. of India).

(c) Publication of Name and Address [Section 147]

(i) The name and the address of the registered office must be painted or affixed on the outside of every office or place of business in legible characters of one of the languages in general use in that locality.

(ii) The name and the address of the registered office must be mentioned in legible characters in all its business letters, bill heads, letter papers, notices and other official publications.

(iii) The name must be engraved in legible characters on its seal.

(iv) The name must be mentioned in all bills of exchange, hundies, promissory notes, endorsements, cheques and orders for money or goods, bills of parcels, receipts and letters of credit.

7.0 REGISTERED OFFICE CLAUSE [SECTION 13(1)(b) AND SECTION 146]

7.1 Legal Requirements

(a) Name of the State [Section 13(1)] The Memorandum of every company must state the name of the State in which the registered office of the company is to be situated. It may be noted that the exact address of the registered office need not be stated in the Memorandum.

(b) Time Limit within which the Company must have its Registered Office [Section 146(1)] A company must have a registered office as from the day on which it commences business or as from the 30th day after the date of its incorporation whichever is earlier.

(c) Notice of Situation [Section 146(2)] Notice of the situation of the registered office and of every change therein must be given to the Registrar (otherwise than through a statement as to the address of the registered office in the Annual Report) within 30 days of the date of the incorporation or of the date of change.

7.2 Importance All communications and notices are to be addressed to the registered office [Section 146(1)]. Every company must keep proper books of account at its registered office [Section 209(1)]. The domicile and the nationality of the company and the jurisdiction of the court is determined by the situation of its registered office.

8.0 OBJECTS CLAUSE [SECTION 13(1)(d)]

8.1 Division of Object Clause into two Sub-Clauses

The Company registered after the commencement of the Companies (Amendment) Act, 1965 must divide its object clause into two sub-clauses, namely:

(a) Main Objects

This sub-clause covers the following two:

(i) Main Objects of the Company to be pursued on its incorporation, and

(ii) Objects incidental or ancillary to the attainment of the main objects.

(b) Other Objects

This sub-clause covers the other objects which are not included in 'Main Objects'.

Notes:

(i) If more than one activity is proposed to be pursued, a separate paragraph should be provided for each activity.

(ii) Under 'Objects incidental or ancillary to the attainment of main objects' all activities essential for the attainment of main objects such as opening of a Bank Account, Appointment of agents, officers, purchase and sale of raw material and finished goods etc., are to be included. These are also terms as *implied powers*.

(iii) The test to be applied whether a power is implied or not, is not the benefit which the transaction is expected to confer on the company but whether it can reasonably be regarded as arising from the main object of the company. In case of *London Country Council* v. *Attorney General* (1902) A.C. 165, the council having a statutory power to work tramways was restrained from running omnibuses in connection with the tramways. The court held that the council could not undertake the omnibus business as it was in no way incidental to the business of working tramways, however beneficial it might prove to the original business.

In case of *Evans* v. *Brunner Mond & Co.* (1921) 1 Ch. 359, where a company expended money on scientific research while its main object was the business of chemical manufacturing, it was held that the act was conducive to attainment of the main object of the company and therefore very much within its powers.

(iv) Wherever the object clause includes the words such as "to do all such things as are incidental or ancillary to the attainment of the main objects", these words do not increase the area of the company's express powers as defined by the 'Main objects'. These words should be construed as being limited to the doing of such things as are legitimate necessary to the attainment of the objects previously specified.

(v) In case of companies (other than trading corporations), with object not confined to one state, the states to whose territories the object extends. [Section 13(1)(e)].

8.2 Restrictions on the Selection of Objects

The subscribers to the memorandum may choose any 'objects' for the purposes of their company subject to the following restrictions:

(a) The objects must **not include anything** which is **illegal or contrary** to general law e.g. floating a company for dealing in lotteries [*Ex-parte More,* (1931) 2 K.B. 197].

(b) The objects must **not include anything** which is **against public policy** e.g. trading with alien enemies [*Daimler & Co.* v. *Continental Tyre Co.*, (1916) 2 A.C. 307] or objects which are in restraint of trade [*Mac. Ellis* v. *Calligot etc. Company,* (1919) A.C. 459].

(c) The objects must **not include anything** which is **prohibited by the Companies Act, 1956**.

8.3 Importance of Objects Clause

The objects clause is of fundamental importance to its members as well as its non-members. In the *first place*, it give protection to subscribers (members) who learn from it the purposes to which their money can be applied. In the *second place*, it gives protection to outsiders dealing with the company who learn from it what its powers are and what is the range of its activities. The narrower the objects appended in the memorandum, the lesser is the subscribers' risks, the wider these objects, the greater is the security of those who transact business with the company.

9.0 LIABILITY CLAUSE [SECTION 13(2)]

9.1 The liability clause states the nature of the liability of members.

9.2 The legal requirements regarding this clause in respect of various types of companies are as follows:

Type of company	*Legal requirement*
(a) ***In case of a company limited by shares***	Liability clause must state that the liability of its members is limited. It means means that liability of a member is limited to the nominal value of shares held by him. In case the shares are partly paid, then no member can be called upon to pay more than the amount that remains unpaid on his shares. Thus, a member is liable to pay only the unpaid amount on his shares and no further. For example, a shareholder holds a Rs 10 share and has paid Rs 8 on its so far. He can be called upon to pay Rs 2 and nothing more. In this example, if he holds a fully paid-up share, then his liability is nil.
(b) ***In case of a company limited by guarantee***	Liability clause must state that the liability of a member is limited to the amount which he has agreed to contribute to the assets of the company in the event of winding up.

Notes:

(i) In case of an unlimited company, liability clause is not required.

(ii) In a limited company, the liability of directors or of any director or manager may be made unlimited by providing so in the memorandum. [Section 322]

(iii) Where a company has carried on business with fewer members than the statutory minimum for more than 6 months, every member who is aware of this fact is severally liable for the entire debts of the company contracted after a period of 6 months and may be severally sued therefor. [Section 45]

10.0 CAPITAL CLAUSE [SECTION 13(4)]

10.1 In case of limited companies by shares, this clause must state the amount of share capital with which the company is to be registered and the division thereof into shares of fixed amount.

10.2 Such capital is called *'Authorised'* or *'Nominal'* or *'Registered'* capital. The fixed amount of a share is known as *'Par'* or *'Nominal'* value of a share.

10.3 The stamp duty and registration fee are payable on the basis of amount of authorised capital.

Notes:

(i) In case of an unlimited company having a share capital, the capital clause is not required in its memorandum. But Section 27(1) provides that the amount of share capital with which the company is to be registered must be stated in the Articles of Association of an unlimited company having a share capital.

(ii) In case of company having no share capital, the capital clause is not required in its memorandum.

(iii) Division of the authorised capital into different classes of shares (if any) and the rights of various clauses of shareholders need not be stated in the capital clause. Instead, these details may be given in the Articles of the company.

(iv) The effect of capital clause is that the company cannot issue more shares than are authorised for the time being by the memorandum.

11.0 ASSOCIATION OR SUBSCRIPTION CLAUSE [SECTIONS 12(1), 13(4)(B), (C) AND 15(C)]

11.1 Legal Requirements

(a) Each of the subscribers must give in his own handwriting his name with surname, address, description (by the name of father, husband or wife as the case may be). [Section 15(c)]

(b) In case of a company having share capital, the each of the subscriber must also write in his own handwriting opposite to his name, the number of shares agreed to be subscribed by him. Each subscriber must take at least one share. [Section 13(4)(b), (c)]

(c) that such declaration must be signed by at least 7 persons (in case of a public company) or 2 persons (in case of a private company). [Section 12(1)]

(d) that an agent may sign the memorandum of association on behalf of subscriber if he is authorised by a power of attorney to do so.

(e) that the signatures of the subscribers must be attested by at least one witness who must not be from among the subscribers. [Section 15(c)]

(f) that each of the witnesses must give in his own handwriting, his name, with surname, the description and occupation, if any. [Section 15(c)]

(g) Such clauses must be strictly in accordance with such one of formats given in Tables B, C, D and E of Schedule I as may be applicable to the case of company.

Notes:

(i) Only individuals or only a person can be a signatiory to the memorandum. It follows therefore that a firm cannot be signatory to the memorandum, because it is not a person having an individuality separate from that of its partners.

(ii) Only individuals or other legal entities can be members of a company [*Ganesh Dass* v. *R.G. Cotton Mills Co.,* [1974] C.W.N. (345)]. But under Section 25(4), a firm may continue to be member of licensed company. Thus, it is an exception to the generality of the law which precludes the firm being accepted as a share holder of a company.

11.2 Specimen of Subscription Clause in Case of Memorandum of a Company Having a Share Capital

"We the several persons whose names and addresses are subscribed, are desirous of being formed into a company in pursuance of the Memorandum of Association and we respectively agree to take the number of shares in the capital of the company set opposite to our respective names".

12.0 ALTERATION OF THE MEMORANDUM

A company may alter the conditions contained in this memorandum in the cases, in the mode and to the extent for which express provision is made in the Act [Section 16(1)]. Let us now discuss the procedure for making alternations in the different clauses of the memorandum.

13.0 ALTERATION OF THE NAME CLAUSE

13.1 Procedure for Changing the Name Clause

The procedure for changing the name of the company is given below:

Case	*Legal Requirements*
(i) ***Where the only change in the name of the Company is the deletion therefrom the words 'private' consequent on the conversion of a private company into a public company. [Proviso to Section 21]***	(a) The company may change its name by passing a special resolution at a general meeting of the members. (b) A copy of resolution is required to be filed with the Registrar within 30 days of passing the resolution.
(ii) ***Where the only change in the name of the company is the addition thereto the words 'private' consequent on the conversion of a public company into a private company. [Proviso to Sections 21 and 31(1)]***	(a) The company may change its name by passing a special resolution. However, *to alter the Articles in this case*, the approval of Central Government would be necessary in addition to special resolution. (b) A copy of resolution is required to be filed with the Registrar within 30 days of passing the resolution. (c) A copy of order of the Central Government's approval is required to be filed with the Registrar within 3 months of the order.
(iii) ***To change the name which is identical with or too nearly resembles the name of an already registered existing company or on an application by a registered proprietor of a trade mark, is in the opinion of Central Government identical with or too nearly resembles, a registered trade mark of such proprietor under Trade Marks Act, 1999. [Section 22(1)(a)]***	(a) The company may change its name by passing an ordinary resolution and with the previous approval of the Central Government signified in writing. (b) A copy of resolution is required to be filed with the Registrar within 30 days of passing the resolution. (c) A copy of order of the Central Government's approval is required to be filed with the Registrar within 3 months of the order.
(iv) ***To change the name on direction by the Central Government within 12 months of registration of name/new name. [Section 22 (1)(b)]***	(a) The company must change its name by passing a ordinary resolution and with the previous approval of the Central Government within a period of 3 months from the date of direction or such longer period as the Central Government may think fit to allow. (b) A copy of resolution is required to be filed with the Registrar within 30 days of passing the resolution. (c) A copy of order of the Central Government's approval is required to be filed with the Registrar within 3 months of the order.
(v) ***To change the name, including or consisting of the omission of the words 'Limited' or the words 'Private Limited' in case of licensed companies. [Section 25(3)]***	(a) The company may change its name by passing a special resolution. (b) A copy of resolution is required to be filed with the Registrar within 30 days of passing the resolution.
(vi) ***To change the name in any other case. [Section 21]***	(a) The company may change its name by passing a special resolution and with the written approval of the Central Government. (b) A copy of resolution is required to be filed with the Registrar within 30 days of passing the resolution. (c) A copy of order of the Central Govern-ment's approval is required to be filed with the Registrar within 3 months of the order.

Note: Application by a registered proprietor of trade mark should be considered after 5 years of coming to notice the registration of the company. [Proviso to Section 22(1)]

13.2 Registration of Change of Name [Section 23]

The provisions relating to the registration of change of name are given below:

(a) A copy of the resolution passed at the general meeting must be filed with the Registrar within 30 days of passing the resolution.

(b) A copy of the order of the Central Government's approval (whenever if any required) must be filed with the Registrar within 3 months of the order.

(c) The Registrar shall enter the new name on the Register in the place of the former name and shall issue a fresh certificate of incorporation with the necessary alterations embodied therein. [Section 23(1)]

(d) The change of name shall be complete and effective only on the issue of such a certificate. [Section 23(1)]

(e) The Registrar shall also make the necessary alteration in the Memorandum of association of the company. [Section 23(2)]

(f) The change of name shall not affect any right or obligations of the company. [Section 23(3)]

(g) The change of name shall not render defective any legal proceedings by or against it. Any legal proceedings which might have been continued or commenced by or against the company by its former name may be continued by its new name. [Section 23(3)]

14.0 ALTERATION OF REGISTERED OFFICE

14.1 Procedure for changing the Registered Office

The procedure for changing the registered office of the company is given below:

Case	*Legal Requirements*
(i) ***Change from one place to another within the same city, town or village [Section 146(2)]***	(a) A resolution of the Board of Directors isrequired to be passed. (b) Notice of new location must be given to the Registrar within 30 days of the change. [Section 146(2)]
(ii) ***Change from one city, town or village to another within the jurisdiction of the same ROC within the same State.***	(a) **Special Resolution** A special resolution is required to be passed at a general meeting of the shareholders. [Proviso to Section 146(2)] (b) **Filing of Copy of Special Resolution with ROC.** A copy of the special resolution, as aforesaid, is to be filed with the Registrar *within 30 days* in Form No. 23. (c) **Notice of New Location** Notice of the new location must be given to the Registrar within 30 days of change. [Section 146(2)]
(iii) ***Change from the jurisdiction of one ROC to the jurisdiction of another ROC within the same State.***	(a) **Special Resolution** A special resolution is required to be passed at a general meeting of the shareholders. [Proviso to Section 146(2)]

(*Contd.*)

(*Contd.*)

	(b) **Confirmation of Regional Director** Confirmation of Regional Director is to be obtained where the *change is from Registrar of Companies.* The Regional Director must convey his confirmation within 4 weeks from the date of receipt of application for such change. (c) **Filing of Copy of Special Resolution with ROC.** A copy of the special resolution, as aforesaid, is to be filed with the Registrar *within 30 days* in Form No. 23. (d) **Filing of Certified Copy of Confirmation together with altered Memorandum with ROC** A certified copy of the confirmation by Regional director together with a printed copy of the altered memorandum of association *must be filed* with the *Registrar of Companies* within 2 *months* of the date of confirmation. The Registrar is required to register the same and certify the registration within 1 month from the date of filing of the said document. The certificate shall be conclusive evidence that all the requirements of the Act with respect to the alteration and confirmation have been complied with and henceforth the memorandum as altered shall be the memorandum of the company. (e) **Notice of New Location** Notice of the new location must be given to the Registrar within 30 days of change. [Sec. 146(2)]
(iv) ***Change from one state to another***	(a) **Substantive Limits** Such change must be for any one of the following purposes (i) to carry on its business more economically or more efficiently; (ii) to attain its main purpose by new or improved means; (iii) to enlarge or change the local area of its operations; (iv) to carry on some business which under existing circumstances may conveniently or advantageously be combined with the business of the company; (v) to restrict or abandon any of the objects specified in the memorandum; (vi) to sell or dispose of the whole, or any part, of the undertaking or of any of the undertakings, of the company; or (vii) to amalgamate with any other company or body of persons. [Section 17(1)] **Procedure Limits** (b) A special resolution is required to be passed by the company at its general meeting. [Section 17(1)]

(*Contd.*)

(*Contd.*)

	(c) Such alteration must be confirmed by the Company Law Board **Note:** The C.L.B. has the power either to confirm or refuse to confirm alteration relating to the change of registered office. [Section 17(2)] (d) Notice must be given to every debenture- holder and to every other person or class of persons where interests are likely to be affected by the alterations. [Section 17(3)(a)]. However CLB may dispense with this requirement [Proviso to Section 17(3)] (e) Notice must be given to the Government of the State where the registered office is at present situated. [Rule 36 of CLB] (f) The company is required to give an advertisement in the newspapers indicating the change proposed to be made. [Rule 36 of CLB] (g) *Either* dissentient creditor's (i.e. creditor who objects to the alteration) consent must be obtained or his debt or claim must be discharged or secured.

14.2 Registration of Alteration of Registered Office [Sections 18 and 19]

The provisions relating to the registration of alteration of registered office are given below:

(a) A copy of the special resolution passed by the company at its general meeting must be filed with the Registrar within 30 days of passing of the resolution.

(b) A certified copy of the order of the Company Law Board together with a printed copy of the altered Memorandum must be filed with the Registrar within 3 months from the date of order [Section 18(1)]. However, the Company Law Board may extend this time by such period as it thinks proper. [Section 18(4)]

(c) The Registrar shall register the name and certify the registration within 1 month from the date of the filing of such documents. [Section 18(1)]

(d) A certified copy of the order of the Company Law Board is also required to be filed with the Registrar of the other state who shall register the name and certify the registration thereof. [Section 18(3)]

(e) The Registrar of the State from which such office is transferred shall send to the Registrar of the other State all documents relating to the company registered, recorded or filed in his office. [Section 18(3)]

(f) A notice of the new location of the registered office must be given to registrar at the state to which office has been shifted within 30 days after the change of office. [Section 146(2)]

14.3 Effect of Failure to Register

(a) No such alteration shall have any effect until it has been duly registered in accordance with the provisions of Section 18. [Section 19(1)].

(b) If the certified copy of order of Company Law Board together with a printed copy of altered memorandum is not filed within 3 months from the date of order, such alteration and the order and all proceedings connected therewith shall at the expiry of 3 months become void and inoperative. [Section 19(2)].

(c) However, the Company Law Board may revive its order if: (a) sufficient cause is shown, (b) an application is made within a further period of 1 month. [Proviso to Section 19(2)]

14.4 Leading Case Laws

1. In case of *Orient Paper Mills Limited* v. *State*, AIR (1959) Orissa 232, Orissa High Court held that the State in which the registered office of the company is situated could oppose the shifting of the registered office to place outside that State on the ground of loss of revenue and employment opportunities.
2. On the contrary, in case of *Rank Film Distributors of India Ltd.* v. *The Registrar of Companies*, AIR (1969) Cal. 32, the Calcutta High Court held that the State has no right to oppose the shifting of registered office from one State to another on the ground of loss of revenue. Loss of one State could be balanced by gain to another State and after all the country was one and indivisible. The consideration of loss of revenue is not only irrelevant but if it is accepted, it would deprive the company of the statutory power conferred on it by Section 17. The State may however object as a creditor in respect of arrears of revenue due to it. In case of *Mineral Mills* v. *Government of Maharashtra* (1975) 45 Comp. Cas. 1, the Bombay High Court also took a similar view.
3. In case of *Orissa Chemicals and Distilleries (P) Ltd.,* AIR (1961) Orissa [621] a company proposing to change the location of registered office from Orissa to Andhra Pradesh had relied on Section 17(1)(a) for the change on the ground of more direct and economic administration but had failed to clarify how the expenses would be curtailed or how the administration from Andhra Pradesh could be more direct while the factory was in Orissa. It was held that *bona fides* of the company's application for the change were questionable.

15.0 ALTERATION OF OBJECTS CLAUSE

Section 17 of The Companies Act lays down the substantive and procedural limits on the powers of alteration to the objects clause. These limits have been shown below:

Limits on the Power of Alteration of Objects Clause

Substantive Limits i.e. Change must be for any of the following specified purposes:	**Procedural Limits**
(a) to carry on its business more economically or more efficiently, (b) to attain its main purpose by new or improved means, (c) to enlarge or change the local area of its operations. (d) to carry on some business which under the existing circumstance may be conveniently or advantageously combined with the business of the company. (e) to restrict or abandon any of the objects specified in the memorandum, or (f) to sell or dispose of the whole, or any part of the undertaking of the company, (g) to amalgamate with any other company or body of persons.	1. Passing of the special resolution. 2. Filing within 1 month from date of resolution the following documents: (a) A copy of special resolution (b) A printed copy of altered memoran-dum.

Let us discuss in detail:

15.1 Substantive Limits Section 17(1)

Section 17(1) permits a company to alter its objects clause for the under mentioned purposes only:

(a) To Carry on its Business more Economically or more Efficiently Under this clause, keeping the same business as before, the company is permitted to alter the mode of conducting the business which enables the company to do so more economically or efficiently.

In *Re Scientific Poultry Breeders' Association Ltd.*, (1933) Ch. 227, the main object of the company was to encourage and improve the breeding of poultry. Its memorandum also prohibited payment of remuneration to or division of profits among the members of the governing body. When the business and membership of the company increased, it was found that members of the governing body were unable to give proper attention to the management of its affairs unless some remuneration was paid to them. It passed a special resolution for payment of equitable remuneration to the members of the governing body. When the petition was presented to the court for sanction, it was held that the alteration did not affect the main object of the company and would enable it to carry on its business more economically or efficiently.

(b) To Attain its Main Purpose by New or Improved Means Under this clause, keeping the same business as before, the company is permitted to alter the means of constructing its business which enable it to take advantage of new scientific discoveries and inventions.

(c) To Enlarge or Change the Local Area of its Operations Under this clause, keeping the same business as before the company is permitted to change the area of its operations. Re *Indian Mechanical Gold Extracting Co.*, (1891) 3 Ch. 538, the memorandum confined the area of its operations to India. The company passed a special resolution deleting the words "in India" from the memorandum so as to enlarge its area of operation. The court confirmed the alteration on the ground that it would enable the company to enlarge its area of operations. The court also directed that the company should change its name in such a manner that it did not give the impression that its business operations were confined only to India.

(d) To Carry on some Business which under the Existing Circumstances may Conveniently or Advantageously be Combined with the Business of the Company Under this clause, keeping the same business as before the company is permitted to take up any new business which can conveniently or advantageously be combined with the existing business of the company at the date of the proposed alteration.

Re Parent Tyre Co., (1923) 2 Ch. 222, it was held that the additional business which a company, by alteration of its memorandum, may carry on may be wholly different from and bear no relation to its existing business, provided it is capable of being conveniently and advantageously combined with it. Moreover, it should not be destructive or inconsistent with the existing business. Whether a business is such or not is for the company's shareholders and managers to judge. In this case a tyre company was authorised to conduct the general business of bankers and financiers. The company in this case had never manufactured tyres as it had always been a holding company. All its funds were invested in Dunlop Rubber Co. Ltd., and it wished to spread its investment risks over a wider range of securities.

In case of *Punjab Distillery Industries Ltd.* v. *Registrar of Companies,* (1963) Comp. Cas. 81, a company which was formed for carrying on distillery business and other allied objects to that business was not permitted to undertake cinema business as the new business could not conveniently or advantageously be combined with the existing business of the company.

Re Cyclist Touring Club, (1907) 1 Ch. 269, a company was incorporated to protect and promote the interests of pedal cyclists on public roads. The company passed a special resolution so as to include all vehicles including motors. The court disallowed the alteration as it was in consistent with the objects of the company because cyclists had to be protected against danger from motorists. The court held that the company would find itself in the impossible position of having to protect one class of members from another.

(e) To Restrict or Abandon any of the Objects Specified in the Memorandum Under this clause, the company is permitted to restrictor abandon any of the objects specified in the memorandum.

(f) To Sell or Dispose of the Whole or Any Part of the Undertaking Under this clause, the company is permitted to sell or dispose of the whole or any part of the undertaking of the company.

(g) To Amalgamate with any other Company or Body of Persons Under this clause, the company is permitted to amalgamate with any other company or body of persons.

15.2 Procedural Limits

The following procedure must be followed for altering the objects clause:

(a) Special Resolution

Special resolution authorising such alteration is required to be passed by the company at its general meeting. [Section 17(1)]

(b) Registration of Alteration

(i) A copy of special resolution passed by the company together with a printed copy of altered memorandum must be filed with the Registrar within 1 month from the date of such resolution.

(ii) The Registrar shall register the name and certify the registration within 1 month from the date of the filling of such documents. [Section 18(1)]

(iii) The Registrar's certificate shall be conclusive evidence that all the requirements with respect to alteration have been complied with and memorandum so altered shall be the memorandum of the company. The alteration is effective from the date of registration of the alteration.

15.3 Effect of Failure to Register [Section 19(2)]

If the documents required to be filled with the Registrar u/s 18 are not filed within 1 month, the alteration shall at the expiry of such period, become void and inoperative.

15.4 Steps to be taken by a Public Company for starting a Business for which there is no provision in the Objects Clause of the Memorandum of Association. [Section 149(2A)]

Case	*Legal Requirements*
(a) To Commence a new business which is not germane to the business which the company was carrying on at the commencement of Companies (Amendment) Act, 1965 in case of companies registered before the Commencement of Companies (Amendment) Act, 1965.	(i) Special resolution is required to be passed by the company [Section 149(2A)] or Ordinary Resolution and approval of Central Government are required. [Section 149(2B)] (ii) A duly verified declaration by one of its directors or its secretary in the prescribed form is required to be filed with the registrar. [Section 149(2A)]
(b) To set up a business in relation to any object other than its main object or ancillary to it, in case of companies registered after the Commencement of Companies (Amendment) Act, 1965.	Same as above.

16.0 ALTERATION OF LIABILITY CLAUSE

16.1 Effect of Increase in Members' Liability [Section 38]

The provisions relating to change of liability are given below:

Case	*Provision*
(i) ***Where the Company is neither a club nor any other association and the alteration requires the member to take or subscribe for more shares than the number held by him at the date of alteration or in any way increases his liability.***	No member of the company shall be bound by such alteration unless he agrees in writing to do so *either* before *or* after the alteration.
(ii) ***Where the company is a club or any other association and the alteration requires the members to pay sub-scription or charges at a higher rate.***	Member is bound by such alteration even though he does not agree in writing to be bound by the alteration.

16.2 Registration of Unlimited Company as Limited Company [Section 32]

Section 32 permits the registration of an unlimited company as a limited company. The registration of an unlimited company as a limited company shall not affect any debts, liabilities, obligations or contracts incurred or entered into by or on behalf of the company before such registration.

16.3 Alteration to make the Liability of Directors Unlimited [Section 323]

A limited company, if so authorised by its articles, may alter the Memorandum by a special resolution so as to make the liability of its director or directors or manager unlimited. Any person holding the office of director or manager before the alteration shall not be bound by this alteration until the expiry of his present term or unless he has accorded his consent in writing to such alteration.

17.0 ALTERATION OF CAPITAL CLAUSE [SECTIONS 94 TO 97]

The provisions relating to the alteration of Share Capital are given below:

1. **Authority in Articles** A company may alter the capital clause of its memorandum only if it is authorised by its articles of association to do so.
2. **Manners of Alteration** A company may alter the capital clause in the following manner:
   (a) by increasing its share capital by issue of new shares; [e.g. from 1 crore to 5 crore]
   (b) by consolidating the existing shares into shares of larger amount than its existing shares; [e.g. Conversion of Shares of Rs 10 each into shares of Rs 100 each]
   (c) by Converting fully paid shares into stock or *vice versa*;
   (d) by sub-dividing the existing shares into shares of smaller amount than its existing shares; [e.g. Conversion of shares of Rs 100 each into shares of Rs 10 each]
   (e) by cancelling its unissued shares.
3. **Passing of Resolution** An ordinary resolution is required to be passed at its general meeting.
4. **Filing of Notice** A notice specifying alteration made must be given to the Registrar within 30 days of alteration.

5. **Duty of Registrar** The Registrar shall make the necessary alteration in the memorandum or articles.
6. **Consequences of Default** If default is made in filing the notice as aforesaid, the company and every officer of the company who is in default shall be punishable with the fine upto Rs 500 per day during which the default continues.

18.0 DOCTRINE OF ULTRA VIRES

18.1 Meaning of Ultra Vires

The term '*ultra*' means '*beyond*' and the term '*vires*' means the '*powers*', Thus, *ultra vires* a company means '*beyond the powers of a company*'. Any act which is beyond the objects stated in the memorandum is ultra vires the company and, therefore, null and void. The company shall not be bound by such acts which are *ultra vires* the company. The purpose of the doctrine of *ultra vires* is to protect the interests of members, outsiders and creditors.

In order to protect the interest of the shareholders and the third parties which enter into contracts with the company's activities are confined to the objects given in the Memorandum of Association. It cannot do anything beyond the objects clause and if it does, it will be considered *ultra vires* (beyond capacity) and *void ab-initio*. Thus, in case of a company whatever is not permitted expressly or by implication, by the constituting instrument, is prohibited not by any express prohibition of the legislature, but by the doctrine of *ultra vires.*

18.2 Meaning of Doctrine of Ultra Vires

The term '*ultra vires*' means beyond one's power or authority. Where exercises of powers vested in a person arises, the question as to the scope of such powers becomes the matter for consideration as to whether a person is acting within the limits of authority conferred on him. If the person exercising the power goes beyond the jurisdiction of his powers, the person is said to have acted *ultra vires*. The doctrine of *ultra vires* thus contemplates two things:

1. that the person exercising the power is not having an unlimited or infinite power to do all acts or things at his will and pleasure; and
2. that the person exercising the power derived the same from some other person or persons on behalf of whom the person acts. The power may be delegated to him by an express or implied act of the said person or persons.

As far as a company is concerned, any act beyond the objects mentioned in the Memorandum of Association is *ultra vires* and void. This important rule of law was laid down in *Ashbury Railway Carriage Co.* v. *Riche,* (1875) [L.R. 7 H.L. (653)].

The acts of the company are subject to the provisions contained in the Act in terms of which it is incorporated and its two-constitutional documents, namely, the Memorandum and Articles of Association.

18.3 Types and Validity of Ultra Vires Acts

Ulta vires acts can be divided into the following four categories:

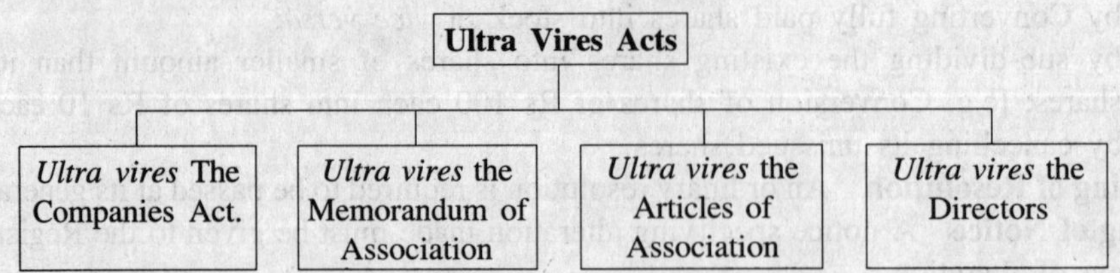

Let us discuss, these *ultra vires* acts one by one.

1. **Acts Ultra Vires The Companies Act** Any act done contrary to or in excess of the scope of The Companies Act will be *ultra vires* the Act. Such an act shall be void and cannot be ratified even by an unanimous resolution of all the shareholders.
   A few examples of such acts are as follows:
   (a) Payment of dividend out of capital,
   (b) Free distribution of bonus shares, and
   (c) Reducing the share capital without complying with the legal formalities.
2. **Acts Ultra Vires the Memorandum** The Memorandum defines and confines the powers of the company. The object of the company is determined by the Memorandum. A company cannot do anything which is beyond the purview of the objects clause. Any act done in contravention of the object clause shall be *ultra vires* the Memorandum and shall be void and it cannot be ratified even by an unanimous resolution of all the shareholders.

   The doctrine of *ultra vires* was first applied in the famous case of *Ashbury Railway Carriage and Iron Co.* v. *Riche*. In this case the company was incorporated to make, and sell, or lend on hire, railway carriages and wagons and to carry on the business of mechanical engineers and general contractors.

   The directors of the company entered into a contract with *Riche*, a firm of Railway contractors to finance the construction of a railway line in Belgium. The contract was ratified by the company by passing a special resolution at a general meeting. Later, the contract was repudiated by the company on grounds of its being *ultra vires* and it was sued for breach of contract. The House of Lords held that the contract was *ultra vires* the Memorandum and therefore void. It could not be ratified by the shareholders, as the contract was *ultra vires* the objects clause.

   In case of *Simpson* v. *West Minister Palace Hotel Co.*, (1861) 20 Beav. 40, a hotel company temporarily let part of its premises not required for its business. This was held to be *ultra vires*.

   In case of *Attorney General* v. *G.N. Railway Co.*, (1860) 1 Dr. & Sm. 154, a railway company was working coal mines and selling coal at a profit. This was held to be *ultra vires*.

   In case of *London Country Council* v. *Attorney General*, (1902) A.C. 165, the council having a statutory power to work tramway, proposed to run omnibuses in connection with the tramways, however beneficial it might prove the original business. It was considered *ultra vires*.

   In case of *A. Laxmanswami Mudaliar* v. *LIC of India*, contribution to a trust for promoting technical and business knowledge was held to be *ultra vires*. The court held that the power to make charitable contribution available to the company in its Memorandum does not entitle it to make grant of every kind. Such grant will be valid when it is *bona fide*, relating to company's business or welfare of employees and useful for attainment of company's own objects.
3. **Acts Ultra Vires the Articles** Acts which are *ultra vires* the Articles of Associations but are within the power of the company are termed as *ultra vires* the articles. For example, payment of interest on 'advance calls' at a rate higher than allowed by the articles. Such act shall also be void, but the company in General Meeting may alter the articles by a special resolution and ratify unauthorised acts with retrospective effect in accordance with the provisions of Section 31.
4. **Acts Ultra Vires the Director** Acts which are beyond the powers of the directors but are within the powers of the company are terms as acts *ultra vires* the director. Such acts are not altogether void. Such acts can be ratified and made valid by altering its Articles by a special resolution at its general meeting with retrospective effect so as to give directors the powers beyond which they have exceeded. When the acts are so ratified the company becomes liable for such acts. *For example*, if the company has power to borrow, but it restricts the authority of the directors to borrow upto a certain sum. If the directors exceed their authority and borrow more than what they are authorised to borrow, then the company may, if it wishes, ratify the directors' act, in which case the loan binds both the lender and the company as if it had been made with the company's authority in the first place.

18.4 Effects of Ultra Vires Transactions

The effects of *ultra vires* transaction are summarised as under:

1. Act which is *ultra vires* the company shall be *void-abinitio* and cannot be ratified even by an unanimous resolution of all the members.
2. A company *cannot be sued* on an *ultra vires* transactions.
3. A company *cannot sue* on an *ultra vires* transactions.
4. **Injunction** Any member can bring injunction against the company to restrain it from doing *ultra vires* acts.
5. **Personal Liability of Directors** The directors of the company can be held personally liable for any loss caused by an *ultra vires* transaction. If a director makes an *ultra vires* payment, he can be compelled to make good the funds used [*Re Sharpee,* (1892) 1 Ch. 154]. But the directors who refunded the money could get indemnity as against the person who received the payment with the knowledge that payment to him was *ultra vires.* [*Russell* v. *Wakefield Water Works Co.* (1975) L.R. 20 Eq. 474]
6. **Liability for Breach of Warranty of Authority** The directors can be held personally liable for breach of warranty of authority if it can be established that their act amounts to an implied misrepresentation of facts and not of law.

   Where the Memorandum of Association of a non-trade company did not give any power to borrow but its directors borrowed, directors are not personally liable since their act amounts to an implied misrepresentation of law as a non-trading company has no implied power to borrow.

   Where the Memorandum of Association of a trading company did not give any power to borrow but its directors borrowed, directors are personally liable since their act, amounts to an implied misrepresentation of fact as a trading company has implied power to borrow.

   In case of *Weeks* v. *Property*, (1873): LR 8 CP 427, the directions having power to borrow up to £ 60,000, further borrowed £ 500. Loan of £500 was held to *ultra vires* and void and therefore not binding on the company. The directors were held personally liable for breach of warranty of authority.
7. **On Ultra Vires Lending by Company** If money is lent by a company having no power to lend, the company can sue the debtors for the recovery of loan since the debtors will be estopped from taking the plea that the company had no power to lend. [*Re. Coltman* (1818) 119 Ch. D. 64]
8. **On Ultra Vires Borrowing by the Company** The effect on *ultra vires* borrowing by company depends upon whether the money borrowed has been expended or not.

   Where the company has no borrowing power, any borrowing and where the memorandum fixes a limit on borrowing powers of the Board of Directors of a Company, any borrowing in excess of that limit is known as *ultra vires borrowing.* Such borrowings are void and the securities given for them are inoperative. In such a case the lender cannot sue the company because it does not create any relation of debtor and creditor. The borrowings which are *ultra vires* cannot be ratified by a resolution passed at a general meeting.

Case	*Effect*
(a) ***If ultra vires borrowings have not been used.***	**Right of Restitution** The lender may bring injunction against the company to restrain it from using the amount of loan since the lender remains the owner of the money which is *ultra vires* the company, he can take back the property in specie. [*Sinclair* v. *Borughman,* (1914) A.C. 398]

(Contd.)

(b) ***If ultra vires borrowings have been used to pay-off lawful debt of the company.***	**Right of Subrogation** The lender steps into the shoes of paid off creditor and consequently he would be entitled to recover him loan to that extent from the company [*Naeth Building Society* v. *Luce* (1889) 43 Ch. D. 158] But he cannot claim any right to any securities held by the original creditor. *[Re. Wrexham Rly. Co.* (1889) 1 Ch. 440].
(c) ***If ultra vires borrowings have been used for the purchase of any asset or assets.***	The lender may claim repayment of his money out of the the asset or assets purchased out of his money. In addition to aforesaid rights, the lender can sue the directors for breach of warranty of authority.

9. **On Ultra Vires Torts** A company will be liable for tort of its employees if—
   (a) the tort is committed in pursuance of its stated objects, and
   (b) the tort is committed by employees within the course of their employment.

In other words, a company will not be liable for any torts committed outside its objects. For example, a company having power to run tramways, started operating omnibuses and a driver of one such bus negligently injured a person who sued the company for damages. It was held that the company could not be held liable for damages because having no existence outside the Memorandum, it could not have appointed the driver.

18.5 The Doctrine of Ultra Vires is an Illusory Protection to the Shareholders and Pitfall to Outsiders

The doctrine of *ultra vires* is intended to protect the shareholders who invest money in the capital of the company and the creditors who deal with it on the basis of range of company's permitted activities as set out in the Memorandum of Association. Any act beyond the permitted area of operation is void and has no legal effect. But the corporations have always endeavoured to escape the limitations imposed by the doctrine of *ultra vires* by drafting the objects clause of Memorandum in very wide terms be as to incorporate all conceivable objects. Alongwith the objects, they usually spell out several powers which companies will be entitled to exercise in carrying out its objects. The result is the every form of conceivable activity and power is included in the memorandum somewhere beneath the mass of words. This protects the acts of company from challenged as *ultra vires.*

Further, where any acts of the company is *ultra vires* the Articles but is *intra vires* the memorandum the company may alter its Articles and ratify the act, if the act of directors is *ultra vires* the authority delegated to them, the company may ratify such act by an ordinary or special resolution, as the case may be, provided such acts are not *ultra vires* the company. Such ratifications can be prejudicial to the outsiders.

Consequently, the protection afforded by the doctrine of *ultra vires* to the shareholders and the third parties dealing with the company has became illusory to some extent.

EXERCISES

VERY SHORT ANSWER TYPE QUESTIONS

1. What is 'Memorandum of Association'?
2. What is 'Name Clause'?
3. (a) What is 'Registered office clause'?

(b) Is it essential to mention the name of the city of the state in which registered office is likely to be situated?

4. (a) What is 'Objects clause'?
   (b) Enumerate the two categories of main objects.
5. What is liability clause? Name the company in which this clause is not required.
6. (a) What is capital clause?
   (b) Name the company in which case the capital clause is not required.
   (c) Is it essential to mention the division of authorised capital into different classes of shares and rights of various clauses of shareholders?
7. (a) What is subscription clause?
   (b) Can a firm be signatory to the memorandum?
8. What is meant by 'Doctrine of Ultra Vires'?

SHORT ANSWER TYPE QUESTIONS

1. State the purpose of Memorandum of Association.
2. State the form in which the Memorandum of Association must be prepared.
3. State the provisions relating to printing and signature of Memorandum.
4. State the contents of Memorandum.
5. State the legal requirements as to the name clause.
6. State the legal requirements as to the registered office clause.
7. (a) State the legal requirements as to the objects clause.
   (b) Also state the importance of object clause.
8. State the legal requirements as to the liability clause.
9. State the legal requirements as to the capital clause.
10. State the legal requirements as to the Association or Subscription clause.
11. State the procedure for changing the name of the company.
12. Comment on the following:
    (a) The memorandum is a charter of the company.
    (b) The memorandum of a company defines as well as confines its objects.
    (c) A company's object clause is of fundamental importance not only to members but also to non-members.
    (d) Act *ultra vires* the company can be made binding upon the company by a unanimous vote of all the members of the company.
    (e) The doctrine of *ultra vires* is illusory protection to the shareholders and pitfall for third parties.
    (f) Alteration of Memorandum invariably involves passing of a special resolution.
    (g) Each company must have capital and liability clause in its Memorandum.
    (h) A firm can never be a member of a company.

LONG ANSWER TYPE QUESTIONS

1. Discuss the meaning, importance and contents of Memorandum of Association.
2. Explain the procedure for changing the name of the company.
3. (a) Why is it necessary to have registered office?
   (b) Explain the procedure for changing the registered office of the company.
4. (a) Explain the procedure for changing the objects clause of the Memorandum.
   (b) When does the alteration takes effect?
   (c) What is the effect of the failure to register the alteration?

5. Explain the provisions relating to:
   (a) Increase in Members' Liability.
   (b) Registration of unlimited company as limited company.
   (c) Alteration to make the liability of directors unlimited.
6. Explain the procedure for changing the capital clause of the Memorandum.
7. (a) What is 'Doctrine of Ultra Vires'?
   (b) Explain the validity of acts *ultra vires* (i) the Company (ii) Directors (iii) Articles
   (c) Explain the effects of *ultra vires* transaction.
   (d) Describe the liability of a company and its agents for *ultra vires* acts.
8. 'The doctrine of *ultra vires* is an illusory protection to the shareholders and pitfall to outsiders'. Comment.
9. Explain the importance of Registered Office Clause and Objects Clause.
10. State the procedural requirements in the following cases:
    (a) To delete the words 'Private' from the name of company.
    (b) To add the words 'Private' to the name of company.
    (c) To change the name which in the opinion of Central Govt. is identical.
    (d) To change the name of licensed company.
    (e) To change the name in any other case.
    (f) To change Registered office from one place to another within the same city.
    (g) To change Registered office from one city to another within jurisdiction of the same ROC within the same State.
    (h) To change the Registered office from the jurisdiction of one ROC to the jurisdiction of another ROC within the same State.
    (i) To change the Registered office from one State to another.
    (j) To alter Objects Clause.
    (k) To alter Liability Clause.
    (l) To alter Capital Clause.
11. Follwing are the procedural legal requirements
    (a) An ordinary resolution is required to be passed at the general meeting of the members.
    (b) A special resolution is required to be passed at the general meeting of the members.
    (c) Company Law Board's confirmation is required.
    (d) Central Govt's Approval is required.
    (e) A copy of special resolution passed is required to be filed with the Registrar within 30 days of passing the resolution.
    (f) A certified copy of the order of Company Law board is required to be filed with the Registrar within 3 months of the order.
    (g) A certified copy of the order of Central Government is required to be filed with the registrar within 3 months of the order.
    (h) A printed copy of the altered memorandum is required to be filed with the Registrar.

    State which of the above is/are required in each of the following cases:
    (i) To change the existing name 'Jalan Ltd.' to 'Tulsian Ltd.'
    (ii) To change the Registered office from Mumbai to Delhi.
    (iii) To make some of other Objects as part of 'Main Objects'.
    (iv) To cancell unissued shares.

CHAPTER

5

Articles of Association

1.0 MEANING OF ARTICLES OF ASSOCIATION

Section 2(2) of the Companies Act defines Articles **"as the Articles of Association of a company as originally framed or as altered from time to time in pursuance of any previous companies law or of this Act".** This definition is not sufficient to explain its meaning. Let us look at some of the observations made in judicial cases.

1. The Articles of Association of a company are the internal rules and regulations to the management of its internal affairs. [*Guinness* v. *Land Corporation of Ireland,* (1882) 22 Ch. D. 349]
2. 'The articles play a part subsidiary to memorandum of association. They accept the memorandum of association as the Charter of Incorporation of the company and so accepting it, they proceed to define the duties, rights and powers of governing body as between themselves and the company at large and the mode and form in which the business of the company is to be carried on and the mode and form in which changes in the internal regulation of the company may from time to time be made." [*Ashbury Railway Carriage Co. Ltd.* v. *Riche,* (1875) L.R. 7. H.L. 653, p. 670]
3. The document containing the articles of association of a company is a business document; hence it has to be construed strictly. It regulates domestic management of a company and creates certain rights and obligations between the members and the company. [*S.S. Rajkumar* vs. *Perfect Castings (P.) Ltd.,* [1968] 38 Camp. Case 187]
4. The Articles of Association are in fact the bye-laws of the company according to which director and other officers are required to perform their functions as regards the management of the company, its accounts and audit.

Thus, the memorandum lays down the objects for which the company is formed, the articles lay down rules and regulations for the attainment of those objects.

2.0 WHICH COMPANIES ARE REQUIRED TO REGISTER ITS ARTICLES [SECTION 26]

According to Section 26, the following companies are required to register its Articles alongwith the memorandum of association:

1. An Unlimited Company (Whether Public or Private).
2. A Company Limited by Guarantee (Whether Public or Private).
3. A Private Company Limited by Shares.

3.0 WHICH COMPANY NEED NOT HAVE ITS OWN ARTICLES [SECTION 28]

A public company limited by shares need not necessarily have its own articles. A public company limited by shares may either have its own articles or it may adopt *either* wholly *or* partly Table A of Schedule I of the Companies Act. Even if it does register Articles of its own, Table A will still apply automatically unless it has been excluded or modified. In other words, there are three possible alternatives in which a public company limited by shares may adopt Articles of Association. These are:

(i) It may adopt Table A in full; or

(ii) It may wholly exclude Table A and set out its Articles in full; or

(iii) It may set out its own Articles and adopt part of Table A.

If such a company goes in for the first alternative, then it is not necessary to get any Articles of Association registered. It has only to endorse on the face of the Memorandum of Association that it has adopted Table A as its Articles of Association. The advantage in adopting the regulations of Table A is that its provisions are legal beyond any doubt. [*Lock* v. *Queensland Investment & Land Mortrage Co.,* (1896) Cl. 397]

4.0 SPECIFIC REGULATION REQUIRED IN THE ARTICLES OF SPECIFIC COMPANIES

As per Section 27, the specific regulations required in the Articles of specific companies are given below:

Type of company	*Specific regulation required*
1. ***In case of an unlimited company***	Its Articles must state the number of members with which the company is to be registered and if it has a share capital, the amount of share capital with which it is to be registered. [Section 27(1)] **Note:** Its Articles must be in the Form given in Table E.
2. ***In case of a company limited by guarantee but not having share capital***	Its Articles must state the number of members with which it is to be registered. [Section 27(2)] **Note:** Its Articles must be in the Form given in Table C.
3. ***In case of a company limited by guarantee and having share capital***	Its Articles must state the number of members. [Section 27(2)] **Note:** Its Articles must be in the Form given in Table D.
4. ***In case of a Private Company having share capital***	Its Articles must contain the following four restrictions as contained in Section 3(1)(iii)— (a) Restricting the right to transfer its shares, (b) limiting the number of its members to 50 excluding the past and present employees of the company. (c) prohibiting any invitation to the public to subscribe for any shares in or debentures of the company. [Section 27(3)] (d) prohibiting any invitation or acceptance of deposits from persons other than its members, directors or their relatives.
5. ***In case of a Private Company having no share capital***	Its Articles must contain the following three restrictions as contained in Sub-clauses (b), (c) and (d) of Section 3(1)(iii): (a) limiting the number of its members to 50 excluding the past or present employees of the company. (b) prohibiting any invitation to the public to subscribe for any shares in or debentures of the company. (c) prohibiting any invitation or acceptance of deposits from persons other than its members, directors or their relatives.

5.0 FORM OF ARTICLES [SECTION 29]

According to Section 29, the Articles of Association of a company must be in one of the forms given in Schedule I as may be applicable to the case of the company or in a form as near thereto as circumstances admit.

The Tables in Schedule I to the Act specify the following forms applicable to different types of companies as under:

Table C: Articles of Association of a company limited by guarantee and not having a share capital.

Table D: Articles of Association of a company limited by guarantee and having a share capital.

Table E: Articles of Association of an Unlimited Company.

Note: Additional matters which are not inconsistent with the provisions contained in the form in any of the Tables C, D and E may be included in the Articles. [Proviso to Section 29]

6.0 PRINTING AND SIGNATURE OF ARTICLES [SECTION 30]

The Articles must be—

(a) printed,

(b) divided into paragraphs numbered consecutively, and

(c) signed by at least 7 persons in case of a public company and by at least 2 persons in case of a private company. The person signing the Articles are known as 'Subscribers'. Each subscriber must give his address, description and occupation (if any). The signature of each subscriber must be attested in the presence of at least one witness. The witness must attest the signature and give his address description and occupation (if any).

7.0 CONTENTS OF ARTICLES OF ASSOCIATION

The Articles of Association may contain any regulation for the attainment of objects stated in the memorandum subject to the following restrictions:

(a) The Articles must not include anything which is illegal or contrary to general law.

(b) The Articles must not include anything which is against public policy.

(c) The Articles must not include anything which is prohibited by the Companies Act, 1956.

Articles usually contain provisions relating to the following matters:

(a) Share Capital and Right of Shareholders, Variation of these rights

(b) Allotment of Shares

(c) Calls on Shares and Lien on Shares

(d) Transfer of Shares

(e) Transmission of Shares

(f) Forfeiture of Shares

(g) Conversion of Shares into Stock

(h) Share Warrants and Shares Certificates

(i) Alteration of Capital

(j) General Meeting and proceedings thereat

(k) Voting Rights, Voting and Poll and Proxies

(l) Directors, their appointment, remuneration, qualification, powers and proceedings of Board of Directors

(m) Manager/Secretary

(n) Seal

(o) Dividend and Reserves

(p) Capitalisation of Profits

(q) Accounts, Audit and borrowing powers

(r) Winding up

(s) The extent to which Table A of Schedule I of the Act is to apply or not to apply.

8.0 ALTERATION OF ARTICLES OF ASSOCIATION

Section 31 empowers the company to alter or add to its Articles. This fundamental power of the company to alter its Articles is subject to the following limitations:

1. **Special Resolution** The alteration must be affected by passing a special resolution at the general meeting of the company [Section 31(1)]. A copy of the special resolution authorising such alteration must be filed with the Registrar within 30 days of passing the resolution and a *printed copy of altered articles must be filed with the Registrar within 3 months of passing the resolution*. The effect of change must be incorporated in all copies of articles of association issued after the date of alteration. [Section 40]
2. **Approval of Central Government in Case of Conversion of Public Company into Private Company** No alteration having the effect of converting a public company into a private company shall have effect unless approved by the Central Government [Proviso to Section 31(1)]. In this case, a printed copy of the altered articles must be filed with the Registrar within 1 month of the date of receipt of the order of approval [Section 31(2A)]
3. **Valid as if Originally Contained** Any alteration made in the Article shall subject to the provisions of this Act, as valid as if originally contained in the Articles. [Section 31(2)]
4. **Not inconsistent with Any Act** The alteration must not be inconsistent with any provisions of the Companies Act or any other statute.
5. **Not Inconsistent with Memorandum** The alteration must not be inconsistent with any provisions of the Memorandum of Association. Articles being subordinate to the memorandum must not override.
6. **Not Inconsistent with CLB Order** The alteration must not be inconsistent with an order of Company Law Board.

   Where the company amends articles on order of CLB (on application u/s 397 or u/s 398 for relief in case of oppression or mismanagement), the subsequent alteration thereof which is inconsistent with such an order can be made by the company only with leave of the Company Law Board. [Section 404(1)]
7. **Not Permit any Illegal Thing** The alteration must not permit anything which is illegal.
8. **Undertaking in Writing [Section 38]** No alteration having the effect of increasing the liability of a member shall be binding upon him unless he agrees in writing either before or after the alteration. However, in case of a company which is a club/any other association, the alteration requiring the member to pay subscription/charges at a higher rate shall be binding upon him although he does not agree in writing to be bound by the alteration. [Section 38]
9. **Reserve Capital** A reserve capital once created in pursuance of Section 99 cannot be unreserved but may be cancelled as a reduction of capital [*Midland Railway Carriage Wagon Co.* (1907) W.N. 175].
10. **Retrospective Effect** The alteration may be regarded as having a retrospective effect so long as it does not affect the things already done by the company and alteration is for the benefit of the company as whole [*Allen* v. *Gold Reef of West Africa* (1909) S.C. 732]. In the case of *Allen* v. *Gold Reefs of West Africa,* the original Articles gave the company a lien on all shares "not fully paid-up" for calls due to the company. '*S*' was the only member holding some fully paid-up shares, but he also owned money to the company for calls due on other shares. '*S*' died and his shares were inherited by his legal representatives. The company, thereafter, altered its Articles enabling the company to exercise lien on all shares—whether fully paid or not. Now the question arose whether the company could exercise lien even on fully paid-up shares. It was held that company could do so as it was done *bona fide* for the benefit of the company as a whole.

11. **Bona Fide** The alteration must be *bona fide* for the benefit of the company as a whole. Such alteration shall be valid even though the private interests of some members may be affected adversely. In case of *Sidebottom* v. *Kershaw, Leese & Co., Ltd.* (1920) 1 Ch. 154], the alteration of articles empowered the directors to require any member who carried on a business competing with that of the company to sell his shares at a fair price to persons nominated by the directors. The validity of the resolution was challenged on the ground that the alteration will not be for the benefit of the company as a whole.

The court held that it was in the interest of the company as a whole to be protected against competition and upheld the resolution. The court was of the view that it was very much in the interest of the company as a whose to get rid of such members who were carrying on a competing business as they always had the chance to exploit the company's secrets for their personal benefit and at its cost.

12. **Not Constitute a Fraud on Minority** The alteration must not constitute a fraud on minority. An alteration the effect of which is to discriminate between the majority shareholders and minority shareholders so as to give the former an advantage of which the latter have been deprived, would constitute a fraud on minority.

In *Menier* v. *Hooper's Telegraph Works Ltd.,* (1874) 9 Ch. App. 350, Two Companies *A* and *B* were in rivalry. The Majority shareholders of company A were also the shareholders of Company *B*. Company A had filed a suit against Company *B*. Later, shareholders of company A passed a resolution to compromise the action against Company *B* in such manner that the terms of compromise were favorable to Company *B* and unfavourable to Company A. The minority shareholders questioned the power of the majority to make the said compromise and the court set aside the same. It observed: "It would be a shocking thing, if that could be done and that majority should have nothing to do with it, then the majority have put something in their pockets at the expense of the minority".

Re *Cook* v. *Deeks,* (1916) A.C. 554, the directors of railway construction company obtained a contract in their own names to construct a railway line. The contract was obtained under circumstances which amounted to breach of trust by the directors who then used their voting powers to pass a resolution of the company declaring that the company had no interest in the contract. It was held that the benefit of the contract belongs in equity to the company and that the directors could not benefit themselves at the expense of the minority. If it were not checked, this would be tantamount to allowing a majority to oppress the minority.

In *Brown* v. *British Abrasive Wheel Co.,* (1919) 1 Ch. 290, the majority shareholders holding 98% of the shares were willing to subscribe further capital which the company badly needed but only if they were able to acquire the shareholdings of the minority. They passed a special resolution to alter the articles to enable them to purchase the minority shares compulsorily on certain terms. The plaintiff refuced to sell its shares and challenged the validity of the majority resolution. It was decided that the alteration was not for the benefit of the company but for the benefit of the majority and accordingly an injunction was granted against the company prohibiting it from carrying out the resolution.

13. **Not Cause Breach of Contract with an Outsider** Alteration must not cause a breach of contract with an outsider. The company shall remain liable for damages for its breach.

Murac Rubber Syndicate v. *Alperton Rubber Co. Ltd.* (1915) Ch. 186. In this case an agreement was made between Company A and Company *B*. Company *A* had the right to nominate two directors on Company *B*'s board as long Company *A* held 5,000 shares in Company B. This was incorporated in the articles. Company A nominated two persons as directors and they were disapproved by Company *B*. Company *B* also made an attempt to alter the clause of articles which provided Company *A* the right of nomination. The court granted on injunction restraining Company *B* from making the said alteration on the ground that it would constitute a breach of contract with an outsider.

But later in case of *Chittambram Chettiar* v. *Krishan Aiyanger,* I.L.R. 30 Mad. 36, it was held that a company may alter its articles even if it causes breach of contract with the outsider. It has statutory power to do so. Where the contract with the outsider is wholly dependent on articles, alteration would be operative, and accordingly, the person accepting appointment purely on the terms of the articles takes the risk of those terms being altered, and will be bound by the altered article.

But the situation will be different if apart from the articles, there is an independent contract. In *Southern Foundries Ltd.* v. *Shirlaw, 'S'* was appointed Managing Director in a company for ten years by an agreement dated 21.12.1933. Subsequently, the company was amalgamated with another company and new articles were adopted. The latter gave power to the company to dismiss a director and accordingly *S* was removed from office as director and the company treated him as having ceased to be one. He sued the company for wrongful repudiation of the contract. It was held that dismissal was breach of contract and therefore the company was liable for damages.

14. Not to take Away Statutory Power to Alter The powers to alter articles of association is a statutory power and it cannot be taken away by any provision in the memorandum or articles. [*Walker* v. *London Tramways Co.,* (1879) 12 Ch. D. 705]

9.0 DISTINCTION BETWEEN MEMORANDUM AND ARTICLES

The Memorandum of Association differs from the Articles of Association in the following respects:

Basis of Distinction	*Memorandum of Association*	*Articles of Association*
1. ***Contents***	It contains the fundamental conditions upon which alone the company is allowed to be incorporated.	It contain the internal rules and regulations relating to management of internal affairs.
2. ***Fundamental/ Subordinate document***	It is a fundamental document.	It is subordinate to the Memorandum.
3. ***Compulsory or optional***	Every company must have its own memorandum.	A public company limited by shares need not have its own Articles. It may adopt Table A as its articles.
4. ***Relationship defined***	It defines the relationship between the company and outsiders.	It defines the relationship between the company and its members as members only and as members *inter se*.
5. ***Alteration whether easy or difficult***	The memorandum cannot be so easily altered. The company has to follow the strict procedure for the alteration of its clauses. In some cases alteration requires the approval of the Company Law Board.	Articles can be easily altered by passing a special resolution.
6. ***Binding Effect of ultra vires act***	An act which is beyond the powers given in the Memorandum is *ultra vires* and void and it cannot be ratified even by the unanimous consent of all the members.	An act which is *intra vires* the Memorandum but *ultra vires* the Articles may be ratified by shareholders by passing a special resolution.
7. ***Remedy in case of ultra vires contracts***	In case of the contracts *ultra vires* the memorandum, outsiders have no remedy against the company.	In case of contracts *ultra vires* the Articles, outsiders can enforce the contract against the company provided they had no knowledge of irregularity.

10.0 BINDING EFFECTS OF MEMORANDUM AND ARTICLES [SECTION 36]

Section 36 provides that the Memorandum and Articles shall, when registered, bind the company and the members thereof to the same extent as if they respectively had been signed by the company and by each member, and contained covenants on its and his part to observe all the provisions of the Memorandum and of the Articles. Thus, the Memorandum and Articles constitute a binding contract between the company and each of its members. The legal effects can be studied under the following headings:

10.1 Members Bound to the Company

Since the Memorandum and Articles constitute a contract between the members and the company, the members are bound to the company by whatever is contained in these documents. Accordingly, the company is entitled to sue its members for enforcement of the articles and can restrain its members through court from violating any provisions contained therein.

In case of *Boreland's Trustee* v. *Steel Brothers and Co. Ltd,* [(1901) 1 Ch. 279], the Articles of the company provided that the shares of any member who became bankrupt would be sold to other persons at a price fixed by the directors. B, a shareholder became bankrupt and his trustee in bankruptcy claimed that he was not bound by the articles and could therefore, sell those shares at their true value. But it was held, that the trustee in bankruptcy was bound by the Articles as it constituted a binding contract between the members and the company.

Similarly in case of *Bradford Banking Company* v. *Brigs,* (1886) 12 A.C. 29, where the articles give the company a lien upon each share for debts due by shareholders to the company, and where a shareholder mortgages his shares and the mortgagee serves notice thereof upon the company, the mortgagee would have priority over the company, only if the shareholder had incurred a liability to the company after the notice of the mortgage was given to the company. If, on the other hand, the sahreholder had incurred a liability before the notice of mortgage was given to the company, the company would have the priority.

10.2 Company Bound to the Members

Since the memorandum and articles constitute a contract between members and the company, the company is bound to its members by whatever is contained in these documents. Accordingly, the members are entitled to sue the company for enforcement of the Articles and can restrain the company through court from violating any provisions contained therein. Views differ on the questions as to whether and how far the memorandum and articles bind the company to the members. The views expressed in various judicial cases are given below:

(a) "The company is bound to the extent that any member can sue it so as to prevent any beach of the article which is likely to affect his right as a member of the company". [*Hickman* v. *Kent Sheepbreeder's Association* (1885) 1 Ch. 88]

Thus, "An individual member can file a suit against the company to enforce his individual rights e.g. right to contest election for directorship of the company, right to get back his shares wrongfully forfeited, right to receive a share certificate, notice of general meetings etc." [*Pender* v. *Lushirgton* (1817) Ch. D. 70, *Nogaffa* v. *Madras Race Club,* AIR 1951 Mad. 83, *C.L. Joseph* v. *Los,* AIR 1965 (Ker.) 68]

(b) "The member suing in cases sues not in the rights of a member but in his own right to protect from invasion of his own individual right as a member". [*Edwards* v. *Halliwell,* (1950) 2 All ER 1964 at p. 1067]

(c) In case of *Johnson* v. *Lyttle Iren Agency,* (1877) 5 Ch. D. 687, a forfeiture of shares irregularly effected by a company was set aside at the instance of the aggrieved member as the company did not comply with the provisions of the Articles.

(d) In case of *Wood* v. *Odessa Water Works,* 6 (1884) 42, Ch. D. 636, the articles empowered the company to declare a dividend to be paid to the shareholders with the approval in the general meetings. A resolution was passed to pay the dividend by issue of debenture bonds and not in cash. At the instance of a member, the court grants an injunction restraining the director from acting on the resolution.

(e) Thus, the member can sue the company for the breach of the Articles in the following cases:

   (a) When the company does an *ultra vires* illegal act,
   (b) For the enforcement of personal rights e.g. right to receive declared dividend,
   (c) when majority plays fraud on minority, and
   (d) for submitting the petition to court for its order for preventions of oppression and mismanagement under Sections 397 and 398.

10.3 Between Members *inter se*

Although there is no express agreement between the members of the company, yet articles regulate their rights *inter se.* Such rights can only be enforced by or against a member through the company or through the liquidator representing the company but no member has as between himself and another member any right beyond that which the contract with the company gives him [*Weltan* v. *Saffary* (1897) A.C. 315]. But the contrary view was taken in case of *Royfield* v. *Hands and others,* (1852) 2. W.L.R. 851. In this case, the articles provided that every member who intends to transfer his shares must inform the directors and directors must take the said shares equally between them at a fair value. The plaintiff informed the directors of his intention to transfer his shares. But the directors refused to take the shares and argued that the articles could not impose such obligation upon them in their capacity as directors. The court held that the directors were bound to take the shares since the articles imposed obligation upon them in their capacity as members and thus obligation was a personal one which could be enforced against them by other members directly without joining the company as a party.

It may also be noted that the articles constitute a contract between members only as regards matters arising out of the company relationship of members as members. They cannot regulate rights arising out of any other contracts in which other members have no interest. In case of *Khusi Ram* v. *Hanut Mal,* (1949) 53, C.W.N. 305, where a member had a commercial dispute of private nature with another member, an arbitration clause in the articles of the company was not allowed to be invoked.

10.4 Between the Company and Outsider

Since the memorandum and Articles do not constitute a contract between the company and outsider, an outsider is not entitled to sue the company for enforcement of the Articles even the articles provide certain rights to him.

The following case of *Eley* v. *Positive Government Life Assurance Co. Ltd.,* (1876) 1 Ex. D. 88 illustrates this point.

"The Articles of the company contained a provision that Eley would be the solicitor of the company for life and would not be removed from office except for misconduct. Eley acted as solicitor to the company and also became a member of the company. The company, however, terminated his services. Thereupon, he sued the company of damages for breach of contract. Held, the Articles cannot be the basis of a contract between the company and an outsider. It would be noted here that he was trying to *Exercise his Right as an Employee and not as a Member. A Person can be a Member of* the company and at the same time may be a creditor or employee of the company. In the above case, he was trying to exercise his right as an employee of the company. There was no independent contract between the company and Eley apart from whatever was contained in the Articles. Therefore, his suit was dismissed.

Similarly in case of *Re Rotherham Alum & Co.,* (1883) 25 D. 103, where the articles provided for remuneration to be paid promoters, it was held that this clause did not give any right of action to promoters against the company.

It may also be noted that where articles are deemed to have formed a part of outsider's contract with the company, the outsider is entitled to maintain a suit on the basis of that contract. In case of Re. *New British Iron Co., (1898) 1 Ch. 324,* where an individual entered into a contract with a company to serve as a director and the articles of the company required the director to have a share qualification and fixed his remuneration, it was held that director was entitled to recover his remuneration as fixed by the articles because the terms of articles were deemed to have formed a part of his contract with the company.

Though the articles and memorandum do not constitute a contract between the company and an outsider, still the outsider is entitled to assume that all the necessary formalities have been duly compiled with in internal workings of the company. [*The Royal British Bank* v. *Turquand*]

11.0 MEANING OF DOCTRINE OF CONSTRUCTIVE NOTICE

(a) Since the Memorandum and Articles of Association on their registration with the Registrar become public documents and are available for public inspection in the Registrar's office on payment of prescribed fee [Section 610], every person dealing with the company is presumed to have the knowledge of the contents of these documents and also to have understood them according to their proper meaning. [*Earnest* v. *Nicholls* (1857) 6 H.I.C. 401, *Griffith* v. *Poget,* (No. 2) (1877) 6 Ch. D. 517, *Oak Bank Oil* v. *Crum,* (1882) 8 A.C. 65]. This type of presumed knowledge of these documents is termed as 'Constructive Notice of Memorandum and Articles of Association.

(b) Accordingly, if a person supplies goods to a company in which it cannot deal according to its objects clause, he will not be able to recover the price from the company. The supplier cannot in his defence take the plea that he did not have the knowledge of the contents of the memorandum of Association of the company. Thus, if a person enters into a contract which is *ultra vires* the company, he must do so at his peril.

(c) The doctrine of constructive notice is not a positive one but a negative one like that of estopple of which it forms part. It operates only against the person who has been dealing with the company but not against the company itself. Consequently, he is prevented from alleging that he did not know that the constitution of the company rendered a particular act or particular delegation of authority *ultra vires*. Thus, **the doctrine of constructive notice protects the company and not the outsiders**. Thus, this doctrine is a 'Cloud' for the strangers.

12.0 PRINCIPLE OF OSTENSIBLE AUTHORITY

A third party dealing with the company in good faith, assumes that the person who is dealing with him has the required authority to deal on behalf of the company. For example if a person is dealing with a director in a matter in which normally a director have power to act for the company, then that person can presume that latter has 'ostensible authority' or 'apparent authority on that matter on behalf of the company. Person dealing with the company is not under obligation to inquire that whether the person to whom which he is dealing really has the authority. In such cases, it is not material whether the person had actual knowledge of company's articles. Of course, the person concern should at least have 'ostensible authority' e.g. a purchase manager can be said to have ostensible authority to issue purchase orders, but he cannot have ostensible authority to sign cheques on behalf of the company.

Notes:

(i) The director repaid their personal loan through the company's account by using company cheques. The lender knew from the cheques that the amount is from company account and not from his personal account. In this case the act of director are *ultra vires*. A director cannot be presumed to have ostensible authority to repay his personal loan from company account. Hence, lender is liable to repay the amount to the company.

(ii) A director has no ostensible authority to institute a suit on behalf of the company. Such authority has to be specifically conferred by a resolution [*Indian Commerce* v. *Swadharma Swarajya Sangha* (1998)].

(iii) Filing of suit cannot be done with specific authority [*BOC India Ltd* v. *Zinc Products* (1997)].

(iv) Suit filed by the secretary under general power of attorney, later ratified by Board if valid [*Turner Marrison & Co.* v. *Hunger Ford Investment,* 42 Comp Cas 512 (SC) 85 ITR 607, AIR 1972 SC 1311].

13.0 DOCTRINE OF INDOOR MANAGEMENT

13.1 Meaning of Doctrine of Indoor Management

The doctrine of indoor management is an ***exception to the doctrine of constructive notice***. This doctrine protects the outsiders against the company by entitling them to assume that the provision of the Articles of Association have been duly complied with by the company in its internal working. This doctrine is based on the principles of justice and public convenience. In case of *Pacific Cost Mines Ltd.* v. *Arkuthnd,* (1971) A.C. 607, the Court held "An outsider is presumed to know the constitution of a company but not what may or may not have taken place within the doors that are closed to him." Therefore, if the contract is within the powers of the company, then company will be bound to the outsider and will not be allowed to escape liability by showing that there was some irregularly in following procedure. This is known as the Doctrine of Indoor Management or *Rule in Royal British Bank* v. *Turquand,* (1856) 6 E & B 327. The facts of this case are as follows:

The directors of a company were authorised by the articles to borrow on bond such sums of money, as authorised from time to time, by a resolution of the company, in General Meeting. The directors borrowed money from Turquand and issued a bond to him. No resolution of the company, as was required to be passed according to the Articles of Association was passed. Decision, Turquand could sue the company on the bond, as he was entitled to assume that the resolution of the company in General Meeting authorising the directors to borrow money on the basis of bond had been passed.

13.2 Exceptions to the Doctrine of Indoor Management

The doctrine of indoor management is subject to the following limitations:

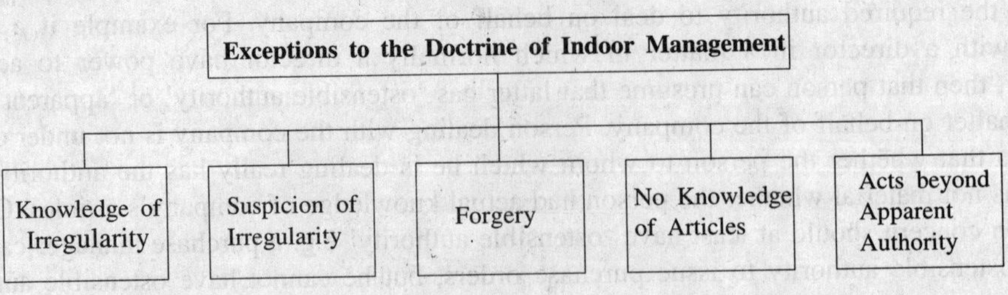

Let us discuss these exceptions one by one.

1. **Knowledge of Irregularity**
   Where the person dealing with the company has knowledge of an irregularity regarding the internal management of the company, he cannot claim protection provided by this doctrine. The knowledge of irregularity may be actual or constructive. In this connection the case of *Howard* v. *Pokent Ivony Co.* is relevant. The directors were empowered to borrow money upto £1,000 and sanction of the shareholders was required for an amount in excess of this. The directors themselves lent to the company an amount in excess of the borrowing powers without the consent of the shareholders. It was held that the directors had the notice of the internal irregularity and therefore the company was liable to them only for £1,000.
2. **Suspicion of Irregularity**
   Where the person dealing with the company is put upon an enquiry, he cannot claim protection under this doctrine in the circumstances under which he would have discovered irregularity if he had made the proper enquiries. In case of *Underwood* v. *Bank of Liverpool,* (1924) I.K.B. 775, the sole director paid a cheque drawn in company's name, into his own bank account. It was held that the bank was put upon inquiry and was not entitled to rely upon the ostensible authority of the director. Likewise, a person dealing with the company may be put upon enquiry by reason of the unusual magnitude of the transactions having regard to the position of the agent who is acting for the company. [*Houghton & Co.* v. *Nothard Howe & Wills,* [(1917) I.K.B. 147, 149]
3. **Forgery**
   A person dealing with the company cannot claim protection under this doctrine where forgery is involved. A company can not be held liable for forgeries committed by its officers.

   In case of *Rubben* v. *Great Fingal Consolidated,* (1906) A.C. 439, the secretary of the company issued a share certificate in favour of Rubben by forging the signatures of two directors under the seat of the company. '*R*' wanted to be registered as a member but the company refused to register him as a member. '*R*' contended that since signatures were part of internal management and he had no means to ascertain the genuineness of the signatures, therefore he should be protected. The court held that the share certificate is not binding on the company since the doctrine of indoor management applies to *irregularities* and *not illegalities* (i.e. forgery).
4. **No Knowledge of Articles**
   Where the person dealing with the company has no knowledge of articles, he can not claim protection under this doctrine since this doctrine is based on the principle of estoppel and the person who did the act without consulting the Articles, can not be said to have relied upon the articles.

   The company's articles contained a clause 'the directors may delegate any of their powers other than the power to borrow and make calls to committee consisting of such members of their body as they think fit. One '*T*', an active director of the company entered into a contract with 'Rama Corporation' under which he took a cheque from 'Rama Corp.' In fact, 'Rama Corp. had not inspected the defendant's articles, therefore he did not know of the existence of delegate authority.

   It was held that defendant company was not bound by the agreement since the power was never delegated to '*T*'.

   In the opinion of Justice Slade, J. 'the knowledge of article is essential because the rule of 'Indoor management' is based upon the principle of estoppel. He observed, "A person who at the time of entering into a contract with a company, has the knowledge of the company's Articles of Association, cannot rely on those articles as conferring ostensible of apparent authority on the agent of the company with whom he dealt"

5. Acts Beyond Apparent Authority

Where an officer of the company does something, which would not ordinarily be within his powers, the person dealing with him must make proper inquiries and satisfy himself as to the officer's authority. If he fails to make proper inquiry in spite of suspicious circumstances, he cannot claim any protection under the doctrine of indoor management.

In case of *Anand Bihari Lal* v. *Dinshaw & Co.,* AIR (1942), the accountant of the company transferred some property of the company to the plaintiff. The transfer was held by the Court to be void, because the power to transfer property could not be considered within the apparent authority of the accountant. The plaintiff were put upon an enquiry before entering into the transaction as they should have insisted on seeing the power of attorney executed in favour of the accountant. Even a delegation clause in the Articles is not enough to validate the transaction unless the accountant was in fact authorised.

Similarly in case of *Kredit Bank Case* v. *Scchenkers,* (1927) K.B. 826, where a branch manager of a bank drew and endorsed bills on behalf of his company without any authority, it was held that drawing of bills was not within the ordinary ambit of power of this branch manager and company was not bound unless such authority was in fact delegated to him.

EXERCISES

VERY SHORT ANSWER TYPE QUESTIONS

1. What is 'Articles of Association'?
2. Is it necessary for every company to have its own articles?
3. What is 'Doctrine of constructive notice'?
4. What is 'Doctrine of Indoor Management'?
5. Name the doctrine which protects company.
6. Name the doctrine which protects outsiders.
7. Name the exception to the doctrine of constructive notice.
8. Enumerate the exceptions to the doctrine of constructive notice.
9. Can articles be altered to deprive a company of its powers to amend articles?

SHORT ANSWER TYPE QUESTIONS

1. State the companies which are required to register its Articles.
2. State the companies which need not have its own Articles.
3. State the various alternatives in which a public company limited by shares may adopt Articles.
4. State the specific regulation required in the articles of:
   (a) an unlimited company,
   (b) company limited by guarantee but not having share capital,
   (c) company limited by guarantee and having share capital,
   (d) private company having share capital, and
   (e) private company having no share capital.
5. State the form in which Articles of a company must be prepared.
6. State the provision relating to printing and signature of Article.
7. State any ten contents of Articles.
8. Comment on the following:
   (a) The Articles are subordinate to and are controlled by the Memorandum of Association.

(b) Articles constitute a contract between the member *inter se* and between the company and the members qua members.

(c) Every person dealing with the company is deemed to have notice of the contents of its memorandum.

(d) Doctrine of Indoor Management is an exception to the doctrine of constructive notice.

(e) Power to alter the Articles conferred by the Companies Act is very wide yet it is subject to a large number of limitations.

(f) The doctrine of indoor management in silver lining to strangers dealing with the company.

LONG ANSWER TYPE QUESTIONS

1. Explain the procedure for the alteration of Articles of Association. Discuss the limits on the powers of a company to alter its Articles.
2. Distinguish between memorandum and Articles of Association.
3. Discuss the binding effects of memorandum and Articles of Association.
4. (a) Explain the doctrine of constructive notice.
   (b) Explain the doctrine of indoor management and its exceptions.
5. What is the legal effect of the Articles between—
   (a) Members and the company,
   (b) Members *inter se*, and
   (c) Company and outsiders.
6. Outline the Turquand Rule or rule in *Royal British Bank* v. *Tarquand.* Are there any exceptions to this rule? If yes, discuss them also.

CHAPTER

6 Prospectus

1.0 MEANING OF PROSPECTUS [SECTION 2(36)]

According to Section 2(36) prospectus means **"any document described or issued as prospectus and includes any notice, circular, advertisement or other document inviting deposits from the public or inviting offers from the public for the subscription or purchase of any shares in, or debentures of, a body corporate."** In simple words, the term 'Prospectus' means a document which invites deposits from the public or invites offers from the public to subscribe or buy the shares or debentures of the company. Thus, a prospectus is *not an offer* in itself but an *invitation* to make an offer. Application for making a deposit or for purchase of shares or debentures constitues an offer by the applicant to the company. It is only on the acceptance of the offer, by the company, a binding contract comes into existence.

The prospectus must be in writing. An oral invitation to subscribe for shares will not be considered prospectus. Television or film advertisement cannot be treated as prospectus.

2.0 MEANING OF INVITATION TO THE PUBLIC [SECTION 67]

2.1 From the definition of prospectus, it is clear that a document can be regarded as a prospectus only when it invites offers from the public. According to Section 67(1) and (2), the term 'public' includes any section of the public whether selected as members or debentureholder of the company concerned or as clients of the person issuing the prospects or in any other manner. According to Section 67(3), no offer or invitation shall be treated as made to the public in *either* of the following two circumstances:

1. If it is not calculated to result in the shares/debentures becoming available by persons other than those receiving the offer or invitation.
2. If it can properly be regarded as being a domestic concern of the persons making and receiving the offer or invitation.

Thus, to determining whether or not an offer has been made to the public, the test is not who receives the offer or the invitation but who can accept it. If the invitation can be accepted by any one whether the prospectus was addressed to him or not, then it should be regarded as invitation being made to the public. If the invitation can be accepted only by those to whom it has been made, then it should not be regarded as invitation being made to the public. Some of the decided cases are given below:

(a) An offer by directors to a few of their friends, relatives, customers by sending them a copy of prospects marked "not for publication" was not considered an offer to the public. [*Sherwell* v. *Combined Incandescent Syndicate,* (1970) W.N. 110]

(b) An offer of shares to the kith and kin of a director is not an invitation to the public. [*Rattan Singh* v. *Moga Transport,* A.I.R. 1959 Punj, 196]

(c) A single private communication does not amount to an invitation to the public.

A managing director of a company sent to his co-director several copies of a document marked "*strictly private and confidential*" and containing particulars of a proposed issue of shares, accompanied by share application forms. One of the copies was sent by the co-director to a solicitor, who in turn, gave it to a client who passed it on to a relation. The allottee (relative of the client of the solicitor) filed a suit for compensation for the loss sustained by him by reason of an omission in the document. It was held that the document did not amount to "prospectus issued to the public", as it was marked "strictly private and confidential". [*Nash* v. *Lynde,* (1929) A.C. 158]

2.2 When is an Offer not Treated as Private Issue? [Poviso to Section 67(3)]

If an offer is made to 50 or more persons, it will not be treated as private issue, i.e. it will be treated as public issue. However this proviso is not applicable to —

(a) Non Banking Finance Companies referred to in Section 45-I(f) at the RBI Act, orr

(b) Public Financial Institutions as defined in Section 4A of Companies Act.

Special Provisions for Non-Banking Finance Companies [NBFC] and Public Financial Institution [PFI] [Section 67 (3A)].

According to Section 67(3A), NBFC and PFI can make private offer over to 50 or more members, without issuing a prospectus as per guidelines notified by SEBI in consultation with RBI.

2.3 Meaning of the Term 'Subscription or Purchase of Shares'

The term 'subscription or 'Purchase of shares' means taking or agreeing to take shares for cash. In case of *Government Stock and other Securities Investment Co. Ltd.* v. *Charistopper* (*1956*), All E.R. 490, an offer was made by Company *X* to the members of Companies *Y* and *Z* to acquire all their shares in these companies in exchange for allotment of shares in the company. It was held that the offer could not be said to have been made to the public on the following two grounds:

(a) It did not invite subscription for shares since subscription means taking shares for cash (as it was an exchange offer).

(b) It could be accepted only by members to whom it was made.

2.4 Initial Offer of Securities to be in Dematerialised form in Certain Cases [Section 68B]

Every listed public company, making initial public offer or any security for a sum of rupees ten crores or more, shall issue the same only in dematerialised form by complying with the requisite provisions of the Depositories Act, 1996 and the regulations made thereunder.

3.0 SIGNIFICANCE OF PROSPECTUS

Prospectus is an important document because of the following reasons:

1. **Invitation** It serves as an invitation by the company to the public to invest through making deposit or subscribing shares or debenture.
2. **Advertisement** It acts as a medium of advertisement since it informs the public about its present operations and future prospects.
3. **Authentic Record** It serves as an authentic record of the terms and conditions of the issue of deposits, shares or debentures.
4. **Protection** It protects the interests of the investors who invest on the faith of the prospectus since any misstatement in the prospectus attracts both civil and criminal liability for persons who authorise the issue of prospectus.

4.0 WHEN PROSPECTUS IS NOT REQUIRED TO BE ISSUED [SECTION 56]

The issue of a prospectus is not necessary in the following cases:

1. Where shares are not offered to the public. [Section 56(3)]
2. Where a person is *bona fide* invited to enter into an underwriting agreement. [Section 56(3)]
3. When shares or debentures are offered to existing holders of shares or debentures. [Section 56(5)]
4. When the issue relates to shares or debentures uniform in all respects with shares or debentures previously issued and dealt in or quoted in a recognised stock exchange. [Section 56(5)]

5.0 REQUIREMENTS AS TO PROSPECTUS [SECTION 55 TO 61 AND 66]

The various requirements as to issue of prospectus are given below:

1. **Dating of Prospectus [Section 55]** Every prospectus issued by the company must be dated. This date must be taken as at the date of the publication of the prospectus unless contrary is proved.
2. **Signature of Prospectus [Section 60(1)]** A copy of prospectus to be delivered to the Registrar for registration must be signed by every person who is named in the prospectus as a director or proposed director or his agent authorised in writing.
3. **Delivery of Prospectus [Section 60(1)]** A copy of prospectus must be delivered to the Registrar for registration on or before the date of publication of prospectus.
4. **Endorsement or Attachment** The copy of the prospectus must have endorsed on or attached to it the following:
   (a) The written consent of the expert to the issue of the prospectus, if his report has been included therein and such expert must not be connected or interested in the formation, promotion or management of the company.
   (b) A copy of every contract appointing or fixing the remuneration of managerial personnel.
   (c) A copy of every material contract unless it is entered into in the ordinary course of business within 2 years before the date of issue of the prospectus.
   (d) When the persons making the reports relating to profits and losses, assets and liabilities, etc. have made adjustments to them, a signed statement by them stating the adjustments and the reasons for the same.
   (e) The written consent of the person if any named in the prospectus as the auditor, adviser, attorney, solicitor, banker of the company to act in that capacity.
   (f) A duly signed report required by Part II of Schedule II relating to adjustments regarding the figures of any profits/losses, or assets or liabilities.
5. **Matters to be Stated on the Face of Prospectus [Section 60(2)]** Every prospectus must state on face of it—
   (a) that a copy thereof has been delivered for registration, and
   (b) the documents required to be endorsed on or attached to the copy delivered for registration.
6. **Time Limit within which Prospectus is to be Issued [Section 60(4)]** The prospectus must be issued within 90 days after the date on which a copy of the same is delivered to the Registrar. If it is issued after 90 days after its registration, it shall be deemed to be a prospectus a copy of which has not been delivered to the Registrar.

Penalty for Issue of Prospectus without Registration [Section 60(5)]

The company and every person who is knowingly a party to the issue of prospectus without registration shall be punishable with fine up to Rs 50,000.

6.0 APPROVAL OF PROSPECTUS BY VARIOUS AGENCIES

6.1 Authorities who Approve the Prospectus

The draft prospectus is required to get approved by the following authorities before it is filed with ROC for registration.

(a) All the lead managers to the issue (who must be authorised by SEBI);

(b) Each of the Stock Exchanges where the shares of the company are listed and where the shares/debentures are proposed to be listed.

(c) The lead financial institutions underwriting the issue (if applicable). (Authorised by SEBI)

6.2 Vetting by SEBI

The draft prospectus is required to get vetted by SEBI to ensure adequacy of disclosures. However, vetting by SEBI does not amount to approval of prospectus. SEBI does not take any responsibility for the correctness of the statements made or opinions expressed in the prospectus.

6.3 Duty of ROC

The ROCs must ensure that merchant bankers to the issue whether as lead manager, Co-managers, advisers or consultants are only those authorized by SEBI. Each merchant banker has been given a code number. ROC must not register a prospectus if prior registration, SEBI informs ROC that the contents of prospectus filed are in contravention of any law or statutory rules and regulations.

7.0 SHELF PROSPECTUS [SECTION 60A]

7.1 What is Shelf Prospectus?

"Shelf prospectus" means a prospectus issued by any financial institution or bank for one or more issues of the securities or class of securities specified in that prospectus.

7.2 Who is Required to File a Shelf Prospectus [Section 60A(1)]

Any public financial institution, public sector bank or scheduled bank whose main object is financing shall file a shelf prospectus.

"Financing" means making loans to or subscribing in the capital of, a private industrial enterprise engaged in infrastructural financing or, such other company as the Central Government may notify in this behalf;

7.3 Benefit of Filing Shelf Prospectus [Section 60A(2)]

A company filing a shelf prospectus with the Registrar shall not be required to file prospectus afresh at every stage of offer of securities by it within a period of validity of such shelf prospectus.

7.4 Obligation of a Company Filing a Shelf Prospectus [Section 60A(3) and (4)]

A company filing a shelf prospectus shall be required to file an information memorandum on all material facts relating to new charges created, changes in the financial positions as have occurred between the first offer of securities, previous offer of securities and the succeeding offer of securities within such time as may be prescribed by the Central Government, prior to making of a second or subsequent offer of securities under the shelf prospectus.

An information memorandum shall be issued to the public along with shelf prospectus filed at the stage of the first offer of securities and such prospectus shall be valid for a period of one year from the date of opening of the first issue of securities under that prospectus:

Provided that where an update of information memorandum is filed every time an offer of securities is made, such memorandum together with the shelf prospectus shall constitute the prospectus.

8.0 INFORMATION MEMORANDUM [SECTION 60B]

8.1 When Information Memorandum may be Circulated [Section 60B(1)]

A public company making an issue of securities may circulate information memorandum to the public prior to filing of a prospectus.

8.2 What is Red-herring Prospectus?

"Red-herring prospectus" means a prospectus which does not have complete particulars on the price of the securities offered and the quantum of securities offered.

8.3 Obligations of Company Filing Information Memorandum

1. A company inviting subscription by an information memorandum shall be bound to file a prospectus prior to the opening of the subscription lists and the offer as a red-herring prospectus, at least three days before the opening of the offer.
2. The information memorandum and red-herring prospectus shall carry same obligations as are applicable in the case of a prospectus.
3. Any variation between the information memorandum and the red-herring prospectus shall be highlighted as variations by the issuing company.
4. Every variation as made and highlighted in accordance with Sub-section (4) above shall be individually intimated to the persons invited to subscribe to the issue of securities.
5. In the event of the issuing company or the underwriters to the issue have invited or received advance subscription by way of cash or post-dated cheques or stock-invest, the company or such underwriters or bankers to the issue shall not encash such subscription moneys or post-dated cheques or stock-invest before the date of opening of the issue, without having individually intimated the prospective subscribers of the variation and without having offered an opportunity to such prospective subscribers to withdraw their application and cancel their post-dated cheques or stock-invest or return of subscription paid.
6. The applicant or proposed subscriber shall exercise his right to withdraw from the application on any intimation of variation within seven days from the date of such intimation and shall indicate such withdrawal in writing to the company and the underwriters.
7. Any application for subscription which is acted upon by the company or underwriters or bankers to the issue without having given enough information of any variations, or the particulars of withdrawing the offer or opportunity for cancelling the post-dated cheques or stock-invest or stop payments for such payments shall be void and the applicants shall be entitled to receive a refund or return of its post-dated cheques or stock-invest or subscription moneys or cancellation of its application, as if the said application had never been made and the applicants are entitled to receive back their original application and interest at the rate of fifteen per cent from the date of encashment till payment of realisation.
8. Upon the closing of the offer of securities, a final prospectus stating therein the total capital raised, whether by way of debt or share capital and the closing price of the securities and any other details as were not complete in the red-herring prospectus shall be filed in a case of a listed public company with the Securities and Exchange Board and Registrar, and in any other case with the Registrar only.

9.0 DEEMED PROSPECTUS OR PROSPECTUS BY IMPLICATION OR OFFER FOR SALE [SECTION 64]

9.1 Meaning of Deemed Prospectus

Where the company allots or agrees to allot any shares or debentures to issuing house and others with a view to such shares being offered to public for sale, any document by which the offer for sale to public is made shall be deemed to be a prospectus issued by a company and all provisions applicable to prospectus shall apply with specified modification. [Section 64(1)]

9.2 Presumption

It will be presumed that an allotment or an agreement to allot shares or debentures to the issuing houses was made with a view to offer them to public if it is shown—

(a) that the shares were offered to the public for sale within 6 months after they were allotted or agreed to be allotted to issuing house, or

(b) that the whole consideration in respect of shares/debentures had not been received by the company. [Section 64(2)]

9.3 Additional Matters to be Stated

In addition to the matters required by Section 56, the deemed prospectus issued by an issuing house under Section 64(1) must state the following two matters:

(a) The net amount of consideration received or to be received by the company in respect of these shares or debentures.

(b) The place and time at which the contract of allotment may be inspected.

10.0 APPLICATION FORMS TO BE ACCOMPANIED BY AN ABRIDGED PROSPECTUS [SECTION 56(3)]

10.1 Meaning of Abridged Prospectus

Abridged prospectus means a memorandum containing such salient features of a prospectus as may be prescribed. [Section 2(1)]

10.2 Application form to be Accompanied

Every application form for shares in or debentures of a company must be accompanied by an abridged prospectus containing all the prescribed features except in the following cases where the form of application is issued—

(a) to person who is **bona fide** invited to enter into an underwriting agreement. [Section 56(3)(a)]

(b) in relation to shares or debentures which were not offered to the public. [Section 56(3)(b)]

(c) to existing members or debentureholders of the company whether with or without the right of renunciation. [Section 56(5)(a)]

(d) in relation to shares or debentures which are—

   (i) uniform in all respects with shares or debentures previously issued, and

   (ii) dealt in or quoted at a recognised stock exchange. [Section 56(5)(b)]

The logic behind the first two exceptions is that the public are not involved, hence no needs of protection. In case of last two exceptions, the offeree being already a member for the shares being quoted one, must have enough information about the company to protect himself.

10.3 Form of Abridged Prospectus

The Government has prescribed a Form 2A of abridged prospectus. The abridged prospectus and the share application form must bear the same printed number.

10.4 Duty to Furnish Prospectus

A copy of prospectus must be furnished on a request being made by any person before the closing of the subscription list. [Provision to Section 56(3)]

10.5 Penalty for Default [Section 56(3)]

If any person acts in the contravention of the provisions of Section 56(3), he shall be punishable with fine which may extend to Rs 50,000.

11.0 EXPERT'S CONSENT [SECTIONS 57–58–59]

11.1 Meaning of Expert [Section 59(2)]

The expression 'expert' includes an engineer, a valuer, an accountant and any other person whose profession gives authority to a statement made by him.

11.2 Expert to be Unconnected [Section 57]

The statement of an expert must not be included in the prospectus if he is in any way connected with the formation or promotion or management of the company. In other words, the person must be independent to function as an expert.

11.3 Conditions for Issue of Prospectus Containing Expert's Statement [Sec. 58]

The statement of an expert must not be included in the prospectus unless—

(a) The expert has given his written consent to the issue of the prospectus.
(b) The expert has not withdrawn such consent before the delivery of a copy of the prospectus for registration.
(c) A statement that he has given and has not withdrawn his consent, appears in the prospectus.

11.4 Penalty for Default [Section 59(2)]

Every person who is knowingly a party to the issue of prospectus in contravention of Section 57 or Section 58, shall be punishable with fine upto Rs 50,000.

11.5 Terms of Contracts Mentioned in Prospectus not to be Varied [Section 61]

A company must not vary the terms of contract mentioned in the prospectus or statement in lieu of prospectus, except with the approval of the members in general meeting.

11.6 Legal Significance [Section 56(2)]

Any condition in the prospectus which requires or binds an applicant for shares or debentures to waive compliance with any of the requirements relating to statutory matters and reports, shall be void. Similarly, the condition which has the effect of affecting him with the notice of any contract, document or a matter not specifically referred to in the prospectus, shall be void.

11.7 Expert's Right to be Indemnified [Section 62(3)]

Where an expert has given his consent to the inclusion of his report in the prospectus and has withdrawn his consent before the issue of the prospectus and inspite of this the prospects has been issued, the directors of the company and every other person who authorised the issue of the prospectus shall be liable to indemnify the expert against all damages, costs and expenses which he may have incurred on account of his being associated with the issue of the prospectus as an expert.

12.0 EFFECT OF ACCEPTING APPLICATION WITHOUT COMPLYING WITH THE REQUIREMENTS OF SECTION 56

In case the company accepts the application for shares or debentures without complying with the requirements of Section 56, the applicant can *neither* ask for the rescission of the contract *nor* the rectification of the register. But he can sue the person responsible for the issue of the prospectus for any damages which he may have suffered. [*South of England Natural Gas and Petroleum Co.*, (1911) Ch. 573]

13.0 MATTERS TO BE STATED IN THE PROSPECTUS [SECTION 56]

Every prospectus must state the matters specified in Part I of Schedule II and set out the reports specified in Part II and the said Part I and Part II have effect subject to provisions contained in Part III of that Schedule.

Keeping in view the requirements of Schedule II of The Companies Act, 1956 and the SEBI guidelines for disclosure and investor protection, the prospectus to be issued by companies should provide for the following matters:

1. General Information

(a) Name and address of registered office of the issuer company;
(b) Details of letter of intent/industrial licence obtained and declaration of the Central Government about non-responsibility for financial soundness or correctness of statements;
(c) Disclaimer clause of SEBI.
(d) Disclaimer Statement from the Issuer
(e) Office of Board and ROC
(f) Names of stock exchanges where listed (if applicable) and where listing applications have been made for the issue;
(g) Provisions of Section 68A(1) of The Companies Act, 1956 regarding fictitious applications;
(h) Minimum Subscription Clause:

(i) For Non-underwritten Public Issues:
"If the company does not receive the minimum subscription of 90% of the issued amount on the date of closure of the issue, or if the subscription level falls below 90% after the closure of issue on account of cheques having being returned unpaid or withdrawal of applications, the company shall forthwith refund the entire subscription amount received. If there is a delay beyond 8 days after the company becomes liable to pay the amount, the company shall pay interest as per Section 73 of the Companies Act 1956."

(ii) For Underwritten Public Issues:
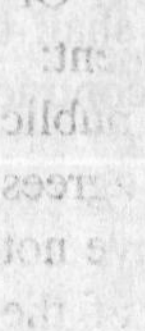
"If the company does not receive the minimum subscription of 90% of the net offer to public including development of Underwriters within 60 days from the date of closure of the issue, the company shall forthwith refund the entire subscription amount received. If there is a delay beyond 8 days after the company becomes liable to pay the amount, the company shall pay interest prescribed under Section 73 of the Companies Act, 1956."

For Composite Issues:
The Lead Merchant Banker shall ensure that the requirement of "minimum subscription" is satisfied both jointly and severally, i.e., independently for both rights and public issues.

If the company does not receive the minimum subscription in either of the issues the company shall refund the entire subscription received.

(i) Offer for sale

The requirement of minimum subscription shall not be applicable to offer for sale.

(j) Public issues by infrastructure companies.

The requirement of minimum subscription shall not be applicable to an eligible infrastructure company, provided disclosures regarding the alternate source of funding is made in the offer documents.

(k) Declaration about the issue of allotment letters or refunds within a period of 10 weeks and interest in case of any delay in refund at the prescribed rate under Section 73(2)/ 73(2A) of the Companies Act, shall be mentioned.

(l) Dates of opening, closing and earliest closing of the issue;

(m) Names and addresses of lead managers, co-managers, trustees (if applicable), legal advisers to the company, auditors, bankers to the issue, brokers to the issue and the secretary.

(n) Whether or not credit rating from any other recognised agency has been obtained for the proposed issue of debt (including convertible instruments) should be mentioned. If rating is obtained, it should be indicated, preferably with implications of the rating symbol. In terms of SEBI guidelines, rating of a credit agency is mandatory for debentures with maturity period of more than 18 months.

(o) Underwriting arrangements made for the issue, names of underwriters, amount underwritten and declaration by Board of Directors and the lead managers that in their opinion the resources of the underwriters are sufficient to discharge their underwriting obligations.

(p) Compliance Officer:

(a) The name, address, telephone number, fax and E-mail number and address of Compliance Officer.

(b) The investor's attention shall also be invited to contact the compliance officer in case of any pre-issue/post-issue related problems such as non-receipt of letters of allotment/share certificates/refund orders/cancelled stockinvests, etc.

2. Capital Structure of the company and Issue Details

(a) Authorised, issued, subscribed and paid-up capital of the company.

(b) Size of the issue with break up of reservation for preferential allotment to promoters, shareholders of group/associate companies, financial institutions, mutual funds, NRI, permanent employees, etc. The lock-in-period in respect of shares/debentures to be allotted to promoters and shareholders of group and associate companies/employees/ financial institutions should be mentioned. The maximum number of shares/debentures that can be allotted to each employee and the number of permanent employees in the company should be mentioned.

(c) Paid-up capital after the present issue and after conversion of debentures, if applicable.

(d) Securities Premium Account (before and after the issue)

3. Terms of the Present Issue

Terms of payments

(a) The caption "Interest in Case of Delay on Despatch of Allotment Lettters/Refund Orders in Case of Public Issues" shall appear and shall contain the following statement: "The company agress that as far as possible allotment of securities offered to the public shall be made within 30 days of the closure of public issue. The company further agrees that it **shall** pay interest @15% per annum if the allotment letters/refund orders have not been despatched to the applicants within 30 days from the date of the closure of the issue. However, applications received after the closure of issue in fulfilment of underwriting obligations to meet the minimum subscription requirement, shall not be entitled for the said interest."

(b) Arrangements for Disposal of Odd Lots

(c) Rights of the instrument holders.

(d) How to apply—availability of forms, prospectus and mode of payment.

(e) Disclosures about Stockinvests:

(i) The disclosures regarding manner of obtaining and mode of drawing stockinvests, non-utilisation of stockinvests by third party, time period for utilisation of stockinvests by the purchasers and disposal of applications accompanied by stockinvest as specified by the RBI shall be incorporated at the appropriate places in the offer document.

(ii) Name of the bank through which the stockinvests shall be realised, shall be given in the prospectus.

(iii) The following paragraph shall be incorporated at the appropriate places in the prospectus:

"Registrars to the Issue have been authorised by the company (through resolution of the Board passed on ....) to sign on behalf of the company to realise the proceeds of the stockinvest from the issuing bank or to affix non-allotment advice on the instrument or cancel the stockinvest of the non-allottees or partially successful allottees who have enclosed more than one stockinvest. Such cancelled stockinvest shall be sent back by the Registrars directly to the investors."

(f) **Despatch of Refund Orders**

The following clause shall be incorporated in the prospectus:

"The company shall ensure despatch of refund orders of value over Rs 1,500 and share/debenture certificates by Registered Post only and adequate funds for the purpose shall be made available to the Registrars by the issuer company."

(g) Undertaking by the Issuer Company.

(h) Utilisation of Issue Proceeds

(i) Any special tax benefits for company and its shareholders.

4. **Particulars of Issue**

(a) Objects

(b) Project cost

(c) Means of financing

(d) Appraisal

(e) Deployment of funds in the project

5. **Details about the Company Management and Project**

(a) History, main objects and present business of the company.

(b) Subsidiaries of the company.

(c) Promoters and their background.

(d) Key Managerial Personnel.

(e) Names, addresses and occupation of manager, managing director and other directors including nominee directors, whole-time directors and their directorships in other companies.

(f) Cost of the project, Means of financing and Location of the project.

(g) Plant and machinery for the project, technology adopted and process of manufacture.

(h) Collaboration, performance guarantee or assistance in marketing by the collaborators.

(i) Infrastructure facilities for raw materials and utilities like water, electricity, etc.

(j) Schedule of implementation of the project, with separate details of land acquisition, civil work, installation of plant and machinery and the progress till the date of the prospectus.

(k) Expected date of trial production and commercial production.
(l) Nature of the products, consumer/industrial and end users and approach to marketing and proposed marketing set up.
(m) Export possibilities and export obligation.
(n) Expected capacity utilisation during the first 3 years from the date of commencement of production for each of the major product groups.
(o) Expected year when the company would be able to earn cash profits and net profits and the expected cash profits and net profits for the next 3 years.
(p) High/Low equity prices of the shares/debentures of the company for each of the last 3 years and monthly high/low prices for the last 6 months (applicable to existing listed companies).

6. Management discuss and Analysis of the financial conditions and result of the operations as reflected in the financial statements.
7. Financial information of Group Companies.
8. **Information about Companies Under the Same Management Covered u/s 370(1)(B)**
In respect of any issue made by the company and other listed companies under the same management, the following details:
(a) Name of the company;
(b) Year of issue;
(c) Type of issue (Public/Private/Composite);
(d) Amount of issue;
(e) Date of Closure of issue;
(f) Date of completion of delivery of share/debenture certificates/letters of allot-ment; and
(g) Date of completion of the project, where the object of the issue was for financing a project;
(h) Rate of dividend paid.
9. Promise vis-a-vis Performance
10. The following information shall be disclosed for all issues irrespective of the issue price:
(a) Earnings per share, i.e., EPS pre-issue for three years (as adjusted for changes in capital);
(b) P/E pre-issue and comparison thereof with industry P/E where available (giving the source from which industry P/E has been taken);
(c) average return on net worth in the last three years;
(d) minimum return on increased net worth required to maintain pre-issue EPS;
(e) Net Asset Value per share based on last balance sheet;
(f) Net Asset Value per share after issue and comparison thereof with the issue price:
Provided that the projected earnings shall not be used as a justification for the issue price in the offer document:
Provided further that the accounting ratios disclosed in the prospectus in support of basis of the issue price shall be calculated after giving effect to the consequent increase in capital on account of compulsory conversions outstanding, as well as on the assumption that the options outstanding, if any, to subscribe for additional capital will be exercised;
(g) An illustrative format of disclosure in respect of basis for issue price is given in *Schedule XV*.
(i) The issuer company and the lead merchant banker shall provide the accounting ratios as mentioned above to justify the basis of issue price:
Provided that, the lead merchant banker shall not proceed with the issue in case the accounting ratios mentioned above, do not justify the issue price.

(ii) In case of book built issues, the offer document shall state that the final price has been determined on the basis of the demand from the investors.

11. **Outstanding Litigation Pertaining to:**
    (i) Matters likely to affect operation and finances of the company, including disputed tax liabilities; and
    (ii) Criminal prosecution launched against the company and directors for alleged offences under the following statutes:
    The Indian Stamp Act, 1899
    The Central Excises Act, 1944
    The Imports and Export (Control) Act, 1951
    The Industries (Development and Regulation) Act, 1951
    The Prevention of Food Adulteration Act, 1954
    The Essential Commodities Act, 1955
    The Companies Act, 1956
    The Wealth-tax Act, 1957
    The Income-tax Act, 1961
    The Customs Act, 1962
    The Monopolies and Restrictive Trade Practices Act, 1969
    The Foreign Exchange Management Act, 1999.
12. Risk Factors and Management perception as the same, if any.
13. Disclosure on Investor Grievances and Redressal System.
14. **General Information**
    (a) Consent of directors, auditors, solicitors/advocates, managers to the issue, Registrar to the Issue, Bankers to the company, bankers to the issue and experts.
    (b) Expert opinion obtained, if any.
    (c) Change, if any, in directors and auditors during the last three years, and reasons thereof.
    (d) Authority for the issue and details of resolution passed for the issue.
    (e) Procedure and time of schedule for allotment and issue of certificates.
    (f) Names and addresses of the company secretary, legal adviser, lead managers, co-managers, auditors, bankers to the company, bankers to the issue and brokers to the issue.
15. **Financial Information**
    A report from the auditors on:
    (a) **Profits and Losses** of the company (where there is no subsidiary company) and the combined profits and losses of the subsidiaries or individual profits and losses of each subsidiary for each of the five financial years preceding the issue of prospectus (where there are subsidiaries);
    (b) **Assets and Liabilities** of the company (where there is no subsidiary company) at the last date to which the accounts are made up and the combined assets and liabilities of the subsidiaries or individually with the assets and liabilities of each subsidiary (where there are subsidiaries); and
    (c) **Rates of the Dividends** paid by the company in respect of each class of shares for each of the five financial years preceding the issue of prospectus.

    If no accounts have been made up in respect of any part of the period of five years ending three months before the date of issue of prospectus, the report should contain a statement of the fact. Further, a statement of accounts of the company should be made in respect of a part of the said period upto a date not earlier than six months of the date of issue of prospectus and the assets and liabilities position as at the end of that period. There should be a certificate from the auditors that such accounts have been examined and found correct by them.

The report should distinguish items of a non-recurring nature and indicate the nature of provisions or adjustments made or are yet to be made.

16. **Statutory and other information**
   (a) Minimum subscription, as laid down in the SEBI guidelines.
   (b) Expenses of the issue giving separately fees payable to advisers, registrars to the issue, managers to the issue and trustees for debentureholders.
   (c) Underwriting commission and brokerage.
   (d) Previous issue for cash or consideration otherwise than for cash.
   (e) Details of public or right issue during the last five years:
      (i) Date of allotment and refund;
      (ii) Date of listing on the stock exchange; and
      (iii) Amount of premimum or discount, if applicable.
   (f) Details of premium received in respect of any issue of shares made in the two years preceding the date of issue of prospectus or to be made stating the proposed date of the issue, the reasons for differentiation of premium for different categories, if applicable and the disposal of premium received or to be received.
   (g) Commission or brokerage paid on previous issue.
   (h) Debentures and redeemable preference shares and other instruments outstanding on the date of prospectus and the terms of their issue.
   (i) Option to subscribe. The details of options to subscribe for securities to be dealt with in a depository.
   (j) Particulars of property purchased or proposed to be purchased from vendors to be paid for wholly or partly out of the proceeds of the issue and the interest of the promoters or directors in any transaction relating to the property within the last two years.
   (k) Details of directors, proposed directors, whole-time directors, their remuneration, appointment and remuneration of the managing director(s).
   (l) Interests of directors, their borrowing powers and qualification shares.
   (m) Any amount or benefit paid or given within the two preceding years or intended to be paid or given to any promoter or officers and consideration for the payment or giving of the benefit.
   (n) The dates of, parties to, and general nature of—
      (i) every contract of appointment or remuneration of a managing director or manager; and
      (ii) every other material contract, not being a contract entered into in the ordinary course of business of the company or entered into more than two years prior to the date of prospectus.

      Reasonable time and place for inspection of the contract should be provided for.
   (o) Full particulars of the nature and extent of interest of every director or promoter:
      (i) in the promotion of the company; or
      (ii) in any property acquired by the company within two years of the date of the prospectus or proposed to be acquired by it.
   (p) Rights of members regarding voting, dividend, lien on shares, modification of rights and forfeiture of shares/debentures.
   (q) Restriction on transfer and transmission of shares/debentures and on consolidation splitting.
   (r) Revaluation of assets, if any, during the last 5 years.
   (s) Material Contracts and Inspection of Documents.
   (t) Particulars of default in meeting statutory dues, institutional dues, dues to holders of instruments like debentures, fixed deposits and arrears of cumulative preference shares, pertaining to the company and/or other companies promoted by the same promoters, which are listed on stock exchanges.

(u) Any material development after the date of the last balance sheet and its impact on the performance and prospects of the company.

14.0 MISLEADING PROSPECTUS

14.1 Meaning of Misleading Prospectus [Section 65]

The prospectus may be described as 'misleading prospectus if it contains untrue statement. The prospectus is said to have contained untrue statement in the following circumstances:

(a) where it contains a statement which is misleading in the form and context in which it is included, and

(b) where it omits any matter which is calculated to mislead.

Thus, the term 'untrue statement' has been used in a broader sense. It covers *not only false statement, but also concealment of material statements.*

14.2 Rule of Golden Legacy

Justice Kindersley, V.C. in *New Brunswick and Canada Rly. and Land Co.* v. *Muggeridge,* [(1860), 3 Lt 651: 30 LJ Ch. 242] observed: "Those who issue a prospectus hold out to the public that great advantages will accrue to persons who will take shares. Public is invited to take shares on the faith of the representation contained in the prospectus. Therefore, they are bound to state everything honestly and faithfully. They must not only abstain from stating something as a fact when it is not actually so but also must not omit a fact the existence of which might in any degree affect the nature or quality of the privileges and advantages which the prospectus holds out as an inducement to take shares."

The above stated rule is popularly known as **'Rule of Golden Legacy'**.

15.0 REMEDIES IN CASE OF MISLEADING PROSPECTUS

The remedies available to person who subscribe for shares on the faith of misleading prospectus are as given below:

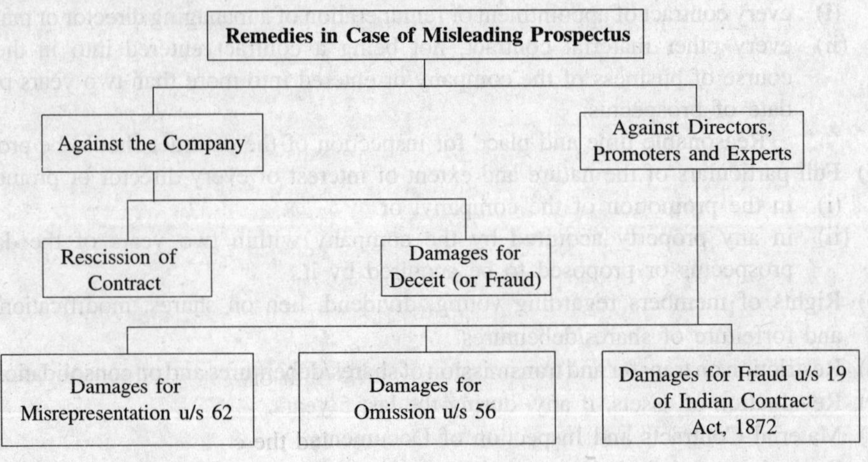

Let us discuss these remedies one by one.

15.1 Remedies Against the Company

(a) Rescission of the Contract

Where a prospectus contains misstatements (whether made innocently or fraudulently), the contract to subscribe for shares becomes voidable at the option of the aggrieved subscriber. In other words, subscriber to the shares can file a suit against the company to rescind the contract under the general law of contract. The right of rescission of contract can be exercised subject to the following conditions:

(i) The prospectus must have been issued by the company or by someone authorised by the company in this behalf.

(ii) There must be misrepresentation or omission of a fact. In other words, a mere opinion, a statement of expression or intention does not amount to misrepresentation.

(iii) The misrepresentation must of fact and not of law.

(iv) The misrepresentation or omission of a fact must be misleading.

In case of *Arnison* v. *Smith,* (1889) 40 Ch. D. 569, A statement in the prospectus that share capital has been subscribed when it has only been allotted in fully paid shares to the company's contractors, was held to be untrue.

In case of *Rex* v. *Kylsant*, (1932) I.K.B. 442, the company issued a prospectus which did not contain any untrue statement. One of the statements disclosed the rates of dividends paid for a number of years. This was a factual statement which was true. But the dividends had not been paid out of trading profits but out of realised capital profits. This fact was not disclosed in the prospectus. The prospectus was held to be misleading not because of what is stated but because what it concealed or omitted.

Further, if a statement was true when it was made but subsequently became untrue when shares were allotted, the contract to subscribe for shares can be rescined. [*Re Scottish Petroleum Co.,* (1823) 23 Ch. D. 413]

(v) The *misrepresentation* must be *material* to the contract of taking shares. A fact can be considered as material if it is likely to influence the judgement of a prospective investor in deciding whether he should purchase shares in the company or refrain from doing so. In the various, judicial decisions, the misrepresentation was held to be a material facts.

(a) A statement that two leading businessmen of repute have agreed to become directors of the company when they had only expressed their willingness to help the company. [*Re Metropolitan Coal Consumer's Association,* (1892) 3 Ch. 2]

(b) A statement that the proceeds of the issue of debentures were to be utilized for improving and developing the business whereas the real object of issuing debentures was to pay-off past liabilities. [*Edington* v. *Fitzmaurice,* (1885) 29 Ch. D. 459]

(c) A statement that directors and their friends have subscribed a large portion of the capital of the company and that they now offer the remaining shares to the public whereas the fact was that they had only subscribed ten shares each. [*Handerson* v. *Lacon,* (1867) 5 Eq. 249]

(vi) The aggrieved party must have relied upon the prospectus while applying for shares. A purchaser of shares in the open market has no remedy against the company or any other persons even if he might bought the shares on the faith of misrepresentation in the prospectus. *[Peek* v. *Gurney,* (1870 L.R. 6 H.L. 377)]

(vii) The aggrieved party must exercise the right to rescind the contract within a reasonable time of becoming aware of a mis-statement in the prospectus and before the company goes into liquidation. *[Shiromani Sugar Mills Ltd.* v. *Debi Prasad, AIR* (1950) All 508]

(viii) The aggrieved party must exercise the right to rescind the contract before he affirms his contract for purchase of shares. In the following cases, it has been held that the subscriber has affirmed the contract:
  (a) where he has received dividend or paid calls *[Scholey* v. *Central Railway,* (1868) L.R. 9 Eq. 266],
  (b) where he attends and votes at general meetings [*Shrpley v. Louth Etc. Co.* (1876) 2 Ch. D. 663],
  (c) where he executes a transfer of his shares [*Crowley's case* (1869) L.R. 4 Ch. App. 322].
  It may be noted that a transfer of part of shares before discovery of misrepresentation does not affect his right as to the rest. [*Re Mount Morgan Etc. Ltd.,* (1887) 56 L.T. 622]

(b) Damages for Fraud (Deceit)

The subscriber can recover damages for any loss which he may have suffered if he was induced to take shares based on a fraudulent misrepresentation of material facts. Lord Herschall in *Derry* v. *Peek,* (1889) 14 A.C. 337, said:' "To support an action for deceit, fraud must be proved and nothing less than fraud will do. Fraud is proved where it is shown that a false statement has been made (a) knowingly, or (b) without belief in its truth, or (c) recklessly, carelessly whether it is false or true".

The right to claim damages may be exercised subject to the fulfilment of the following conditions:

(i) There must be fraudulent misrepresentation,
(ii) The fraudulent misrepresentation must relate to facts which are material to the contract of purchasing shares,
(iii) The aggrieved party must have actually relied on the misstatements,
(iv) The aggrieved party must have taken shares directly from the company, and
(v) The aggrieved party must have suffered some loss.

It may be noted that the right to claim damages may be exercised against the company after rescinding the contract of allotment and against the persons who authorized the issue of prospectus without rescinding the contract of allotment. The House of Lords in *Houldsworth* v. *City Glargow Bank,* (1880) 5 A.C. 317, held that if a shareholder wants to sue the company for damages, he must first rescind the contract. He can not sue the company for damages while he remains a shareholder.

15.2 Remedies Against Directors and Promoters

(a) Damages for Misrepresentation Under Section 62(1)

The following persons are liable to compensate all those who subscribe for shares on the faith of the prospectus for any loss sustained by them by reason of any untrue and misleading statement included in the prospectus.

(i) Every person who is director of the company at the time of the issue of the prospectus.
(ii) Every person who has authorised himself to be named and is named in the prospectus as a director or as one having agreed to become a director, either immediately, or after an interval of time.
(iii) Every promoter of the company.
(iv) Every person who has authorised the issue of the prospectus.

Notes:

(a) The action for damages must be taken within 3 years from the date of the allotment of the shares.

(b) A shareholder who bought shares from an existing shareholders or from the share market, cannot bring an action for deceit against directors. [*Peek* v. *Gurney*]
(c) The subscribers may institute a suit for damages against those responsible for the issue of the prospectus, inspite of the fact that the contract to purchase shares has been repudiated. This is an action for deceit under the general law. [*Derry* v. *Peek,* (1889) 14 A.C. 337]
(d) The action for damages can be taken even if the remedy by way of rescission (as against the company) has been last through negligence or even if the company goes into liquation.

Defences Available to Directors etc. [Section 62(2)]

No person shall be liable under this section, if he proves:

(i) that, he having consented to become a director, had withdrawn his consent to become director before the issue of prospectus and that it was issued without his authority; or
(ii) that the prospectus was issued without his knowledge or consent and that on becoming aware of its issue, he immediately gave reasonable public notice to that effect; or
(iii) that after the issue of the prospectus and before, allotment, he, on becoming aware of any untrue statement in it, had withdrawn his consent to the prospectus and gave reasonable public notice of the withdrawal and his reasons for doing so; or
(iv) that he had reasonable ground to believe and until allotment did believe that the statement was true. This statement pertains to every untrue statement not purporting to be made on the authority of expert or of a public official document or statement or
(v) that the statement was a correct and fair representation of the statement made by an expert and he had reasonable ground to believe and until issue of prospectus did believe that the person making the statement was competent to make it and that the expert had given his consent and had not withdrawn that consent before delivery of a copy of the prospectus for registration or to the defendant's knowledge, before allotment; or
(vi) that if the statement is a copy of or exract from an official document or is made by an official person, it was a correct and fair copy of the document or a fair representation of the statement.

15.3 Remedies Against Expert [Section 62(3)]

The form 'expert' includes an engineer, a valuer, an accountant and any other person whose profession gives authority to a statement made by him [Section 59(2)].

An expert is liable to compensate only in respect of his own untrue statement, wrong report or valuation made by him and included in the prospectus.

(a) Defences Available to an Expert

An expert shall not be liable if he proves—

(i) having given his consent, he withdrew it in writing before delivery of a copy of the prospectus for registration with the Registrar of Companies; or
(ii) after delivery of prospectus for registration with the Registrar of Companies but before allotment, he on becoming aware of the untrue statement, withdrew his consent in writing, and gave reasonable public notice of the withdrawal and his reasons therefor; or
(iii) he was competent to make the statement, and believed on reasonable grounds that it was true.

Measure of Damages The measure of damages is the loss suffered by reason of the false statement, that is to say, the difference between the value which the shares would have had if the company had processed the advantages stated in the prospectus (but not exceeding the price paid) and the true value of the shares at the time of allotment in the circumstances which in fact existed. [*McConnnel* v. *Wright,* (1903) 1 Ch. 546]

Right of Indemnity Every such director or expert who has escaped liability on the above grounds is entitled to be indemnified by other directors or experts who continue to be liable against all damages, costs and expenses which he may incur in defending himself against any legal proceedings brought against him. [Section 62(4)]

Right of Contribution If any subscriber realises any damages from any director or officer of the company for untrue statement in the prospectus, the directors and officers who authorised the issue of untrue prospectus shall contribute and pay their share of damages to the director who has made the payment. *[Gerson* v. *Simpson,* (1903) 2 K.B. 197]

(b) Damages for Omission u/s 56

In case of any omission of required matter in the prospectus, the subscriber can sue the persons responsible for the issue of prospectus if he can prove—

(a) that he would not have purchased shares if there had been no such omissions, and
(b) that he has actually suffered a loss.

Notes:

(i) omission does not entitle the subscriber to rescind the contract unless it amounts to fraud or misrepresentation. *[Shiromani Sugar Mills* v. *Debi Prasad, AIR* (1950) All. 508]
(ii) Subscriber can sue even if omission does not make the prospectus misleading.

Defences Available [Section 56(4)]

A director or any other person sued under this section shall not be liable, if—

(a) he proves that he had no knowledge of any matter not disclosed; or
(b) he proves that the non-compliance or contravention arose from an honest mistake of fact; or
(c) in the opinion of the court, the matter not disclosed was immaterial; or
(d) that the non-compliance or contravention ought to be excused with regard to all the circumstances of the case.

Criminal Liability for Misstatement [Section 63]

Every person who had authorised the issue of prospectus containing an untrue statement shall be punishable with imprisonment for a term upto 2 years or with fine upto Rs 5,000 or with both unless he proves either—

(a) that the statement was immaterial; or
(b) that he had reasonable ground to believe and did upto the time of issue of prospectus that the statement was true.

16.0 PENALTY FOR FRAUDULENTLY INDUCING PERSONSTOINVEST MONEY [SECTION 68]

Any person who, by making (either knowingly or recklessly) any false, deceptive or misleading statement, promise or forecast or by any dishonest concealment of material facts, induces or attempts to induce another person to enter into, or to offer to enter into—

(a) any agreement for, the acquisition, disposal, subscribing for, or underwriting shares or debentures; or
(b) any agreement for the purpose of securing any profit to any of the parties from the yield of shares or debentures, or from fluctuations in the value of shares or debentures;

shall be punishable with imprisonment for a term upto 5 years, or with fine upto Rs 1,00,000 or with both.

17.0 PERSONATION FOR ACQUISITION, ETC., OF SHARES. [SECTION 68A(1)]

Any person who—

(a) makes an application to a company for acquiring, or subscribing for, any shares therein, in a fictitious name or

(b) otherwise induces a company to allot, or register any transfer of, shares therein to him, or any other person in a fictitious name,

shall be punishable with imprisonment for a term upto **5 years.**

Disclosure in Prospectus [Section 68A(2)]

The provisions of Section 68A(1) must be prominently reproduced in every prospectus issued by the company and in every form of application for shares which is issued by the company to any person.

18.0 ISSUE OF SECURITIES ONLY IN DEMAT FORM [SECTION 68B]

Initial Public officer of Securities of at least Rs 10 crore must be only in Dematerialised form, by complying with the requisite provisions of the Depositories Act, 1996 and Regulations made thereunder. According to SEBI Guidelines company can make an issue of securities to the public or on right basis only in demat form, while this new section implies that only with regard to *initial offer* it should be in demat form, whereas for any subsequent issue it could be in physical form.

19.0 STATEMENT IN LIEU OF PROSPECTUS [SECTION 70]

19.1 When Required

When the public company having share capital decides to raise the capital privately (say from relatives and friends) without inviting offers from the public. It is required to issue a statement in lieu of prospectus.

19.2 Contents of Statement in Lieu of Prospectus

The statement in lieu of prospectus shall contain the particulars and reports as set out in Schedule III to the Companies Act.

19.3 Signature

The statement to be delivered to the Registrar for registration must be signed by every person who is named in the statement as director or proposed director or his agent authorised in writing.

19.4 Delivery

The statement must be delivered to the Registrar for registration at least 3 days before the allotment of the shares or debentures.

19.5 Penalty for Default

The company and every director of the company, who willfully authorises or permits contravention, shall be punishable with fine upto Rs 10,000.

19.6 Liability for Misstatement

The liability for any misstatement in a Statement in lieu of prospectus is the same as in case of a prospectus.

19.7 Is a Private Company Required to Issue Prospectus or Statement in Lieu of Prospectus?

A private company is *neither* required to issue a prospectus *nor* a statement in lieu of prospectus since it cannot invite public to subscribe for its shares or debentures as per restrictions of Section 3(1)(iii).

EXERCISES

VERY SHORT ANSWER TYPE QUESTIONS

1. What is 'Prospectus'?
2. Where is a company not required to issue a prospectus? What is meant by 'public'?
3. What is meant by 'Invitation to the public'?
4. What is meant by 'Subscription or purchase of shares'?
5. Name the various agencies who approve the Prospectus?
6. Name the agency by whom the prospectus is to get vetted?
7. What is 'Misleading Prospectus'?
8. What is 'Rule of Golden Legacy'?
9. What is 'Statement in lieu of prospectus'?
10. Who is deemed to be an expert?
11. What is the limitation period for bringing an action against director on ground of misstatement in the prospectus?

SHORT ANSWER TYPE QUESTIONS

1. State the significance of prospectus?
2. State the requirement to prospectus?
3. What is meant by 'Deemed prospectus'?
4. 'Every application from is to be accompanied by an is Abridged Prospectus'. Comment?
5. State the provisions relating to expert's comment?
6. State the effect of accepting application form without complying with the requirements of Section 56?
7. Explain the remedies available against the company to a person who subscribe for share on the faith of misleading prospectus.
8. Explain the remedies available against the directors and experts on the faith of misleading prospectus.
9. State the defences available to directors and experts in case of misleading prospectus.
10. Write a short note on the following:
    (a) Rule of Golden Legacy.
    (b) Deemed Prospectus.
    (c) Statement in lieu of Prospectus.
    (d) Misleading Prospectus.
    (e) Application and Allotment of shares in fictitious name.
    (f) Shelf Prospectus
    (g) Abridged Prospectus

LONG ANSWER TYPE QUESTIONS

1. State the matter to be stated in the prospectus?
2. (a) What is 'Misleading Prospectus'?
   (b) Discuss the various remedies available to a person who subscribe for shares on the faith of misleading prospectus?
3. (a) Who is deemed to be an expert in relation to the prospectus of a company?
   (b) What conditions must be satisfied before a report by an expert can be published therein?
   (c) Is there any remedy available to the allottee who has been induced to take shares on the faith of an untrue statement of an expert in the prospectus?
   (d) Are there any defences available to such an expert?
4. Define 'prospectus'. Discuss briefly the contents of 'prospectus'. What guidelines have been issued by SEBI in this regard?
5. Bogo Ltd. issued a prospectus which contained some misleading statements. Mr. Yogi knowing the fact did not subscribe to the issue. But he purchased some shares from open market and claimed compensation from the company on the ground that the prospectus issued for the shares contained misleading statements. Can he succeed? Give reasons.
6. When and in what manner may a company be permitted to furnish an abridged form of prospectus? Under what circumstances such abridged prospectus is not required to be accompanied with the share application form?

CHAPTER 7

Shares

1.0 MEANING OF ALLOTMENT

Allotment is an acceptance by the company of the offer to take shares made by an applicant. The term 'Allotment' means the appropriation out of the previously unappropriated capital of the company, of a certain number of shares to a person. That is why, the reissue of forfeited shares is not an allotment since reissue occurs as a result of sale of forfeited shares which had already been allotted and not allotment thereof. It is on allotment that shares come into existence. The amount payable on allotment is called 'Allotment Money'.

1.1 General Provisions as to Allotment

Since the allotment is the acceptance of an offer to take certain number of shares, the general provisions relating to valid acceptance of an offer must be followed. The general provisions regarding allotment of shares are as follows:

1. **Proper Authority** The allotment must be made by proper authority. It is the duty of the Board of directors to allot the shares. However, the Board may delegate this authority to some other person or persons as per the provisions of the articles of association. Allotment of shares made by an improper authority will make it void.
2. **Reasonable Time** The allotment should be made within a reasonable time. The offer to take shares of the company must be accepted within a reasonable time otherwise the applicants may refuse to take shares because after a reasonable time the offer lapses. What is the 'reasonable time' is a question of fact in each case. [*Ramlgate Victoria Hotel* v. *Montefiare*, (1866)]
3. **Communication** It must be communicated. The allotment of shares should be communicated to the applicants. Posting of a properly addressed and stamped letter of allotment will be taken as a valid communication. Even if this letter of allotment is delayed or lost in transit, the allottee will be liable, 'G' applied for certain shares in a company. The letter of allotment was despatched to him but it never reached. It was held that 'G' was liable as a shareholder (*Household Fire Insurance Co. Ltd.* v. *Grant*). A mere entry in the name of applicant on the Register of Members is not sufficient for the purpose [*Radhesham* v. *Prabhu Dayal* A.I.R. 1936, Lah. 16]. The allotment may be communicated to the applicant either in writing or verbally or by contract. [*Gunn's* case (1867) L.R. 3 Ch. App 40]
4. **Absolute and Unconditional** It must be absolute and unconditional. The allotment of shares must conform to the terms and conditions of the application. If the allotment is not according to the terms and conditions, the applicant may refuse to accept the shares even though allotment has been made to him. If the conditions are not fulfilled, the applicant must reject the shares promptly. His silence or acceptance will debar him from this right. Thus, where the applicant pledged his shares, he lost his right to insist on the condition. [*Hargopal* v. *People's Book of Northern India Ltd.*, AIR 1935 Lah. 691]

In case of *Motilal Chunilal* v. *Thakorlal,* (1912) 14 Bom. L.R. 648, an applicant was allotted certain shares in a company on the condition that he would pay for them only when the company paid dividends, it was held that he was bound by allotment even though the company went into liquidation before paying any dividend.

2.0 RESTRICTIONS AS TO THE ALLOTMENT OF SHARES BY PUBLIC COMPANIES UNDER THE COMPANIES ACT

2.1 When no Public Offer is Made [Section 70]

Where a public company does not offer its shares to the public but arranges the capital privately the company cannot proceed with the allotment unless it files with the Registrar of Companies at least 3 days before the first allotment, a statement in lieu of prospectus. If the allotment is made in contravention to this provision, it will be termed as 'irregular allotment' and it shall be voidable at the option of the allottee. In addition to this, every officer of the company, who is a party to such allotment shall be punishable with fine which may extend to Rs 10,000.

2.2 When Public Offer is Made

1. **Registration and Issue of Prospectus** Where a public company offers its shares to the public, a copy of prospectus must be filed with the Registrar for registration on or before the date of publication of the prospectus [Section 60(1)]. The prospectus must be issued to the public within 90 days of its registration with the registrar otherwise it will be deemed to be a prospectus a copy of which has not been delivered to the Registrar. [Section 60(4)]
2. **Time of the Opening of Subscription List** No allotment can be made until the beginning of the 5th day or such later time as may be specified in the prospectus. The 5th day is to be counted from the day when the prospectus was published in a newspaper or was otherwise notified to the public. The beginning of the fifth day is known as 'the time of the opening of the subscription lists'. The object of this provision is to enable the public to go through the contents of the prospectus and to decide whether to apply for shares.

   Vailidity The validity of an allotment shall not be affected by any contravention of the foregoing provisions of this section; but, in the event of any such contravention, the company, and every officer in default, shall be punishable with fine upto Rs 5,000. [Section 72(3)]

   Revocation of Offer An application for shares is not revocable untill the end of the 5th day from the opening of subscription list. [Section 72(5)]
3. **Time of Closing of Subscription Lists** The Companies Act is silent about the time for which the subscription list must be kept open.

   Minimum Time According to Stock Exchange regulation, where the shares are listed on any stock exchange the subscription list must be kept open for at least 3 working days and disclosure to this effect must be made in the prospectus.

   Maximum Time According to the Ministry of Finance, Stock Exchange Division, the subscription list for public issues can be kept open for a maximum period of 21 working days where the issue is not underwritten and for a maximum period of 10 working days where the issue is underwritten.
4. **Minimum Subscription in Case of First Allotment of Shares [Section 69(1)]** No allotment shall be made unless the amount stated in the prospectus as the minimum subscription has been subscribed and the sum payable on application for the stated amount has been received by the company. The minimum subscription refers to the amount which, in the opinion of directors, must be raised by issue of shares in order to provide for the following:

(i) the purchase price of any property purchased or to be purchased which is to be met out of the proceeds of the issue of shares;

(ii) any preliminary expenses payable by the company and any commission payable in connection with the issue of shares;

(iii) the repayment of any money borrowed by the company in respect of any of the above two matters;

(iv) working capital; and

(v) any other expenditure stating the nature and purposes thereof and the estimated amount in each case.

Note: The amount of minimum subscription shall be exclusive of any amount payable otherwise than in money.

Position as Per SEBI Guidelines In view of the existing SEBI guidelines for the issue of shares/debentures, the aforesaid provision of The Companies Act, 1956 has practically become redundant. As per SEBI Guidelines, the minimum subscription in respect of public and right issues (excluding the offer for sale of securities) is 90% of the issued amount.

5. **Minimum Application Money [Section 69(3)]** It is the amount which is payable on each share alongwith the application for purchase of shares. The amount payable on application on each share must be at least 5% of the nominal amount of the share.

6. **Application Money to be Deposited in a Scheduled Bank [Section 69(4)]** All the money received from applicants must be deposited in a scheduled bank.

(a) until the certificate to commence business is received.

(b) until the minimum subscription has been received where certificate to commence business has already been received.

7. **Refund of Application Money** If minimum subscription is not received within 120 days from the date of issue of prospectus, the company must refund the application money within 130 days without interest and with interest @ 6% p.a. for the delayed period beyond 130 days for date of issue of prospectus. [Section 69(5)]

Position as per SEBI Guidelines As per SEBI Guidelines, in case of non-receipt by the company of 90% of the issued amount from public subscription *plus* accepted devolvement from underwriters or from other sources in case of under subscribed issues, within 60 days from the date of closure of the issue, thc company must refund the subscription amount in full within 78 days without interest and with interest @ 15% p.a. for the delayed period beyond 78 days from the date of closure of the issue.

8. **Compulsory Listing of All Public Issues [Section 73]**

Application before Issue Every company intending to offer shares or debentures to the public for subscription by the issue of a prospectus must, before such issue, make an application to one or more recognised stock exchanges for permission for the shares or debentures intending to be so offered to be dealt with in the stock exchange or each such stock exchange. [Section 73(1)]

Name of Stock Exchange in Prospectus Where a prospectus states that an application has been made for permission for the shares or debentures offered thereby to be dealt in one or more recognised stock exchanges, such prospectus must state the name of the stock exchange or, as the case may be, each such stock exchange.

Allotment to be Void in Case of No Listing Permission Any allotment made shall be void if the permission has not been granted by the stock exchange or each such stock exchange, as the case may be, before the expiry of 10 weeks from the date of the closing of the subscription lists. However, where an appeal against the decision of any recognised stock exchange refusing permission for the shares or debentures to be dealt in on that stock exchange has been preferred under section 22 of the Securities Contracts (Regulation) Act, 1956 (42 of 1956), such allotment shall not be void until the dismissal of the appeal.

Refund in case of No Permission Where the permission has not been applied or, such permission having been applied for, has not been granted, the company shall repay without interest all moneys received from applicants, and, if any such money is not repaid within 8 days after the company becomes liable to repay it, the company and its every director in default shall, be jointly and severally liable to repay that money with interest at such rate, not less than 4% and not more than 15%, as may prescribed for the delayed period beyond the expiry of 8th day. [Section 73(2)]

Refund in case of over subscription Where permission has been granted by the recognised stock exchange and the issue is over subscribed, the company must repay the moneys to the extent of such excess without interest, and if such money is not repaid within 8 days, from the day the company becomes liable to pay it, the company and its every director in default shall, be jointly and severally liable to repay that money with interest at such rate, not less than 4% and not more than 15%, as may be prescribed, for the delayed period beyond the expiry of 8th day. [Section 73(2A)]

Penalty If default is made in complying with the provisions of Sub-section (2A), the company and its every officer in default shall be punishable with fine upto Rs 50,000, and where repayment is not made within 6 months from the expiry of the 8th day, also with imprisonment for a term upto 1 year. [Section 73(2B)]

Application Money to be Deposited in Schedule Bank [Section 73(3)]

All application moneys received must be kept in a separate bank account maintained with a Scheduled Bank until the permission has been granted, or where an appeal has been preferred against the refusal to grant such permission, until the disposal of the appeal, and where the permission has not been applied for as aforesaid or has not been granted, the money standing in such separate account must be repaid within the time and in the manner specified in Sub-section (2); and if default is made in complying with this sub-section, the company, and its every officer in default, shall be punishable with fine upto Rs 50,000. [Section 73(3)]

Restriction on Use of Application Money [Section 73(3A)]

Moneys standing to the credit of the separate bank account shall not be utilised for any purpose other than the following purposes namely:

(a) adjustment against allotment of shares, where the shares have been permitted to be dealt in on the stock exchange or each stock exchange specified in the prospectus; or

(b) repayment of moneys received from applicants in pursuance of the prospectus, where shares have not been permitted to be dealt in on the stock exchange or each stock exchange specified in the prospectus, as the case may be, or, where the company is for any other reason unable to make the allotment of share.

It will be deemed that permission has not been granted, if the application for permission, where made, has not been disposed of with the time specified in Section 73(1). [Section 73(5)]

2.3 Subsequent Allotment of Shares

The provision regarding the subsequent allotment of shares are same as discussed above except the provisions relating to minimum subscription.

3.0 IRREGULAR ALLOTMENT

3.1 Meaning of Irregular Allotment

An allotment is said to be irregular if it is made in contravention of the provisions of Section 69 or 70. The allotment of shares is irregular in the following, cases:

1. Where an allotment is made without receiving the minimum subscription. [Section 69(1)]
2. Where an allotment is made without receiving at least five per cent of the nominal value of shares as application money. [Section 69(3)]
3. Where an allotment is made without depositing the application money in a scheduled bank. [Section 69(4)]
4. Where if the allotment is made without filing with the Registrar the 'Statement is lieu of prospectus' at least three days before the first allotment of shares in the case of a public company which does not invite public to subscribe its shares. [Section 70]

3.2 Effects of Irregular Allotment [Section 71]

1. Allotment voidable [Section 71(1)]

An irregular allotment is voidable at the option of the applicant within the time specified by Section 71(1). The time specified is given below:

Case	*Time limit within which allotment is voidable*
(a) ***Where the allotment is made before the statutory meeting***	Within 2 months after the holding of statutory meeting and not later
(b) ***Where no statutory meeting is required to be held***	Within 2 months after the date of allotment and not later
(c) ***Where the allotment is made after the statutory meeting***	Within 2 months after the date of allotment and not later

Notes:

(i) The allottee must inform the company that he avoids the allotment within 2 months.

(ii) It is not necessary that the allottee should commence legal proceedings within the said period provided he has given notice of avoidance within 2 months.

(iii) But Legal proceedings should be reasonably prompt thereafter if they are to be brought. [*Re National Motor Mail Coach Co.*, (1908) 2 Ch. 228]

(iv) If the applicant takes steps for avoiding the allotment within this period, it does not matter that winding up proceeding has intervened during this period. [*Blanche Fonseca* v. *Jupiter Airways Ltd.*, AIR (1953) Bom. 407]

2. Suit for Compensation Against the Directors [Section 71(3)]

If any director of a company knowingly contravenes, or wilfully authorises or permits the contravention of, any of the provisions of Section 69 or Section 70 with respect to allotment, he shall be liable to compensate the company and the allottee respectively for any loss, damages or costs which the company or the allottee may have sustained or incurred thereby. The proceedings to recover any such loss, damages or costs must be commenced before the expiration of 2 years from the date of the allotment.

Note: As the allotment is only voidable at the option of the shareholder, the shareholder may keep the shares and yet sue the directors who have knowingly contravened either of the two Sections (69 and 70) to compel them to make good the loss to him as a result of the irregular allotment.

3. **Penalty [Section 69(4) and 70(4)]**
   (a) In the event of any contravention of Section 69(4) regarding deposit of money in a scheduled Bank, every promoter, director or other person who is knowingly responsible for such contravention shall be punishable with fine upto Rs 50,000. [Section 69(4)]
   (b) If a company acts in contravention of Section 70(1) or (2), the company and its every director who wilfully authorises or permits the contravention, shall be punishable with fine upto Rs 10,000. [Section 70(4)]

4.0 RETURN OF ALLOTMENT [SECTION 75]

4.1 Meaning of Return of Allotment A report in the prescribed Form No. 2 about the allotment of shares is known as 'Return of Allotment'.

4.2 When is Return of Allotment required When a company having a share capital makes any allotment of its shares, it is required to file the 'Return of Allotment'.

4.3 When is Return of Allotment not Required In the following 3 cases return of allotment is not required to be filed.

(a) In case of reissue of shares forfeited for non-payment of calls since reissue of forfeited shares amounts to resale of shares and not the allotment of shares [Section 75(5)]
(b) In case of issue of shares to signatories to the Memorandum of association.
(c) In case of allotment of debentures.

4.4 Time Limit for Filing Return of Allotment [Section 75(3)] The company must file the return of allotment within 30 days of the allotment or period extended by the Registrar. The period for filing return of allotment can be extended by the Registrar on an application made by the company either before or after the expiry of 30 days of allotment.

4.5 Contents of Return of Allotment

The return of allotment must contain the prescribed particulars as under:

1. *In case shares are allotted in cash* [Section 75(1)(a)]
   (a) the number and nominal amount of the shares allotted;
   (b) the names, addresses and occupations of the allottees and the amount, if there be any, paid or due and payable on each shares.

   But the company must not show shares as having been allotted for cash, if cash has not been actually received by it.
2. *In case shares allotted are not bonus shares and allotted as fully or partly paid up otherwise than in cash* [Section 75(1)(b)]. The company must produce for the inspection and examination of the Registrar the following documents.
   (a) a contract in writing constituting the title of the allottee; and
   (b) any contract of sale or contract of service or other consideration in respect of which the allotment was made.

   These documents must be duly stamped. Also along with these documents the company must file with the Registrar:

(i) copies of the said contracts after verifying them in the prescribed manner, and
(ii) a return stating the number and nominal amount of the shares so allotted, the extent to which they are to be treated as paid-up and the consideration for which they have been allotted.

Under Rule 5 of the Companies (Central Government's) General Rules and Forms, 1956 these copies of contracts must be verified by affidavit of a responsible officer of the company. Where such a contract is not in writing, the company must within 30 days after allotment, file with the Registrar a document embodying the said particulars of the contract. The document must bear the same amount of stamp duty as would have been payable if the contract had been in writing.

3. *In the case of issue of bonus shares* [Section 75(1)(c)(i)]:
   (a) the number and nominal amount of shares allotted,
   (b) the names, addresses and occupations of the allottees, and
   (c) resolution authorising the issue of bonus shares.
4. *In the case of issue of shares at a discount* [Section 75(1)(c)(ii)]. The return must be accompanied:
   (i) by a copy of the company's resolution authorising such an issue,
   (ii) by copy of the order of court which sanction the issue, and
   (iii) where the maximum rate of discount exceeds 10 per cent, a copy of the Central Government's order permitting the issue at a higher percentage.

4.6 Penalty for Default [Section 75(4)]

Case	*Penalty*
(a) ***In case of contravention of the provisions to Section 75(1)(a) regard-ing showing shares as having been allotted for cash if the cash has not been actually received by it.***	Every officer and every promoter who are guilty of the contravention shall be punishable with fine upto Rs 50,000.
(b) ***In case of contravention of any other provision of Section 75***	Every officer who is in default shall be punishable with fine upto Rs 5,000 for every day during which the default continues.

5.0 UNDERWRITING COMMISSION AND BROKERAGE [SECTION 76]

5.1 Meaning of Underwriting Agreement An underwriting agreement is an agreement between the company and certain party (known as underwriter) under which the latter agrees to take up the whole or part of the shares which may not be subscribed by the public for an agreed consideration (known as underwriting commission). It is in the nature of an assurance against the risk involved in placing the shares before the public.

Note: An underwriting agreement is enforceable against the executors of deceased underwriter. [*Wasner Engineering Co.* v. *Benan* (1913) 307 L.R. 191]

5.2 Purpose for which Underwriting Commission may be Paid [Section 76(1)(a) & (b)]

A company may pay a commission to any person in consideration of—
(a) his subscribing or agreeing to subscribe, whether absolutely or conditionally, for any shares in, or debentures of, the company, or

(b) his procuring or agreeing to procure subscriptions, whether absolute or conditionals for any shares in, or debentures of, the company.

5.3 Conditions for Payment

A company may pay if the following conditions are fulfilled, namely:

(i) The payment of the commission must be authorised by the articles;

(ii) The commission paid or agreed to be paid does not exceed in the case of shares, 5% of the price at which the shares are issued or the amount or rate authorised by the articles, whichever is less, and in the case of debentures, $2\frac{1}{2}$% of the price at which the debentures are issued or the amount or rate authorised by the articles, whichever is less;

(iii) The amount or rate per cent of the commission paid or agreed to be paid must be disclosed in the prospectus or in the statement in lieu of prospectus or in a statement in the prescribed form signed in a like manner as a statement in lieu of prospectus and filed before the payment of the commission with the Registrar.

(iv) The number of shares or debentures underwritten by each of the underwriters must be disclosed in the prospectus or statement in lieu of prospectus.

(v) A copy of the contract for the payment of the commission must be delivered to the Registrar at the time of delivery of the prospectus or the statement in lieu of prospectus for registration.

5.4 Can Commission be Paid to Any Person on Shares or Debentures Which are not Offered to Public for Subscription?

According to Section 76(4A), no commission shall be paid to any person on shares or debentures which are not offered to the public for subscription.

Exception Proviso to Section 76(4A) provides an exception to the above rule. Accordingly, a company may pay commission to the underwriter in respect of shares or debentures already subscribed if the following two conditions are simultaneously fulfilled:

(i) where a person has subscribed or agreed to subscribe for any shares in, or debentures of, the company and before the issue of the prospectus or statement in lieu thereof any other person or persons has or have subscribed for any or all of those shares or debentures, and

(ii) that fact together with the aggregate amount of commission payable under this section in respect of such subscriptions is disclosed in such prospectus or statement.

Brokerage It is the sum paid to a person by the company for placing the shares (i.e. for finding the person who will take shares). Section 76(3) empowers the company to pay lawful brokerage. Lawful brokerage means reasonable brokerage payable to a person carrying on the business of a broker and not to the person who had casually induced others to subscribe. [*Andreae* v. *Zinc Mines of Great Britain Ltd.,* (1918) 2 K.B. 454]

5.5 Difference between Brokerage and Underwriting Commission

1. **Nature of Agreement** Broker enters into an agreement to place shares i.e. he agrees that he will procure other persons to take the shares. Underwriter enters into an agreement to take unsubscribed shares.
2. **Purpose of Payment** Brokerage is paid to brokers for procuring other persons who will take shares or debentures where underwriter commission is paid to the underwriters for agreeing to take up the whole or part of shares or debentures which may not be subscribed by the public.
3. **Personal Liability** If broker fails to place any share, he is not personally liable to take them nor he is entitled to any brokerage. On the other hand, the underwriter is bound to take up the shares which have not been subscribed by public.

5.7 Penalty for Default [Section 76(5)]

If default is made in complying with the provisions of this section, the company, and its every officer in default, shall be punishable with fine upto Rs 5000.

6.0 ISSUE OF SHARES AT A PREMIUM [SECTION 78]

6.1 Meaning of Issue of Shares at a Premium

Shares are said to be issued at a premium when they are issued at a price higher than the face value. The excess of issue price over the face value is called as the amount of 'Securities Premium' e.g. if a share of Rs 10 is issued at Rs 15, it is said that the share has been issued at a premium of Rs 5.

6.2 Implied Power to Issue Shares at a Premium

A company may issue shares at a premium even though there is no express authority in its Articles since the company has an implied power to issue shares at a premium.

6.3 Transfer of Premium to Securities Premium Account

Where a company issues shares at a premium, whether for cash or otherwise, a sum equal to the aggregate amount or value of the premiums on those shares must be transfered to an account, to be called the Securities Premium Account. The word 'amount' refers to cash premium and the word 'value' refers to a premium other than cash. Securities issued for consideration other than cash will be treated as having been issued at a premium if the value of the assets in consideration of which they are issued is more than the nominal value of the securities.

6.4 Purposes for which Securities Premium can be utilized

(a) Though there are no restrictions in the Companies Act, 1956 on the issue of shares at a premium but there are restrictions on the application of Securities Premium. According to Section 78 of the Companies Act, 1956, the Securities Premium may be applied only for the following purposes:
   (i) To issue fully paid bonus shares to the members;
   (ii) To write off preliminary expenses of the company;
   (iii) To write off the expenses of or the commission paid or discount allowed on any issue of shares or debentures of the company.
   (iv) To provide for the premium payable on the redemption of any redeemable preference shares or of any debentures of the company;

(b) According to Sec 77A, a company may buy back its own shares or other specified securities out of Securities Premium Account.

(c) The use of Securities Premium Account for purposes other than those mentioned above requires the compliance of the provisions of the Act relating to reduction of share capital.

Notes:

(i) The amount of securities premium may be demanded alongwith the application money/allotment money/call money.

(ii) The amount of securities premium may be demanded either in lumpsum or in instalments e.g. partly with application money and balance with allotment money.

(iii) Even when the shares are issued at a premium for consideration other than cash, a sum equal to the amount of premium must be transferred to the 'Securities Premium Account'. [*Head Henry & Co. Ltd.* v. *Ropher,* (1951) 2 All. E.R. 994]

(iv) There is no prohibition in the Act against issue of securities at different premiums. [*CIT.* v. *Standard Vacuum Oil Company,* AIR (1966) SC 1963]

7.0 ISSUE OF SHARES AT A DISCOUNT [SECTION 79]

7.1 Meaning of Issue of Shares at a Discount

Shares are said to be issued at a discount when they are issued at a price lower than the face value. The excess of the face value over the issue price is called as the amount of discount e.g. if a share of Rs 10 is issued at Rs 9, it is said that the share has been issued at a discount of Re 1.

7.2 Six Conditions for Issue of Shares at Discount [Section 79(2)]

According to Section 79 of the Companies Act 1956, a company may issue the shares at a discount only if the following conditions are fulfilled:

(i) The shares must belong to a **class** of shares **already issued**;

(ii) The issue must be authorised by an **ordinary resolution** of the company;

(iii) The **sanction of the *Central Government** must be obtained;

(iv) The resolution must **specify the maximum rate of discount** at which the shares are to be issued. No resolution shall be sanctioned by the *Central Government if the maximum rate of discount specified in the resolution exceeds 10% unless it is of opinion that a higher percentage of discount may be allowed in the special circumstances of the case;

(v) **At least 1 year** must have elapsed since the date on which the company was entitled to commence business;

(vi) The issue must be made **within 2 months** from the date of receiving the sanction of the *Central Government or within such extended time as the *Central Government may allow.

7.3 Disclosure Requirements [Section 79(4)]

Every prospectus relating to the issue of the shares shall contain particulars of the discount allowed on the issue of the shares or of so much of that discount as has not been written off at the date of the issue of the prospectus.

7.4 Consequences of Improper Issues of Shares at a Discount

1. **Penalty for Default [Section 79(4)]** In case of default, the company, and its every officer in default, shall be punishable with fine upto Rs 500.
2. **Directors Liabilities** The directors render themselves liable to compensate the company to the extent of the amount of discount. [*Hirsche* v. *Sims*, [1894] A.C. 654].
3. **Members Liability** Even the acceptor of shares, in such a case has to pay back to the company the amount of discount if he holds the shares [*Re. Pitkin (James) & Co.,* [1916] 95 L.J. Ch. 318]. This he would have to do if the conditions of Section 79 are not satisfied, despite the fact that he did not know the legal effect of his contract to take shares at a discount or that the memorandum or articles give the directors the power to issue shares at a discount [*Welden* v. *Saffery,* [1897] A.C. 229; Re *Pitkin Supra*]. But the allottee may avoid liability to take the shares if he applies on discovery of illegality of the discount allowed without delay, before commencement of the winding up of the company, to have his name removed as a shareholder provided he has not otherwise agreed to keep the shares [Re *Midland Electric Co.*, [1889] 60 L.T. [1892] Bom. 7].

* After the Companies (Amendment) Act, 2002

8.0 ISSUE OF SWEAT EQUITY [SECTION 79A]

8.1 Meaning of Issue of Sweat Equity

Sweat equity shares means equity shares issued by the company to employees or directors at a discount or for consideration other than cash for providing know-how or making available right in the nature of intellectual property rights or value additions, by whatever name called. (Explanation II to Section 79A)

8.2 Conditions for Issue of Sweat Equity

According to Section 79A(1), a company may issue sweat equity shares if the following conditions are fulfilled, namely:

(a) the shares must belong to a **class** of shares **already issued**;

(b) the issue must be authorised by a **special resolution** passed by the company in the general meeting;

(c) the resolution must **specify** the number of shares, current market price, consideration, if any, and the class or classes of directors or employees to whom such equity shares are to be issued;

(d) **at least 1 year** must have elapsed since the date on which the company was entitled to commence business;

(e) the sweat equity shares of a company whose equity shares are listed on a recognised stock exchange must be issued in accordance with the regulations made by the Securities and Exchange Board of India in this behalf:

Provided that in the case of a company whose equity shares are not listed on any recognised stock exchange, the sweat equity shares are issued in accordance with the guidelines as may be prescribed.

8.3 Meaning of Company for the Purpose of Section 79A

The expression "a company means the company incorporated, formed and registered under this Act and includes its subsidiary company incorporated in a country outside India".

Applicability of other provisions—All the limitations, reiterations and provisions relating to equity shares shall be applicable to such sweat equity shares.

9.0 CALLS ON SHARES

9.1 Meaning of Call

A call may be defined as a demand upon the shareholders to pay the whole or part of the balance remaining unpaid on their shares.

Notes:

(i) Only the registered shareholder can be made liable in respect of calls and it makes no difference whether he is a benamidar or the beneficial owner of the shares or a mere trustee. [*Murshidabad Loan Office* v. *Satish Chandra* AIR, (1943) Cal. 440]

(ii) Reserve capital can be called up only in the event and for the purposes of winding up of company.

9.2 Who Can Make a Call

The following persons can make a call:

Case	*Who can make a call?*
(a) ***Before the commencement of winding up of the company***	The Board of Directors
(b) ***After the commencement of winding up of the company***	—The Court (in case of compulsory winding up by the Court ups 433) —The liquidator (in other cases of winding up)

9.3 Liability of Members in respect of a Call

All money payable by any member to the company under the Memorandum or Articles shall be a debt due from him to the company [Section 36(2)]. But the liability to pay will arise when a valid call has been made. [*Pabha Dhanabhanders Co.* v. *Fayezuddin*, AIR 1932 Cal. 714]

9.4 Requisite of a Valid Call

The requisites of a valid call are as follows:

1. **Resolution of the Board of Directors** A call must be made under a resolution of the Board of Directors passed at a duly constituted meeting of the Board and not under the resolution by circulation. This power cannot be delegated to a director or to a committee of directors or to any other officer of the company.

   Contents of Resolution The resolution must state:
   (a) time or times allowed for its payment;
   (b) place of payment;
   (c) the amount of the call per share.

Note: Where the directors passed a resolution fixing the amount of a call but omitted to fix the date of payment, this call was held to be invalid. [*E&W Insurance Co. Ltd.* v. *Mrs. Kamla Mehta* AIR, (1966) Bom. 537]

2. **On Uniform Basis [Section 91]** The call must be made on a uniform basis on all shares falling under the same class. Shares of the same nominal value on which different amounts have been paid up shall not be deemed to fall under the same class. [Section 91].

   This means that if a call is made on some shareholders and not others, the call is invalid. In *Galloway* v. *Halley Concerts Society*, (1915) 2 Ch. 233, a shareholder paid the first two calls after a great delay and neglected to pay the third call. The directors got annoyed and called upon him to pay the whole amount on his shares without making a similar call on other shareholders. The court held that the call was invalid as it did not require all the members to pay the full amount due on their shares.

3. **In accordance with the provisions of the Articles of the Company** The call must be made strictly in accordance with the provisions of the provisions of the Articles. If the Articles are silent, then Regulations 13–18 of Table 'A' shall be applicable. Table 'A' provides the following regulations:
   (i) The amount of call must not exceed 25% of the nominal value of the shares;
   (ii) **At least 1 month** must have elapsed since the date which was fixed for the payment of the last preceding call.
   (iii) At least fourteen days' notice specifying the time and place of payment must be given to each members.

(iv) A call may be revoked as postponed at the discretion of the Board.

(v) The joint holders of a share shall be jointly and severally liable to pay all calls in respect thereof.

4. **Bona Fide and for the Benefit of the Company** The power to make calls is a power in the nature of a trust and it must be exercised for the general benefit of the company. The amount uncalled should be called only when it is necessary for the promotion of the objects of the company.

However, if the call is made by the directors to serve their personal ends and not for the benefit of the company, shareholders can prevent its enforcement by an injunction. [*Lambus. Sambas Rubber Etc. Co.*, (1908) 1 Ch. 845]

A shareholder complaining against the director must establish *mala fide* in such a case. The court will not interfere with the discretion of the directors in making a call in the absence of proof of *mala fide*. [*Odessa Tramways Co.* v. *Mendel*, (1878) 8 Ch. D 235]

10.0 CALLS-IN-ARREARS

10.1 Meaning of Calls-in-arrears

Calls-in-arrears refer to the amount called up by the company which has not yet been paid by the shareholders till the last day fixed for the payment thereof. For example, if a company has called up a final call of Rs 2 on a share of Rs 10 each and a shareholder has not paid the final call on 100 shares held by him, then Rs 200 are said to be calls-in-arrears.

10.2 Rate of Interest on Calls-in-arrears

The interest on calls-in-arrears is recoverable according to the provision in this regard contained in the Articles of the company. If the Articles are silent, Regulation 16 of Table 'A' shall be applicable which prescribes that if a sum called in respect of a share is not paid before or on the day appointed for payment thereof, the person from whom the sum is due shall pay interest thereon from the day appointed for payment thereof to the time of actual payment at five per cent per annum or at such lower rate, if any, as the Board may determine and the Board shall be at liberty to waive payment of any such interest wholly or in part.

10.3 Effect of Non-Payment of a Call

In the event of non-payment of a call the Board may forfeites such shares in accordance with the provisions of the Articles. If Articles are silent, Regulations 29 to 32 of Table A shall apply.

Articles of company may also provide that a member who has not paid call on shares held by him shall not exercise voting rights in respect of shares held by him. [Section 181]

Non-payment of a call by a person for 6 months will disqualify him from holding the office of a director of the company. [Section 274]

11.0 CALLS-IN-ADVANCE

11.1 Meaning of Calls-in-advance

Calls-in-Advance refer to the receipt of the amount which has not been called up by the company. For example if a company has called up a first call of Rs 3 per share and a shareholder has paid the final call of Rs 2 per share alongwith the first call on 100 shares held by him, then Rs 200 are said to be calls-in-advance.

11.2 Provisions relating to Call-in-Advance

The various provisions relating to calls-in-advance are as follows:

(i) **Authorised by Articles** A company may, if so authorised by its articles, accept from any member the whole or a part of the amount remaining unpaid on any shares held by him although no part of that amount has been called up [Section 92 (1)]. If the Articles are silent, Regulation 18(a) empowers the Board to receive the Calls-in-advance.

(ii) **No Voting Right** The member is not entitled to voting rights in respect of the moneys so paid by him until the same becomes presently payable. [Section 92(2)].

(iii) **Dividend on Call-in-advance** A company may, if so authorised by its articles, pay dividends in proportion to the amount paid-up on each share where a larger amount is paid-up on some shares than on others. [Section 93]

If the Articles are silent, then Regulation 88(2) of the Table A shall apply which does not permit so.

(iv) **Rate of Interest** The interest on calls-in-advance is payable according to the provision contained in the Articles of the company. If the Articles are silent, then the Regulation 18(b) of the Table 'A' shall be applicable which prescribes that the Board may pay interest at such rate not exceeding, (unless the company in general meeting shall otherwise direct), 6% per annum, as may be agreed upon between the Board and the members paying the sum in advance. The Board may pay such interest from the date of the receipt of such amount till the date when such amount becomes due for payment.

(v) **Payment of Interest as Charge** The payment of interest on calls-in-advance is a charge against the profits and therefore it must be paid irrespective of whether there are profits or not since the shareholders becomes the creditor of the company in respect of this amount.

(vi) **Calls-in-advance Not refundable** The amount received in advance of calls is not refundable except in the event of winding up. In the event of winding up the shareholder making the advance payment will be entitled to refund of their amount with interest before the other shareholders are paid-off.

(vii) **Extinguishment of Liability** The liability of the shareholder in respect of the call for which the amount is paid in advance is extinguished.

(viii) **Bona fide and for the Benefit of the Company** The power to accept calls-in-advance must be exercised bona fide and for the benefit of the company [*Re. Syke's case,* (1872) L.R. 13 Eq. 255]. Where the directors knew that the company was insolvent and paid the amount unpaid on their shares in advance and applied it in the payment of their own shares, they were still liable for the amount unpaid on their shares. [*Re. European Central Renil Co.,* (1872) L.R. 13 Eq. 255]

12.0 SHARE CERTIFICATE [SECTION 113]

12.1 What is Share Certificate?

Share certificate is a document under the common seal of the company specifying that member is the holder of the specified number of the shares of the company.

12.2 Time of Issue of Share Certificate [Section 113]

Case	Time
(1) ***In case of allotment of shares. [Section 113(1)]***	Within 3 months of the allotment
(2) ***In case of Transfer of shares. [Section 113(1)]***	Within 2 months after the application for registration of valid transfer of shares.
(3) ***In case shares are issued in demat form [Section 113(4)]***	Issue of Share Certificate is not required. However the company must intimate details of allotment of shares to depository immediately after the shares are allotted.

12.3 Penalty for Default

In case of default, the company, and its every officer in default shall be punishable with fine upto Rs 5,000 for every day during which default continues.

12.4 Object and Effect of Share Certificate [Section 84(1)]

The object and effect of share certificate are as follow:

(a) Estoppel as to Title The company is estoppel from denying the title of the shareholder on number of shares specified in the share certificate. Hence share certificate is *prima facie* evidence of the title of member to such shares.

(b) Estoppel as to Payment The company is estopped from denying that the shares are paid upto the extent stated in the share certificate.

12.5 Judicial Rulings

(i) If an officer of the company, who has no authority to issue certificates, issues a forged certificate, then there is no estoppel [*Rubpen* v. *Great Fingal Consolidated*, [1906] A.C. 439; *South London Greyhound Racecourses Ltd.* v. *Wake*, 1931 Ch. 496].

(ii) Where a company states that shares are fully paid up, it cannot later contend that they were not, unless the person relying upon the certificate knew that the shares were not in fact fully paid up [*Bloomenthal* v. *Ford*, [1897] A.C. 156].

(iii) The *bona fide* holder of the share certificate, who had no notice that the shares were not actually paid up fully, could sell those shares away as fully paid to a person who knew that they were not fully paid so as to give the latter a good title to shares as fully paid because the latter derived title from the transferor who had a good title [*Re. Gulabdas's,* [1982] 17 Bom 672].

(iv) A certificate, however, does not confirm the existence of an equitable interest in the share and as such, the company owes no obligation to a person who holds such an interest. The title of mortgagee, with whome a share certificate and bank transfer have been deposited, may be defeated by the borrower selling all the shares and procuring the registration of the purchaser by obtaining a duplicate certificate. The purchaser in such cases would obtain priority over the mortgagee, since the mortagee would have no remedy against the company [*Reinford* v. *James Keith Blackman and Co.,* [1905] 1 Ch. 296].

(v) The certificate is not conclusive proof of the title of the member, specified in the certificate, to certain shares mentioned therein. A share certificate, however cannot be described as "share". It is just *prima facie* evidence of the title to a share or shares represented by the certificate [*Gopal Paper Mills Ltd.* v. *CIT Central Calcutta,* [1966] 1 Com. L.J. 1 174].

12.6 Issue of duplicate Share Certificate [Section 84(2)]

A certificate may be renewed or a duplicate of a certificate may be issued if such certificate

(a) is proved to have been lost or destroyed, or

(b) having been defaced or mutilated or torn, is surrendered to the company.

Procedure for issue of duplicate share certificate:

(i) Consent of Board is given (in case of loss or destruction of certificate) or certificate in lieu of which it is being issued is surrendered to the company and is cancelled.

(ii) Payment of fees for issue of duplicate certificate is made by the shareholder. However this fee is not to exceed Rs 2 per share certificate.

(iii) Proper evidence and indemnity to the satisfaction of the company is furnished.

(iv) Out-of-pocket expenses estimated to be incurred by the company investigating the evidence, as the Board may think fit, are deposited with the company.

(v) The words "duplicate issued in lieu of share certificate No. . . ." are rubber stamped on its face and also on counterfoil. The word "Duplicate" may either be rubber stamped or punched.

(vi) Mutilated, defaced or torn certificate surrendered must be defaced by a cancellation mark and destroyed after 3 years with the authority of the Board.

12.7 Penalty for Renewing a Certificate or Issue of Duplicate Certificate by the Company with Intention of Fraudulent Motive [Section 84(3)]

If a company with intent to defraud renews a certificate or issues a duplicate thereof, the company shall be punishable with fine which may extend to Rs 10,000 and every officer of the company who is in default shall be punishable with imprisonment of a term which may extend to 6 months, or with fine which may extend to Rs 1,00,000.

12.8 Penalty for Personation of Shareholder [Section 116]

If any person impersonates or obtain certificate fraudulently, he may be liable to imprisonment up to 3 years and also fine.

12.9 Sealing and Signing of Share Certificate

According to Rule 6 of the Companies (Issue of Share Certificates) Rule, 1960, every share certificate shall be issued under the common seal of the company, which shall be affixed in presence of

(i) two directors or persons acting on behalf of the directors under a duly registered Power of Attorney.

(ii) the secretary or some other person appointed by the Board for the purpose.

Two directors or their attorney and the secretary or other person shall sign the share certificate.

In case the composition of Board permits, at least one of the aforesaid director shall be person other than the managing or whole-time director.

However in practice, where a managing or whole time director exist, the share certificate is signed by such director along with any other director.

Note: The Company (Issue of Share Certificate) Rules, 1960 have been given in Appendix II at the end of chapter.

13.0 SHARE WARRANT [SECTION 114 AND 115]

13.1 Which company can issue Share Warrant? [Section 114(1)]

A public company limited by shares may issue share warrant if:

(i) It is authorised by the articles.
(ii) Previous approval of Central Government has been obtained.
(iii) It is in respect of fully paid up share.
(iv) It is issued under common seal of the company.

13.2 May Company Provide for the Payment of Future Dividends on the Shares Specified in the Warrant?

Yes, the company may provide for the payment of future dividends on the shares specified in the warrant by coupons or otherwise.

13.3 Effect of Share Warrant to Bearer [Section 114(2)]

A share warrant shall entitle the bearer thereof to the shares specified therein and the shares may be transferred by delivery of the warrant. Thus, a share warrant is a bearer document of title to share specified therein which can be transferred by mere delivery of share warrant. To that extent, it is a negotiable instrument.

13.4 What are the Conditions to be Fulfilled on Conversion of Share into Share Warrant? [Section 115(1)]

On conversion of share into share warrant the following conditions are required to be complied by the company:

(1) Striking out the name of the shareholder to whom share warrant is issued from Register of Members.
(2) Enter in the register the following particulars:
  (a) the fact of issue of warrant;
  (b) a statement of the shares specified in the warrant, distinguishing each share by its number; and
  (c) the date of the issue of the warrant.

13.5 Reconversion of Share Warrant into Shares [Section 115(2), (3), (4)]

1. The bearer of warrants shall subject to the Articles, be entitled to have his name entered as a Member in the Register of Members if—
   (i) he surrenders his warrant to the company.
   (ii) he pays the prescribed fees.
2. If company enters the name of the bearer of share warrant in respect of shares specified therein, without the warrant being surrendered and cancelled, then the company shall be responsible for any loss that may be occurred to any person in this regard. [Section 115(3)]
3. Until the warrant is surrendered, the particulars specificed in Section 115(1) shall be deemed to be particulars to be entered in the register of members and, on the surrender, the date of surrender shall be entered in the register of members. [Section 115(4)]
4. The bearer of a share warrant is not a member of the company. But if the articles provide and subject to this Act, he shall be deemed to be member of the company for any purpose defined in the articles. [Section 115(5)]

Notes: Holding of a share warrant does not operate as a qualification for being a director of a company, where such is required under the articles.

13.6 Distinction between Share Certificate and Share Warrant

Share certificate differ from share warrant in the following respects:

Basis of Distinction	*Share Certificate*	*Share Warrant*
1. *Which company can issue*	It can be issued by **any** company.	It can only be issued by **public** company **limited by shares.**
2. *Provision in the articles*	For issuing share certificate **no** provision in this regard is required.	For issuing share warrant specific provision in this regard is **required**.
3. *Prior approval of central government*	**No** such approval is required.	Prior approval of central government is **required**.
4. *In respect of which shares*	Share certificate can be issued in respect of **partly paid up or fully paid** up shares.	Share warrant can be issued **only** in respect of **fully paid up** shares.
5. *Membership*	Holder of share certificate is a **member** of the company.	Share warrant holder **ceased to be member** of the company.
6. *Transfer*	Transfer is not complete unless **registered** by the company.	Transfer is complete merely **by delivery** and no registration of transfer with the company is required.
7. *Stamp duty*	Stamp duty is **payable** in respect of transfer of share.	**No** stamp duty is payable on transfer.
8. *Negotiability*	Share certificate is **not** used as negotiable instrument.	Share warrant is used as **negotiable instrument**.
9. *Share qualification for directorship*	It **constitutes** qualification for directorship	It **does not constitute** qualification for directorship.
10. *Petition for winding up*	Holder of share certificate **can present** petition for winding up.	Holder of share warrant **cannot present** petition for winding up.

14.0 TRANSFER OF SHARES

14.1 Meaning of Transfer of Shares

Transfer of Shares means the voluntary conveyance of the ownership rights from a member who wishes to cease to be a member to a person who wishes to become a member. The shares or other interests of a member of company are movable properties transferable in the manner prescribed by the Articles of the company [Section 82]. The articles of a public company cannot contain such absolute provision by which the right to transfer shares is altogether taken away. The right of a shareholder to transfer his shares in a company is absolute and inherent in the ownership of shares. [*Thenappa Chettiar* v. *Indian Overseas Bank Ltd.*, (1943) 13 Comp. as 2002]

14.2 Procedure for Transfer

In addition to comply with the provisions of the Articles, the following procedure must be followed before a company can lawfully register a transfer:

1. **Prescribed Form and Presentation to the Prescribed Authority** The instrument of transfer must be in the prescribed form i.e. Form No. 7B and presented to the prescribed authority (i.e. the Registrar), before it is signed by the transferor or transferee and before any entry is made in it. The prescribed authority shall stamp or otherwise endorse on the instrument the date on which it is so presented.
2. **Execution** The instrument must—
   (i) be duly stamped.
   (ii) be executed by or on behalf of the transferor and the transferee
   (iii) be completed in all respects
   (iv) specify the name, address and occupation if any, of the transferee.
   (v) be signed by both the transferor and the transferee.
3. **Share Certificate/Letter of Allotment** The instrument must be accompanied by share certificate or letter of allotment (if no such certificate is in existence).
4. **Time Limit for Delivery** The instrument must be delivered to the company for registration—
   (i) In case of listed shares at any time before the date of closure of Register of Members for the first time after the date of the presentation to the prescribed authority, *or* within 12 months from the date of such presentation whichever is later.
   (ii) In any other case, within 2 months from the date of presentation to the prescried authority.

   Extension of Time Limit The Central Government is empowered to extend the aforesaid time limit on an application made *either* before *or* after the expiry of aforesaid period. [Section 108(1D)]
5. **Transfer by Legal Representative [Section 109]** A legal representative of a decreased member although he may not be a member, can validly transfer shares.
6. **Notice in the Case of Transfer of Partly Paid Shares [Section 110]** Where the transferor makes an application for registration of partly paid shares, transfer must not be registered unless the company gives notice of the application to the transferee and the transferee makes no objection to the transfer within 2 weeks from the receipt of the notice. [Section 110(2)]

Note: Notice to the transferee shall be deemed to have been duly given if it is despatched by prepaid registered post to the transferee at the address given in the instrument of transfer and shall be deemed to have been duly delivered at the time at which it would have been delivered in the ordinary course of post. [Section 110(3)]

7. **Time Limit for Registration of Transfer** The Board of Directors considers the application and if found alright in all respects, registers the transfer. An endorsement is made on the back of the share certificate recognising the transferee as the new member. In Register of Members, the name of the transferer is strike off and the name of the transferee is entered. The share certificate is required to be despatched to the transferee within 2 months of the application for registration.

14.3 Notice of Refusal and Remedy Against Refusal [Section 111]

1. **Notice** If a company refuses to register a transfer, it must send the notice of refusal giving reasons to the transferor and the transferee, within 2 months of the date of delivery of the instrument of transfer.

2. **Remedy** The transferor or transferee may file an appeal with the National Company Law Tribunal as follows:

Refusal/failure	*Time limit for Appeal*
(a) ***Refusal to register the transfer***	Within 2 months of the receipt of notice of refusal
(b) ***Failure to register within 2 months or for not giving reason for refusal***	Within 2 months from the expiry of 2 months of date of delivery of instrument of transfer.

3. **Penalty** For default in registration of transfer within 2 months or for not giving reason for refusal. The company and its every officer in default is punishable with fine upto Rs 500 for every day of default.
4. **Power of NCLT** The National Company Law Tribunal may *either* dismiss the appeal *or* direct the company to register the transfer within 10 days of the receipt of the order.
5. **Penalty for Non-compliance of Order** For default in complying with the NCLT's order, the company and its every officer in default is punishable with fine upto Rs 10,000 and with a further fine of Rs 1,000 for every day of continuing default.

15.0 TRANSFER OF SECURITIES OF A PUBLIC COMPANY [SECTION 111A]

1. The Board of directors of a company or the concerned depository has no direction to refuse or withhold transfer of any security. The transfer has to be effected by the company/depository automatically and immediately.
2. **Right to Appeal** Where the transfer of security effected in contravention of the SEBI Act, 1992 or SICA, 1985 a depository, company, participant or investor or SEBI may make an appeal to Company Law Tribunal to rectify the register or records of the company or depository within 2 months from the date of transfer of securities or from the date on which the instrument of transfer or the intimation of transmission was delivered to the company as the case may be.
3. **Power of CLB** The Company Law Tribunal—
   (a) may direct the company or the depository to rectify the register or the records of ownership if after making enquiry, if it is satisfied that the contravention has taken place.
   (b) may suspend the voting rights in respect of the securities subject to enquiry if enquiry has not yet completed.
4. **Right of Transferee** During the pendency of the application before the CLT, the transferee can transfer the security and such further transfer would entitle the transferee to voting rights also unless voting rights in case of transferee have also been suspended by CLT.

16.0 CERTIFICATE OF TRANSFER [SECTION 112]

1. **Lodging Certificate** Where a member wishes to transfer only a part of his shareholding or wishes to sell them to two or more persons, he is required to lodge the share certificate with the company. This is known as lodging the certificate.
2. **Certification** Where he has already lodged the share certificate alongwith an instrument of transfer for a part of his shareholding, he may request the company to certify on the instrument of the transfer that the share certification for the shares covered by the instrument of transfer has been lodged with the company. An act of noting on the instrument that share certificate in respect of shares to be transferred has been lodged with the company is called **certification**. An

instrument of transfer shall be deemed to be certified if it bears the words 'Certificate lodged' or the words to the like effect. [Section 112(3)(a)]

Note: The company is under no obligation to certify any instrument of transfer of shares at all.

3. **Balance Ticket** When only a part of the shares is transferred, the company issues a ticket for the balance of shares not transferred. Such a ticket is known as 'Balance Ticket'.
4. **What Certificate represents** [Section 112(1)] Certification merely represents that the documents showing the prima facie title to the shares mentioned in the instruments have ben produced to the company. It does not represent that the transferor has any title to the shares.
5. **Co.'s Liability** The company will be responsible for the certification only if:
   (a) the person issuing the instrument is authorised to issue such instrument on the company's behalf, and
   (b) the certificate is signed by any officer or servant of the company or any other person authorised to certify transfer on the company's behalf.
6. **Liability in Case of Wrong Certification** Where any person acts on the faith of an erroneous certification made by a company negligently, the company shall be liable to him in a manner as if the certification has been made fuauduently.

   Practical Illustration The secretary of X Ltd. after certifying the transfer negligently returns the original certificate to the transferor. If transferor pledges the same, the company shall not be liable to the pledge because of two reasons:
   (i) it covers no duty to the pledgee,
   (ii) the immediate cause of his loss was not the issue of the certificate.
   [*Longman* v. *Bath Electric Tramways*, (1905) Ch. 646]

17.0 BLANK TRANSFER

17.1 Meaning of Blank Transfer

Blank transfer is an instrument of transfer in which only the name and signature of the seller are filled in and the name and signature of buyer and the date of sale are not filled in.

17.2 Effects of Blank Transfers

1. Indefinite circulation of the instrument of transfer.
2. Avoidance of stamp duty on transfer.
3. Concealment of beneficial owners behind their nominees.
4. Evasion of tax by suppression of secret profit invested in holdings on blank transfer.

17.3 Present Position

Now, the blank instrument of transfer is required to be presented to the prescribed authority who will stamp the instrument alongwith the date of presentation. Such instrument can then remain in circulation for 12 months or upto the closure of the registar of members whichever is later.

18.0 FORGED TRANSFER

1. If a company registers a forged transfer and removes the name of the true owner from the Register of Members, the true owner can compel the company to restore his name to the register and can claim any dividend which may not have been paid to him during the intervening period. [*Boston* v. *North Staffordshire Railway Co.*, 38 Ch. D. 456]

2. If a company registers a forged transfer and issues a new certificate to the subsequent buyer for value acting in good faith (i.e. without the knowledge of forgery), it would be liable to compensate him since it cannot deny the liability accruing from its own act. [*Balkin Consolidated Co.* v. *Tamkinser*, (1982) A.C. 1961]
3. If a transferee gets a certificate from the company on a forged transfer, he will be liable to indemnify the company against its liability to the true owner of the shares. [*Sheffield Corporation* v. *Barelay*, (1905) B.C. 393]
4. If a transferee without any negligence brings about a transfer is liable to indmnify the company against its liability to the true owner of shares. [*Starkey* v. *Bank of England*, (1903) A.C. 104]
5. If a share certificate was issued fraudulently by forging the signatures of the directors, the share certificate was rendered void. Forgery is nullity and cannot be a source of a valid transfer of title and thus, it confers no rights upon a subsequent buyer and the company may deny being liable towards him. [*Ruben* v. *Great Fingal Consolidated*]

19.0 EFFECTS OF TRANSFER

The transferee does not acquire a legal title to the shares untill his name has been entered in the Register of Members. Position during the intervening period may be summarised as follows:

1. **Legal Title** The transferor continues to the legal owner of the shares but on the principle of equity he holds them in trust for the transferee.
2. **Call** If any call is demanded by the company before transfer is registered, the transferor must pay the calls in the first instance and may later recover the amount from the transferee.
3. **Dividend** If dividends are declared and paid before transfer is registered, the company must pay it to the transferor. The tranferor is required to retain dividends where shares have been sold ex-dividend and is required to return dividends to transferee where shares have been sold-cum-dividend.
4. **Voting Rights** If voting rights are to be exercised before transfer is registered, the transferor must vote as the transferee directs where transfere has already paid the price and may vote as he likes where transferee has not paid the price.

20.0 TRANSMISSION OF SHARES

20.1 Meaning of Transmission of Shares

Transmission of shares means the transfer of shares under the operation of law.

20.2 When does Transmission of Shares take place.

It takes place—

1. if a registered member dies, or
2. if a registered member is adjudged as insolvent, or
3. if a member being a company goes into liquidation.

20.3 Effects of Transmission

1. Upon death, the shares of the deceased vest in his executors or administrators and the executors become liable for calls if shares are partly paid up.
2. Upon insolvency, the shares of the insolvent vest in the Official Assignee or the Receiver.
3. Upon liquidation of company, the shares vest in the Liquidator.

20.4 Other Provisions

1. No instrument of transfer is to be executed.
2. No stamp duty is payable.
3. It does not involve any consideration.
4. It is always subject to original liabilities attached to shares so transmitted.

20.5 Distinction between Transfer and Transmission

Transfer differs from transmission in the following respects:

Basis of Distinction	*Transfer*	*Transmission*
1. *Results*	Transfer is the result of *deliberate act* of a member.	Transmission is the result of *opeartion of law* on the death/insolvency of a member. or liquidation of a member being a company.
2. *Instrument of transfer*	Instrument of transfer is *required* to be executed.	*No* Instrument of transfer is required to be executed.
3. *Stamp Duty*	Stamp Duty is *payable.*	*No* Stamp Duty is payable
4. *Consideration*	It generally *involves* consideration.	It *does not involve* any consideration.

21.0 FORFEITURE OF SHARES

21.1 Meaning of Forfeiture of Shares

Forfeiture of shares is compulsory termination of membership of a member and confiscation of his shares as a penalty for non-payment of a call or other sum due on shares.

21.2 Power to Forfeit Shares

Power to forfeit the shares can be exercised only if the Articles expressly so provide. Such power must be exercised bona fide (i.e., in good faith) and for the benefit of the company. *It must not be collusive or fraudulent.* Such power should not be exercised to expel a member or relieve a friend or relative from liability. Such power must be exercised, strictly according to be the procedure stated in the Articles.

21.3 Grounds for Forfeiture of Shares

The Articles may provide for forfeiture of shares not only for non-payment of call but also for other grounds say non-compliance of any other arrangement according to the prescribed condition. But such grounds must not be opposed to statute or public policy. [*Calcutta Stock Exchange* v. *S.N. Nandy & Co.,* (1950) (Cal)]

In *Naresh Chander Sanyal* v. *The Calcutta Stock Exchange,* (1971) (SC), where the Articles provide for forfeiture if a member failed to carry out the arrangement according to the prescribed conditions. The forfeiture was held to be valid.

21.4 Procedure for a Valid Forfeiture

Regulations 29, 30, 31 and 34 of Table A of Schedule I of the Companies Act, 1956 provides for the procedure to be followed for forfeiture:

1. **As per Articles** Power of forfeiture must be exercised only on the basis of various grounds specified in Articles.

2. **Notice** Notice must be served upon the defaulting member. Such notice must—
   (a) require the member to pay unpaid call together with an accrued interest (if any)
   (b) mention a day at least 14 days ahead from the date of service of the notice on or before which the payment is required to be made.
   (c) state that if the payment is not made on or before the date mentioned in the notice, the shares in respect of which call was made would be liable to be forfeited.

Note: A notice is deemed to be served if sent by registered post with acknowledgement due (A.D.) at the registered address of the members. But where a notice, though sent, came back unserved, the company must make enquiry at the proper address of the member whose shares are to be forfeited.

3. **Resolution** The directors must pass a resolution before actual forfeiture is exercised.

21.5 Effects of Forfeiture

1. On forfeiture of shares, member ceases to be a member of the company.
2. Liability of Ex-member

If the Company goes into liquidation	*Liability of Ex-Members*
(a) *Within 1 year of forfeiture*	He may be put on 'B' list of contributories
(b) *After 1 year but within 3 years of forfeiture*	He may be held liable as an ordinary debtor but not as a contributor.

3. **Reduction of Capital** Forfeiture of shares results in reduction of capital unless the shares are reissued.
4. Forfeited shares become the property of the company.
5. The annual return must specify the total number of shares forfeited [Section 159]

21.6 Re-issue of Forfeited Shares

1. The forfeited shares may be reissued in accordance with the provision of Articles.
2. The reissue does not amount to allotment. It is merely a sale of forfeited shares. Hence, no return is to be filed in respect of reissue of forfeited shares.
3. Re-issue price cannot be less than the amount unpaid on those shares.
4. Profit on reissue of partly paid up forfeited shares belong to the company and not to the defaulter.
5. Profit on re-issue of fully paid up forfeited shares may be refunded to the defaulter. [*Naresh Chandra Sanyal* v. *The Calcutta Stock Exchange*]

22.0 SURRENDER OF SHARES

22.1 Meaning of Surrender of Shares

Surrender of shares is voluntary return of shares for the purpose of cancellation.

22.2 Power to accept Surrender of Shares

Power to accept the surrender of shares can be exercised only if the Articles expressly so provide.

22.3 Condition for a Valid Surrender of Shares

Surrender of shares in accordance with Articles is valid—

(a) in case of partly paid up shares if it is accepted to avoid the formalities for a valid forfeiture only. [*Bellerby* v. *Rewland & Marwood's Steamship & Co. Ltd.* (1902)]

(b) In case of fully paid up shares, if it is accepted in exchange of new shares of the same nominal value. [*Rowell* v. *John Rowell & Sons Ltd.* (1912)]

22.4 Invalid Surrender of Shares

The surrrender of shares is invalid if—

(a) it involves reduction of share capital

(b) it amounts to a purchase by the company of its own shares

(c) it releases the member from further liability in respect of shares. [*Collector of Muradabad* v. *Equity Insurance Company,* (1948)]

22.5 Effects of Surrender of Shares

Surrender of shares has the same effect as forfeiture of shares has.

22.6 Distinction between Forfeiture and Surrender of Shares

Forfeiture of shares differs from surrender of shares in the following respects:

Basis of Distinction	*Forfeiture of Shares*	*Surrender of Shares*
1. *Meaning*	Forfeiture of shares is **compulsory** termination of membership of a penalty for non-payment of a call.	Surrender of shares is a **voluntary** return of shares for the purposes of cancellation.
2. *Instance*	It is at the instance of **company**.	It is at the instance of **member**.
3. *Purpose*	Its purpose is **to penalise** the defaulter.	Its purpose is **to avoid the formalities** for a valid forfeiture.
4. *Notice*	Notice precedent to forfeiture is **required**.	**No** such notice is required.
5. *Provision in the Act & Table A*	Both the Act and Table A **provide** for forfeiture.	Both the Act and Table A are **silent** on surrender.

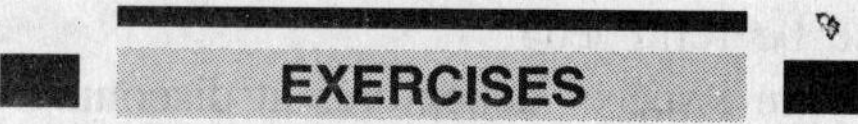

EXERCISES

VERY SHORT ANSWER QUESTIONS

1. (a) What is meant by 'Allotment'?
   (b) Is the reissue of forfeited shares an allotment?
2. What is the maximum and minimum time of opening of subscription list?
3. When can application for shares be revoked?
4. What is the minimum and maximum time of closing of subscription list?
5. When is application money required to be refunded (a) without interest (b) with interest? Answer this question as per the Companies Act and as per the SEBI Guidelines.
6. When is application money required to be refunded (a) without interest (b) with interest in the following cases:
   (a) where the listing permission is not granted
   (b) where shares are oversubscribed
7. When will it be deemed that the listing permission has not been granted?
8. Is the condition of minimum subscription applicable to subsequent allotment of shares?
9. Is there any difference between the restriction applicable to first allotment of shares and subsequent allotment of shares?

10. What is "Irregular Allotment"?
11. (a) What is return of allotment?
    (b) What is the time limit to file return of allotment?
    (c) Is it required in case of re-issue of forfeited shares?
    (d) Is it required for allotment of debentures?
    (e) Is it required for allotment of shares to signatories to Memorandum?
12. (a) What is meant by 'Underwriting Agreement'?
    (b) What is meant by 'Underwriting Commission'?
    (c) What is meant by 'Brokerage'?
13. (a) Can a company issue shares at premium even if there is no express authority in its Articles?
    (b) Can the shares be issued at different premiums?
    (c) Name the account to which premium received on shares must be transferred.
    (d) Can shares at a premium be issued for consideration other than cash?
14. What are sweat shares?
15. (a) What is meant by a call on share?
    (b) Who can make a call on shares before and after the commencement of winding up of a company?
    (c) What is the liability of a member in respect of a call?
16. (a) What is maximum rate of interest which is to be charged on calls-in-arrears according to Table A?
    (b) Can the directors waive the interest on calls in arrears wholly?
17. (a) Can a company accept calls-in-advance if the Articles are silent?
    (b) What is the maximum rate of interest which may be allowed on calls-in-advance according to Table A?
    (c) Is the payment of interest on calls-in-advance a charge against the profits?
    (d) Is the member entitled to voting right is respect of calls-in-advance?
    (e) Can dividend be paid on calls-in-advance?
    (f) Can call-in-advance be refunded?
18. Are there any restriction an issue of debentures at discount?
19. What are the statutory periods for the application of permission for listing and for the actual grant of the permission for listing?
20. (a) What is share certificate?
    (b) Who can sign share certificate?
    (c) State the time limit for issue of share certificate.
        (a) In case of allotment of shares
        (b) In case of transfer of shares
21. (a) What is share warrant?
    (b) Which company can issue share warrant?
    (c) How may a bearer of share warrant transfer the shares?
22. (a) Is registration of transfer optional with the company?
    (b) Can the instrument of transfer be in any form?
    (c) Can the instrument be signed by the transferor or can any entry be made in the instrument before it is presented to prescribed authority?
    (d) What is the prescribed authority required to do with the instrument?
    (e) What is the next step to be taken in this regard and by whom?
    (f) Will it be sufficient legal compliance if the instrument of transfer of shares is executed only by the transferor?

(g) Is it necessary to specify the name, address and occupation of the transferee in the transfer-deed?
(h) Does instrument of transfer need stamping?
(i) The law requires the instrument of transfer to be delivered to the company along with the certificate relating to the shares transferred. But if no such certificate is in existence, then what should the parties do?
(j) When is the instrument to be presented to the company (a) when shares are quoted on a recognised stock exchange and (b) where it is not quoted?
(k) When all the requirements relating to transfer are compiled with what should the company do?
(l) Can registration of transfer of shares be refused by the company on any ground?
(m) State the period within which the notice of refusal must be communicated to both the transferor and the transferee?
(n) What is the remedy of the parties in case of refusal?
(o) Can the Company Law Tribunal compel the company to register the transfer?

SHORT ANSWER TYPE QUESTIONS

1. Write short note on the following:
   (a) Minimum Subscription
   (b) Irregular Allotment
   (c) Return of Allotment
   (d) Calls-in-arrears
   (e) Calls-in-advance
2. When is return of allotment not required?
3. Distinguish between the following:
   (a) Brokerage and underwriting commission
   (b) Void Allotment and Irregular Allotment
4. Comment on the following:
   "Commission can be paid on shares or debentures which are not offered to public for subscription."
5. State two legal effects of a share certificate.
6. When can a duplicate share certificate be issued ?
7. State the conditions for the issue of share warrants.
8. Is the bearer of share warrant a member?
9. Distinguish between share certificate and share warrant.

LONG ANSWER TYPE QUESTIONS

1. Discuss the general provisions and statutory provisions on to the allotment of shares by the public company when public offer is made.
2. (a) What is an allotment of shares?
   (b) Explain the situation when allotment of shares is void, voidable and valid.
3. (a) What is 'Irregular Allotment'?
   (b) What is the effect of irregular allotment?
   (c) What are the rights of an allottee in such a situation?
4. (a) Explain the purpose for which and conditions under which a company may pay underwriter commission.
   (b) Can a company pay brokerage?

5. State the purposes for which the balance of securities premium can be utilized.
6. (a) State the conditions for the issue of shares at discount.
   (b) State the consequences of improper issue of shares at discount.
7. (a) What are sweat shares?
   (b) State the conditions for the issue of sweat shares.
8. (a) What is meant by call on shares?
   (b) Explain the requisites of a valid call on shares.
9. State the procedure for the issue of duplicate share certificates.
10. Distinguish between the following:
    (a) Share Certificate and Share Warrant
    (b) Transfer and Transmission of Shares
    (c) Forfeiture and Surrender of Shares
    (d) Share and Stock
    (e) Underwriter and Broker
11. Write short notes on the following:
    (a) Irregular Allotment
    (b) Blank Transfer
    (c) Forged Transfer
    (d) Certificate of Transfer
    (e) Lien on Share
    (f) Minimum Subscription
    (g) Return of Allotment
12. Comment on the following:
    (a) "A director can hold a share warrant for share qualification of his directorship."
    (b) "The holder of a share warrant cannot be called as member of the company."
    (c) "A company cannot refuse to register a transfer of shares."
    (d) Surrender of shares is always lawful.
    (e) "No Commission can be paid on shares or debentures which are not offered to public for public subscription."
    (f) "Return of Allotment is required in case of issue of securities."
13. "Surrender is a short-cut to forfeiture". Explain
14. Explain the meaning of a share warrant. How far is the bearer of a share warrant a member of a company?
15. (a) Explain the procedure for effecting a transfer of shares in a limited company.
    (b) Explain the legal position of transferor and transferee of shares pending registration of transfer by the company.
16. What is a forged transfer? What would be the legal position of the parties involved in it?
17. When can a company refuse to register a transfer of shares?
18. Explain the law relating to restrictions on the acquisition and transfer of shares.
19. Explain clearly the meaning of the term share 'certificate'. What is the time limit under the provisions of the Companies Act, 1956, for the issue of such certificates for shares alloted by a company? State as to how and under what circumstances can a company issue duplicate share certificates.
20. What is meant by 'sweat equity shares'. What are the conditions to be fulfilled by a company proposing to issue 'sweat equity shares' under the Companies Act, 1956.
21. A public company proposes to purchase its own shares. State the source of funds that can be utilised by the company for purchasing its own shares and the requirements to be complied with by the company under the Companies Act before and after the shares are so purchased.

CHAPTER 8

Share Capital

1.0 SHARE CAPITAL

1.1 Meaning of Share Capital

Share Capital means the capital raised by the issue of shares. The amounts invested by the shareholders towards the face value of shares are collectively known as 'Share Capital' which is quite distinct from the capital put in by individual shareholders.

1.2 Categories of Share Capital

The share capital is divided under the following three heads:

(a) **Authorised Capital** Authorised Capital refers to that amount which is stated in the 'Capital Clause' of the Memorandum of Association as the share capital of the company. This is the maximum limit of the company which it is authorised to raise and beyond which the company cannot raise unless the capital clause in the Memorandum is altered in accordance with the provisions of Section 94 of the Companies Act, 1956.

(b) **Issued Capital** Issued Capital refers to the nominal value of that part of authorised capital, which has been (i) subscribed for the signatories to the Memorandum of Association, (ii) allotted for cash or for consideration other than cash and (iii) allotted as Bonus shares.

(c) **Subscribed Capital** Subscribed Capital refers to the paid-up value of the issued capital.

Other terms used under the Companies Act, 1956 are:

(d) **Unissued Capital** Unissued Capital refers to that portion of the authorised capital which has not yet been issued.

(e) **Uncalled Capital** Uncalled capital refers to that portion of the issued capital which has not yet been called up by the company.

(f) **Reserve Capital** It refers to that portion of uncalled share capital which shall not be capable of being called up except in the event and for the purposes of the company being wound up (Section 99). A limited company may, by a special resolution, determine a portion of its uncalled capital as reserve capital. Reserve capital should not be confused with capital reserve.

Notes:

(i) Reserve Capital cannot be dealt with in any manner even under a power in its Memorandum of Association.

(ii) A company cannot borrow on the security of its reserve capital.

(iii) Reserve capital cannot be turned into uncalled capital without the leave of the court. It is available only for the creditors on the winding up of the company. The company can neither charge it nor cancel it in a reduction of capital. [*Re Midland Rly. Carriage Co.* (1904) W.N. 175]

2.0 DISTINCTION BETWEEN AUTHORISED CAPITAL AND ISSUED CAPITAL

Authorised Capital and Issued Capital can be distinguished as follows:

Basis of distinction	*Authorised capital*	*Issued capital*
1. *Meaning*	It refers to that amount which is stated in the Memorandum of Association as the share capital of the company.	It refers to the nominal value of that part of authorised capital which has been (i) subscribed for by the signatories to the Memorandum of Association, (ii) allotted for cash or consideration other than cash, (iii) allotted as Bonus issue
2. *Determination*	Its amount is determined after considering **present and future requirements.**	Its amount is determined after considering the **present requirements.**
3. *Disclosure in Memorandum of Association*	Its amount is **required** to be disclosed in the Memorandum of Association.	Its amount is **not required** to be disclosed in the Memorandum of Association.
4. *Is it Basis of Stamp Duty*	Stamp Duty is **payable** on the basis of authorised capital.	**No** stamp duty is payable.
5. *Is it Basis of Company registration fees*	Company registration fee is payable on the **basis** of authorised capital.	Issued capital is **not the basis** for registration fees.
6. *Does the change amount to an Alteration of Memorandum*	Any change in the amount of authorised capital **amounts** to an alteration of the Memorandum of Association.	Any change in the amount of issued capital **does not amount** to an alteration of the Memorandum of Association.
7. *Whether one can exceed other*	It **can exceed** issued capital.	It **cannot exceed** authorised capital.

Illustration 1

X Ltd. was formed with a capital of Rs 5,00,000 divided into shares of Rs 10 each. Out of these, 2,000 shares were issued to the vendors as fully paid as purchase consideration for a building acquired, 1,000 shares were issued to signatories to the Memorandum of Association as fully paid. The directors offered 6,500 shares to the public and called up Rs 6 per share and received the entire called up amount on shares allotted. Calculate Issued capital and subscribed capital in each of the following two cases:

Case (a) If the public applied for 7,000 shares.

Case (b) If the public applied for 6,000 shares.

Solution:

Case (a): Calculation of Issued Capital

	Rs
2,000 shares of Rs 10 each allotted to vendors	20,000
1,000 shares of Rs 10 each allotted to signatories to the Memorandum of Association	10,000
6,500 shares of Rs 10 each allotted to public	65,000
	95,000

Case (b): Calculation of Issued Capital

	Rs
2,000 shares of Rs 10 each allotted to vendors	20,000
1,000 shares of Rs 10 each allotted to signatories to the Memorandum of Association	10,000
6,000 shares of Rs 10 each allotted to public	60,000
	90,000

Note: The face value of shares actually allotted is considered and not the face value of shares offered.

Illustration 2

Calculate (a) Authorised Capital (b) Issued Capital (c) Unissued Capital (d) Subscribed Capital, (e) Called-up Capital, (f) Uncalled Capital (g) Paid-up Capital (h) Calls-in-arrears in each of the following alternative cases:

Case (i) X Ltd. was formed with a capital of Rs 10,00,000 divided into shares of Rs 10 each. *X* offered the entire shares and *called up fully* on application. The subscribers paid Rs 20,00,000.

Case (ii) X Ltd. was formed with a capital of Rs 10,00,000 divided into shares of Rs 10 each. It offered 90% shares and *called up fully* on application. The subscribers paid Rs 20,00,000.

Case (iii) X Ltd. was formed with a capital of Rs 10,00,000 divided into shares of Rs 10 each. It offered 90% shares and *called up fully* on application. The subscribers paid Rs 8,50,000.

Case (iv) X Ltd. was formed with a capital of Rs 10,00,000 divided into shares of Rs 10 each. It offered 90% shares and *called up* 60% on application. The subscribers paid Rs 5,10,000.

Case (v) X Ltd. was formed with a capital of Rs 10,00,000 divided into shares of Rs 10 each. It offered 90% shares called up 40% on application and 20% on allotment. The subscribers paid Rs 3,40,000 on application and Rs 1,69,000 on allotment.

Solution:

Calculation of Various Types of Capital

Type of Capital	*Case (i)*	*Case (ii)*	*Case (iii)*	*Case (iv)*	*Case (v)*
A. Authorised Capital	10,00,000	10,00,000	10,00,000	10,00,000	10,00,000
B. Issued Capital	10,00,000	9,00,000	8,50,000	8,50,000	8,50,000
C. Unissued Capital [A – B]	Nil	1,00,000	1,50,000	1,50,000	1,50,000
D. Subscribed Capital	10,00,000	9,00,000	8,50,000	5,10,000	5,09,000
E. Called-up Capital	10,00,000	9,00,000	8,50,000	5,10,000	5,10,000
F. Uncalled Capital	Nil	Nil	Nil	3,40,000	3,40,000
G. Paid-up Capital	10,00,000	9,00,000	8,50,000	5,10,000	5,09,000
H. Calls-in-arrears	Nil	Nil	Nil	Nil	1,000

3.0 DISTINCTION BETWEEN RESERVE CAPITAL AND CAPITAL RESERVE

Reserve Capital should not be confused with Capital Reserve which is created out of profits. Reserve Capital and Capital Reserve can be distinguished as folllows:

Basis of Distinction	*Reserve capital*	*Capital reserve*
1. *Meaning*	It refers to that portion of uncalled share capital which shall not be capable of being called up except in the event and for the purpose of the company being wound up. [Section 99]	It refers to those amounts which are not regarded as free for distribution by way of dividend through Profit and Loss Account.
2. *Creation—Optional mandatory*	It is ***not mandatory*** to create Reserve Capital.	It is ***mandatory*** to create Capital Reserve in case of profit on forfeited shares.
3. *Disclosure in Balance Sheet*	It is ***not required*** to be disclosed in the company's Balance Sheet.	It is ***required*** to be disclosed as the 1st item under the head 'Reserves and Surplus' on the liabilities side of the Balance Sheet.
4. *Time when it can be used*	It can be used only at the time of ***winding up***.	It can be used during the ***life*** of the company.
5. *Realised vs. Unrealised*	It refers to the amount which has *neither been called* up ***nor been received***.	It (excluding items like revaluation profit) refers to that amount which has already been ***realised***.
6. *Can it be used to write off of capital losses*	It ***cannot*** be used to write off capital losses.	It ***can*** be used to write off capital losses.
7. *Can it be used to declare source of share bonus*	It ***cannot*** be used to declare a share bonus.	It (excluding items like revaluation profit) ***can*** be used to declare a share bonus.

4.0 SHARE

4.1 Meaning of Share

A 'Share' is one of the units into which the capital of the company is divided. Section 2(46) of the Companies Act, 1956 defines a share as "a share in the share capital of a company, and includes stock except where a distinction between stock and share is expressed or implied". *For example*, where a company has a share capital of Rs 1,00,000 divided into 10,000 units of Rs 10 each, then each unit of Rs 10 is called a share of Rs 10 each and a person who has taken 10 shares of that company is said to have share in the share capital of the company to the extent of Rs 100. A share thus represents such proportion of the interest of the shareholders as the amount paid up thereon bears to the total capital payable to the company. A share may be partly paid up or fully paid up. It is a measure of the interest in the company's assets to which a person holding a share is entitled.

4.2 Nature of Share

A share is not a sum of money but is an interest measured by a sum of money and made up of various rights contained in the contract [*Borland Trustees* v. *Steel Bros. & Co Ltd.*]. It must be noted that a shareholder has not only contractual rights against the company but also certain other rights which accrue to him according to the provisions of the Companies Act. It may also be noted that the shareholders are not, in the eyes of law, part owners of the undertaking. The undertaking is somewhat different from the totality of the shareholders.

5.0 STOCK

5.1 Meaning of Stock

"Stock" is an aggregate of fully paid shares that have been legally consolidated. The consolidated amount is divisible into fractions of any amount, regardless of the nominal value of the shares that have been consolidated. It thus represents a part of the capital of the company which is fully paid. According to Section 94(1)(c), a company limited by shares, may if so authorised by its Articles, by a resolution passed in a general meeting, convert all or any of its fully paid shares into stock. However the notice of such conversion must be given to Registrar within 30 days of the conversion. Upon receipt of such notice the registrar shall record the notice and make necessary alteration in the memorandum or articles or both. [Section 95]. According to Section 96, all the provisions of Companies Act which are applicable to shares only, shall cease to apply as to so much of share capital as is converted into stock.

5.2 Advantage of Stock

The main advantage claimed for stock is that it is transferable in any denomination which is not merely limited to the nominal value of the share converted into a stock. However, this advantage may be limited by making such regulation in the Articles as contained in the proviso to Regulation 37 of Table A. Proviso to Regulation 37 runs as under: "Provided the Board may from time to time fix the minimum amount of stock transferable so however that such minimum shall not exceed the nominal amount of the shares for which the stock arose."

6.0 DISTINCTION BETWEEN STOCK AND SHARE

The difference between a share and stock may be noted as follows:

Basis of Distinction	**Share**	**Stock**
1. *Fully paid or partly paid*	Shares may be fully paid up or partly paid up.	Stock must be fully paid up.
2. *Transfer in fraction*	Shares transferable only in its entirety.	Stock is transferable in fraction also.
3. *Direct Issue*	Shares can be directly issued.	Stock cannot be issued directly. Stock comes into existence as a result of conversion of fully paid up shares.
4. *Serial No.*	Shares are serially numbered.	Stock is not serially numbered.

7.0 NATURE OF SHARES OR DEBENTURES [SECTION 82]

The shares [or debentures] or other interest of any member in a company are the movable properties, transferable in the manner provided by the articles of the company.

8.0 NUMBERING OF SHARES [SECTION 83]

Each share in a company having a share capital must be distinguished by its appropriate number: **Provided** that nothing in this section shall apply to the shares held with a depository.

9.0 KINDS OF SHARE CAPITAL [SECTION 86]

The share capital of a company limited by shares shall be of two kinds only namely:

(a) Equity share capital—

  (i) with voting rights, or

  (ii) with differential rights as to dividend, voting, or otherwise in accordance with such rules and subject to such conditions as may be prescribed.

(b) Preference Share Capital.

10.0 MEANING OF AN EQUITY SHARE

An equity share is a share which is not a preference share. In other words, it is a share which does not carry two preferential rights (viz., right to receive dividend and right to receive repayment of capital) attached to a preference share. The capital raised through equity shares is called equity share capital and the persons who contribute money through equity shares are called equity shareholders. The main features of these shares as discussed below:

1. Payment of equity dividend is made after the payment of preference dividend.
2. Repayment of equity share capital is made after the repayment of preference share capital in the event of winding up of the company.
3. The equity shareholders generally enjoy voting rights. They have right to elect directors and to participate in the management.

Note: After the commencement of The Companies (Amendment) Act, 2000, the company can issue equity shares without voting rights.

4. The rate of equity dividend is not fixed and may vary from year to year depending upon the profits available and the decision of directors (at board meeting) and members (at annual general meeting).
5. The equity share capital is generally not redeemable during the life of the company unless the company decides to buy back its shares.
6. Equity shareholders enjoy various rights as members, which include, *inter alia*, the following rights:
   (a) Right of pre-emption in the matter of fresh issue of capital [Section 81].
   (b) Right to apply to the Court to have any variation of their rights set aside [Section 107].
   (c) Right to receive a copy of the statutory report [Section 165].
   (d) Right to apply to Central Government to call an annual general meeting when the company fails to call such a meeting [Section 167].
   (e) Right to apply to CLB for calling an extraordinary general meeting of the company [Section 186].
   (f) Right to receive copies of annual accounts along with auditor's report [Sections 210 and 219].

11.0 MEANING OF A PREFERENCE SHARE

According to Section 85 of the Companies Act, 1956, a preference share is one which carries the following two rights:

1. **a right to receive dividend** at a stipulated rate or of a fixed amount before any dividend is paid on equity shares; and
2. **a right to receive repayment of capital** on winding up of the company, before the capital of equity shareholders is returned.

12.0 KINDS OF PREFERENCE SHARES

In addition to the aforesaid two preferential rights, a preference share may carry some other rights. On the basis of additional rights, preference shares can be classified into seven types as under:

(a) Cumulative Preference Share is the share on which arrears of dividend accumulate. Unless stated otherwise in Articles or Terms of Issue, a preference share is always deemed to be a cumulative share. They carry the right to cumulative dividends if the company fails to pay the dividend in a particular year. The accumulated arrears of dividends shall be paid, if any dividend is declared in subsequent years, before any dividend is paid to the equity shareholders. If the company goes into liquidation, no arrears of dividends are payable unless either the Articles contain an express provision to this effect or such dividends have been declared. Of course the arrears of undeclared dividends shall be payable, even if the Articles are silent, out of any surplus left, after returning in full the preference and equity share capital.

(b) Non-cumulative Preference Share is the share on which, arrears of dividends do not accumulate as per the express provision in the Articles of Association. If no dividend is paid in any particular year, it lapses.

(c) Participating Preference Share is that share which, in addition to two basic preferential rights, also carries one or more of the following rights as per the articles of association:

(i) a right to participate in the surplus profits left after paying dividend to equity shareholders; and

(ii) a right to participate in the surplus assets left after the repayment of capital to equity shareholders on the winding up of the company.

Note: The right to participate in the surplus profits does not automatically entitle the preference shareholders to participate in the surplus assets on the winding up of the company. [Re. *Isle of Thanet Electric Supply Co.,* (1949) 2 All. E.R. 1060]

(d) Non-participating Preference Share is the share which is not a participating share. Unless stated otherwise, a preference share is always deemed to be a non-participating preference share.

(e) Convertible Preference Share is the share which confers on its holder a right of conversion into equity share.

(f) Non-convertible Preference Share is the share which does not confer on its holder a right of conversion into equity share. Unless stated otherwise, a preference share is always deemed to be a non-convertible share.

(g) Redeemable Preference Share is the share which is redeemable in accordance with the provisions of Section 80 and 80A of the Companies Act, 1956. Paying back of capital is called the redemption. After the commencement of the Companies (Amendment) Act, 1996, no company limited by shares shall issue any preference share which is redeemable after the expiry of a period of 20 years from the date of its issue.

(h) Irredeemable Preference Share is the share which is not redeemable during the life time of the company. After the commencement of the Companies (Amendment) Act, 1988, no company limited by shares can issue any preference share which is irredeemable.

(i) Cumulative Convertible Preference Shares (CCP) These shares were introduced in 1985. The objects of the issue of such shares should be for setting up new projects, expansion or diversification of existing projects, capital expenditure for modernisation and working capital requirements. The amount of issue of CCP shares will be to the extent the company would be offering equity shares to the public for subscription. These shares are deemed to be equity issue for the purpose of calculating debt-equity ratio. The entire issue would be convertible into equity shares between the end of 3 years and 5 years. The rate of dividend payable on CCP would be 100 per cent. The face value of these shares will ordinarily be Rs 100 each, and the holders are entitled to receive arrears of dividend, if any, even after conversion.

13.0 DISTINCTION BETWEEN AN EQUITY SHARE AND A PREFERENCE SHARE

An equity share and a preference share can be distinguished as follows:

Basis of Distinction	*An Equity Share*	*A Preference Share*
1. *Preferential right as to the payment of dividend*	Payment of equity dividend is made after the payment of dividend.	Payment of preference dividend is made before the payment of equity dividend.
2. *Preferential right as to the repayment of capital*	Repayment of equity share capital is made after the repayment of preference share capital.	Repayment of preference share capital is made before the repayment of equity share capital.
3. *Fluctuations in the rate of dividend*	The rate of equity dividend may vary from year to year depending upon the decision of directors and members.	The rate of preference dividend is fixed.
4. *Arrears of dividend*	In case of an equity share, arrears of dividend cannot accumulate in any case.	In case of preference shares, arrears of dividend may accumulate.
5. *Convertibility*	It cannot be convertible.	It may be convertible.
6. *Redeemability*	It is not redeemable during the lifetime of the company unless the company decides to buy-back its shares.	It is redeemable during the lifetime of the company.
7. **Premium on redemption**	It cannot carry a right to receive premium on redemption.	It may carry a right to receive premium on redemption.
8. **Voting rights**	Equity shareholders generally enjoy voting rights.	Preference share holders do not have any voting rights except at their class meetings.

14.0 MEANING OF DEFERRED SHARES

Deferred shares are also known as 'founders' share' or 'Management Shares' because these shares are issued to the promoters or founders of the company. The main features of these shares are as follow:

(a) **Last to Receive Dividend** These shares carry the right as to the payment of dividend only after the payment of dividend on all other kinds of shares.

(b) **Last to Receive Repayment of Capital** Similarly in case of winding up these shares carry the right as to the repayment of capital only after the payment of capital of all other kinds of shares issued.

(c) **Disproportionate Voting Rights** These shares usually carry disproportionate voting rights so that the management may be controlled by small investment and it is for this reason that they are also known as 'Management Shares'.

No public company or private company which is subsidiary of a public company can issue deferred shares [Sections 86 and 88]. However, an independent private company is still entiltled to issue deferred shares [Section 92(2)]. Such shares are not all common now-a-days.

15 ALTERATION OF SHARE CAPITAL CLAUSE

The provisions relating to the alteration of Share Capital are given below:

1. **Authority in Articles** A limited company having a share capital may alter the Capital Clause of its memorandum only if it is authorised by its articles of association to do so. [Section 94(1)]
2. **Manner of Alteration** A company may alter the Capital Clause in the following manner:
   (a) by increasing its nominal share capital by issue of new shares; [e.g. from 1 crore to 5 crore]
   (b) by consolidating the existing shares into shares of larger amount than its existing shares; [e.g. Conversion of Shares of Rs 10 each into shares of Rs 100 each]
   (c) by Converting fully paid shares into stock or vice versa;
   (d) by sub-dividing the existing shares into shares of smaller amount than its existing shares; [e.g. Conversion of shares of Rs 100 each into shares of Rs 10 each]
   (e) by cancelling its unissued shares.

Note: A cancellation of shares under Section 94 shall not be deemed to a reduction of share capital within the meaning of the Act.

3. **Passing of Resolution** An ordinary resolution is required to be passed at its general meeting. [Section 9(2)]
4. **Filing of Notice** A notice specifying alteration made must be given to the Registrar within 30 days of alteration. [Sections 95(1) and 97(1)]
5. **Duty of Registrar** The Registrar shall make the necessary alteration in the memorandum or articles or both. [Section 95(2)]
6. **Consequences of Default** If default is made in filing the notice as aforesaid, the company and every officer in default must be punishable with the fine upto Rs 500 for every day during which the default continues. [Sections 95(3) and 97(3)]
7. **In Applicability of Provisions to Stock** Where a company has converted any of its shares into stock, such provisions of the Act as are applicable to shares shall cease to apply to such shares which have been converted into stock. [Section 96]
8. **Notice of Increase** Notice of increase in authorised capital or number of members beyond registered number in case of a company not limited by shares must be given to the Registrar. [Section 97]

Note: Notice of increase must be given to the registrar even when the new shares may not have been issued to any shareholders. [*Mahalaxmi Mills Co. Ltd.* v. *State,* (1969) Comp. Case 342]

16.0 REDUCTION OF SHARE CAPITAL [SECTION 100 TO 105]

16.1 Meaning of Reduction of Share Capital

Reduction of share capital may involve reduction in respect of that portion of:

(a) issued capital which has been subscribed, called up and paid up, or
(b) issued capital which has been subscribed but not called up.

16.2 To which Company the Restriction as to Reduction of Share Capital do not Apply.

The restriction as to reduction of share capital apply to the following two categories of companies:

(a) A company limited by shares

(b) A company limited by guarantee having share capital.

Thus, such restrictions do not apply to unlimited companies whether having share capital or not and companies limited by guarantee not having share capital.

16.3 Manner of Capital Reduction

A company may reduce its share capital in any way and in particular:

(a) by extinguishing or reducing the liability of members in respect of capital not paid up. e.g. where the shares of Rs 100 each with Rs 75 paid up are reduced to Rs 75 fully paid up shares, the shareholders are relieved from liability on the uncalled capital of Rs 25 per share.

(b) by cancelling any paid up share capital which is lost or is unrepresentated by available assets, with or without extinguishing or reducing liability of members.

(c) by paying off any paid up share capital which is in excess of the wants of the company with or without extinguishing or reducing liability.

Example I Where the fully paid shares of Rs 100 each are reduced to Rs 75 fully paid up shares and Rs 25 are returned to the members. Thus, in this case nominal value of the share is reduced and not merely the paid up value.

Example II Where the fully paid shares of Rs 100 each are reduced to Rs 75 paid up and Rs 25 are returned to the members on the condition that when required, the company may call it up again. Thus, in this case the paid up value of share is reduced and not the nominal value.

Note: Interest of creditors is really involved only in the circumstances referred to in (a) and (c).

16.4 Procedure for Reduction of Capital

The procedure for reducing the capital is given below:

1. **Authorised by Articles** The articles must authorise the company to reduce the share capital. If the articles do not so authorise, then these must be altered by a special resolution first.
   Note: It is not enough to provide this authority in the Memorandum.
2. **Special Resolution** A special resolution must be passed at a general meeting.
3. **Court's Order** After passing the special resolution, the company has to apply to the court for an order confirming the reduction.

   Mandatory and Discretionary Powers of the Court The mandatory and discretionary powers of the Court are as under:

   (i) After the petition for the court's confirmation has been filed, the Court must settle the list of creditors who are entitled to object in accordance with Section 101(2)(a) (e.g. the creditors having a debt or claim admissible on a winding up). [Section 101(2)(b)]

   (ii) For settling the list of creditors, the court must ascertain the names of those creditors and the nature and amount of their debts or claims. [Section 101(2)(b)]

   (iii) The court may publish notices fixing a day or days within which the creditors not entered on the list are to claim to be so entered or are to be excluded from the right of objecting to the reduction. [Sec 101(2)(b)]

   (iv) Where a creditor entered on the list whose debt or claim is not discharged or has not determined does not consent to the reduction, the court may dispense with the consent of that creditor if the company secures the payment of his debt or claim by appropriating the full amount or the amount fixed by the court. [Section 101(2)(c)]

(v) The court has discretionary power having regard to any special circumstances of the case to direct that the provisions of Section 101(2) shall not apply as regards any class(s) of creditors. [Section 101(3)]

Note: Special circumstances must be such as would convince the court that with reasonable foresight it can be said the proposed reduction of capital would not adversely affect the relevant creditor and would not render him any worse off than if he had attended and objected to the application for confirmation.

[*Re Lucanic Tempscule Billard Hall (London) Ltd.*, 1965 3 All E.R. 879]

(vi) The court may make an order confirming the reduction on such terms and conditions as it think fit if the court is satisfied that either the consent of every creditor who is entitled to object to the reduction, has been obtained or his debt or claim has been discharged or has been determined or has been secured. [Section 102(1)]

(vii) The court may order that the words 'And Reduced' be added to the name of the company for a certain period. [Section 102(2)(a)]

(viii) The court may require the company to publish the reason for the reduction and the causes which led to the reduction. [Section 102(2)(b)]

4. Registration of Order and Minutes of Reduction

(i) The Registrar must register the order and minute—

(a) on the production of an order of the court confirming the reduction of the share capital, and

(b) on the delivery of a certified copy of the order and of a minute approved by the court. [Section 103(1)]

(ii) On the registration of the order and minute and not before, the resolution shall become effective. [Section 103(2)]

(iii) The notice of registration must be published in such a manner as the court may direct. [Section 103(3)]

(iv) The Registrar shall issue a certificate which shall be conclusive evidence that all the requirements of the Act as to the reduction have been complied with and that the share capital is such as is stated in the minute. [Section 103(4)]

(v) The minutes shall be deemed to be substituted for the corresponding part of the memorandum thereby altering the memorandum within the meaning of Section 40. [Section 103(5) and (6)]

5. Liability of Members in Case of Reduced Share Capital [Section 104] On the reduction of share capital the extent of the liability of any past or present member on any call or contribution shall not exceed the difference between (a) the amount already paid on the share or the reduced amount if any which is deemed to have been paid thereon by the member and (b) the amount of the shares as fixed by the minute of the reduction.

In the event any creditor entitled to object to the reduction of capital is not entered on the list of creditors by reason of his ignorance and after such reduction, the company is unable to pay his debt or claim:

(a) every member at the time of registration of court's order for reduction, shall be liable to contribute for the payment of that debt or claim an amount not exceeding the amount which he would have contributed on the day before registration of the order.

(b) In case the company is wound up, the court on the application by the creditor and on proof of his ignorance may settle a list of contributories and make and enforce calls and orders on the contributories settled on the list as if they were ordinary contributories in a winding up.

It is further provided that, if any officer of the company conceals the name of any creditor entitled to object to the reduction, he shall be liable to be punished with imprisonment up to one year, or with fine or with both [Section 105].

17.0 DISTINCTION BETWEEN REDUCTION OF SHARE CAPITAL AND DIMINUTION OF SHARE CAPITAL

Reduction of capital may involve reduction in respect of issued capital which has been subscribed but not called up and paid up, or issued capital which has been subscribed but not called up but diminuation involves cancellation of that portion of the issued capital which has not been subscribed. [Section 94(1)(e)]

Reduction of share capital differs from the diminution of share capital in the following respects:

Basis of Distinction	*Reduction of Share Capital*	*Diminution of Share Capital*
1. ***Which capital is involved***	It involves reduction in respect of issued capital which has been subscribed.	It involves reduction in respect of authorised capital.
2. ***Type of resolution required***	It can be effected by a **special** resolution. [Section 100]	It can be effected by an **ordinary** resolution. [Section 94]
3. ***Court's confirmation***	It **needs** the Court's confirmation. [Section 101]	It needs **no** confirmation by the Court. [Section 94(2)]
4. ***Order for 'and reduced works***	The court **may order** to add the words 'And Reduced' to the name of the company. [Section 102(3)]	**No** such provision exists in this case.
5. ***Documents to be filed with the Registrar***	It requires the registration of the following with the Registrar: (a) the **court's order** confirming reduction (b) **minutes** approved by the court	It requires **only a notice** to the Registrar.
6. ***Time limit for filing the documents with the Registrar***	There is **no time limit** specified in the Act for filing the documents with the Registrar.	Notice to Registrar must be given within **30 days** from the date of cancellation.

18.0 VARIATION OF SHAREHOLDERS' RIGHTS [SECTION 106]

Where the share capital of a company is divided into different classes of shares, the rights attached to the shares of any class may be varied subject to the following provisions:

1. **Authorisation or No Prohibition** There must be provision with respect to variation in the memorandum or articles or in the absence of such provision, such variation must not be prohibited by the terms of issue of the shares of that class.
2. **Written Consent of 75% Holders or Special Resolution** The rights can be varied only if—
   (a) Written consent of the holders of at least $\frac{3}{4}$th of the issued shares of that class is obtained, or

(b) the special resolution sanctioning the variation is passed at a separate meeting of the holders of the issued shared of that class.

3. **Rights of Dissentient Shareholders [Section 107]**

(a) The holders of at least 10% of the issued shares of that class, who did not consent to or vote in favour of the resolution for the variation, may apply to the court to have the variation cancelled. [Section 107(1)]

(b) Such applicantion is to be made within 21 days after the consent is obtained or the resolution is passed. [Section 107(2)]

(c) Where any such application is made, the variation shall not have effect unless and until it is confirmed by the court. [Section 107(1)]

(d) If the court, after hearing the applicant and any other person interested in the application is satisfied that the variation would unfairly prejudice the shareholders of that class, it may disallow the variation and shall confirm the variation if not so satisfied. [Section 107(3)]

(e) The decision of the court on any such application shall be final. [Section 107(4)]

(f) The company must forward a copy of court's order on any such application, to the Registrar within 30 days after the service of the order on the company. If default is made, the company and every officer of the company who is in default shall be punishable with fine which may extend to Rs 500. [Section 107(5)]

Notes:

(i) Sub-division of shares is not tantamount to variation.

(ii) The variation which affects only the enjoyment of a right without modifying the right itself does not amount to variation within the meaning of Section 106. [*Re Hindustan General Electric Corporation,* AIR (1959) Cal. 672]

(iii) A proposed issue of new preference and ordinary capital to the ordinary stockholders does not affect the rights or privileges of the exiting preference stockholders though in fact, it lessens the latter's voting power. [*White* v. *Bristal Aeroplane Co. Ltd.,* (1953) 1 All E.R. 40]

(iv) Once the variation is effected in strict consonance with the provisions of Section 106, it is complete, no further steps are necessary to adopt it. [*Re Ramuria Cotton Hills Ltd.,* 53 C.W.N. II]

(v) In the event of the variation of right being a part of a scheme or arrangement with the intervention of the court under Section 391, Section 106 will be inapplicable. [*Re. Hindustan General Electrical Corporation,* ATR (1959) 190, Cal. 672]

19.0 REDEMPTION OF REDEEMABLE PREFERENCE SHARES [SECTION 80]

19.1 Which Company can Issue Redeemable Preference Shares

A Company limited by shares may, if authorised by its Articles, issue redeemable preference shares.

19.2 Can a Company Issue Irredeemable Preference Shares after the commencement of the Companies (Amendment) Act, 1988

No Company limited by shares shall issue irredeemable preference shares. [Section 80(5A)]

19.3 What can be the Maximum Period of Redemption

After the commencement of the Companies (Amendment) Act, 1988, no company limited by shares shall issue any preference share which is redeemable after the expiry of a period of 20 years from the date of issue. [Section 80(5A)]

19.4 What are the Restrictions on the Redemption of Redeemable Preference Shares

According to Section 80, the redemption of preference shares is subject to the following restrictions:

(i) **Fully paid**—Such shares can be redeemed only if they are fully paid.

(ii) **Two Sources of Redeeming such shares**

Such shares can be redeemed only out of the following **two** sources:

(a) **Divisible Profits** i.e. Profit available for distribution as dividend. Some of the examples of Divisible Profits are as under:

1. General Reserve
2. Reserve Fund
3. Dividend Equalisation Fund
4. Insurance Fund
5. Workman's Compensation Fund
6. Workman's Accident Fund
7. Profit and Loss Account

(b) **Proceeds of fresh issue of shares** (whether Equity or Preference) made for the purpose of redemption.

What constitute the proceeds is explained as follows:

In case of fresh issue of shares	*What constitute the proceeds*
(a) At Par	Nominal value of shares issued
(b) At Premium	Nominal value of shares issued
(c) At Discount	Net amount received (i.e. Nominal Value *less* discount on issue of shares)

Note: These shares may be Equity shares or Preference shares.

(iii) **Two Sources of providing Premium if any, payable on redemption.**

The premium, if any, payable on redemption must be provided for out of any of the following two sources:

(a) Securities Premium Account

(b) Profits (whether divisible or not) e.g. Capital Reserve

(iv) **Transfer to CRR A/c**—Where any such shares are redeemed out of divisible profits, an amount equivalent to the nominal value of the shares so redeemed, must be transferred out of divisible profits to **Capital Redemption Reserve Account.**

(v) **Utilization of CRR**—The Capital Redemption Reserve Account may be applied by the company in issuing fully paid bonus shares to the members of the company.

(vi) The provision of this Act relating to the reduction of share capital of a company shall apply to Capital Redemption Reserve Account as if it is paid up share capital of the company. [Section 80(1)(d)]

19.5 Does the Redemption of Preference Shares Constitute Reduction of Authorised Share Capital

The redemption of preference shares by a company shall not be taken as reducing the amount of its authorised share capital. [Section 80(3)]

19.6 Has Company Power to Issue New Shares

Where in pursuance of this section, a company has redeemed or is about to redeem any preference shares, it shall have power to issue shares upto the nominal amount of the shares redeemed or to be redeemed as if these shares have never been issued. [Section 80(4)]

19.7 Does the Issue of New Shares Constitute an Increase of Authorised Share Capital

For the purpose of calculating the fees payable u/s 611, the share capital shall not be deemed to be increased by the issue of new shares under this section.

Where new shares are issued before the redemption of old shares, the new shares shall not , so far as relates to stamp duty be deemed to have been issued unless the old shares are redeemed within one month after the issue of the new shares. [Section 80(4)]

19.8 Penalties for Contravention

If a company fails to comply with the provisions of Section 80, the Company and every officer of the company who is in default shall be punishable with fine which may extend to Rs 10,000. [Section 80(6)]

20.0 FURTHER ISSUE OF CAPITAL—RIGHTS SHARES [SECTION 81]

20.1 Meaning of Pre-emptive Right

Section 81 gives pre-emptive rights to existing equity shareholders in case of further issue of shares. Pre-emptive rights mean that further shares must be offered to the existing shareholders in proportion as nearly as the circumstances admit to the capital paid up on those shares at that date. Such shares are called 'Rights Shares'.

20.2 When Pre-emptive Right is Available

Pre-emptive right is available when it is proposed to increase the subscribed capital of the company by allotment of further shares at any time after the expiry of 2 years from the formation of a company or after the expiry of 1 year from the first allotment of shares, whichever is earlier.

20.3 Provisions Applicable to Pre-emptive Rights or Right Offer

The provisions applicable to right offer are given below:

1. **Offer to be made by Notice** The right offer must be made by notice. Such notice must specify—
   (a) the number of shares offered,
   (b) the time limit (at least 15 days from date of offer within which the offer may be accepted.
   (c) The fact that if the offer is not accepted within the specified time, it will be deemed to have been declined.
   (d) Unless the articles otherwise provide, the fact that the shareholder has the right to renounce the offer in whole or in part in favour of any other person.
2. **Power of Board in Case of Refusal** After the expiry of the time specified in the notice aforesaid, or on receipt of earlier intimation from the person to whom such notice is given that he declines to accept the shares offered, the Board of directors may dispose of them in such manner as they think most beneficial to the company.

20.4 Circumstances Under which New Shares can be Offered to the Outsiders before Offering them to the Existing Shareholders

In the following circumstances new shares can be offered to the outsiders before offering them to the existing shareholders:

1. Where the **special resolution** to that effect is passed by the company in general meeting.
2. Where the **ordinary resolution** to that effect is passed by the company in general meeting and the **Central Government** has sanctioned such issue after being satisfied that the proposal is most beneficial to the company.
3. Where the existing shareholder to whom the offer is made or the person(s) in whose favour the renunciation if any, is made, does not accept the offer within the specified time.
4. Where allotment of further shares is made at any time before the expiry of 2 years from the formation of a company or before the expiry of one year from the limit allotment of shares, whichever is earlier.

Practical Illustration 1

Date of formation of company 1.4.20X1.
Date of first allotment of share 1.5.20X1.

State whether the further shares need to be offered to the existing shareholders under Section 81 if the date of second allotment is (a) 30.4.20X2 (b) 31.3.20X3.

Solution:

Case	*Where further shares need to be offered to the existing shareholders under Section 81*
(a)	No, since neither 1 year has expired from the date of first allotment nor 2 years have expired from the date of formation.
(b)	Yes, since 1 year has expired from the date of first allotment even though 2 years have not yet expired from the date of formation.

Practical Illustration 2

Date of formation of company 1.4.20X1
Date of first allotment of shares 1.5.20X2

Date of first allotment of shares need to be offered to the existing shareholders under Section 81 if the date of second allotment is (a) 31.3.20X3 (b) 30.4.20X3.

Solution:

Case	*Whether further shares need to be offered to the existing shareholders under Section 81*
(a)	No, since neither 1 year has expired from the date of first allotment nor 2 years have expired from the date of formation.
(b)	Yes, since 2 years have expired from the date of formation even though 1 year has not expired from the date of first allotment.

20.5 Case where Provisions of Section 81 do not Apply [Section 81(3)]

The provisions of Section 81 do not apply—

(a) to a private company

(b) to the increase of the subscribed capital of a public company caused by the exercise of an option attached to debentures issued or loan raised by the company.
Such option must be—
   (i) to convert such debentures or loan into shares in the company, or
   (ii) to subscribe for shares in the company.

Terms Providing for Option

(a) The terms of issue of such debentures or the terms of such loans must include a term providing for such option;

(b) Such term either must be approved by the Central Government before the issue of debentures or the raising of the loans, or must be in conformity with the rules, if any, made by that Government in this behalf;

(c) In the case of debentures or loans other than debentures issued to, or loans obtained from, the Government in this behalf, such term must also be approved by a special resolution passed by the company in general meeting before the issue of the debentures or the raising of the loans.

21.0 RESTRICTION ON FINANCIAL ASSISTANCE FOR THE PURCHASE OF SHARES [SECTION 77]

No public company and no private company (which is subsidiary of a public company) can give any financial assistance in any form to any person for the purchase of its own shares or shares of its holding company except in the following 3 cases:

1. Where a banking company lends money in the ordinary course of its business; but not on the security of its own shares.
2. Where provision of money is made by a company in accordance with any scheme to enable the trustee to purchase or subscribe fully paid shares in the company or its holding company for the benefit of employees (including director holding a salaried office or employment).
3. Where loan is made by the company to persons (other than directors or managers) bona fide in the employment of the company to enable them to purchase or subscribe for fully paid shares for an amount not exceeding his salary or wages for a period of 6 months.

Penalty In case of default, the company and its every officer in default shall be punishable with fine upto to Rs 10,000. [Section 77(4)]

22.0 PROVISIONS RELATING TO BUY BACK OF SHARES [SECTION 77A]

22.1 Meaning of Buy-back of Shares

The term buy-back of shares implies the act of purchasing its own shares by a company.

22.2 Three Sources of Funds for Buy-Back [Section 77A(1)]

A company may purchase its own shares or other specified securities out of—

(i) its free reserves; or
(ii) the securities premium account; or
(iii) the proceeds of any shares or other specified securities;

Provided that no buy-back of any kind of shares or other specified securities shall be made out of the proceeds of an earlier issue of the same kind of shares or same kind of other specified securities.

"Specified securities" includes employees' stock option or other securities as may be notified by the Central Government from time to time.

22.3 Buy-back from Whom? [Section 77A(5)]

The buy-back under Sub-section (1) may be—

(a) from the existing security holders on a proportionate basis; or
(b) from the open market; or
(c) from odd lots, that is to say, where the lot of securities of a public company, whose shares are listed on a recognised stock exchange, is smaller than such marketable lot, as may be specified by the stock exchange; or
(d) by purchasing the securities issued to employees of the company pursuant to a scheme of stock option or sweat equity.

22.4 Conditions for Buy-Back

1. **Authorised by Articles**—The buy-back must be authorized by the **Articles**

2. **Special Resolution/Board's Resolution**—The **special resolution** must be passed in the General Meeting of shareholders.

OR

The Board must pass a resolution at its meeting where the buy-back does not exceed 10% of the total equity paid up capital and free reserves of the company.
3. **Minimum Time Interval between Two buy-back**—No offer of buy back must be made within a period of 365 days from the date of preceding offer of buy-back.
4. **Maximum Limit**—The buy-back of the shares must **not exceed 25%** of total paid-up capital and free reserves.
5. **Maximum Limit**—The buy-back of equity shares in any financial year must not exceed 25% of its total paid up equity capital
6. **Maximum Debt-Equity Ratio**—The debt-equity ratio must **not be more than 2:1** after such buy-back.

   Here Debt = Secured + Unsecured Debt and Equity = Capital + Free Reserves Free Reserves = Free Reserves as per Sec 372A + Securities Premium as per Sec 78.
7. **Fully Paid Shares**—All the shares for buy-back must be fully paid-up.
8. **Time Limit**—The buy-back must be completed within **12 months** from the date of passing the special resolution
9. **Solvency Declaration**—The company must file **solvency declaration** with the Registrar and SEBI in the form of an affidavit signed by at least two directors of the company. The affidavit must state that the Board has made full inquiry into the affairs of the company as a result of which they have formed an option that the company is capable of meeting its liabilities and will not render insolvent within a period of one year from the date of declaration adopted by the Board [77A(6)].
10. **Transfer of Certain Sums to Capital Redemption Reserve Account**—Where a company purchases its own shares out of free reserves, than a sum equal to the nominal value of the share so purchased shall be transferred to the capital redemption reserve account referred to in Clause (d) of the proviso to Sub-section (1) of Section 80 and details of such transfer shall be disclosed in the balance sheet.
11. **As per SEBI Guidelines**—Buy-back must be as per SEBI Guidelines

22.5 Proportionate Buy-back

In case the number of securities tendered for buy-back are more than the number of securities to be bought back, the number of securities to be bought back from each member shall be determined as follows:

$$\frac{\text{Acceptance tendered by a Member}}{\text{Total Acceptance tendered by Member}} \times \text{No. of Securities to be bought back}$$

22.6 Extinguishment of Certificates [Sec 77A(7)]

Where a company buys-back its own shares, it must extinguish and physically destroy the securities so bought back within 7 days of the last date of completion of buy-back in the presence of merchant bankers or Registrar or Statutory auditor.

22.7 Cooling Period [Section 77A(8)] Where a company completes a buy-back of its shares or other specified securities under this section, it must not make further issue of same kind of shares (including allotment of further shares under section 81 (1)(a) or other specified securities *within a period of 6 months* except by way of bonus issue or in the discharge of subsisting obligations such as conversion of warrants, stock option schemes, sweat equity or conversion of preference shares or debentures into equity shares.

22.8 Register of Buy-back [Section 77A(9)] Where a company buys back its securities under this section, it must maintain a register of the securities so bought, the consideration paid for the securities bought-back, the date of cancellation of securities, the date of existing and physically destroying of securities and such other particulars as may be prescribed.

22.9 Filing of Buy-back Return [Section 77(A)(10)] A company must, after completion of the buy-back under this section, file with the Registrar and the SEBI, a return containing such completion, as may be prescribed;

Provided that **no return** is to be filed with the SEBI by a company whose shares are **not listed** on any recognised stock exchange.

22.10 Prohibition of Buy-back in Certain Circumstances [Section 77B] No company shall directly or indirectly purchase its own shares or other specified securities—

(a) through any subsidiary company including its own subsidiary companies; or
(b) through any investment company or group of investment companies; or
(c) if a default, by the company, in repayment of deposit or interest payable thereon, redemption of debentures or preference shares or payment of dividend to any shareholder or repayment of any term loan or interest payable thereon to any financial institutions or bank, is subsisting; or
(d) in case such company has not complied with provisions of Sections 159, 207 and 211.

22.11 Penalty for Default [Section 77A(11)] In case of default the company or its officer in default shall be punishable with imprisonment for a term upto 2 years, or with fine upto Rs 50,000 or with both.

22.12 Procedure before Buy-back [Section 77A(3)] The notice of the meeting at which special resolution is proposed to be passed must be accompanied by an explanatory statement stating—

(a) a full and complete disclosure of the all material facts;
(b) the necessity for the buy-back;
(c) the class of security intended to be purchased under the buy-back;
(d) the amount to be invested under the buy-back; and
(e) the time limit for completion of buy-back.

23.0 BOOK BUILDING

23.1 Meaning of Book Building

Book Building is a process by which the issue price of securities is determined by the issuer company and the Book Runner on the basis of bids received from various investors during bid period. The bid may vary from floor price (i.e. minimum price) to 120% of floor price. The issue price is determined after the bid closing date.

23.2 Reason for Book Building

Book Building facilitates the evaluation of the intrinsic worth of the securities and creditability of the company.

23.3 Steps in Book Building Process

1. **Book Runner**—Appoint a lead merchant banker as Book Runner.
2. **Draft Prospectus**—Prepare draft prospectus and file with SEBI.
3. **Syndicate Members**—Appoint Syndicate members to underwrite the issues to the extent of 'net offer to the public'.

4. **Circulation**—Circulate the copy of draft prospectus to the institutional investors and syndicate members.
5. **Building up an Order Book**—Build up an order book showing the demand for the securities at various prices.
6. **Issue price**—Determine the issue price.
7. **Issue size**—Determine the issue size of (a) placement portion and (b) public offer portion.
8. **Allocation**—Allocate securities to various bidders.
9. **Final Prospectus**—File the final prospectus with the Registrar of companies within 2 days of the determination of issue price and receipt of acknowledgement card from SEBI.

23.4 Advantages of Book Building Process

1. **Low Cost of Issue**—Book Building process minimises the cost of issue because of limited number of investors.
2. **No Risk**—It avoids the risk of failure of issue because of underwriting of the issue.
3. **Easy Evaluation**—It facilitates the evaluation of the intrinsic worth of the securities and creditability of the company.
4. **Realistic Issue Price**—It facilitates to determine the realistic issue price since it is based on the floor price which is fixed just 1 *or* 2 weeks before the opening of the issue.
5. **Reflects Market Price**—Since issue price is based on actual offers made by various bidders, it reflects real market price.

23.5 Limitations of Book Building Process

1. It is suitable for mega issues only.
2. There must be well organised stock exchanges.
3. Issuer company must be well known to investors.
4. There is Risk of Price Rigging on listing of securities.

24.0 DEMATERIALISATION

24.1 Meaning of Demat Shares

Demat shares represent the electronic shares standing to the credit of demat account of the holder of shares which is maintained with depository participant.

24.2 Meaning of Dematerialisation

Dematerialisation is the process of converting physical certificates into electronic holdings maintained in a demat account opened with a depository participant.

24.3 Steps in the Process of Dematerialisation

Step 1 → An investor opens a Demat Account with a Depository Participant (DP) and submits his physical certificates alongwith Dematerialisation Request Form to the DP.

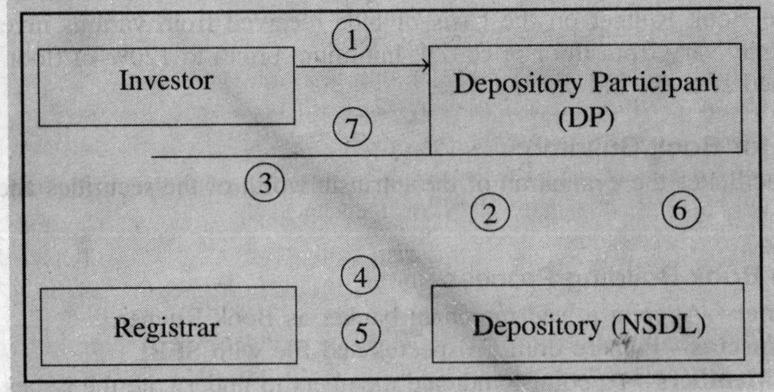

Process of Dematerialisation

Step 2 → DP intimates NSDL of the investor's request.
Step 3 → DP forwards the physical certificates to the Registrar.
Step 4 → Registrar confirms the request.
Step 5 → Registrar processes the request, updates the records and informs NSDL.
Step 6 → NSDL credits DP's Account and informs DP.
Step 7 → DP credits the investor's account and informs investor.

24.4 Meaning of Rematerialisation

Rematerialisation is the process of converting the electronic holdings into physical certificates.

24.5 Advantages of Demat Shares or Electronic Shares (E-Share)

1. No Tearing/Mutilation of Shares
2. No Risk of Loss of Shares due to theft/fire etc.
3. No Risk of Loss-in-transit
4. No Risk of Forged Certificates
5. No Risk of Bad Deliveries
6. Immediate delivery within a day after the settlement
7. Next working day settlement
8. No need to send shares for registration while buying the shares
9. No stamp duty for registration of shares in own name

Thus, E-share offers a faster, easier and safer solution to the ownership, trading and transfer of shares.

EXERCISES

VERY SHORT ANSWER TYPE QUESTIONS

1. What is meant by 'Share Capital'?
2. What is meant by 'Authorised Capital'?
3. What is meant by 'Issued Capital'?
4. What is meant by 'Subscribed Capital'?
5. What is meant by 'Unissued Capital'?
6. What is meant by 'Uncalled Capital'?
7. What is meant by 'Reserve Capital'?
8. What is meant by 'Share'?
9. What is meant by 'Stock'?
10. What is meant by 'Equity Share'?
11. What is meant by 'Preference Shares'?
12. What is meant by 'Cumulative Preference Shares'?
13. What is meant by 'Non-cumulative Preference Shares'?
14. What is meant by 'Participating Preference Shares'?
15. What is meant by 'Non-Participating Preference Shares'?
16. What is meant by 'Convertible Preference Shares'?
17. What is meant by 'Non-convertible Preference Shares'?
18. What is meant by 'Cumulative Convertible Preference Share'?
19. What is meant by 'Deferred Shares'?
20. What is meant by 'Reduction of Share Capital'?
21. Name the companies to which the restriction as to reduction of share capital apply.
22. What is meant by pre-emptive right?
23. When is pre-emptive right available?

24. Is the authorisation under Articles required to issue redeemable preference shares?
25. Does the option to redeem the redeemable preference shares lie with the holders thereof?
26. Can partly paid preference shares be redeemed?
27. Name the reserve to be created on redemption of preference shares out of profits?
28. Name the resolution required to authorise (a) the alteration of capital clause; (b) the reduction of share capital.
29. Who are the creditors likely to be hit by the company's contemplated reduction?

SHORT ANSWER TYPE QUESTIONS

1. Distinguish between the following:
   (a) Reserve Capital and Capital Reserve
   (b) Authorised Capital and Issued Capital
   (c) Share and Stock
   (d) An Equity Share and a Preference Share
   (e) Reduction of Share Capital and Diminution of a Share Capital.
2. State the nature of a share.
3. State the advantage of stock.
4. State the kinds of shares.
5. Comment on the following;
   (a) A company can offer new shares to outsiders before offering them to the existing shareholders.
   (b) Preference shareholders cannot vote on every resolution.
   (c) A public company cannot buy its own shares.
   (d) A public company cannot provide financial assistance for the purchase of its shares.
   (e) Variation of shareholders' rights is permissible only when authorised by the Memorandum or Articles.
   (f) Rights attaching the class cannot be varied after passing the special resolution at separate meeting of the shareholders of that class.
6. Write short notes on the following:
   (a) Book Building
   (b) Dematerialisation

LONG ANSWER TYPE QUESTIONS

1. Describe the various kinds of preference shares.
2. Explain the provisions relating to the alteration of share capital clause of the memorandum.
3. Explain the provision relating to the reduction of share capital.
4. Explain the liability of members in case of reduced share capital.
5. Explain the provisions relating to variation of shareholders' right's.
6. Explain the provision relating to the redemption of redeemable preference shares.
7. Explain the provisions relating to pre-emptive right?
8. (a) State the circumstances under which new share can be offered to the outsiders before offering them to the existing shareholders.
   (b) State the cases where provision of Section 81 do not apply.
9. Explain provisions relating to the conversion of loan into shares.
10. Discuss the voting rights of equity shareholder and preference shareholders.
11. (a) When does dividend on preference shares become due?
    (b) What should be the basis of voting rights of preference shareholders?
    (c) What are the restrictions on exercise of voting rights?
12. What are the restrictions on financial assistance for the purchase of shares?
13. Explain the provisions relating to buy-back of shares.

CHAPTER

9 Membership

1.0 MEMBER AND SHAREHOLDER

1.1 Definition of Member [Section 41]

Section 41 covers the following persons as member:

1. **Subscribers to Memorandum** The subscribers to the Memorandum of a company shall be deemed to have agreed to become members of the company and on its registration, shall be entered as members in its register of members.
2. **Every Other Person** Every other person who agrees in writing to become a member of a company and whose name is entered in its register of members, shall be a member of the company.
3. **Beneficial Owner in Records of Depository** Every person who holds equity share capital of company and whose name is entered as beneficial owner in the records of the depository shall be deemed to be a member of the concerned company.

Note: A person may also become a member through transfer or transmission of shares (to be discussed later on)

1.2 Judicial Rullings

1. The subscriber to the memorandum becomes a member, on registration of the company, even without the shares having been allotted to him and is liable as a contributory when the company is wound up [*Universal Transport Co.* v. *Jagjit Singh*, (1965) Comp. Case. 36; *Babulal* v. *Naraina Sugar Mill*, (1958) Comp. Case. 155].
2. Since his agreement needs to be in writing, one cannot be deemed to be a member on ground of estoppel, simply because his name appears in the register of members.
3. Where, however, a person's name is there in the register and he has, in fact, accepted the position and acted as a member, the agreement will be presumed to be in writing until the presumption is rebutted by proof to the contrary

1.3 Definition of Shareholder

The term 'shareholder' refers to a person who holds share in a company.

1.4 Distinction between Member and Shareholder

Though the two terms 'Members' and 'Shareholder' are used synonymously, yet there is a difference between the two. In some cases, a person may be a member but not a shareholder or he may be shareholder but not a member.

1.5 All Shareholders need not be Members

Under the following circumstances, a person is a shareholder and not a member:

(a) Holder of share warrant is a shareholder and not a member because holder's name is struck off from the Register of Members on the issue of share warrants. However, the articles may give membership rights to holders of share warrants. [Section 115(1)]

(b) A transferee or legal representative of a deceased member is a shareholder and not a member unless he applies for registration of transfer/transmission of the shares and his name is entered into the Register of Members.

1.6 All Members Need not be Shareholders

Under the following circumstances, a person is a member and not a shareholder:

(a) Subscribers to the Memorandum of a company become members on registration of the company even before any shares are allotted to them.

(b) Members of a company limited by guarantee having no share capital or an unlimited company having no share capital.

(c) A transferee of shares ceases to be a holder of those shares but continues to be the member of the company until his name is replaced by the name of the transferee.

(d) A deceased member continues to be the member of the company until his name is removed from the register of member.

(e) List 'B' contributories who ceased to be members within 12 months before the commencement of winding up, are treated as part members even though they are not shareholders.

2.0 MODES OF ACQUIRING MEMBERSHIP

The various modes of acquiring membership are shown below:

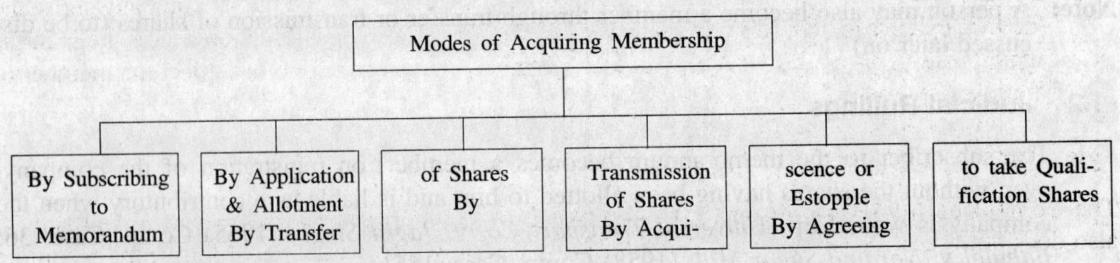

Let us discuss these modern one by one:

1. **By Subscribing to Memorandum** A subscriber to the memorandum automatically becomes a member of the company on its registration.

Notes:

(i) Neither application form nor allotment of shares is necessary. Even an absence of entry in the register of members cannot deprive him of his status as member. [*Official Liquidator* v. *Suleman Bhai*, AIR (1955) M.B. 166]

(ii) A subscriber cannot rescind the contract for purchase of shares even on the ground of fraud or misrepresentation on the part of promoters. [*Re Metal Constituents Co. Lord Husgan's* case (1902) 1 Ch. 707]

(iii) A subscriber cannot refuse to take shares on the ground that his name does not appear in the register of members.

2. **By Application and Allotment of Shares** Every person other than the subscribers to the Memorandum becomes the member on fulfilment of the following two conditions:

(a) He must have agreed in writing to become a member. In other words, there must be an offer to take shares by way of written application and acceptance of that offer by way of allotment. The general law of contract applies to this agreement. If a person applies for shares subject to certain conditions, the allotment by the company must be made according to those conditions otherwise the allottee shall not be bound to accept the shares. Where a person applies for shares but withdraws his application before acceptance and the company allots the shares and puts his name in the register, he may rescind the contract.

(b) His name must have entered in the registers of members.

3. **By Transfer** A person may become a member by acquiring shares in the open market and by having the transfer registered and getting his name placed on the register of members. It may be noted that the shares are movable property and are transferable as determined by the Articles of the company.

4. **By Transmission** A person may become a member by operation of law on the happening of such events as the death, insolvency or lunacy of a member. On the death of a member, his legal representatives have the right to get the shares of the deceased member registered in their name.

   Similarly the Official Receiver or Official Assignee is entitled to be a member in place of member who has been declared insolvent. No instrument of transfer is necessary in this case.

5. **By Acquiescence or Estoppel** Acquisition of membership by this method is the direct result of the doctrine of acquiescence or estoppel. A person is deemed to be a member if he allows his name, apart from any agreement to become a member, to be on the register of members or otherwise holds himself out or allows himself to be held out as a member. In such a case, he is estopped from denying that he is registered with his consent. He can, however, escape liability by taking prompt action to have his name removed from the register on some permissible ground.

6. **By Agreeing to Take Qualification Shares** When a director of a public company signs and files with the Registrar an undertaking to take and pay for his qualification shares, he is in the same position as subscriber to the memorandum and he is deemed to have become member of the company on incorporation.

3.0 WHO CAN BECOME A MEMBER?

The Companies Act does not specifically lay down as to who can be a member of a company. It also does not prescribe any disqualification for any person which would debar him from becoming a member of a company. The Act simply provides that any person who agrees in writing to become a member of a company can become a member. As the contract to purchase shares in a company is like any other contract. Therefore, only such persons can become members of a company who are competent to contract. However, as regards competency of a member, the provisions of the Indian Contract Act shall apply. This means that minors, persons of unsound mind and those who have been disqualified by law from contracting, cannot become members of a company.

The membership rights of some special categories of persons are discussed below:

1. **Minor** Can minor become a member?

   (a) **Incompetent to Contract** According to Section 11 of the Indian Contract Act, a minor is incompetent to contract, therefore, he cannot enter into an agreement to become a member of the company. In *Palaniappa* v. *Official Liquidator, Pasupati Bank Ltd.* an application was made by a father as guardian of his minor daughter describing her as minor. The company went into liquidation. It was held that the allotment was void and neither the minor nor her guardian could be held liable as contributories.

(b) Right to Repudiate the Allotment during Minority

(i) Both the company and minor can repudiate the allotment.

(ii) In either case, the company has to refund all moneys received from minor in respect of the shares allotted to him.

(iii) The question of whether or not the minor can be compelled to restore the benefits received from the company would be for the court to decide considering the circumstances of each case.

(iv) If neither party repudiates allotment, the name of the minor shall continue to appear on the register of members, but even then a minor incurs no personal liability.

(c) Right to Repudiate the Allotment after Attaining Majority

Case	*Whether Right to Repudiate available*
(a) ***If he has not received dividend after attaining majority***	He **can repudiate** his liability on the shares even if he had received dividends during his minority and if he does so the company cannot plead estoppel on the plea that he had received dividends during his minority or that he had fraudulently misrepresented his age in his application for shares [*Sadiq Ali* vs. *Jay Kishore*, 30 Bomb. L.R. B 46(1)]
(b) ***If he has received dividend after attaining majority***	He **cannot repudiate** his liability on the shares because he would be deemed to have intentionally led the company to believe him to be a shareholder and on the faith of such belief to pay him the dividend [*Fazalbhoy* v. *The Credit Bank of Public*, (1914) 39 Bom. 331]

(d) Right to become Transferee of Fully Paid Share

There is nothing in the Act to bar a minor from becoming a transferee of fully paid shares. *In Miss Nandita Jain* v. *Bennet Coleman and Company Ltd.*, the Company Law Board held that the contract entered into by a minor for registration of transfer of fully paid shares, through the natural guardian was a valid and binding contract. In such a case the entry in the register of members will be made as follows. "A, (a minor) through . . . guardian".

If shares are transferred to a minor, the transferor will continue to remain liable for all future calls on such shares even if he was ignorant of the minority of the transferee. If the company is aware of the minority of the transferee at the time of transfer, it can refuse to register the transfer in favour of a minor unless the shares are fully paid.

2. Company

(a) A company being a legal person can become a member of another company if it is so authorised by its Memorandum.

(b) A subsidiary company cannot become a member of its holding company except in the following two cases:

(i) where the subsidiary is concerned as the legal representative of a deceased member,

(ii) where the subsidiary is concerned as trustee and the holding company or its subsidiary is not beneficially interested except as lender of money in the ordinary course of business. [Section 42(2)]

(c) A subsidiary which was a member of its holding company at the commencement of the Act or before becoming a subsidiary, may continue to be a member.

(d) But a subsidiary shall not except in two cases mentioned in Section 42(2), have any voting right at the holding company's meeting.

(e) A subsidiary cannot hold shares in holding company even through its nominee. [Section 42(4)]

3. **Partnership Firm** A partnership firm is not a legal entity separate from its members. Therefore, it cannot buy shares in its own name. A firm may hold shares in the names of individual partners who may be entered as joint holders in the register of members. However, it can become member of a non-profit making company licensed under Section 25 of the Act and its membership shall cease on dissolution of firm.
4. **Hindu Undivided Family** A HUF can have shares in a company in the name of its Karta. Thus, the Karta will be a member of a company as his name alone will be entered in the register of members.
5. **Insolvent** If any member is declared insolvent, he remains a member of the company till his name appears on company's register of members. He is entitled to vote in respect of shares held by him, but the dividend on shares will be paid to Official Assignee or Official Receiver.
6. **Foreigners** A foreigner may become a member with the general or special permission of the Reserve Bank of India under the Foreign Exchange Management Act, 1973. But if he becomes an alien enemy, his rights as a member shall be suspended.
7. **Married Woman** A married women is competent to contract and as such can become a member of a company.
8. **Trustee** Section 153 of the Act lays down that no notice of trust, express or implied or constructive, shall be entered in the register of members. Therefore, a trustee cannot become a member of a company in his capacity as such. But a trustee can be a member in his own name.

4.0 TERMINATION OF MEMBERSHIP

A person ceases to be a member of a company when his name is removed from the register of members. A person may cease to be a member in any one of the following ways:

1. **Transfer of Shares** When he transfers all of his shares to another person and the transfer is duly registered by the company, the name of the transferor is removed from the register to members.
2. **Transmission of Shares** When he dies and his legal representative(s), transfer the shares or secures their registration in his/their own name. Until the shares are transmitted he continues to be member and his estate to be liable for any money due on shares. The legal representative of deceased member is entitled to receive dividends and notice of the meeting but cannot vote at the meeting.
3. **Forfeiture of Shares** When his shares are forfeited for non-payment of calls and other reasons contained in the articles. The membership terminates on share forfeiture.
4. **Surrender of Shares** When he validly surrenders his shares to the company, he ceases to be a member.
5. **Redemption of Shares** When a member holds redeemable preference shares, his membership terminates on redemption of such shares.
6. **Repudiation of Contract** When he repudiates the contract to take shares on the ground of misrepresentation or mistake in the prospectus or on the ground of irregular allotment.
7. **Insolvency of Member** When he is declared insolvent, his shares vest in the Official Receiver or Official Assignee. The Assignee or Receiver may sell these shares and when the transferee's name is entered in the register of members, insolvent member ceases to be a member.
8. **Winding up of Company** When the winding up of the company, commences, he ceases to a member but he continues to be liable as a contributory.
9. **Issue of Share Warrants** When share warrants are issued in exchange of fully paid shares, his name is removed from the register of members although he continues to be a shareholder of the company.

10. **Court's Order** When the court passes an order for the purchase of shares of a member under Section 402 of the Companies Act, he ceases to be a member.
11. **On Buy-back of Shares**
12. **Enforcement of Lien** When the company has a lien on the shares and the shares are sold by the company to enforce this lien or if the shares are sold in the execution of a decree of the court, the membership terminates.

The Register of members, however is only *prima facie* evidence as to whether a person is a member or not and if a person's name is improperly removed, all his rights and obligations as a member continue to remain the same.

5.0 RIGHTS OF MEMBERS

A number of rights have been conferred on the members by the Companies Act, some of the important rights are as under:

1. Right to receive copies of memorandum and Articles of Association on request and on payment of the prescribed fee. [Section 39]
2. Right of priority to have shares offered in case of increase of capital. [Section 81]
3. Right to transfer his shares according to the Articles of Association. [Section 82]
4. Right to apply to the court to have any variation or abrogation to his rights set aside by the court. [Section 107]
5. Right to appeal to the Company Law Board where the company refuses or fails to register the transfer of shares. [Section 111]
6. Right to apply to the Company Law Board for rectification of register of members.
7. Right to receive share/stock certificate within the prescribed period. [Section 113]
8. Right to inspect register of members, register of debentureholders, Index and copies of annual returns and to obtain extracts or copy thereof.
9. Right to receive a copy of Statutory Report. [Section 165]
10. Right to make requisition to convene an extra ordinary meeting. [Section 169]
11. Right to request the Company Law Board for calling an annual general meeting when the Board of directors fail to call such meeting or apply for an extraordinary meeting of the company whenever necessary. [Sections 167 and 186]
12. Right to have his name entered in the register of members.
13. Right to receive notice of meetings, to attend, to appoint a proxy and vote at the meeting.
14. Right to demand poll. [Section 179]
15. Right to receive proper notice of resolutions requiring special notice. [Section 196(2)]
16. Right to have on request minutes of proceedings at a general meeting. [Section 192(2)]
17. Right to receive copies of Balance Sheet, Profit and Loss Account and Director's report before the annual general meeting. [Section 210 and 219]
18. Right to participate in the appointment of auditors at the annual general meeting. [Sections 224 and 225]
19. Right to inspect the Auditor's Report at AGM [Section 230]
20. Right to apply to the Company Law Tribunal for ordering an investigation into the affairs of the company. [Section 235 and 237]
21. Right to remove a director by joining with others. [Section 284]
22. Right to present petition to the Company Law Tribunal for relief in cases of oppression and mismanagement. [Section 397 and 398]
23. Right to present petition to High Court for the winding up of the company. [Sections 433 and 484(1) (b)]
24. Right to share in the surplus assets of the company on winding up. [Sections 475 and 511]

25. Right to associate in the declaration of dividends and to apply to the court for an injunction restraining the directors from paying dividends on an ultra vires declaration or out of capital.
26. Right to participate in appointmet and in fixation of remuneration of one or more liquidators in the case of a Member's Voluntary Winding up and to fill any vacancy in the office of a liquidator so appointed by him. [Sections 490 and 492]

6.0 DUTIES AND LIABILITIES OF MEMBERS

6.1 Duties of Members

1. To take shares when they are allotted in due time and in compliance with the provisions of the Act, unless the refusal to accept the shares has been sent on the ground of non-compliance with the provisions of the Act as regards the issue of the prospectus or as regards allotment.
2. To abide by the doing of the majority of members unless the majority acts vindictively, oppressively, *mala fide* or fraudulently.

6.2 Liabilities of Members

1. **In Case of Unlimited Company** Every member of such a company is liable for all debts contracted by the company during the period when he was a member.
2. **In Case of Company Limited by Guarantee** Every member is liable to contribute to the extent of the amount guaranteed by him which is given in the liability clause of the memorandum.
3. **In Case of Company Limited by Shares** The majority of the companies belong to this category. In the case of such companies, the liability of a member is limited to the amount unpaid on the shares held by him. If he has paid full amount on shares, his liability is nil.
4. It may be noted that all money payable by any member to the company under the memorandum or articles are a debt due from him to the company [Section 36]. If a shareholder dies and he was holding partly paid-up shares, then his estate will be liable or the legal representatives will be liable for the unpaid amount.
5. **Unlimited Liability on Reduction of Membership below Minimum:** If at any time the number of members is reduced below the statutory number (seven for public company and two for private company), and the company carries on business for more than 6 months while the number is so reduced, every member becomes severally liable for the debts of the company contracted **after** the said period of 6 months.

7.0 IS A CONTRACT TO TAKE SHARES IN A COMPANY GOVERNED BY THE SAME RULES AS ANY OTHER CONTRACT?

The same rules which govern the contract under the law of contracts also apply to a contract to take shares.

1. **Offer by Applicant** An application to subscribe shares/debentures in response to a prospectus (which is an invitation to make an offer) is treated as an offer made by the applicant to the company.
2. **Revocation of Offer**
   (a) The applicant can revoke his application, before the notice of the allotment is put in the course of transmission to him e.g. by post. [*Wallance's* case (1920)].
   (b) The aforesaid application generally cannot be revoked untill after the expiry of the 6th day after the opening of the subscription list, or the giving, of a public notice by some responsible person u/s 62 having the effect of excluding, limiting or diminishing the responsibility of that person before the expiry of said 5th day.

3. **Acceptance of an Offer** Allotment to the applicant with the notice thereof constitutes an acceptance of an offer. Acceptance must be communicated to the applicant in some way whether by writing or verbally or conduct. [*Gun's* case (1867)]
   (a) Even a notice of allotment brought to the applicant, not from the company but elsewhere will be binding on him. [*Wall's* case (1863)]
   (b) Where shares have been applied for prior to the company's incorporation, allotment and notice thereof after incorporation in response to such application constitute a complete contract because the application operates as a continuing offer and when the company accepts it after incorporarion, it matures into a binding contract. [*Lawarence's* case (1866)]
4. **Application Subject to Condition**
   (a) Where the application has been made subject to a condition precedent, the applicant becomes a member only when the condition is complied with
   (b) where the application has been subject to a condition subsequent, the applicant becomes a member in present, when he accepts the notice of allotment and his name is placed on the Register of Members. If the company goes into liquidation before the fulfilment of condition by the company, he cannot escape his liability as contributory. He may be entitled to damages against the company for its failure in carrying out the condition. [*Fishes's* case (1885)]

   Since the liability of a contributory arises *exlege and net ex contracts*, he cannot set up the non-fulfilment of the condition as a defence against his statutory liability as a contributory, which is the direct result of his being a member of the company. [*Hansraj* v. *Astana* 35]
5. **Entry on Register of Members** The applicant by agreeing to take shares, merely agrees to become a member but does not actually become a member, he becomes a member only when his name is entered on the Register of Members. [*Odessa Tramways Co.* v. *Mande* (1878)]

Conclusion Now it may be conclued that the statement that "a contract to take shares in a company is governed by the same rules as any other contract" is fully correct.

8.0 REGISTER OF MEMBERS [SECTION 150]

8.1 Which Company is Required to Maintain Register of Member

Every company must keep a register of its members containing the following particulars:

8.2 Contents of Register of Members

The Register of Members must contain the following particulars:

(i) the name, address and occupation, if any, of each member.
(ii) the shares held by each member with their individual numbers and the amount paid or agreed to be considered as paid on the shares of each member;
(iii) the date on which each person was entered in the register as a member;
(iv) the date on which each person ceased to be a member; and
(v) where the shares have been converted into stock, the register show the amount of stock held by each member instead of the amount and particulars relating to shares.

Notes:
(i) In the case of joint shareholders, names of all joint shareholders must be entered in the register and the notices etc., be sent to the first named joint shareholder.
(ii) No notice of any trust, express or implied is allowed to be entered on the register of members.

8.3. Consequences of Default

In case of default, the company and its every officer in default, is punishable with a fine which upto Rs 500 for every day during which the default continues.

The register must be kept up-to-date containing all changes that might be taking place from time to time.

8.4. Place of Keeping the Register [Section 163(1)]

The register must be kept at the registered office of the company unless some other place (though it must be in the city, town or village where the registered office is situated) has been approved by a special resolution in the general meeting and the Registrar of Companies has been given in advance a copy of the proposed special resolution.

8.5. Prima Facie Evidence

Section 164 of the Act provides that the register of members shall be a *prima facie*, but not conclusive, evidence of membership. It is a *prima facie* evidence of matters required or authorised to be contained therein. The court will accept the same as correct until rebutted.

8.6 Form of Register

The form of the register is prescribed by the government. The companies can either adopt this form or any other form closely resembling to this. Separate registers in different colours should be maintained for different types of shares.

9.0 INDEX OF MEMBERS

9.1 Which Company is Required to Maintain Index of Members

Every company having more than 50 members must keep an index unless the register serves the purpose of index.

9.2. Place of Keeping the Index

The index must be kept at the same place as the register of members.

9.3. Contents of Index of Members

The index must contain sufficient indication to enable the account of each member in the register of members to be easily found.

9.4. Entry of Alteration

If any alteration is made in the register of members, the company must make the necessary alteration in the index within 14 days after the date on which the alteration is made in the register.

9.5. Consequences of Default

In case of default the company and its every officer in default, is punishable with a fine which upto Rs 500 for every day during which the default continues.

10.0 RESISTER AND INDEX OF BENEFICIAL OWNERS [SECTION 152A]

The register and index of beneficial owners maintained by the depository under Section 11 of Depositories Act, 1996 shall be deemed to a register and index of member.

11.0 INSPECTION OF REGISTER

11.1 Public Document [Section 163(2)]

(a) A company's register of members is a public document and open to public inspection.
(b) The register of members and index must be open to inspection by members free and by any other person on payment of Rs 10 for each inspection.
(c) The register must remain open for at least 2 business hours each day except when the register is closed under the provisions of the Act.
(d) The right to inspect also includes the right to make extracts from the register.

11.2 Duty of Company [Sections 163(3) and 163(4)]

The company must supply a copy of the register, index etc. within 10 days, exclusive of non-working days on payment of Re 1 for every 100 words or fractional part thereof required to be copied.

11.3 Penality for Default [Section 163(5)]

If inspection is refused or a copy is not sent within a period of 10 days, the company and its every officer in default shall be punishable in respect of each offence with fine upto Rs 500 for every day during which the default continues.

Notes:

(i) The object of inspecting the register is immaterial.
(ii) The right to inspect ceases upon the circumstances of winding up and if an inspection is required after that, an order of the court must be obtained under Section 549. [*Re Rent Coalfield Syndicate*, (1898) 1. Q.B. 754]

12.0 NO NOTICE OF TRUST IN REGISTER OF MEMBER [SECTION 153]

No notice of trust, express or implied or constructive shall be entered in the Register of members [Section 153]

This expression means "In the Register of Members only the name of registered shareholder must be entered without mentioning the name of beneficial owner on whose behalf registered shareholder is holding the shares.

Example—If X purchases shares in the name of Y, X wil be beneficial owners and Y will be a trustee. In Register of Member the name of Y only will be included without any mention of his being a trustee on X's behalf.

13.0 CLOSURE OF REGISTER

According to Section 154 of the Act, a company may close the register of members for a period not exceeding 45 days in a year but not exceeding 30 days at any one time. For closing the register at least 7 day's notice must be given by advertisement in some newspaper circulating in the district in which the registered office of the company is situated.

It is compulsory to close the register of members before annual general meeting of the shareholders and before declaring the bonus issue. During the period of closure of the register of members, no transfer of shares is registered. Contravention of these provisions will entail a fine of Rs 5,000 for each day of wrong closure.

14.0 FOREIGN REGISTER OF MEMBERS [SECTION 157]

1. A company, may, if so authorised by its articles, keep in any state or country outside India a branch register (called as foreign register) of its members resident in that state or country.
2. The company must within 30 days from the date of the opening of any foreign register notify the Registrar about the place where such register is kept.
3. Any change in the situation of the office or of its discontinuance shall be duly notified to the Registrar within 30 days of the date of change or discontinuance.
4. A foreign register shall be deemed to be part of the company's register of members.
5. The company must keep a duplicate of every foreign register.
6. A copy of every entry made in the foreign register must be transmitted to the head office in India.
7. The head office in India must record the same in the duplicate register maintained by it.

15.0 RECTIFICATION OF REGISTER [SECTION 111(4)]

15.1 Power of CLT

The Company Law Tribunal is empowered to order the rectification of the register of members in the following cases:

(a) Where the name of a person is entered, without sufficient cause, or

(b) Where the name of person having been entered in the register, is, without sufficient cause, omitted therefrom,

(c) Where default is made or unnecessary delay taken place in entering in the register the fact of any person having become or ceased to be a member.

15.2 Who can Apply for Rectification

The person aggrieved or any member of the company or the company may apply to the Company Law Board for rectification of the registers.

15.3 Power of CLB

The Company Law Board shall hear the concerned parties and after hearing them may either dismiss the appeal or reject the application or by order direct the rectification of the register. The CLB may also direct the company to pay damages, if any, sustained by the aggrieved party.

EXERCISES

VERY SHORT ANSWER TYPE QUESTIONS

1. Who is called a member?
2. Who is called a shareholder?

SHORT ANSWER TYPE QUESTIONS

1. Name the persons who are called members.
2. All shareholders need not be members. Comment.
3. All members need not be shareholders. Comment.
4. Enumerate the various modes of acquiring membership.
5. Who can become a member?
6. A subsidiary company can become member of its holding company. Comment.
7. Write short notes on the following:
   (a) Register of members
   (b) Index of members
   (c) Inspection of Register
   (d) Closure of Register
   (e) Rectification of Register
   (f) Foreign Register of Member.
8. Comment on the following:
   (a) A minor may become a member of a company.
   (b) A company cannot become a member of another company.
   (c) Every shareholder is a member but every member is not necessarily a shareholder.
9. Who may apply for rectification of the register of member and under what circumstances?
10. When does the liability of a member of a limited company become unlimited?
11. Distinguish between a members and shareholders.

LONG ANSWER TYPE QUESTIONS

1. Explain the various modes of acquiring membership.
2. (a) Can minor or lunatic become a member?
   (b) State the position when shares are allotted to a minor and his name appears on the Registers of Members.
   (c) State the position after attaining majority.
   (d) State the position of minor as transferee of fully paid shares.
3. State the position of a company as a member of another company.
4. Explain the ways in which a person may cease to be a member.
5. Enumerate any 10 statuary rights of members.
6. Explain the liabilities of members.
7. In what ways may a person (i) become (ii) cease to be a member of a company.
8. State giving reasons as to whether the following can become member in a company:
   (a) A Minor (b) A Company (c) A Firm
   (d) A Foreigner (e) An Insolvent
9. What are the provisions of the Companies Act as regards maintenance, location, inspection and closing of the company's register of members?
10. What is meant by rectification of register of members? What are the remedies open to a person where his request for rectification is refused by the company?

CHAPTER

10 Dividend, Interest and Bonus Shares

1.0 MEANING OF DIVIDEND

Dividend ordinarily means that portion of divisible profits or reserves which is distributed among the shareholders of a company which is a going concern.

In case of a liquidating company, dividend means a division of the realised assets among the creditors and contributories according to their respective rights. [*CIT* v. *Girdhar Dass & Co. (P) Ltd.* Supreme Court]

The Institute of Chartered Accountants of India has defined 'dividend' as a "a distribution to shareholders out of profits or reserves available for this purpose." [*Guidance Note on terms used in Financial Statements*]

2.0 CAN A COMPANY DECLARE AND DISTRIBUTE DIVIDEND IF THE MEMORANDUM AND ARTICLES ARE SILENT?

Yes, a company can declare and distribute dividend even if its Memorandum and Articles are silent because it has an inherent power to declare and distribute dividend. Such power need not expressly be given by the Memorandum or Articles though the Articles may regulate the manner in which dividends are to be distributed.

3.0 LEGAL PROVISIONS RELATING TO DIVIDEND

3.1. Sources from which Dividends can be Declared or Paid [Section 205(1)]

Section 205(1) of the Companies Act, specifies the following **three sources** from which dividends can be declared or paid:

(i) out of profits of current financial year;

(ii) out of undistributed profits of the previous financial year or years;

(iii) out of moneys provided by the Central Government or State Government for payment of dividend in pursuance of a guarantee given by that government.

3.2. Provision for Depreciation [Section 205(1)(a), (1)(c), (2)]

(a) Before declaring any dividend, the company must provide for:

(i) depreciation for current financial year, and

(ii) arrears of depreciation for previous financial year or years after the commencement of The Companies (Amendment) Act, 1960

(b) **Exception to above [Section 205(1)(c)]** The Central Government may allow any company to declare dividend without providing for depreciation if it thinks necessary to do so in the public interest.

(c) **Methods of Depreciation [Section 205(2)]**
Section 205(2) provides that depreciation must be provided *either*—
  (i) to the extent specified in Section 350, or
  Section 350 provides that depreciation should be written off at the rates specified for different assets in Schedule XIV to the Companies Act, 1956. Provision is required only for the normal depreciation (including extra and multiple shift allowance) and not for any initial depreciation or any development rebate. Further, when the asset is sold, discarded, demolished or destroyed in any financial year, the excess of the written down value over its sale proceeds as scrap, if any should be written off in the same financial year.
  (ii) equal to an amount arrived at by dividing 95% of the original cost of the asset by such number of years at the end of which at least 95% of original cost of the asset would have been provided for, or
  (iii) on any other basis approved by the Government by which 95% of the cost of each depreciable assets will be written off on the expiry of specified period; or
  (iv) As regards any other depreciable asset for which no rate of depreciation has been laid down by the Act, or any rules made thereunder, on such basis as may be approved by the Central Government.

Note: A company need not provide for depreciation if it does not want to declare dividends. In such a case, the fact that depreciation has not been provided for or written off, together with the quantum of arrears of depreciation [computed as per Section 205(2)], must be stated in the Profit and Loss Account.

3.3. Provision relation to Past Losses [Section 205(1)(b)]

Before declaring any dividend, the company must provide for—
 (i) the amount of loss, or
 (ii) the amount of depreciation provided in that year or those years whichever is less.

Thus, past losses to the extent the losses are due to depreciation provided, must be provided for.

Practical Illustration 1

	Rs (in lakh)		
	20X1	*20X2*	*20X3*
1. Profit (Loss) before charging Depreciation	(5)	6	16
2. Depreciation Chargeable u/s 205	3	7	6
3. Profit (Loss) after charging depreciation	(8)	(1)	10

Required Calculate the divisible profits for the year 20X3

Solution:

Divisible profit for the year 20X3 is Rs 6,00,000 as shown below:

	Rs (in lakh)
A. Profits for the year 20X3	16
B. *Less:*	
(a) Depreciation for 20X3	(6)
(b) Past Loss of Rs 8 lakh or Depreciation of Rs 3 lakh whichever is lower (for 20X1)	(3)

(c) Past loss of Rs 1 lakh or Depreciation of Rs 7 lakh whichever is lower (for 20X2) (1)

C. Divisible Profits for the year 20X3 6

3.4 Transfer of Profits to Reserves [Section 205(2A)]

(a) Minimum Transfer

According to The Companies (*Transfer of Profits to Reserves*) Rules, 1975, a company declaring or paying a dividend exceeding 10% out of current profits, must transfer the prescribed % of current profits to reserve as follows:

Rate of proposed dividend (as % of paid up capital)	*Minimum % of current profits to be transferred to reserve*
(i) *Where the Rate of Proposed dividend exceeds 10% but not 12.5%*	2.5%
(ii) *Where the Rate of Proposed Dividend exceeds 12.5% but not 15%*	5.0%
(iii) *Where the Rate of Proposed Dividend exceeds 15% but not 20%*	7.5%
(iv) *Where the Rate of proposed Dividend exceeds 20%*	10%

Notes:

(i) Meaning of the term 'Dividend' The term '**Dividend**' implies only equity dividend and that portion of dividend relating to participating preference shares which is over and above the fixed rate of preference dividend. [*Circular No. 8/76 dated 18.5.1976 of the Deptt. of Company Affairs*]

(ii) Meaning of the term 'Current Profits' The term '**Current Profits**' implies profits after tax after statutory transfer to Development rebate reserve (Investment Allowance Reserve) and arrears of depreciation. [*Circular No. 8/76 dated 18.5.1976 of the deptt. of company affairs, Govt. of India*]

(iii) Meaning of the Term 'Reserves' The term '**Reserves**' implies only free reserves and does not include Development Rebate Reserve, Capital Reserve or any Special Reserve. [*Circular No. 8/76 dated 18.5.1976 of the Deptt. of Company Affairs, Govt. of India*]

Practical Illustration 2

TULSIAN Ltd provides you the following information as at 31st March 20X5:

12%, 10,000 Preference Shares of Rs 100 each

40,000 Equity of Rs 10 each fully paid up

30,000 Equity Shares of Rs 10 each fully called up [(call @ Rs 2 unpaid on 5,000 equity shares)

20,000 Equity Shares of Rs 10 each. Rs 8 per share called up and paid up

Profit and Loss Account (as on 1.4.20X4) Rs 8,00,000

General Reserve (as on 1.4.20X4) Rs 3,00,000

Profit after Interest and Tax for the year 20X4-20X5 Rs 2,40,000

Required Calculate the minimum amount required to be transferred to Reserve for the year 20X4-20X5, if the Board of Directors proposes an equity dividend of (a) 10% (b) 12.5% (c) 15% (d) 20% (e) 21%.

Solution:

Case	Rate of Equity Dividend	Minimum % of current profit to be transferred to Reserve	Amount of Profits to be transferred to Reserve
(a)	10%	0%	0% of Rs 2,40,000 = 0
(b)	12.5%	2.5%	2.5% of Rs 2,40,000 = Rs 6,000
(c)	15%	5%	5% of Rs 2,40,000 = Rs 12,000
(d)	20%	7.5%	7.5% of Rs 2,40,000 = Rs 18,000
(e)	21%	10%	10% of Rs 2,40,000 = Rs 24,000

(b) Can a Company Transfer more than 10% of its Current Profits to Reserves?

A company can transfer more than 10% of its current profits to reserve if it satisfies the following two conditions:

Condition 1. If a dividend is declared, the dividend rate must be at least equal to the average dividend rate of the company in the 3 years immediately preceding the financial year. In case bonus shares have been issued in the financial year in which the dividend is declared or in the 3 years immediately preceding the financial year, the total dividend amount should be at least equal to the average amount of dividends declared over the 3 years immediately preceding the financial year. However, if the current net profits after tax are lower by 20 per cent or more, as compared to the average net profits after tax of the 2 financial years immediately preceding, it shall not be necessary to ensure the minimum distribution.

Condition 2. Where no dividend is declared, the amount proposed to be transferred to the reserves from the current profits must be lower than the average amount of the dividends to the shareholders declared by the company over the 3 years immediately preceding the financial year.

Practical Illustration 3

Tulsian Ltd. provides you the following information:

Year	Rate of dividend	Amount of paid up equity share capital
20X1-20X2	10%	1,00,000
20X2-20X3	15%	1,00,000
20X3-20X4	17%	1,00,000

Profits after interest and tax for 20X4-20X5 – Rs 2,00,000.

Required Can the company transfer profits of Rs 22,000 to reserves if the rate of dividend declared by the company is (a) 0% (b) 13% (c) 14%?

Solution:

Case (a) If Rate of Dividend declared is 0%

Decision: The company can not transfer profits of Rs 22,000 to reserves.

Provision: Where no dividend is declared, the amount proposed to be transferred to the reserves from the current profits should be lower than the average amount of dividends to the shareholders declared by the company over the 3 years immediately preceeding the financial year.

Reason: Average Amount of Dividend
= (Rs 10,000 + Rs 15,000 + Rs 17,000)/3 = Rs 14,000
Since proposed transfer of Rs 22,000 exceeds the average amount of Rs 14,000 the company cannot transfer Rs 22,000.

Case (b) If Rate of Dividend declared is 13%

Decision: The company cannot transfer profits of Rs 22,000 to reserves.

Provision: Where dividend is declared, the dividend rate should be at least equal to average dividend rate during the 3 years immediately preceeding the financial year.

Reason: Average Rate of Dividend = (10% + 15% + 17%)/3 = 14%
Since the actual rate of dividend (i.e. 13%) is lower than the average rate of dividend of 14%, the company can not transfer Rs 22,000 to reserves.

Case (c): If Rate of Dividend declared is 14%

Provision: Where dividend is declared, the dividend rate should be at least equal to average dividend rate during the 3 years immediately preceding the financial year.

Reason: Average Rate of Dividend = (10% + 15% + 17%)/3 = 14%
Since the actual rate of dividend (i.e. 14%) is equal to the average rate of dividend of 14%, the company can transfer Rs 22,000.

3.5. Declaration of Dividend out of Reserves [Section 205A(3)]

According to The Companies (*Declaration of Dividend out of Reserves*) Rules, 1975, in the event of inadequacy or absence of profit in any year, dividend may be declared by a company for that year out of the reserves as at the beginning of that year, subject to the following 3 conditions:

(i) the rate of the dividend declared must not exceed the average rate of dividend declared in 5 years immediately preceding that year or 10% of its paid-up capital, whichever is less:

(ii) the total amount so drawn from the reserves must not exceed 10% of the sum of its paid up capital and free reserves and the amount so drawn shall first be utilised to set off the losses incurred in the financial year before any dividend in respect of preference or equity is declared; and

(iii) the balance of reserves after such drawal must be at least 15% of its paid up share capital.

Practical Illustration 4

X Ltd. provides you the following information:

Year	*Rate of dividend declared*	*Paid up capital*
20X1-20X2	9%	Rs 1,00,000
20X2-20X3	8%	Rs 1,00,000
20X3-20X4	10%	Rs 1,00,000
20X4-20X5	7%	Rs 1,00,000
20X5-20X6	6%	Rs 1,00,000

Reserves as on 1.4.20X6 Rs 50,000

Loss after charging depreciation for the year 20X6-20X7 Rs 6,000

Depreciation for year 20X6-20X7 Rs 6,000

Required: X Ltd. desires to declare divided for the loss year 20X6-20X7. Can it do so? If yes, at what rate, it may declare dividend?

Solution:

Step 1 Maximum withdrawal of Reserve if condition (iii) is satisfied

A. Opening Balance of Reserves in the beginning of the year	50,000
B. *Less:* Closing Balance of Reserve being 15% of paid up share capital	15,000
C. Reserve available (A – B)	35,000

Step 2 Maximum withdrawal of Reserve if condition (ii) is satisfied
= 10% of Paid up Capital and free reserves
= 10% of (Rs 1,00,000 + 50,000) = Rs 15,000

Step 3 Permissible withdrawal of Reserve if conditions (ii) and (iii) are satisfied
= Rs 15,000 (being lower of limits as per Step 1 and Step 2)

Step 4 Maximum Permissible Divisible Profits

A. Permissible withdrawal of Reserve (*as per Step 3*)	15,000
B. *Less:* Loss to the extent of depreciation	6,000
C. Maximum Permissible Divisible profit [A – B]	9,000

Step 5 Actual Permissible Rate of Dividend

A. Maximum Permissible Rate of Dividend $\left(\frac{\text{Rs } 9000}{\text{Rs } 1,00,000} \times 100\right) = 9\%$

B. Average Rate of Dividend based on 5 years [(9% + 8% + 10% + 7% + 6%)/5]	8%
C. Maximum Rate of Dividend as % of paid up capital	10%
D. Actual Permissible Rate of Dividend being lowest of three i.e.	8%

3.6. No Default in Compliance of Section 80A [Section 205(2B)]

A company which fails to redeem its redeemable preference shares in accordance with Section 80A of the Act, cannot declare any dividends on its equity shares so long the default continues.

3.7. Dividend in cash [Section 205(3)]

Dividend must be payable except in cash. But this shall not in any way affect the company's right to capitalise its profits or reserves for purposes of issuing fully paid-up bonus shares or paying up any unpaid amount on any shares held by the members of the company.

3.8. Dividend through Cheque or Warrant [Section 205(5)(b)]

Any dividend payable in cash may be paid by cheque or warrant sent through the post directed to the registered address of the shareholder entitled to the payment of the dividend. In case of shares held jointly it may be sent to the registered address of the joint shareholder named first on the register of members, or to such person and to such address as the shareholder or the joint shareholders may in writing direct.

3.9. To whom Dividend is to be Paid [Section 206]

Dividend is to be paid only to the registered holder of shares or to his order or to his banker. In the case of share warrants dividend is payable to the bearer of such warrant or to his bankers.

3.10 Deposit in Separate Bank Account [Section 205(1A) and (1B)]

The dividend declared must be deposited in a separate bank account within 5 days of its declaration and the same shall be used for payment of dividend.

3.11 Time Limit for Payment and Penalty [Section 207]

(a) **Time limit**—The dividend must be paid or the dividend warrant must be posted within 30 days of the declaration of the dividend of the company.

(b) **Penalty**—If a company fails to pay or post the dividend warrant within the stipulated period of 30 days, every director who is knowingly a party to such default shall be punishable with imprisonment upto 3 years and also a fine Rs 1,000 for everyday during which such default continues and the company shall be liable to pay simple interest @ 18% per annum for the period of default.

(c) **Defences**—But no offence shall be deemed to have been committed:

(a) where the dividend could not be paid by reason of the operation of any law.

(b) where a shareholder has given direction to the company regarding the payment of the dividend and those directions cannot be compiled with.

(c) where there is a dispute regarding the right to receive any dividend.

(d) where the dividend had been lawfully adjusted by the company against any sum due to it from the shareholder.

(e) where for any other reason, the failure to pay the dividend or to post the warrant within the period aforesaid was not due to any default on the part of the company.

3.12 Unpaid/Unclaimed Dividend [Section 205A, 205B or C]

(a) **Duty of Company to Transfer to Special Dividend Account**

The company must transfer the total amount of dividend which remains unpaid/unclaimed within 30 days of its declaration, to a special account 'Unpaid Dividend Account of ... Company limited/Company (Private) Limited, within 7 days of the expiry of aforesaid 30 days. This account is to be opened in a Scheduled Bank.

(b) **Penalty for Default in Transfer [Section 205A(4)]**

If unpaid/unclaimed dividend is not transferred to unpaid dividend account within the stipulated period of 7 days, the company shall be liable to pay interest @ 12% p.a. The interest accruing on such an amount shall ensure to the benefit to the members of the company, in proportion to the amount remaining unpaid to them.

(c) **Payment of Unclaimed/unpaid Dividend [Section 205B]**

Any person claiming to be entitled to any money transferred to the unpaid/unclaimed dividend account may make an application to the Central Government within 7 years form the date of transfer for an order for payment of money claimed after taking such security from him as it may think fit.

(d) **Investor Education and Protection Fund [Section 205C]**

(i) **Transfer of Unclaimed/Unpaid Dividend after 7 Years**

If any amount transferred to unpaid dividend account remains unclaimed/unpaid for 7 years, it shall be transferred by the company to the 'Investor Education and Protection Fund'.

(ii) **Objective of the Fund**

The Fund shall be used for promotion of investors' awareness and protection of interests of investors in accordance with such rules as may be prescribed.

(iii) **Power of Central Government to Constitute Committee**

The Central Government shall by notification in the Official Gazette, constitute a committee to administer the Fund, and maintain separate accounts and other relevant records in relation to the Fund in such form as may be prescribed in consultation with the Comptroller and Auditor General of India.

(iv) Power of Committee to Spend

The committee shall be entitled to spend money out of the fund for carrying out the objectives of the fund.

(v) Amount to be Credited to Fund

The following amounts shall be credited to the fund:

(a) Unpaid dividends
(b) Matured deposits with companies
(c) Refund of application money
(d) Matured debentures with the companies
(e) Interest accrued on the amounts referred to in Clauses (a) to (d) above.
(f) Grants and donations given to the fund by the Central Government, State Government, Companies or any other institution.
(g) The interest or other income received out of instruments made from the fund.

4.0 RIGHT TO DIVIDEND, RIGHT SHARES AND BONUS SHARES TO BE HELD IN ABEYANCE PENDING REGISTRATION OF TRANSFER OF SHARES [SECTION 206A]

Where any instrument of transfer of shares has been delivered to any company for registration and the transfer of such shares has not been registered by the company, it shall—

(a) transfer the dividend on such shares to the special account referred to in Section 205A unless the registered shareholder authorises the company in writing to pay such dividend to the transferee;
(b) Keep in abeyance in relation to such shares any offer of right shares u/s 81(1)(a) and any issue of fully paid bonus shares u/s 205(3).

Notes:

(i) Unless otherwise agreed, the buyer is entitled to all benefits (i.e. dividend, bonus, right shares) declared after the date of purchase and the seller is entitled to all benefits declared before the date of sale. *For example*, in case of ex-dividend transfer, the seller and in case of cum-dividend transfer, the buyer have the right to receive dividend.
(ii) The company is liable to pass on these benefits only to the person (whether buyer or seller) whose name appears in the Register of Members as on the 'Record Date' fixed for the purpose.

5.0 DECLARATION OF DIVIDEND

5.1 Who takes Dividend Decision?

The dividend decision is taken by the Board of Directors and is then recommended to the shareholders for their final approval at AGM (i.e., Annual General Meeting) of the company. The shareholders can reduce the amount of dividend even to zero but can not increase the amount of dividend as recommended by the Board of Directors. If the directors decide not to declare and dividend, the shareholders in general meeting cannot themselves declare it.

5.2 Declaration of Dividend at AGM/EGM [Regulation 85 of Table A]

(i) A company usually declares dividend at its annual general meeting. But it may declare dividend at any other general meeting (Regulation 85 and Table 'A') unless the articles provide otherwise.
(ii) A company cannot declare a further dividend after having declared a final dividend at its annual general meeting.

(iii) It may also be noted that there can be no declaration of dividend for past years in respect of which the accounts have already been closed at previous annual general meetings.

5.3 When Dividend becomes a debt?

(a) Dividend becomes a debt due from the company on its declaration by shareholders at AGM and not on its recommendation by the Board of Directors.

(b) Shareholders may sue the company for its recovery after expiry of the period prescribed by Section 207.

(c) Suit for dividend can be filed only at the place where the registered office of the company is situated.

(d) If a company goes into liquidation, a declared unpaid dividend will not rank with other debts due to creditors. It will only be taken into account for adjustment of the rights of shareholders as contributories (Section 426(1)(g)).

(e) Cumulative preference shareholders are entitled to claim the arrears of dividends on the winding up of the company even when the dividends were never declared on such shares.

(f) But a declaration of a dividend subject to a condition precedent like subject to remittances from Pakistan is not a declaration at all as such a declaration will not allow the shareholder to sue the company until the condition if fulfilled and therefore, does not create an immediately payable debt. [*Jhimi Bajoria* v. *CIT* (1920)]

5.4 Revocation of Declared Dividend

Dividends once declared cannot be revoked except with the consent of the shareholders. But the board of directors may revoke it under the following circumstances:

(a) where it has been declared illegally or

(b) where due to certain compelling circumstances such as fire destroying company's property, or the outbreak of a war, or the imposition of a new killing tax burden, it has become necessary to conserve the remaining assets of the company.

6.0 DIVIDEND OUT OF CAPITAL PROFITS

(a) **Three conditions for declaring dividend out of Capital Profits**. A company may distribute its capital profits as dividend provided—

(a) Such profits have been realised in cash,

(b) Such profits exists after *bona fide* revaluation of all the assets and liabilities, and

(c) the articles permit such a distribution amongst shareholders. [*Lubbock* v. *British Bank of South Africa* (1892)]

This implies that where there is appreciation in the value of certain assets and fall in the value of certain others, it is only the net surplus which can be considered for payment of dividend.

In other words, the *all Capital losses* must be provided for before declaring any dividend out of *Capital profits*.

Thus, if Articles permit, capital profits realised in cash may be used to declare any dividend after providing for all capital losses.

(b) Depending upon the results disclosed by such a revaluation, with the approval of the shareholders, the assets, which may have been over depreciated in the past may be written up and the surplus, if any, resulting therefrom utilised for writing down value of other assets, so that the value of each assets is brought closer to its current value (*Ammonia Soda Co.* v. *Chamberlain*).

(c) Where any expenditure of a capital nature has been charged to revenue the company can subsequently reimburse an equal amount of revenue, out of capital. Similarly, when losses can subsequently reinburse an equal amount of revenue and later the value of the capital assets appreciates, the amount so realised would be a revenue profit (*Mills* v. *Northern Railway of Buenos Aires Co.*)

7.0 INTERIM DIVIDEND

7.1 Meaning of An Interim Dividend

Interim dividend is the dividend which is declared between two annual general meetings. It is declared during the current year for the current year.

7.2 No Limit on Number of Interim Dividends [Regulation 86 of Table A]

The Board may from time to time pay to the members such interim dividends as appear to it to be justified by the profits of the company. Thus, there is not limit on the number of interim dividends a company may declare in a year.

7.3 Conditions subject to which Interim Dividends can be Declared?

An interim dividend cannot be declared unless:

(a) it is authorised by articles,
(b) the provision for depreciation for the whole of current year has been made
(c) the past accumulated losses have been set off
(d) the prescribed percentage of the profits as required u/s 205(2A) has been transferred to reserves.

7.4 The term 'dividend' includes interim dividend also [Section 2(14A)].

7.5 All provisions of the Companies Act which apply to dividends have now become applicable to interim dividends also. [Section 205(1C)]

7.6 The amount of dividend including interim dividend shall be deposited in a separate bank account within 5 days of the declaration of such dividend and the same shall be used for payment of dividend. [Section 205 (1A) and (1B)]

7.7 It is declared by the Board of Directors. It does not require approval of members at general meeting. [*Scott* v. *Scott*, (1943)]

7.8 Before declaring an interim dividend, the directors must satisfy themselves that the financial position of the company warrants the payment of such dividend out of its distributable profits because "the declaration of interim dividends depends much more upon estimates and opinions than the declaration of final dividend which is made upon the information contained in a formal balance sheet." [*Lucas* v. *Fitzgarald* (1903)]

7.9 Distinction between Interim Dividend and Final Dividend.

Interim Dividend differs from Final Dividend in the following respects:

Basis of Distinction	*Interim Dividend*	*Final Dividend*
1. ***Meaning***	Interim dividend is the dividend which is declared between two annual general meetings of the shareholders.	Final dividend is the dividend which is declared at annual general meeting of the shareholders.
2. ***Year of Declaration***	It is declared during the current financial year.	It is declared after the end of financial year.
3. ***Who declares?***	It is declared by the Board of Directors.	It is declared by the shareholders.
4. ***Does declaration constitute a liability?***	Its declaration does not creat a liability against the company.	Its declaration creates a liability against the company.
5. ***Revocation/Variation***	After declaration it can be revoked or varied before its payment.	After declaration it can *neither* be revoked *nor* be varied.

8.0 PAYMENT OF DIVIDEND ON PARTLY PAIDUP SHARES [SECTION 93 AND REGULATION 88]

1. A company may, if so authorised by its articles, pay dividends in proportion to the amount paid up on each share where a larger amount is paid up on some shares than on others. But if the articles do not contain any such provision, dividend will have to be paid only in proportion to the nominal value of shares. [*Oak Bank Oil Co.* v. *Crum,* (1882)]

2. Legal Position as to Dividend on Partly Paid up Shares

Case	*Dividend on partly paid shares*
1. ***Where the articles specify provision in this regard***	Dividend is payable on the nominal/called up/paid up amount of shares as per Articles.
2. ***Where the articles are silent in this regard and Table A has not been excluded.***	
(a) *If some amount has been paid on any of the shares of the company.*	Dividend must be declared and paid on the amount paid up (excluding calls-in-advance) on shares. [Regulation 88(1) and (2)]
(b) *If nothing has been paid on any of the shares of the company.*	Dividend may be declared and paid according to the nominal amounts of the shares.
3. ***Where the Articles are silent in this regard and Table A has been excluded.***	Dividend must be declared and paid on nominal amount of shares.

Practical Illustration 5

X Ltd. provide you the following information:

10,000 Equity Shares of Rs 10 each, Rs 6 per share called up	Rs	60,000
Less: Calls-in-arrears on 1,000 shares @ Rs 2 per share	Rs	2,000
	Rs	58,000
Add: Calls-in-advance on 500 shares @ Rs 3 per share	Rs	1,500
	Rs	59,500

The Board of Director recommend a dividend @ 10%.

Required: Calculate the amount of Proposed Dividend in each of the following alternative cases:

Case (a) If no other information is given.

Case (b) If the Articles prescribe the payment on the nominal amount of shares.

Case (c) If the Articles prescribe the payment of dividend on the called up amount of shares.

Case (d) If the Articles prescribe the payment of dividend on the paid up amount of shares.

Case (e) If the Articles are silent and Table A has not been excluded.

Case (f) If the Articles are silent and Table A has been excluded.

Solution:

Case (a) 10% of Rs 58,000 = Rs 5,800

Case (b) 10% of Rs 1,00,000 = Rs 10,000

Case (c) 10% of Rs 60,000 = Rs 6,000

Case (d) 10% of Rs 58,000 = Rs 5,800

Case (e) 10% of Rs 58,000 = Rs 5,800

Case (f) 10% of Rs 1,00,000 = Rs 10,000

9.0 DIVIDEND ON PREFERENCE SHARES

9.1. Holders of preference shares are entitled to receive a dividend at a fixed rate before any dividend is declared on equity shares. They can exercise this right only when there are sufficient divisible profits and a dividend is declared in accordance with the provisions of the Act.

9.2 Arrears of Dividend in Case of Cumulative Preference Shares

(a) ***If the company is a going concern***	Holders of Cumulative Preference Shares are entitled to receive the arrears of dividend out of the profits of subsequent years before any dividend is paid on equity shares.
(b) ***If the company goes into liquidation*** (i) ***Where Articles contain an express provision to that effect.*** (ii) ***Where Articles are silent*** (a) *If such dividends have been declared* (b) *If such dividends have not been declared.*	(i) Arrears of dividend are payable alongwith return of preference share capital before return of equity capital. (ii) (a) Arrears of dividend are payable alongwith return of preference share capital before return of equity capital. (b) Arrears of undeclared dividends are payable out of any surplus if any left after the return of full preference and equity share capital.

9.3. Dividend in case of Non-cumulative Preference Shares Holders of non-cumulative preference shares are not entitled to receive the arrears of dividend out of the profits of subsequent years if no divided is declared in a particular year or years. In other words, they are entitled to receive the dividend only for the year in which the dividend is declared.

9.4. Dividend in case of Participating Preference Shares Holders of Participants Preference shares are entitled to receive their fixed dividend before any dividend is paid on the equity shares *plus* a fixed percentage of surplus profits remaining after a certain fixed percentage of equity dividend has been paid to equity shareholders.

10.0 PAYMENT OF INTEREST OUT OF CAPITAL [SECTION 208]

10.1 When can a Company Pay Interest on Capital? [Section 208(1)(a)]

A company may pay interest on paid up capital where any shares are issued to raise money to defray the expenses of the construction of any work or building or the provision of any plant which cannot be made profitable for a lengthy period.

10.2 How can the Interest on Capital be Treated? [Section 208(1)(b)]

A company may charge the interest so paid to capital as part of the cost of construction of the work or building or the provision of the plant.

10.3 What are the Conditions Subject to which Payment of Interest on Capital may be Made?

(a) Such payment must be authorised by Articles or a Special Resolution.

(b) Previous sanction of the Central Government must be obtained.

(c) Such payment must be made only for such period as may be determined by the Central Government.

But such period cannot extend beyond the close of the half year next after the half year during which the work or building or provision of plant has been actually completed. For example, if the construction is over on 17th January 2005, interest cannot be paid after 31st December 2005.

(d) The rate of interest must not exceed 4% p.a. or rate prescribed by the Central Government (i.e. at present 12%).

10.4 Power of the Central Government [Section 208(4)]

The Central Government may hold on an enquiry at the company' expense before granting its sanction and may require the company to give security for the payment of the costs of the inquiry.

10.5 Shall Payment of Interest Operate as a Reduction of Capital? [Section 208(7)]

The payment of the interest shall not operate as a reduction of the paid up share capital on which it is paid.

10.6 Non-applicability of Section 208

Section 208 does not affect any company to which the Indian Railway Companies Act, 1895 or the Indian Tramways Act, 1902 applies.

11.0 CAPITALISATION OF PROFITS

11.1 Meaning of Capitalisation of Profits

Capitalisation of profits refers to the process of converting profits or reserves into paid up capital.

11.2 How to Capitalise Profits? [Provisio to Section 205(3)]

A company may capitalise its profits. or reserves—

(a) by paying up amounts unpaid on existing partly paid shares so as to make them fully paid up shares, or
(b) by issuing fully paid bonus shares to the existing members.

11.3 Procedure Relating to Issue of Bonus Shares [Regulations 96 and 97 of Table A]

1. **Power to Issue** A company can issue bonus shares if its Articles expressly authorise to do so.
2. **Board's Resolution** A resolution is to be passed by the Board of Directors recommending its decision to issue bonus shares.
3. **Member's Resolution** A resolution is to be passed by the members in the general meeting to approve the Board's resolution recommending the issue of bonus shares. Members' resolution must state—
   (a) an intention to capitalize the profits or reserves, and
   (b) the amount of profits or reserves to be capitalized.
4. **Manner of Application of Profits or Reserves to be Capitalized** The profits or reserves to be capitalized must be applied—
   (a) in paying up amount unpaid on existing partly paid shares so as to make them fully paid up shares, or
   (b) in issuing fully paid bonus shares to the members.

   Note: Such profits or reserves to be capitalized as per resolution must not be paid in cash.
5. **Sources for Capitalization**
   (a) The profits or reserves which otherwise are available for distribution as dividends among the members, may be applied
      (i) in paying up amount unpaid on existing partly paid shares so as to make them fully paid up shares, or
      (ii) in issuing fully paid bonus shares to the members.
   (b) Securities Premium as per [Section 78(2)] and the Capital Redemption Reserve [as per Section 80(5)] which otherwise are not available for distribution as dividend among the members, may be applied in issuing fully paid bonus shares to the members.
6. **Return** A return of the bonus issue alongwith a copy of resolution authorising the issue of Bonus Shares is to be filed with the Registrar within 30 days of the allotment of such shares. Such return must state—
   (a) the number and nominal amount of shares issued
   (b) the names, addresses and occupations of the allottees.

11.4 SEBI Guidelines on Bonus Issues

A listed company proposing to issue bonus shares shall comply with the following:

1. (a) The articles of association of the company must contain a provision for capitalisation of reserves, etc.
   (b) If there is no such provision in the articles the company must pass a resolution at its general body meeting making provision in the articles of association for capitalisation.

2. Consequent to the issue of bonus shares, if the subscribed and paid up capital exceed the authorised share capital a resolution must be passed by the at its general body meeting for increasing the authorised capital.
3. (a) No company shall, pending conversion of FCDs/PCDs, issue any by way of bonus unless similar benefit is extended to the holders of such FCDs/though reservation of shares in proportion to such convertible part of FCDs or PCDs.
   (b) The shares so reserved may be issued at the time of conversion(s) of such debentures on the same terms on which the bonus issues were made.
4. The bonus issue shall be made out of free reserves built out of the profits or securities premium collected in cash only.
5. Reserves created by revaluation of fixed assets are not capitalised.
6. The declaration of bonus issue, in lieu of dividend, is not made.
7. The bonus issue is not to be made unless the partly-paid shares, if any, are made fully paid-up.
8. The company—(a) has not defaulted in payment of interest or principal in respect of fixed deposits and interest on existing debentures or principal on redemption and (b) has sufficient reason to believe that it has not defaulted in respect of payment of statutory dues of the employees such as contribution to provident fund, gratuity, bonus etc.
9. A company which announces its bonus issue after the approval of the Board of directors must implement the proposal within a period of 6 months from such approval and shall not have the option of changing the decision.
10. No bonus issue shall be made within 12 months of public/right issue.

11.5 Distinction between Bonus Shares and Right Shares

Bonus Shares differ from Right Shares in the following respects:

Basis of Distinction	*Bonus Shares*	*Right Shares*
1. **Provisions Applicable**	Sec. 78, Sec. 80, Sec. 205	Sec. 81
2. **Manner of Issue**	These are issued by Capitalizing the accumulated profits or reserves.	These are issued by issuing new share capital.
3. **Consideration**	These are issued without any consideration.	These are issued for cash.
4. **T/f of Right to Receive**	Right to receive bonus shares can not be transferred to another person.	Right to subscribe for right shares can be transferred to another person.
5. **Apply**	Shareholders are not required to apply for bonus shares.	Shareholders are required to apply to subscribe for right shares.
6. **Option**	Shareholders have no option to receive bonus shares less than/ more than those offered.	Shareholders have an option to apply for right shares less than/ more than those offered.
7. **Cash Inflow**	There is no cash inflow.	There is cash inflow.

EXERCISES

SHORT ANSWER TYPE QUESTIONS

1. Distinguish between:
   (a) Bonus Shares and Right Shares
   (b) Interim Dividend and Final Dividend
2. (a) "Dividend can be declared only at annual general meetings". Comment
   (b) "Dividend once declared cannot be revoked" Comment.
   (c) "Interest can be paid out of Capital." Comment.
3. Write a short note on 'Investor Education and Protection Fund'.
4. A company wants to declare bonus by way of (i) converting partly paid shares into fully paid shares, and (ii) issue of fully paid bonus shares.
   State which of the following can be used for this purpose:
   (a) Capital Redemption Reserve
   (b) Securities Premium Account
   (c) Dividend Equalisation Reserve
   (d) General Reserve
   (e) Profit & Loss A/c (Cr.)
   (f) Revaluation Reserve

LONG ANSWER TYPE QUESTIONS

1. "Dividend can be paid only out of profits". Explain with particular reference to the provisions of the Companies Act, 1956.
2. Discuss the provisions of the Companies (Transfer of Profits to Reserves) Rules, 1975.
3. Discuss the provisions of the Companies (Declaration of Dividend out of Reserves) Rules, 1975.
4. Discuss the provisions of the Companies Act, 1956, relating to payment of dividend on shares.
5. How can dividends be paid:
   (a) out of the accumulated profits earned by a company in previous years and transferred by it to reserves?
   (b) out of profits on reissue of the forfeited shares?
   (c) out of the profits of the financial year without transferring any amount to the reserves?
   (d) out of capital profits.
6. What amounts are required to be transferred to Investor Education and Protection Fund? Give provisions of the Companies Act in this regard.
7. Briefly explain the guidelines issued by SEBI in regard to the issue of bonus shares.
8. State the provisions of the Companies Act, 1956 relating to:
   (a) Unpaid/Unclaimed Divided
   (b) Investor Education and Protection Fund
   (c) Interim Dividend
   (d) Payment of Interest out of Capital
   (e) Bonus Shares
   (f) Dividend on partly paid up shares
   (g) Dividend on preference shares

CHAPTER 11

Directors

1.0 DEFINITION OF DIRECTOR AND BOARD OF DIRECTORS

1.1 Definition of Director [Section 2(13) & Explanation 1 to Section 303]

Section 2 (13) defines a director as ***"any person occupying the position of Director by whatever name called."***

This is inclusive and not exhaustive definition. It means that any person who performs the duties of a director will be known as a director irrespective of the name by which he is called. In other words, the persons who direct, conduct, control and manage the affairs of the company are known as Directors. *According to Explanation 1 to Section 303*, ***"any person in accordance with whose direction or instruction, the Board of Directors of a company is accustomed to act, shall also be deemed to be Director of the company."***

1.2 Definition of Board of Directors [Section 252(3)]

The Directors of a company are collectively known as "Board of Directors" or the "Board"

2.0 MINIMUM NUMBER OF DIRECTORS [SECTION 252]

2.1 Minimum Number of Directors

Section 252 has fixed the minimum number of directors which a company must have, as under :—

Type of Company	Minimum number of Directors
(a) ***In case of every Public company***	3
(b) ***In case of every other company***	2

2.2 Election of Directors by Small Shareholders

Provisio to Section 252(1) provides that a public company having—

(a) a paid up capital of at least Rs 5 crores.

(b) at least 1000 small shareholders.

May have director elected by such small shareholders in the manner as prescribed.

Small shareholder means a shareholder holding shares of nominal value of Rs 20,000 or less.

However, director appointed under this proviso shall be counted for minimum limits as prescribed above.

3.0 MAXIMUM NUMBER OF DIRECTORS

The Companies Act has prescribed vide section 252 only the minimum number of Directors but is **silent on the maximum number** of Directors. Subject to the statutory minimum, the Articles of a company may fix the minimum and maximum number of Directors for its Board of Directors.

4.0 CHANGE IN THE NUMBER OF DIRECTORS [SECTION 258 AND 259]

The company may change the number of its Directors as under :—

Type of change	How to effect change
(a) ***In case of increase or decrease within limits fixed by articles.***	The company may increase or reduce the number of its directors by an **ordinary resolution in a general meeting.**
(b) ***In case of increase or decrease beyond limits fixed by articles.***	
(i) *Where the increase in number of directors make the total number of Directors more than 12 in case of a Public company and private company which is subsidiary of a public company.*	1 First alter the Articles by passing a **special resolution** and then pass **ordinary resolution** in a general meeting. 1 Such increase must also be **approved** by the **Central Government.**
(ii) *In other cases*	Procedure mentioned in case (i) except that No approval of Central Government is required.

5.0 WHO CAN BE APPOINTED AS A DIRECTOR [SECTION 253]

Only an individual shall be appointed as Director of a company.

6.0 WHO CANNOT BE APPOINTED AS A DIRECTOR [SECTION 253]

No body corporate, association or firm shall be appointed as Director of a company.

7.0 QUALIFICATION SHARES [SECTION 270]

7.1 Meaning of Qualification Shares

It is that number of shares which a Director is required to hold as per articles of the company.

7.2 Does the Act provide for any Share Qualification for Director ?

The Companies Act does **not** provide for any Share Qualification for a person to be a Director. As such a Director need not hold any shares and need not be a member of the company.

7.3 Does the Table A provide for any Share Qualification for Director ?

Regulation 66 of Table A **provides** that the qualification of Director shall be holding of at least one share in the company.

7.4 Can the Articles of a company provide for any Share Qualification for Director?

The Articles of a **Public company** and **Private company which is subsidiary of a Public** company **may provide** for any Share Qualification for Director but the Articles of an **independent Private company** (i.e. which is not a subsidiary of public company) **cannot provide** for any Share Qualification for Director. [Section 273]

7.5 Time Limit within which Qualification Shares must be obtained. [Section 270(1) and 270 (2)]

Where the Articles provide for Qualification share, such shares must be obtained within **two months** after his appointment as Director. Any provision in the Articles which requires a person to hold the Qualification share before his appointment as a Director or to obtain them within a period shorter than two months after his appointment, shall be void.

7.6 Maximum value of Qualification Shares. [Section 270 (3)]

The nominal value of Qualification shares must not exceed **Rs 5,000 or the nominal value of one share where it exceeds Rs. 5000.**

7.7 Position of Bearer of Share Warrant. [Section 270(4)]

The Bearer of Share Warrant shall **not be deemed to be the holder** of the shares specified in the Warrant for the purposes of Qualification Shares.

7.8 Consequences of not holding Qualification Shares.

(i) **Penalty [Section 272]** — If any person acts as a director of a company when he does not hold qualification shares after the expiry of two months after his appointment, he shall be punishable with a **fine** which may extend to **Rs 500** for every day from the date of expiry of two months to the date up to which he acted as director.

(ii) **Vacation of office [Section 283(1)(a)]** — If a Director fails to obtain Qualification shares within two months from his appointment or thereafter ceases to hold them any time then, his **office** shall become **vacant**.

Notes :—

(i) Directors appointed by the Central Government u/s 408 to prevent oppression or mismanagement need not hold any Qualification shares.

(ii) Qualification shares can be obtained either directly from the company or the market.

(iii) Unless the Articles otherwise provide, a joint holding will be sufficient for Share qualification. [*Grundy Vs. Briggs (1910)1CH. 444)*]

(iv) Until the required number of shares are registered in the name of Director he is not qualified. [*Channel Collieries Trust Ltd. Vs. Dover Light Railway Co.* (*1914*) *2 Ch. 506*]

8.0 DISQUALIFICATIONS OF DIRECTORS [SEC 274]

8.1 Grounds for Disqualifications [Sec 274 (1)]

Sec 274(1) lists the circumstances in which a person cannot be appointed as a director of a company. A person shall not be capable of being appointed director of a company if:

(a) he has been found to be of **unsound mind** by a competent court:

(b) he is an **undischarged insolvent**;

(c) he has applied to be **adjudicated as an insolvent** and his application is pending;

(d) he has been **convicted by a court** of any offence involving moral turpitude and has been sentenced to imprisonment for atleast six months and a period of five years has not elapsed since the expiry of this sentence.

(e) he has **not paid any call** in respect of the shares of the company held by him, whether alone or jointly with others, and six months have elapsed from the last day fixed for the payment of the call;

(f) he has been **disqualified by an order of the Court** under Section 203, of an offence in relation to promotion, formation or management of the company of fraud or misfeasance in relation to the company, unless the leave of the court has been obtained for his appointment in pursuance of Section 203.

(g) he is already a **director of public company which —**

 (a) has not filed the annual accounts and annual returns for any continuous 3 financial years starting on or, after 1st April 1999.

 (b) has failed to repay its deposit on interest thereon on due date or redeem its debentures on due date or pay dividend and such failure continues for 1 year or more.

However such person shall not be eligible to be appointed as a director of any other public company for a period of 5 years from the date on which such public company, in which he is director, failed to file annual accounts and annual returns or has failed repay its deposit or interest or redeem its debentures on due date or pay dividend.

8.2 Power of Central Government to remove disqualification [Sec 274 (2)]

The Central Government may, by notification in the Official Gazette, remove the disqualifications listed under clause (d) and (e) above.

8.3 Power of An Independent Private Company to provide for additional grounds for disqualification [Sec 274 (3)]

A private company which is not a subsidiary of a public company may, by its articles, provide for additional grounds for disqualification. Thus, a public company or a private company which is a subsidiary of a public company cannot provide for additional disqualifications in its articles.

9.0 VACATION OF OFFICE BY DIRECTORS [SEC 283]

9.1 Grounds on which the Office of a Director shall fall vacant

According to Section 283 of the Companies Act, the office of a director shall become automatically vacant if —

(a) he **fails to obtain or ceases to hold the qualification shares**;

(b) he is found to be of **unsound mind** by a competent court;

(c) he applies to be **adjudicated as an insolvent;**

(d) he is **declared insolvent**;

(e) he is **convicted of any offence involving moral turpitude** and sentenced to imprisonment for at least 6 months.

(f) he **fails to pay any call** on shares held by him whether alone or jointly with others within 6 months from the last date fixed for the payment of the call.

(g) he **absents** himself from three consecutive meetings of the Board of directors or from all the meetings of the Board for a continuous period of three months, whichever is longer, without obtaining leave of absence from the Board.

(h) he whether by himself or by any person for his benefit or on his account or any firm in which he is a partner or any private company of which he is a director, **accepts** a **loan** or any **guarantee** or **security** for a loan from the company **without** the **previous** approval of the Central Government;

(i) he **fails to disclose** to the Board his interest in any contract entered into by the company as required by Section 299;

(j) he **becomes disqualified** by an order of the court under Section 203 which restrains fraudulent persons from managing the affairs of companies;

(k) he is **removed** by an ordinary resolution of the company u/s 284

(l) he had been appointed a director by virtue of his holding any office and he **ceases** to **hold** such **office**;

(m) he is **convicted of an offence** in connection with the inspection of books of accounts and other records by the Registrar, or by such officer of the government as may be authorised by the central government or such officers of SEBI as may be authorised by it [Sections 209A(9)]

9.2 Power of An Independent Private Company to provide for additional grounds [Sec 283 (3)]

A private company which is not a subsidiary of a public company may, by its articles, provide for additional grounds on which the office of a director shall fall vacant.

9.3 Power of Central Government to remove the grounds for disqualification

The Central Government may by notification in the Official Gazette, remove the disqualifications listed in clause(f).

9.4 When shall disqualification contained in clause (d), (e) and (j) not take effect

Disqualification contained in clause (d), (e) and (j) shall not take effect —

(a) for 30 days from the date of adjudication, sentence or order

(b) where any appeal or petition is preferred within 30 days aforesaid against the adjudication, sentence or conviction resulting in sentence or order, within 7 days from the date on which such appeal or petition is disposed of.

(c) Where within aforesaid 7 days further appeal or petition is preferred until such appeal or petition is disposed of [Section 283(2)]

9.5 Penalty for functioning as director after vacation of office [Sec 283 (2A)]

If a person functions as a director when he knows that the office of director held by him has become vacant on account of any of the disqualifications specified in Sec 283 (1), he shall be punishable with fine which may extend to **Rs 5,000** for each day on which he so functions as a director.

9.6 Automatic vacation of office

Automatic vacation of office of by directors takes place in the following two cases:

(a) In case of an alternate director when original director in whose place alternate director was appointed returns [Sec 313(2)]

(b) In case a director already holding directorships in 15 companies is appointed as director in other company and he does not give notice of choice before the expiry of 15 days from the date of appointment.

10.0 APPOINTMENT OF DIRECTORS

The directors can be appointed by the following:

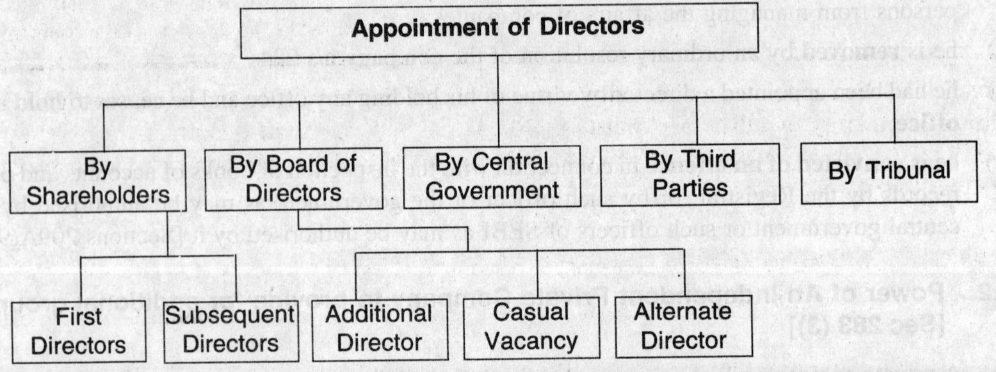

11.0 APPOINTMENT OF FIRST DIRECTORS [SECTION 254 AND REGULATION 64 OF TABLE A]

11.1 Who will be the First Directors?

According to Section 254, in default and subject to provisions in the Articles, subscribers to memorandum who are individuals shall be deemed to be the directors of the company, until the directors are duly appointed in accordance with section 255.

Case	*Who will be first directors*
(1) ***Where Articles contain the names of first directors.***	The persons who are named as first directors in the Articles shall be deemed to be the directors of the company.
(2) ***Where Articles do not contain the names of the first directors but provide that the number of the directors and the names of the First Directors shall be determined in writing, by the subscribers of the memorandum or a majority of them.***	
(a) *If subscribers so appoint.*	Directors appointed in writing, by the subscribers of the memorandum or a majority of them.
(b) *If subscribers do not so appoint.*	Subscribers to memorandum who are individuals shall be deemed to be the directors of the company.
(3) ***Where Articles neither contain the names of the first directors nor provide that the number of the directors and the names of the First Directors shall be determined in writing, by the subscribers of the memorandum or a majority of them.***	
(i) ***In case of a Public company***	
(a) *If subscribers so appoint in accordance*	Directors appointed in writing, by the subscribers of *with Table A* the memorandum or a majority of them.

(b) *If subscribers do not so appoint.*	Subscribers to memorandum who are individuals shall be deemed to be the directors of the company.
(ii) ***In case of a Private company***	Subscribers to memorandum who are individuals shall be deemed to be the directors of the company.

Note : — Where subscribers or majority of them appoint Directors, then in such a case, it has been held that a majority of subscribers must be present and not simply the quorum as required by Articles, before the first directors could be validly appointed. [Re. London & Southern Company Countries etc. 1885]

11.2 Term of Office of First Directors [Section 254]

The first directors shall hold office until the directors are appointed at the first Annual General meeting.

12.0 APPOINTMENT OF SUBSEQUENT DIRECTORS

12.1 How many directors shall be subject to retire by rotation ? [Section 255(1) and 255(2)]

Section 255(1) — Unless the Articles provide for the retirement of all directors at every annual general meeting, at least 2/3 rd of the total number of directors of a public company (including its subsidiaries) shall —

(a) be persons who shall be subject to retirement by rotation.

(b) be appointed by company in its general meeting.

Section 255(2) — The remaining directors in case of any such company and directors of a private company which is not a subsidiary of a public company shall in default of and subject to any regulation in the Articles of the company also be appointed in the general meeting of the company.

Notes :

(i) A public company (including its subsidiaries) may appoint directors up to 1/3rd of the total number of directors on permanent basis if the Articles so provide.

(ii) An Independent Private company may appoint all its directors on permanent basis if the Articles so provide.

Practical Illustration 1

X Ltd. has 15 directors. State how many directors shall be subject to retirement by rotation and how many directors shall be appointed in its general meeting in each of the alternative cases given on next page:

Case (a) If the Articles are silent

Case (b) If the Articles provide that 1/5th of the total number of Directors shall be permanent directors.

Case (c) If the Articles provide that 1/3 rd of the total number of Directors shall be permanent directors.

Case (d) If the Articles provide for the retirement of all directors.

Solution

Case	*No. of Directors subject to retirement by rotation*	*No. of the Directors to be appointed in General Meeting*
(a)	15	15
(b)	2/3rds of 15 = 10	15 – 1/5 th of 15 = 12
(c)	2/3rds of 15 = 10	15 – 1/3 rd of 15 = 10
(d)	15	15

Practical Illustration 2

X Pvt. Ltd. has 15 directors. State how many directors shall be subject to retirement by rotation and how many directors shall be appointed in its general meeting in each of the following alternative cases.

Case (a) If the Articles are silent

Case (b) If the Articles provide that 1/5 th of the total number of Directors shall be permanent directors.

Case (c) If the Articles provide that 1/3 rd of the total number of Directors shall be permanent directors.

Case (d) If the Articles provide for the retirement of all directors.

Case (e) If the Articles provide that all directors shall be permanent directors.

Solution

Case	*No. of Directors subject to retirement by rotation*	*No. of the Directors to be appointed in General Meeting*
(a)	Nil	15
(b)	Nil	15 – 1/5 th of 15 = 12
(c)	Nil	15 – 1/3 rd of 15 = 10
(d)	Nil	15
(e)	Nil	0

12.2 How many Directors shall retire ? [Section 256 (1)]

In case of Public company (including its subsidiaries) 1/3 rd (the number nearest to 1/3 rd) of the Directors liable to retire by rotation shall retire from office at every AGM.

Delhi High Court in B R Kundra vs Motion Pictures Association held that directors can not prolong their office tenure by not holding a meeting in time. The directors due to retire by rotations must vacate office at the latest on the last day on which AGM ought to have been held.

12.3 Who shall retire ? [Section 256 (2)]

Directors who have been **longest in the office** since their last appointment shall first retire but in case the date of appointment is the same the retirement will be determined by an agreement among them and if there is no agreement, it shall be determined by draw of lots.

12.4 How to fill up vacancy caused by the retirement by rotation ? [Section 256 (3)]

The company may fill up the vacancy by appointing the retiring director or some other person.

12.5 Effects of not filling up vacancy. [Section 256 (4)]

(a) If the vacancy caused by the retirement of a director by rotation is not filled up and the meeting has not expressly resolved not to fill up the vacancy, the **meeting shall stand adjourned** till the same day in the next week, at the same time and place or if on that day it is public holiday then on the next succeeding day which is not a public holiday.

(b) If at an adjourned meeting also, vacancy caused by the retirement of a director by rotation is not filled up and the meeting has not expressly resolved not to fill up the vacancy then the **retiring director(s) shall be deemed to have been reappointed at** the **adjourned meeting except** in the following cases :—

(i) when at the meeting or at the previous meeting a resolution for reappointment of such director has been put to the meeting and lost, or

(ii) When such director has declined reappointment in writing, or

(iii) When such director is not qualified or is disqualified for appointment, or

(iv) When a resolution whether ordinary or special is required for his appointment or reappointment.

(v) Where two or more persons have been appointed as directors by a single resolutions. [Proviso to Sec 263(2)]

12.6 How can a person other than retiring director stand for directorship ? [Section 257 (1)]

(a) Notice of 14 days — A person other than the retiring director shall be eligible for appointmentto the office of director if he or some other member intending to propose him has given at least 14 days' before the meeting a notice in writing to the company.

(b) Deposit of Fees — A deposit of Rs. 500 is required to be made with a company and such deposit shall be refunded to the depositor if a person gets elected as director.

12.7 Duty of the company on receipt of such notice. [Section 257 (1A)]

On receipt of such notice, the company is required to inform its members by serving individual notices at least 7 days before the meeting about the candidaturc or intention of member.

12.8 When individual notices are not necessary?

Individual notices to members shall not be necessary if company advertises such candidature or intention of member at least 7 days before the meeting in at least 2 newspapers circulating in the place where the registered office of the company is located of which one is published in the English language and other in regional language.

Notes :—

(i) The aforesaid provisions of Section 257 (1) shall apply only to Public company and its subsidiaries. [Section 257 (2)]

(ii) Section 255 and 256 and 263 do not apply to a company whose Articles provide for election of directors by ballot provided the company does not carry on business for profit or prohibits the payment of dividend to its members. [Section 263A]

12.9 Consent of a candidate for directorship to be filed with company and consent to act as director to be filed with registrar [Section 264]

(a) Person who under section 257 proposed as a candidate for the office of directors, shall sign and file his consent with the company in writing to act as director if appointed.

(b) A person other than—

(i) director reappointed after retirement by rotation immediately on the expiry of his term.

(ii) an additional or alternate, or a person filling casual vacancy in the office of directors u/s 262, appointed as a director or reappointed as additional or alternate director, immediately on expiry of his term or

(iii) a person named as a director of the company under its articles as first registered

shall not act as directors of the company unless he has within 30 days of his appointment signed and filed with Registrar his consent is writings to act as director.

However these provisions do not apply to a private company unless it is a subsidiary of public company.

12.10 Appointment of directors must be voted individually [Section 263]

Each director shall be appointed by a separate resolution in case of a public company and its subsidiary. If a resolution is moved in contravention of aforesaid provision, then such resolution shall be void, whether the objection was raised or not when the resolution was moved.

12.11 When can a resolution appointing more than one director can be made?

Such resolution can be made if has been first agreed unanimously in the meeting. Unanimously means that there is no single vote against it.

12.12 Can a minor be appointed as Director?

There is no provision in the Act, which can expressly disqualify him to act as director. However, since a minor is not competent to contract, he cannot file with the company or with the Registrar any valid consent u/s 264. But as this section only applies to public company and its subsidiaries, there is nothing in the Act which can prevent a minor to become a director of an independent private company.

13.0 APPOINTMENT OF DIRECTORS BY BOARD OF DIRECTORS

(a) ***Additional Directors. [Section 260]***	**Who can appoint :** The Board of Directors if so authorised by its Articles may, within the maximum strength of Board fixed by Articles, appoint additional directors. **Term of Office :** Additional Directors shall hold office up to the date of next annual general meeting.
(b) ***Casual Vacancy. [Section 262]***	**Who can fill up casual vacancy:** The Board of Directors in default and subject to regulation in the Articles, may fill up the casual vacancy occurring amongst the directors at its meeting. **Term of Office:** The Directors so appointed shall hold office upto the unexpired term of office of such director in whose place he is appointed.

	Note: Casual vacancies cannot be filled up by resolution passed by circulation.
(c) *Alternate Directors. [Sec 313]*	**Who can appoint** : The Board of directors may if so authorised by its Articles or by a resolution passed by company in its general meeting, appoint an alternate director to act for a director during his absence for a period at least 3 months from the state in which meetings of Board are ordinarily held. **Term of Office :** Alternate director, shall vacate the office immediately on the return of original director or on the expiry of term of office of original director whichever is earlier. It may be noted that the provision of automatic reappointment of retiring director shall apply to original director and not to alternate director.

14.0 APPOINTMENT OF DIRECTORS BY CENTRAL GOVERNMENT. [SECTION 408 AND 409]

14.1 When the Central Government can appoint

The Central Government may appoint such number of Directors as the Tribunal may by order in writing specify to effectively safeguard the interest of the company or its shareholders or the public interests.

14.2 Term of Office of Govt. Directors.

Such director shall hold office for not more than 3 years on any one occasion.

14.3 When the Tribunal can pass the order

The Tribunal can pass such order in any one of the following three circumstances:—

(a) On a reference made to it by the Central Government,

(b) On the application of at least 100 members,

(c) On the application of the members holding at least 10 % of total voting power.

14.4 Power of Tribunal to direct the company to make fresh appointments by system of proportional representation. [Provision to Section 408 (1)]

In lieu of passing an order aforesaid the Tribunal may direct the company to amend its articles so as to provide for election of directors by system of proportional representation (as provided under section 265) and make fresh appointments of directors in pursuance of amended Articles within the prescribed time.

14.5 Special provisions applicable to Govt. Directors. [Section 408 (3) and 408 (4)]

Any Director (s) appointed by the Central Government shall not be —

(a) considered for the purpose of reckoning 2/3 rd or any other proportion of total number of Directors,

(b) required to hold any qualification shares,

(c) liable to retire by rotation,

(d) removed except by Central Government.

14.6 Subsequent change in the Board to be confirmed by CLB. [Section 408 (5)]

No change in the Board of Directors of the company after the appointment of a director by the Central Government shall have effect unless confirmed by the Tribunal.

15.0 APPOINTMENT OF DIRECTORS BY THIRD PARTIES [SECTION 255(2)]

(a) **Articles may authorise**—According to Section 255 (2), the Articles of the company may authorise the third parties to appoint directors on the Board of Directors of the company. Articles may give such power to Debenture holders, Financial institutions or Banks etc. that has advanced loans to the company.

(b) **Maximum limit of such Directors**—The number of Directors so appointed must not exceed 1/3 rd of the total number of directors in case of a Public company (including its subsidiaries).

(c) **Professional view of Perrins and Jeffrays**—However in this regard **Perrins and Jeffrays** in their Company Law observe "It is doubtful whether the court will grant *either* specific performance *or* an injunction where company refuses to appoint director nominated by third party and probably third party's only remedy in case of breach is an action for damages, since the court can not impose on a company directors whom members do not approve."

16.0 APPOINTMENT OF DIRECTORS BY TRIBUNAL [SEC 388C]

(a) During the pendency of the case before the Tribunal, certain situations might come to its knowledge which might necessitiate the passing of an interim order for the interest of members or creditors as the case may be, restraining the delinquent person.

(b) For this purpose the Tribunal may either on the application of Central Government or on its own motion direct that the delinquent person shall not discharge any of the duties until further order and appoint in his stead another person to discharge duties connected with the office of delinquent person subject to such terms and conditions as the Tribunal may specify in the order.

17.0 APPOINTMENT OF DIRECTORS AND MANAGER WITH UNLIMITED LIABILITY IN LIMITED COMPANY. [SECTION 322 AND 323]

17.1 Legal requirements as to Memorandum, Statement and Notice

In a limited company, any director or manager may be appointed with unlimited liability subject to the following provisions of Section 322 :

(a) The memorandum must provide for unlimited liability of directors or manager, [Section 322 (1)]

(b) A statement that a liability of the person holding the office shall be unlimited, must be added to the proposal by the directors and manager and member who proposes a person for appointment to the office of director or manager. [Section 322 (2)]

(c) A notice in writing that his liability will be unlimited, must be given to him by the following or any one of the following persons:

  (i) The promoters of the company,

  (ii) The directors of the company,

  (iii) The manager of the company,

  (iv) The officers of the company.

17.2 Consequences of default [Section 322 (3)]

(a) The person who makes default in adding the aforesaid statement or in giving the aforesaid notice shall be punishable with fine which may extend to Rs. 10,000 and shall also be liable for any damage which the person so appointed may sustain from the default.

(b) The liability of the person so appointed shall not be affected by the default.

17.3 Alteration of Memorandum [Section 323]

(a) A limited company may, if so authorised by its articles, by special resolution alter its memorandum so as to render the liability of its directors or manager unlimited.

(b) Upon the passing of any such special resolution, the provisions thereof shall be as valid as if they had been originally contained in the memorandum.

(c) **Effect of Alteration on Existing Directors or manager** — No such alteration shall apply to such officer who was holding the office from before the date of alteration until the expiry of his term unless he has accorded his consent to his liability becoming unlimited.

18.0 ASSIGNMENT OF OFFICE BY DIRECTOR [SECTION 312]

Any assignment of his office made by a director of a company shall be void.

Supreme Court has given its view regarding assignment and appointment. It is of view that where an appointment by a director to the office which he previously held but did not hold at the time of appointment is not an assignment. In Parmanand Choudhury vs Smt Shukla Devi Mishra it was held that appointing managing director and giving him sole charge of company's management and other directors were given only advisory role will not result in assignment.

19.0 RESIGNATION OF DIRECTORS

(a) If the articles permit a director to resign at any time, the resignation will be effective from the date of service of notice. There is no need for its acceptance by the Board or company in general meeting.

(b) But where articles contains no provisions as to resignation then the resignation will be effective only when he serves notice on the company or Board and his resignation is accepted.

(c) A verbal resignation is also enough.

(d) No compensation for loss of office shall be paid to directors if he resigns his office. [Section 318]

20.0 MAXIMUM NUMBER OF DIRECTORSHIPS

20.1 Maximum Limit of Directorships

(a) A person shall not hold office at the same time as a director in more than 15 companies. [Section 275]

(b) **Directorship excluded**—However for calculating the limits for above purpose, the directorships of the following companies shall be excluded.

   (i) a private company which is *neither* a subsidiary *nor* a holding company of a public company

   (ii) an unlimited company

   (iii) an association not carrying on business for profit or which prohibits the payment of dividend

(iv) a company in which person concern is only an alternate director u/s 313 [Section 278(1)]

(c) If companies mentioned in (a), (b) and (c) above ceases to fall within the purview of those clauses then directorship shall remain excluded for a period of 3 months from the date of such cessation [Section 278(2)]

20.2 Choice to be made by director of more than 15 companies [Section 276]

If any person holds office as director in more than 15 companies before the commencement of Companies (Amendment) Act, 2000, he shall within 2 months from such commencement.

(a) choose not more than 15 companies in which he wishes to continue to hold office of director.

(b) resign his office as director in other companies

(c) intimate the choice made by him to each company in which he was director before commencement of The Companies (Amendment) Act, 2000, and to the concerned Registrar and Central Government.

20.3 Choice by person becoming director of more than 15 companies. [Section 277]

(a) where a person already holding the office of director in 15 companies, is appointed as a director of any other company, then

(i) such appointment shall not take effect unless person concerned, within 15 days vacates his office as director in any of the companies in which he already holds directorship and

(ii) shall become void immediately on expiry of 15 days if person concern does not vacate his office as director in any of existing companies. [Section 277(1)]

(b) Where a person already holdings office of director in 14 companies or less is appointed as a director of other companies making the total number of directorship more than 15, then person concern shall choose the directorships which he wishes to continue to hold or to accept, so the number of directorship did not exceed 15.

(c) None of the new appointments shall take effect until such choice is made, and all new appointments shall become void if choice is not made within 15 days. [Section 277(2)].

20.4 Penalty [Sec. 279]

Directors holding office in more than 15 companies shall be subject to a fine upto Rs. 50,000 for every company, which they hold after the first 15.

21.0 BOARD MEETING

21.1 When & how many times Board meetings to be held ? [Section 285]

(a) Every company is required to hold a meeting of its Board of directors at least once in every 3 months and at least 4 in every year.

(b) As the word year has not been defined in the act ,it will be taken to mean a calendar year as defined in General Clause Act (GCA). Accordingly 2 stipulations to be complied with u/s 285 shall be as under :

i) At least one meeting must be held in each quarter i.e. between Jan. to Mar., April to June, July to Sep. & Oct. to Dec. each year.[Department's Clarification (No.8/16(1)/61 - PR, dated 9th May 1961)]

ii) At least 4 meeting must be held during a calendar year i.e. Jan. to Dec. of any year irrespective of the financial year of the company.

Practical Illustration 3

	Case A	Case B	Case C
1st Board meeting	1 st Jan	26 th Jan.	26 th Jan.
2nd Board meeting	30 th June	1 st May	15 th Aug.
3rd Board meeting	1 st July	15 th Aug.	2 nd Oct.
4th Board meeting	31 st Dec.	2 nd Oct.	31 st Dec.

Interpretation

According to clarification issued by the Department

In case A both the stipulations are complied with and it is to be noted that there could be a gap of more than 3 months (not exceeding 6 months in any case except of adjourned meeting) between two original meetings (not adjourned) of the Board & there shall be no violation of the provision of the Sec. 285.

In case B both the stipulations are complied with & it is to be noted that a Board meeting can be on any day including public holiday since the Act does not prohibit so specifically anywhere.

However, according to strict interpretation of the section 285 there should not be gap of 3 months between 2 consecutive board meetings, hence there is violation of section 285 in Case A & Case B.

In case C, there is the violation of the provision of the Section 285 since the stipulation of ' at least one meeting must be held in each quarter 'has not been complied with. (There is no meeting in quarter April to June.)

21.2 Is there is any contravention of Section 285 in case of Adjournment of the meeting ?

Section 288 (2) provides that where a Board meeting is duly called but adjourned for count of quorum, there is no contravention of section 285.

Practical Illustration 4

Ist meeting duly commenced on 26 th Jan & duly held.
2nd meeting duly commenced on 1 st May & duly held
3rd meeting duly commenced on 1st July & duly held
4th meeting duly commenced on 31st Dec. but could not be held due to lack of quorum then held on 7 th Jan.

In this case no meeting held in the quarter of Oct. to Dec. & the total no. of the meeting in the year were 3 but in the view of the section 288(2), there is no violation of Section 285 since the meeting was adjourned for lack of quorum.

21.3 Maximum number of Board Meetings

Section 285 provides for minimum number of Board meetings and not for maximum number of meetings. That is why there can be more meetings than provided in section 285.

21.4 Power of Central Government to exempt from section 285

The central Government may by notification in the official gazette , direct that the provision of this section shall apply in relation to or shall apply subject to such exceptions , modifications or conditions as the central government may specify in the notification.

In the pursuance of this power, the central government has permitted the governing bodies of companies licensed u/s 25 to hold one meeting of its governing body every 6 months.

22.0 NOTICE AND AGENDA OF BOARD MEETING (SECTION 286)

22.1 Who is the proper authority to convene the Board meeting ?

A Director may & the Manager or the Secretary on the requisition of a director shall at any time summon a of the Board. However, a meeting convened by the secretary without authority may be ratified by the directors at a board meeting. [Regulation 73 (2)]

22.2 To whom notice is to be given (Section 286)

Notice must be given to all the directors irrespective of whether they are in India or not. In case of the directors not in India , such notice must be served at their usual address in India. The right to receive the notice cannot be waived at any case.

22.3 Should the notice be in writing or oral (Section 286)

Such notice must be in writing

22.4 Default in servicing of notice [Section 288 (2)]

Every officer of the company whose duty is is to serve the notice and who fails to do so shall be punishable with a fine upto Rs. 1,000.

22.5 If Board meeting is to be held on fixed date of every month as provided by the article of association then will it be necessary to serve the notice of the meeting on every director.

No, then it will be not necessary to serve notice of the meeting u/s 288 (1).

[*Arunchalam Chettiar Vs .Kaleshwarar Mills Ltd.*]

But two necessary conditions have also to be fulfilled

(i) all the directors attend the meeting and do not raise any objection to the non - service of the notice.

(ii) where the absent directors make no compliant about the want of notice ,particularly when the proceedings are ratified at the subsequent meeting whereat the absentee directors are present.

[*Re - State of Wymoing Syndicate (1901)*]

22.6 Length of the Notice. (Section 286)

Notice may be given even on the day of the meeting since the act is silent on the point of the length of the notice.

22.7 Agenda of Board Meeting

The Act does not require that notice must state the business to be transacted at the meeting except u/s 316, (to appoint a person as Managing director who is already a Managing director or a manager of another company), 372 (to invest in the shares & debentures in another body corporate), 386 (to appoint a person a manager who is already a manager or managing of another company) which require that the notice of resolution to be moved at the board meeting must be sent to every director in the manner specified in section 286. There is also no violation of law if item which have not been included in the Agenda are considered at the Board meeting.

23.0 PLACE OF BOARD MEETING

The board meetings may be held at any place (whether or not the registered office or within the city, town or village in which the registered office is situated) However, if such meeting is held at a place other than the registered office, it will involve removal of the register of the contracts/ arrangements kept all u/s 310 (5) outside the registered office which shall violate the provision of section 301(5). The Central government has classified that it would be sufficient compliance with the requirement of section 301 (5) if the company gives adequate notice to its shareholders either once for all or from time to time indicating the precise period during business hour and the dates on which they could inspect the register under section 301 (2) at the registered office of the company.

24.0 DAY OF BOARD MEETING

(a) Original Board meeting can be held on any day including a public holiday since the act does not prohibited so specifically.
(b) Board meeting adjourned for lack of quorum must be held on a day which is not a public holiday.
(c) Board meeting adjourned for any reason other than lack of quorum may be held on any day including a public holiday since the act does not prohibit so.

25.0 HOURS OF BOARD MEETING

The Board meeting may be held at any time which may or not fall within business hours since the act does not prohibits so specifically.

26.0 QUORUM FOR BOARD MEETING (SECTION 287)

Quorum for the Board' s meeting shall be 1/3 rd of the total strength (any fraction to be rounded off to 1) or 2 directors whichever is higher. Where at any time the no. of interested directors exceeds or is equal to 2/3 rd of the total strength , the no. of disinterested directors present at the meeting or two director whichever is higher shall be the quorum during such time.

(a) Total strength means the total strength of the board as determined in pursuance of this act after deducting therefrom the no. of the directors if any, whose places may be vacant at the time ; and
(b) 'Interested Director' means any director whose presence cannot by virtue of section 300 , count for the purpose of forming a quorum at the time of discussion or vote at any matter.

Case	Quorum
I *No Vacancy and No interested director*	1/3 rd of the Total strength or 2 whichever is higher *[Refer to Example 1]*
II *Vacancy but no interested director*	1/3 rd of the Total strength (excluding vacancy) or 2 whichever is higher *[Refer to Example 2]*
III *When number of interested director is less than 2/3 rd of the Total strength (excluding vacancy)*	Disinterested 1/3 rd director of the Total strength (excluding vacancy) or 2 disinterested director whichever is higher *[Refer to Example 3]*
IV *When number of interested director is equal to 2/3 rd of the Total strength (excluding vacancy)*	Remaining Disinterested director or 2 Disinterested director whichever is higher. *[Refer to Example 3]*

Case	Quorum
V ***When number of interested director is more than 2/3 rd of the Total strength (excluding vacancy)***	Remaining Disinterested director or 2 Disinterested director whichever is higher. *[Refer to Example 3]*

Example 1

	Cases I	II	III
Total Strength	13	14	15
Vacancy	0	0	0
Quorum	5	5	5

Example 2

	Cases I	II	III
Total Strength	15	16	17
Vacancy	2	2	2
Effective strength	13	14	15
Quorum	5	5	5

Example 3

	Cases I	II	III	IV	V	VI	VII
Total Strength	13	13	13	13	13	13	13
Interested Director	6	7	8	9	10	11	12
Quorum	5	5	5	4	3	2	1*

* Only general meeting can be called up

27.0 CHAIRMAN OF BOARD MEETING [REGULATION 76 OF TABLE A]

The Board may elect a chairman of its meeting & determine the period for which he is to hold office. If no chairman is elected or if at any meeting chairman elected is not present within 5 minutes after the time appointed for holding the meeting, the directors present may choose one of them to be the chairman of the meeting.

28.0 DECISION ON QUESTION [REGULATION 74 OF TABLE A]

28.1 By a Majority of Votes

Except as otherwise provided in the Act, question arising at the board meeting shall be decided by a majority of votes. However in case of equality of votes, chairman can exercise his second or casting vote.

28.2 By Unanimous Consent

The Act provides for the **unanimous consent** of all the directors present at the meeting in the following **three cases** :

i) To appoint a person as managing director who is already a managing director /manager of another company u/s 316(2).

ii) To appoint a person as manager who is already a manging director / manager of another company u/s 386(2).

iii) To invest in the shares or debentures of another body corporate u/s 372(5).

28.3 Not considering the interested director. (Section 300)

The director interested in any contract or arrangement :-

a) shall not be entitled to take part in any discussion or vote on that contract / arrangement.
b) shall not be counted for the purpose of the quorum.
c) his vote shall be void if he votes on such matter in which he is interested.

28.4 Methods of taking decision.

There are two methods of taking decisions:

(a) Passing of resolution by circulation
(b) Passing of resolution at duly called meeting.

28.5 Passing of resolution by circulation

No resolution shall be deemed to have duly passed by the board or by a committee thereof by circulation, unless.

(a) resolution has been circulated in drafts together with necessary papers if any to all the directors or all the number of committee, then in India (not being less than qurum fixed for a meeting of the Board of committee] and to all other directors at their usual address in India and,
(b) has been approved by such of the directors as are in India or by a majority of such of them, as are entitled to vote on resolution

29.0 AUDIT COMMITTEE [SECTION 292A]

29.1 Which company is required to constitute Audit Committee

Every public company having paid up capital of atleast 5 crore is required to constitute a committee of the Board known as 'Audit Committee'.

29.2 Composition of Audit Committee

It shall consist of atleast 3 directors and such number of other directors as the board may determine of which 2/3 directors of the total number of members shall be directors, other than managing or whole time directors.

29.3 Terms of Reference

Every audit committee constituted above shall act in accordance with terms of reference to be specified in writing by the Board. [Section 292A(2)].

29.4 Disclosure in Annual Report

The annual report of the company shall disclose the composition of the Audit Committees [Section 292A(2)]

29.5 Election of Chairman

The members of the audit committee shall elect a chairman from amongst themselves. [Section 292A(3)].

29.6 Invitees—The auditor, the internal auditor if any, and the director-in-charge of the finance shall attend and participate at meetings of the Audit Committee but shall not have right to vote. [Section 292A(5)].

29.7 Duties of Audit Commitee

The audit committee should

(a) have discussions with the auditors periodically about (i) internal control system, (ii) the scope of audit including the observations of the auditors.

(b) Review the half-yearly and annual financial statements before submission to the Board

(c) Ensure compliance of internal control system. [Section 292A(6)]

29.8 Powers of Audit Committee

The audit committee shall have

(a) authority to investigate into any matter in relation to the items specified in the section or referred to it by Board and for this purpose,

(b) full access to information contained in the records of the company and external profession advice if necessary. [Section 292A(7)].

29.9 Binding Effect of Recommendation

The recommendation of the Audit Committee on any mater relating to financial management including audit report, shall be binding on the Board. [Section 292A(8)].

If the Board does not accept the recommendation of the audit committee, it shall record the reasons thereafter and communicate such reasons to the shareholders. [Section 292A (9)]

29.10 Duty of Chairman

The chairman of the audit committee shall attend the annual general meeting of company to provide any clarification on matters relating to audit. [Section 292A(10)].

29.11 Penalty

In case of contravention of above provisions, the company and every officers in default, shall be punishable with imprisonment for a term upto 1 year or with fine which upto Rs 50,000, or with both. [Section 292A(11)].

EXERCISES

VERY SHORT ANSWER QUESTIONS

1. Define Director.

2. Define Board of Directors.

3. What is the minimum number of directors required for a public company?

4. What is the minimum number of directors required for a private company?

5. What is the maximum limit on number of directors in a public company?

6. Can a minor be appointed as director of a public company?

7. Can a partnership firm be appointed as director of a public company?

8. Can a Trust be appointed as director of a public company?

9. Can a Bank be appointed as director of a public company?

10. What is qualification share?

11. (a) Does the Companies Act provide for any share qualification for Director?

(b) Is the director of a public company required to hold qualification shares if its Articles are silent?

(c) Can the Articles of an independent private company provide for any share qualification for director?

(d) State the period within which a director must vacate his office if he fails to obtain qualification shares.

(e) What can be the maximum value of qualificaiton shares?

12. What is the term of office of First Directors?

13. What is the term of office of Additional Director?

14. What is the term of office of Director appointed to fill casual vacancy?

15. What is the term of office of Alternate Director?

16. What is the term of office of Director appointed by Central Government?

17. Who is an additional director?

18. Who is an alternate director?

19. Who is authorised to fill a casual vacancy of a director?

20. How many directors can the Central Government appoint on the Board of Directors of a company?

21. What is the maximum limit of number of directors appointed by third parties?

22. How many directors are liable to retire at first A.G.M.?

23. How many directors of a public company are liable to retire by rotation at A.G.M. unless the Articles provide for retirement of all?

24. Can all the directors of a private company be permanent?

25. Can all the directors of a public company be permanent?

26. Name the persons who are required to file consent to act as directors with the Registrar.

27. Name the persons who are not required to file consent to act as directors with the Registrar.

28. Identify the directors who can not be removed by the shareholders at their general meeting.

29. What is the maximum limit of number of directorships which a person can hold in a public limited company?

SHORT ANSWER TYPE QUESTIONS

1. Comment on the following:

(a) The companies Act does not provide for any share qualification for the directors.

(b) In a limited company a director can be appointed with unlimited liability.

(c) A director as well as his alternate director can be present at a Board Meeting.

2. Give two disqualifications of a director of Directors

3. Give two grounds on which the office of a director fall vacant.

4. Mention two methods of appointing directors of a company.

5. How are the first directors appointed?

6. State the circumstances under which a director retiring at an AGM shall be deemed to have been reappointed even though no such appointment was made.

7. How can vacancies resulting from removal of director be filled?

8. How can the casual vacancy of a director be filled?

9. When can additional directors be appointed and for what period?

10. When can alternate directors be appointed and for what period?

11. When can the Central Government appoint directors and for what period?

11. Can directors be appointed by third parties? Also state the maximum limit on number of such directors (if any).

12. Write short notes on the following:

(a) Additional Directors

(b) Alternate Directors

(c) Government Directors
(d) Permanent Directors
(e) Qualification Shares
(f) Audit Commitee

LONG ANSWER TYPE QUESTIONS

1. Explain the disqualifications of a director.
2. Explain how are the directors appointed.
3. How and when may a director be appointed by the Central Government?
4. When does the office of a director fall vacant?
5. Explain breifly the provisions relating to Board Meetings.

CHAPTER 12

Meetings and Procedures

1.0 MEANING OF MEETING

Meeting is a means of action for the purpose of taking a decision. Unlike a natural person, a company cannot think and express its will or make a decision. A company can express its will and make a decision only through the resolution passed at properly conveyed and constituted meetings. The affairs of a company are conducted by collective action of the members through the general meeting and that of directors through Board meeting.

2.0 CLASSIFICATION OF MEETINGS

Meetings held the Companies Act may be classified as follows:

1. Meetings of shareholders or members:
   (a) Statutory meeting.
   (b) Annual general meeting.
   (c) Extraordinary general meeting.
   (d) Class meetings.
2. Meeting of debentureholders.
3. Meetings of creditors and contributories in winding up.
4. Meeting of creditors otherwise than in winding up.
5. Meeting of directors:
   (a) Board meeting:
   (b) Committee meeting.

3.0 STATUTORY MEETING [SECTION 165]

Statutory meeting is the first meeting of the members of a public limited company having share capital and is held only once during the lifetime of the company.

3.1. Which Company is required to Hold Statutory Meeting?

Every Public limited company having share capital is required to hold such meeting. However, if a private company becomes a public company by virtue of Section 3(i)(iv) or converts itself into a public company 'within period of 6 months from date of its incorporation, it shall be required to hold such meeting.

3.2. To Which Type of Company this Section does not Apply?

(1) Private company (other than banking company) [Section 165(10)]
(2) Government companies
(3) Private company becoming a public company by virtue of Section 3(i)(iv) or on its conversion into a public company after period of 6 months from date of its incorporation
(4) Company not having share capital

3.3 When is to be held?

Such meeting is to be held after the expiry of 1 month but before the expiry of 6 months from the date on which the company is entitled to commence business.

Note: It cannot be held prior to 1 month.

3.4 Object of the Meeting

The object of this meeting is to provide an opportunity to the members of the company to discuss all matters relating to the promotion and formation of the company.

3.5 Place, Date and Hours of Conducting Meeting

Such meeting can be held at any place, any day and at any time because the Act is silent on these points.

3.6 Notice of the Meeting

At least 21 clear days' notice must be given (Section 171). A shorter notice less than 21 days may be given if the consent is obtained thereto—

(a) by the members holding at least 95% of the paid up share capital carrying voting rights in case of the company having share capital.

(b) by member holding at least 95% of the total voting power in case of the company having no share capital.

Note: The notice must state that it is a statutory meeting. [*Gardner* v. *Iredel*]

3.7 Quorum [Section 174]

The term 'Quorum' means the minimum number of members required to constitute a valid meeting and to transact business threat. Unless the articles provide for a larger number, quorum shall be:

Case	*Minimum number required to constitute meeting*
In case of meeting originally held	5 members personally present.
In case of meeting adjourned due to lack of quorum	Members present **Notes:** (i) A single member present shall not constitute quorum at an adjourned meeting. (ii) Even 2 proxies present can constitute quorum at an adjourned meeting.
In case of meeting adjourned due to other reasons	5 members personally present.

In all of the above case, article may provide for the higher number for the purpose of constituting the quorum. But article cannot provide for the shorter number for the purpose of constituting quorum.

3.8 Statutory Report

(i) **Forwarding the Statutory Report to the Member [Section 165(2)]** The Director's must forward at least 21 days before the meeting is held, a statutory report to every member of the company. However such report can be sent at shorter notice provided it was condoned unanimously by members entitled to attend and vote at the meeting.

(ii) Eight Contents of Statutory Report [Section 165(3)]

(a) The total number of shares allotted, distinguishing shares allotted as fully paid or partly paid, otherwise than for cash, and in case of partly paid up share stating the extent to which they are so paid up, and in both cases the consideration for which they have been allotted.

(b) The total amount of cash received in respect of shares allotted for cash.

(c) an abstracts of the receipts and payment A/c up to date within 7 days of the date of report, showing under the different headings the receipts of the company from shares, debentures and other sources, payments made, balance in hand, and an account or estimate of the preliminary expenses of the company, showing separately any commission or discount paid, or to be paid on the issue or sale of shares or debentures,

(d) the names, addresses and occupations of the directors, auditors, manager and secretary, if any and any changes therein, if any occurred since the date of incorporation.

(e) the particulars of any contract, or modifications thereof submitted to the meeting for its approval.

(f) the extent, if any, to which each underwriting contract has not been carried out and the reasons thereof

(g) The calls-in-arrears from every director and manager of the company.

(h) The particulars of any commission or brokerage paid or payable to any director or manager in connection with the issue or sale of shares and debentures.

(iii) Certification by Director [Section 165(4)] The statutory report must be certified by at least 2 directors of the company one of them must be managing director if any.

(iv) Certification by Auditors Auditors are required to certify the statutory report after the certification by directors on the matters which relates to the shares allotted by the company cash received on such shares and the receipts and payments (both capital and revenue) of the company.

(v) Delivery of the Report to Registrar [Section 165(5)] After the copies of the report have been sent to the members of the company, then the company must send the copy of the report to the Registrar of the company for registration.

(vi) In Prescribed Form The statutory report must be in Form No. 22 of the General Forms.

3.9 Procedure at the Meeting

(a) A list showing the names, addresses and occupations of the members of the company and the no. of the shares held by them must be produced at the commencement of the meeting and must be open and accessible to any member during the continuance of the meeting. [Section 165(6)]

(b) Members present may discuss any matter related to the formation of the company or arising out of the statutory report whether previous notice has been given or not, but no resolution can be passed unless notice is given in accordance with the provision of the Act. [Section [165(7)]

(c) **Adjournment of Statutory Meeting**

(i) the statutory meeting may be adjourned from time to time, and at any adjourned meeting, any resolution of which notice has been given in accordance with the provisions of the Act, whether before or after the former meeting, may be passed; and the adjourned meeting shall have-the same power as an original meeting. [Section 165(8)]

(ii) The power to adjourn rests with the decision of the meeting Thus, the chairman may not adjourn without the consent of the meeting, and must adjourn if so directed by the meeting, even if any discretionary power is given to the chairman by the articles. Normally, where the chairman is given a discretion he is not bound to adjourn the meeting even if the majority desires it [*Parashuram* v. *Tata Industrial Bank Ltd.*, (1924)].

(iii) The statutory meeting also provides an exception to the normal rule that only business left unfinished at the original meeting can be transacted at the adjourned meeting [Reg. 53(2), Table A]. Members have a right to introduce new business at the adjourned meeting, since the Act provides that any resolution of which notice has been given in accordance with the provisions of the Act, either *before or after* the former meeting, may be passed, and the adjourned meeting has the same power as an original meeting. If the meeting wishes to pass a resolution on any matter which it is entitled to discuss it may adjourn so that the notice in accordance with the provisions of the Act may be given in the interval.

(d) The provisions relating to Notice, Quorum, Adjournment, Chairman, Proxies and Voting shall be governed by general sections [Sections 171 to 186] as are applicable to the general meetings.

3.10 Consequences of Default

(a) If the default is made in complying with the provisions of Section 165, every officer who is in default shall be punishable with fine upto Rs 5,000. [Section 165(9)]

(b) The court may order for the compulsory winding up of the company if default is made in delivering the statutory report to the registrar or in holding the statutory meeting [Section 433(b)]; or

The court, instead of winding up order, may direct the company to deliver statutory report or hold statutory meeting. [Section 443(3)]

4.0 ANNUAL GENERAL MEETING [SECTIONS 166 TO 168]

4.1 Which Company is bound to Hold?

Every company must hold an 'Annual General Meeting'. [Section 166(1)]

4.2 When is to be held?

First Annual General Meeting

(i) It must be held within 18 months of its 'incorporation. Where the company hold such meeting then the company is not required to hold any annual general meeting in the year of its incorporation or in the following year. [1st Provisio of Section 166(1)]

(ii) It must be held within 9 months of the end of financial year [Section 210(3)]. The period of financial year must not exceed 15 months and may extend to 18 months with special permission of the Registrar. [Section 210(4)]

Practical Illustration 1

	I	II	III
Date of incorporation	31st Dec. 20X1	31st Dec. 20X1	31st Dec. 20X1
Financial year ended	30th Sept. 20X2	31st Mar. 20X3	30th June 20X3*
Last date for holding Annual General Meting	30th June 20X3	30th June 20X3	30th June 20X3

*Here special permission from the Registrar has to be obtained since financial year exceed 15 months.

Subsequent Annual General Meeting

(i) It must be held in each calendar year. [Section 166(1)]

(ii) It must be held within 15 months of previous meeting. [Section 166(1)]

(iii) It must be held within 6 months of the end of the financial year. Financial year of the company must not exceed 15 months and may extend to 18 months where special permission has been granted by the Registrar. [Proviso to Section 210(4)]

These three requirements are cumulative and separate. Failure to comply with any of them constitutes an offence unless an extension of time has been granted for holding the meeting by the Registrar of Companies. The period of such extension is limited to 3 months. If extension has been granted the 6 months period will be increased by such extension.

Practical Illustration 2

Case	*Financial year ended*	*Last date for holding AGM*	*AGM held on*
1st	31st Dec. 20X1	30th June 20X2	1st Jan. 20X2
2nd	31st Dec. 20X2	31st Mar. 20X3	30th April 20X3
3rd	31st Dec. 20X3	30th June 20X4	30th Aug. 20X4*

*2 month's extension was granted by the Registrar of companies

In 2nd AGM there is the violation of the Section 166 since the time gap between two AGM is more than 15 months

In 3rd AGM there is no violation of the Section 166 since the time gap of more than 15 months between two AGM of 20X3 and 20X4 has resulted after approval for extension of time from the Registrar.

Practical Illustration 3

Cases	*Financial year ended*	*Last Date for holding AGM*	*AGM held on*
1st	30/09/20X1	31/03/20X2	31/12/20X1
2nd	30/09/20X2	31/03/20X3	01/01/20X3

In 2nd there is the violation of the Section 166 since no AGM could not be held during the calendar year 20X2.

Practical Illustration 4

Cases	*Financial year ended*	*Last Date for holding AGM*	*AGM held on*
1st	30/06/20X1	31/12/20X1	31/12/20X1
2nd	30/06/20X2	31/12/20X2	31/01/20X3*

*1 month's extension was granted by the Registrar of companies

In 2nd AGM there is no violation of the Section 166 since the AGM could not be held in the year 20X2 because of extension granted by the Registrar.

Practical Illustration 5

Cases	*Financial year ended*	*Last Date for holding AGM*	*AGM held on*
1st	30/06/20X1	31/12/20X1	31/ 09/ 20X1
2nd	30/06/20X2	31/12/20X2	31/ 01/ 20X3*

*1 month's extension was granted by the Registrar of companies

In 2nd AGM there is no violation of the Section 166 since gap of more than 15 months resulted and AGM during calendar year 20X2 could not be held because of extension granted by the Registrar.

4.3 Duty of Board to Lay Final Accounts [Section 210(1)]

At every AGM held in pursuance of Section 106, the Board of Directors shall lay before the company.

(a) a Balance Sheet as at the end of period specified in Section 210(3)

(b) a Profit and Loss Account for that period.

4.4 Period for which Profit and Loss shall be Prepared

The Profit and Loss Account shall relate to:

AGM	*Period*
(a) ***In case of the first AGM***	The period beginning with the incorporation of the company and ending with a day which shall not precede the day of meeting by more than 9 months.
(b) ***In the case of any subsequent AGM***	The period beginning with the day immedi-ately after the period for which the account was last submitted and ending on day which shall not precede the day of meetings by more than 6 months, or in case where an extension is granted u/s 166, by more than 6 months and extension so granted.

4.5 Place, Date and Hours of Conducting Meeting [Section 166(2)]

(a) An annual general meeting must be called for at *any time during business hours*, on a day which is *not a public holiday*, and must be held either at the *registered office* of the company *or* at other some *place within* the city, town or village in which the *registered office* of the company is situated.

(b) The Central Government may exempt any class of companies from this provision subject to such conditions as it may impose. In pursuance of this power, the Central Government has exempted Licensed Companies u/s 25 provided the time, date and place of each AGM are decided before hand by board of directors having regard to the direction if any given in this regard by the company in general meeting.

(c) Public company or a private company which is the subsidiary of a public company by its articles fix the *time* for its Annual general meeting or by resolution passed in previous Annual general meeting can also fix the time for its subsequent Annual general meeting.

(d) An independent Private Company in addition to the power given above can also fix the place for meeting in the similar manner given above. Hence in case of independent private company meeting can be held at any place. It is not a necessary that such a place should be within the city, town or village in which the registered office of the company is situated.

(e) **Meaning of Public Holiday [Section 2(38)]**

(i) "Public holiday" means a public holiday within the meaning of the Negotiable Instrument Act, 1881.

(ii) According to Negotiable Instrument Act the Public Holiday includes Sundays and any other day declared by the Central Government, by notification in the Official Gazette, to be a public holiday.

(iii) If any day is declared by the Central Government as a Public Holiday after the notice calling the meeting has been issued, then such holiday shall not be deemed to be a Public Holiday in relation to such meeting.

4.6 Power of Company Law Tribunal [Section 167]

(i) In case of the default in holding an Annual general meeting in accordance with Section 166, the Company Law Tribunal may on application of any member call/direct the calling of an Annual general meeting and give such ancillary and consequential direction as the Company Law Tribunal think expedient, in relation to the calling, holding and conducting of the meeting.

(ii) Such direction may include a direction that any one member present in member or proxy shall be deemed to constitute meeting.

(iii) Such Annual General Meeting subject to any direction Company Law Tribunal shall be deemed to be an annual general meeting of the company.

Notes on Section 167

(i) If the time prescribed by the articles have been expired but not the time prescribed by Section 166 then this section cannot be invoked.

(ii) When meeting was called but could not be properly commenced because directors abandon it before taking up any business then this section can be invoked.

(iii) If meeting was properly held but some of the resolution has been challenged then this section cannot be invoked.

(iv) If meeting of year 20X1 held in year 20X2 as per CLT order then it should be treated as the meeting of the year 20X1. It can also be treated as the AGM for both the year i.e. 20X1 and 20X2 provided that the company passes resolution and forward the copy of the resolution to the registrar within 30 days. [Section 192(1)]

(v) A member and not a company is empowered to invoke the provision of Section 167. A company cannot seek direction against itself. [*M. Sampath* v. *AKMN Cylinders Pvt. Ltd.*]

4.7 Consequences of Default [Section 168]

If the default is made by the company in holding Annual General Meeting in accordance with Section 166 or in complying in any direction given by Company Law Tribunal under Section 167 then the company and its every officer of the company in default shall be punishable with fine upto Rs 50,000 and in case of the continuing default with a further fine upto Rs 2,500 for every day after the first.

4.8 Adjournment

(i) Annual general meeting can be adjourned.

(ii) It must be held either at the registered office of the company or within the city, town or village in which the registered office of a company is situated. But it can not be held at the place different from the place of original Annual General Meeting.

(iii) The Department of company affairs has also clarified that there is no contravention of Section 166(2) if the adjourned meeting comes to be accidentally held on a public holiday. [Department's Letter No. 8/16(1)/61-PR dated 19th May 1961]

(iv) Adjourned meeting can be adjourned again.

(v) No fresh notice for the adjourned meeting is necessary. However, when the date of adjourned meeting is not decided in original meetings then notice becomes necessary.

4.9 Notice

21 clear days' notice in writing must be given. However a shorter notice than 21 days may be given if the consent of ALL the members entitled to vote had been taken on Form. No. 22A. The notice must state the place, the day and the time of holding the meeting alongwith the details of the business to be transacted.

4.10 Quorum [Section 174]

The term 'Quorum' means the minimum number of members required to constitute a valid meeting and to transact business threat. Unless the articles provide for a larger number, quorum shall be:

Case	*Minimum Number*
In case of a Public company	5 members personally present
In case of a Private company	2 members personally present
In case of meeting adjourned due to lack of quorum	Members present **Notes:** (i) A single member present shall not constitute quorum at an adjourned meeting. (ii) Even 2 proxies present can constitute quorum at an adjourned meeting.
In case of meeting adjourned due to other reasons (i) *Public company* (ii) *Private company*	 5 members personally present 2 members personally present

In all of the above cases article may provide for the higher number for the purpose of constituting the quorum. But article cannot provide for the shorter number for the purpose of constituting quorum.

4.11 Important Judicial Rulings

(i) Meeting held beyond the time prescribed by the Section 166 is not void. As the section only prescribes the limit and is silent about the invalidity of the meeting to be held beyond time. However this act is punishable with a penalty in accordance with section 168. [*Re El Sombrero Ltd.*, (1958)]

(ii) Meeting must be held irrespective of the fact that accounts are ready for the consideration or not. [*Hungerford Investment Trust Ltd.* v. *Tourner Marrison & Co. Ltd.*, (1972)]

"In case the annual accounts are not ready for laying at the appropriate AGM, it is open to the company concerned to adjourn the said AGM to a subsequent date when the annual accounts are expected to be ready for laying. This may be done by a suitable resolution adjourning the said meeting to a specific date or to a date to be specified later on". [*Vide Communique No. 35/9/72-CL III dated 2-2-1974 Department of Company Law Affairs*].

Practical Illustration 6

Previous AGM held on 31/12/20X1
Financial year ended on 30/09/20X2
Accounts are not ready for consideration upto 31/12/20X2

Remedy: Hold meeting on or before 31/12/20X2 and adjourn it for future date when the accounts are to be ready for the consideration. But extension of the time by registrar must be obtained.

Practical Illustration 7

Previous AGM held on 30/09/20X1
Financial year ended on 31/03/20X2
Accounts are not ready for consideration upto 30/09/20X2

Remedy: Hold meeting on or before 31/12/20X2 and adjourn it for future date when the accounts are ready for the consideration, but extension of the time by registrar must be obtained. However the adjourned meeting must be held before the expiry of the extended period so as not to attract the penal provision of Section 168.

If Registrar granted 2 months tension then meeting can be held upto 28.02.20X3. As in this case statutory time limit has not been expired so there would be no penalty under Section 168 but penalty will be attracted under Section 210 because statutory limit as per Section 210 is 6 + 2 = 8 months. So meeting should be held before 30.11.20X2.

(iii) Notice for the meeting must be given even when time and place of the meeting is already fixed by the articles.

(iv) Failure to get accounts audited is not the valid excuse for extension of time by the registrar.

(v) Application for extension of time should be admitted before the expiry of statutory period.

(vi) Convened meeting (Notice for which has been given) cannot be postponed.

(vii) Voting right to be considered at the date of the meeting.

(viii) where all the members of the company were also the members of the board of directors, a meeting of the board could be treated as a general meeting of the company. [*P.V. Damodara Reddi* v. *Indian National Agencies Ltd.,* (1945)]

(ix) If because of circumstances beyond their control (for example, pandemonium in the hall) the directors decided not to hold the meeting, it cannot be said to have been held by mere fact that before the directors' announcement, printed copies of balances sheet and agenda had been distributed to shareholders. [*Selvaraj* v. *Mylapore Hindu Permanent Fund Ltd.,* (1968)]

(x) Directors could not be allowed to escape performance of duties regarding the meeting by a mere plea that they had no real control over the affairs of the company and they did not wilfully permit default; if directors were mere passive spectators and did not have the statutory requirements carried out, they may be considered as having wilfully permitted default (*Sarasvati Printers Limited* v. *State*, (1968)]

(xi) If the registered office is not available, moving to a nearby place and holding meeting there is not a violation of law; It is only an irregularity. [*M.R.S. Rathnavelusami Chettiar* v. *M.R.S. Manickavelu Chettiar,* (1951) 21 Comp. Cas. 93 (Mad.)]

(xii) The company did not function is no excuse for not holding the AGM. [*Madan Gopal* v. *State of West Bengal,* (1968)]

(xiii) Where the account books were seized by the police so on to make it impossible for the directors to hold the meeting, the default was not held punishable. [*Re Asia Udyog (P) Ltd.,* (1961)]

(xiv) Failure to place the statement of account before the AGM and the default in holding the AGM are two distinct and separate offences which are punishable separately under the Act.

5.0 EXTRA ORDINARY GENERAL MEETING [SECTION 169]

5.1 Meaning (Regulation 47 of Table A)

All general meetings other than statutory meeting and Annual General Meeting are termed as "extraordinary general meetings".

5.2 Who can Call Extra Ordinary General Meeting?

Extraordinary General Meeting may be called by Board, Requisitionists or Company Law Tribunal.

5.3 Extra Ordinary Meeting by Board of Directors

(a) On its Own Motion [Regulation 48 of Table A]

The Board may, whenever it thinks fit, call an extraordinary general meeting. If an extraordinary general meeting cannot be convened since number of directors in India is less than the quorum required for Board meeting then any director or any 2 members can call an extraordinary general meeting in the same manner nearly as possible as that in which such a meeting may be called up by the Board. [Regulation 48 of Table A]

Exercise of Directors' Power to Call Extraordinary General Meetings. The directors' power to call general meeting including extraordinary general meeting must, like their other powers, be exercised at a properly convened Board meeting. It is not open to some of the directors to convene a general meeting of their own motion [*Harben* v. *Phillips*, (1883) Ch. D- 14].

If the Articles provide that a resolution in writing signed by all the members of the board without meeting is as effective as a resolution passed at a Board meeting as in normally the case, (Regulation 8 of Table A), a general meeting may be convened on a resolution so signed.

(b) On Requisition of the Members [Section 169]

The Board on the requisition of the specified number of the members can call an extraordinary general meeting. Specified number of members will be as follows:

Case	*Specified Number*
(i) ***In case of company having share capital***	Members having at least 10% of the such of the paid up share capital of the company which carries the voting right regarding that matter as at date of the deposit of requisition.
(ii) ***In case of company having no share capital***	Members having at least 10% of the total voting power of all the members having right to vote at the date of the deposit of requisition

Practical Illustration 8

Following data pertains to *X* Ltd.

10,000 shares of Rs 10 each Rs 8 called up	80,000
Less: Call in arrears on 1000 shares @ Rs 2	2,000
Paid up capital	78,000

State the minimum number of members entitled to make requisition in each of the following alternative cases:

Case (i) Where Articles are silent

Case (ii) Where Articles provide that no member shall be entitled to vote at any general meeting unless all calls or other sums presently payable by him in respect of shares in the company have been paid.

Case (iii) Where articles provides that all members whose names appear in the register of member are entitled to vote at general meeting.

Solution:

Case (i) Where articles are silent on particular point then Table A will be applicable and according to Regulation 59 if any calls or sums payable on shares is not paid then that member shall not be entitled to vote. Hence members having 1/10th of the paid up capital (excluding the amount paid up on 1000 shares on which calls are in arrears) i.e. 1/10th of Rs 72,000 (i.e. Rs 78,000 – Rs 6,000) are entitled to make a requisition.

Case (ii) Same Answer as in case (i) because articles provides similar provision as in Table A.

Case (iii) Members having 1/10th of the paid up capital i.e. 1/10th of Rs 78,000 are entitled to make a requisition.

5.4 Provisions as to Requisition

1. **Form of the Requisition** The requisition may be in the form of a letter addressed to the Board of Directors signed by the requisite number of members or there may be several letters in the like form. Although, the letters need not be identical in language but they should be to the same effect.
2. **Contents of Requisition [Section 169(2)]** The requisition must contain all the matters for consideration of which the meeting is to be called. If any special resolution is intended to be passed at the requisitioned meeting, the Board shall be deemed not to have duly convened the meeting if they do not give such notice thereof as is required by Section 189(2). For each item of the agenda explanatory statement must be given.
3. **Signature of the Requisition [Section 169(3)]** The requisition must be signed by all the requistionists. In case of joint shareholders, a requisition signed one or some of them for the purpose of this section has the same force and effect as though it has been signed by all of them.
4. **Deposit of Requisition [Section 169(2)]** The requisition must be deposited *at the registered office* of the company. The requisition sent by a registered post properly addressed and received by the company at its registered office will amount to deposit of the requisition at the registered office.
5. **Application of the Section to Each Matter Separately [Section 169(5)]** When there are two more distinct matters covered in the requisition, then the provision of the Section 169(4) shall apply separately to each such matter.
6. **Compliance of Requisition [Section 169(6)]** The Board of Directors must proceed within 21 days of the deposit of the requisition to convene a meeting which must be held within 45 days of such deposit of the requisition with the company. The Board shall send out notices within 21 days of the deposit of the requisition giving at least 21 days' notice for the meeting.

5.5 Judicial Rulings Relevant for Requisition

1. The Board of Directors cannot refuse to proceed with a requisitioned meeting merely on the ground that the requisition does not disclose sufficient reasons for the resolution to be put to vote at the meeting, in the explanatory statement. [*Life Insurance Corporation of India* v. *Escorts Limited*, 1986, 59 Comp. Cas 548 (SC)]. Section 73(2) requires the management and not the shareholders, calling the meeting to disclose the reasons for the resolution which they purpose to move at meeting.
2. The word or the adjective 'valid' in Section 169 has no reference to the object of the requisition but rather to the requirement in that section itself. If these requirements indicated in the earlier part of section are satisfied, then the requisition deposited with the company must be regarded as a valid requisition on which directors of the company must act. [*Cricket Club of India Ltd.* v. *Madhav L. Apte,* (1975) Bom.]

3. The shareholders cannot requisition a meeting to compel the company for withdrawing its petition pending before the court for its sanction under Section 392 where an amalgamation scheme has been approved in a statutory meeting under Section 391. [*Centron Industrial Alliance Ltd.* v. *Pravin Kantilal Vakil,* (1985) Bom.]
4. Shareholders could requisition the meeting for proposing a modification to the scheme pending before the court for its sanction under Section 392. [*Pravin Katilal Vakil* v. *Rohini Ramesh Save*]
5. Where a requisition contained a matter which is illegal and invalid, still directors are liable to hold general meeting, if the requisition made is valid. It is a matter of court to decide on the fact that whether proposal is invalid or contrary to the provision of the Act [*Cricket Club of India Ltd.* v. *Madhav L. Apte*]. But Judicial opinion outside India is against the view [*Queensland Press Ltd.* v. *Academy Instrument No. 3 Pvt. Ltd.*].
6. Where a requisition is valid on the ground that it complies with requirements Section 169, still in the case of removal of director a special notice is necessary and the special notice must disclose the grounds for the removal of the director. [*Queens Kuries Loans Pvt. Ltd.* v. *Sheena Jose*, (1993) 'Kerala High Court]
7. Where the Articles of Association of a company prohibited any defaulting shareholder from exercising his right to vote at any general meeting, and certain shareholders had not paid a call made on their shares it was held that they were not entitled to requisition an extraordinary general meeting under Section 169. [*Col. Kuldip Singh Dhillon* v. *Paragaon Utility Financiers (P) Ltd.*, (1986) 60 Camp. Cas 1075 (Punj. & Har)]
8. Shares the holder of which has died will be excluded in counting 1/10th as they have no power on the date of deposit of the requisition.
9. Preferences shareholders can join in the requisition only if their dividends are in arrears for the specified period or if the proposed resolution is likely to affect their interest, e.g., a resolution for winding up of the company.
10. After requisition if any requisition ceases to be a member or withdraws, it will not invalidate the requisitionist.
11. The right of a member to requisition or vote at a meetings not affected by pledge or attachment of his shares or by appointment of Receiver over his shares.
12. Such rights are also not affected by taking over of management under the Industries (Development and Regulation) Act, of the shareholder company [*Balkrishan Gupta* v. *Swadeshi Polytex Ltd.*, (1985) 58 Comp. Cas 563 (SC)]

5.6 Extraordinary Meeting by Requistionists [Section 169(6)]

If the board did not proceed to convene such a meeting within 21 days from the date of receipt of requisition or did not call a meeting within 45 days from the date of receipt of the requisition then such meeting may be called within 3 months from the date of deposit of requisition:

(a) by the requistionists themselves, or

(b) In the case of a company having share capital by the requistionists as representing *either* majority in value of the paid up share capital held by all of them *or* at least 10% of the paid up share capital of the company which carries the voting rights regarding that matter which ever is less, or

(c) In the case of a company not having a share capital by the requistionists representing at least 10% of the total voting power of all the members having right to vote regarding that matter.

Practical Illustration 9

7 members (though only 3 members were sufficient to make a requisition) made a requisition to the board who could not proceed to convene the meeting within 21 days from date of requisition. In this case the following members may call the meeting within 3 months from date of deposit of requisition:

(i) 7 members (Requistionist themselves)

(ii) 4 members (Representing majority of the requistionist)

(iii) 3 members (Requisitionist representing at least 10% total voting power)

5.7 Manner of Calling the Meeting by Requistionists under Section 169(6) [Section (169)(7)]

Where the meeting is called by the requistionists, it shall be called in the same manner as nearly as possible to that in which meetings are to be called by the Board but such meeting must be held before the expiry of 3 months from the date of deposit of requisition. However, there is no violation if the meeting is called within 3 months but adjourned to some other date falling after the expiry of the 3 months.

5.8 Consequences of Absence Quorum If the Quorum is not present within half an hour from the time appointed for holding of the meeting the meeting, shall stand dissolved if it is called on the requisition of the members Section 169(6) [Section 174(3)]. But if the articles provide otherwise then articles will apply.

5.9 Consequences of Board's Default [Section 169(9)] If default is made in calling the meeting by the board then—

(i) The requistionist shall be entitled to claim all reasonable expenses incurred by them for convening a meeting from the company.

(ii) The company shall be entitled to retain such sum so paid from any sum due to the directors by ways of fees or other remuneration for their services in respect of those directors who were in default.

5.10 Judicial Rulings

1. Once a final dividend is declared at an annual general meeting no further dividend can be declared at an extraordinary general meeting. [*Biswanath Prasad Khaitan* v. *New Central Jute Mills Co. Ltd.*]
2. In case of a meeting convened by the directors on requisition or on their default, by the requistionists themselves then—
   (a) the meeting cannot transact any business other than the business for which it has been expressly convened. (*Ball* v. *Metal Industries Ltd.*, (1975) S.C. 315]
   (b) the agenda of general meeting cannot include matters which do not appear in the requisition. [*Patent Wood Key Syndicate Ltd.* v. *Pearse*]
3. Where a company cannot convene a meeting due to stay order issued by a court then on Board's inability to call the meeting requistionist themselves also cannot hold meeting. The proper course of action for the requistionist is to apply to the court for convening the meeting. [*Chaudhary (A.D.)* v. *Mysore Paper Mills Ltd.*]

5.11 Extraordinary Meeting by Company Law Tribunal [Section 186]

(i) Where for any reason it is impracticable to call a general meeting other than Annual General Meeting, the Company Law Tribunal may either on its own motion *suo moto* or on the application of any director (whether or not the member) or any member of the company who is entitled to vote at a meeting, order a meeting to called, held and conducted in such manner as it thinks fit and give such ancilliary and consequential directions as it thinks expedient in relation to the calling, holding and conducting of such meeting.

(ii) Such directions may include a direction that one member present in person or by proxy shall be deemed to constitute the meeting. Such meeting shall be held in the same manner as any other meeting called by the company.

(iii) The Company Law Tribunal may direct for the modification of the provisions of the Act or the articles in relation to the calling, holding and conducting of the meeting or that one member of the company present in person or by proxy may be deemed to constitute a meeting.

(iv) Any meeting called, held and conducted in accordance with the order of the Company Law Tribunal will be deemed, for all purpose, to be a meeting of the company duly called, held and conducted.

Note: It may be noted that where a meeting can be called by recourse to Section 169 or Section 167, the Company Law Tribunal will not grant an application under Section 186. For Section 186 the petitioner would at least have to show that there is no other option but to apply under Section 186.

5.12 Judicial Rulings relevant for Section 186

1. On the Word 'Impracticable'

(a) If a petition was filed under Section 186, but in petition there was no allegation that it is impracticable for a company to hold the meeting, such petition would be not valid. [*Siri Ram* v. *Edward Ganj Public Welfare Association Ltd.*]

(b) The word 'impracticable' must be given a practical meaning. It must be understood to be impracticable from the business point of view. It must not be held impracticable on the slightest excuse that the directors do not agree. [*Bengal & Assam Investors Ltd.* v. *J.K. Eastern Industries*]

(c) The word impracticable does not mean impossible. Thus where it is possible to hold meeting but impracticable to hold meeting in ordinary manner then it would also be treated as impracticable. [*Re Passari Floor Mills Ltd.*, (1962) 32. Comp. Cas 896 (M.P.)]

(d) Impracticability of conducting a meeting also includes impracticability of holding a meeting. For example holding of a meeting is impracticable where the registered office of the company is locked and is not available. [*M.R.S. Rathnavelusami Chettiar* v. *M.R.S Manickavelu Chettiar,* (1951) 21 Comp. Cas 93 (Mad.)]

(e) Impracticable also include a case that where due to the Article of Association, it becomes difficult for a company to get a quorum present. [*Opera Photographic Ltd.* v. *BCLC*]

2. Basic Principles which should Guide Company Law Tribunal

Some basic principles that should guide the Company Law Tribunal were set out *Re. Ruttonjee & Co. Ltd.,* (1968) 2 Comp. LJ ISS (1970) 40 Com. Cases 491 (Cal.).

(a) The Company Law Tribunal would not interfere with the domestic management of a company which should be conducted in accordance with the articles.

(b) The discretion granted under Section 186 should be used sparingly with caution so that the Company Law Tribunal does not become either a shareholder or director of a company trying to participate in internecine squabbles of the company.

(c) The word 'impracticable' means impracticable from a reasonable point of view.

(d) The Company Law Tribunal should take a common sense view of the matter and must act as a prudent man of business. Prudent means that Company Law Tribunal should in ordinarily circumstances keep itself away from indulging in controversy of rival group of directors or members.

(e) Where there are doubts and controversy about who are the directors and rival group convene their own meeting, the situation may render the holding of the meeting impracticable.

(f) The Company Law Tribunal should act in a *bona fide* manner and in a larger interest of a company.

3. An application under Section 186 need not to on behalf of the company since the very language of that section even permits the Company Law Tribunal *suo moto* to call meeting of the company if it has become impracticable to call a meeting other than an annual general meeting. An action need not be in the name of the company for actions concerning injuries personal to the petitioner.
[*Smt. Jain* v. *Delhi Flour Mills Company Ltd. and others*, (1974) 44 Comp. Cas. 228 (Delhi)]
4. In a petition for an order directing the holding of general meeting under Section 186, the Company Law Tribunal will not go to the extent of rectifying the register of member for the purpose of giving directions as to who should vote at such meeting. [*Smt. Jain* v. *Delhi Floor Mills Co. Ltd.*]
5. As directors do not continue to hold office on the failure of calling Annual General Meeting within statutory limits, the Company Law Tribunal can invoke Section 186 to call the meeting for election of directors. [*B.R. Kundra* v. *Mohan Pictures Association*]
6. A meeting which is not conducted according to the direction issued by the Company Law Board is not a valid meeting. [*Re Motion Pictures Association*, (1979) 46 Comp. Cas 298 (Delhi)]
7. Company court which is supervising the scheme under Section 392, can convene the meeting for proper supervision and implementation of scheme under Section 392, and it is not necessary to invoke Section 186. In other words Section 186 is not applicable in cases covered by Section 392. [*India Hardware Ltd*. v. *S.K. Gupta*]
8. The Company Law Board's power under Section 186 is discretionary and not mandatory. It is alternative course of action which may be applied on the failure of company management to hold meeting. [*Bengal & Assam Investors Ltd.* v. *J.K. Eastern Industries*]
9. The use of the word "and" between the word "held" and "conducted" in Section 186(1)(a) clearly shows that the court has no power to make any order regarding the holding and conducting of meeting which has been called up by the board or its members on board's failure to call the meeting. [*Rangachari (R)* v. *S.K. Suppiah*]

5.13 Notice of the Meeting

At least 21 clear days' notice must be given (Section 171). A shorter notice less than 21 days' may be given if the consent is obtained there to—

(a) by the members holding at least 95% of the share capital carrying voting rights in case of the company having share capital

(b) by member holding at least 95% of the total voting power in case of the company having no share capital.

5.14 Quorum [Section 174]

The term 'Quorum' means the minimum number of members required to constitute a valid meeting and to transact business threat. Unless the articles provide for a larger number, quorum shall be:-

Case	*Minimum number*
In case of Public company	5 members personally present
In case of Private company	2 members personally present
In case of meeting adjourned due to lack of quorum	Members present **Notes:** (i) A single member present shall not constitute quorum at an adjourned meeting. (ii) Even 2 proxies present can constitute quorum at an adjourned meeting.
In case of meeting adjourned due to other reasons (i) *Public company* (ii) *Independent Private company*	 5 members personally present 2 members personally present

In all of the above cases article may provide for the higher number for the purpose of constituting the quorum. But article cannot provide for the shorter number for the purpose of constituting quorum.

5.14 Place, Date and Hours of Conducting Meeting

Such meeting can be held at any place, any day and at any time because the Act is silent on these points.

5.15 Kind of the Business [Section 173]

All business to be transacted at such a meeting shall be **special** therefore, an explanatory statement as required by Section 173(2) is required to be annexed to the notice convening such meeting. Such statement shall include amongst other:

(a) All material facts concerning each item of business.
(b) The nature of the concern or interest if any, therein of every director and manager.
(c) If any item of the special business affects any other company, then the extent of shareholding of every director and manager in that company in case their share-holding interest is at least 20% of the paid up share capital of the other company.
(d) The time when and place where the document to be approved at the meeting can be inspected.

Note: The company is not bound to attach any explanatory statement unless the company gives the notice on its own behalf. As long as it is merely forwards the requistionist notice, it does not have to attach any explanatory statements. [*Vijay M. Porwal* v. *Pentokey Organy (India) Ltd.*]

5.16 Kind of Resolution

The resolution can be either *ordinary* or *special* depending on the specific provision in this regard incorporated in the Act or Articles.

5.17 Adjournments, Chairman, Proxies and Voting

The provisions relating to Adjournment Chairman, Proxies and Voting shall be governed by general sections [Sections 171 to 186] unless the article provide otherwise. [Section 170]

6.0 CLASS MEETINGS

The class meetings may be of members *or* debentureholders.

6.1 Class Meetings of Members [Sections 106 and 391]

The class meetings of the members may be convened by the company under Section 106 or by the court under Section 391.

(i) Convened by the Company [Section 106]

Where the share capital of a company is divided into different classes of shares, the rights attached to the shares of any class may be varied in any one of the following two ways:

(a) with the consent in writing of holders of at least 3/4th of the issued shares of that class, or

(b) with the sanction of special resolution at a separate meeting of the holders of the issued shares of that class.

Authority for Variation

(a) Provision with respect to such variation must be contained in the memorandum or articles of the company, or

(b) Such variation must not be prohibited by terms of issue of the shares of that class in the absence of any provision in respect of variation in the memorandum or articles.

(ii) Meeting Convened by the Court [Section 391]

Where a compromise or arrangement is proposed either between the company and its creditors or between a company and its members or any class of them, then court may on the application of the company or of any creditor or member of the company, order a meeting of the creditors or members, or class of members, as the case may be, to be called, held and conducted in such manner as the court may direct. If a majority in number representing 3/4th in value of creditors or class of creditors or members or class of members present and voting either in person or by proxy agree to such compromise or arrangement, then such compromise or arrangement if sanctioned by the court shall be binding on the concerned creditors or members as the case may be. The important rules applicable to such meetings are as follows:

(i) Notice is required to be served on all members and creditors by advertisement in the newspaper in the manner to be directed by the court 21 clear days before the date of meeting in addition to individual service of notice.

(ii) the chairman to be appointed by the court,

(iii) Proxies are entitled to attend and vote.

(iv) Decisions must always be ascertained only by taking a poll.

6.2 Class Meetings of Debentureholders

Where the trust deed provides for convening and holding the meeting where it is proposed to vary any condition relating to debentures, appointment of new trustees and to issue new debentures, a class meeting of concerned debentureholders is required to be held.

The objective of such clause in trust deed is to enable the company to deal with debenture holders as a class and prevent a few adversely affected debentureholders from interrupting a necessary or desirable arrangement. However, this power must be exercised in a bona fide manner. [*British America Nickel Corpn.* v. *O' Brien* (1927)]

Purpose for which Debentureholders' Meeting May be Called These may include the following:

1. to release particular property from the specific charge (with or without the substitution of other property), or

2. to reduce the amount of the debenture interest, or
3. to defer its payment for a time, or
4. to allow the creation of debentures ranking in priority to the existing debentures, or *pari passu* with them, or
5. to release the company for a limited period from all obligations to set apart profits towards a sinking fund, or
6. to effect an exchange of debentures for equity or preference shares.

Applicability of Sections 171 to 186 to Class Meetings [Section 170(2)]
Unless articles otherwise provide, the provision of Sections 171 to 186 with such adaptations and modifications, if any, as may be prescribed, shall apply also with respect to meetings of class of members or of debentureholders or any class of debentureholders in the same manner as they apply to general meetings of such company.

7.0 APPLICABILITY OF SECTIONS 171 TO 186 TO MEETINGS [SECTION 170]

1. The provisions of Sections 171 to 186 shall apply to all public companies and private companies which are subsidiaries of public companies even if anything is contrary in the Articles.
2. The provision of Section 174(1) relating to minimum quorum shall also apply to all independent private companies.
3. The provision of Section 182, (relating to restriction on exercise of voting right) are not applicable to independent private companies.
4. Unless the Articles otherwise provide, the provisions of Sections 171 to 181 and Sections 183 to 186 shall also apply to all independent private company companies. In other words, an independent private company may make special provisions in its articles in respect of any of the matters covered by these sections.
5. Section 176 with such adaptations and modifications if any, may be prescribed shall apply to—
   (a) meetings of any class of members
   (b) meetings of debentureholders
   (c) meetings of any class of debentureholders
6. Unless the Articles otherwise provide or a contract binding on the persons concerned otherwise provide, Sections 171 to 186 apply to—
   (a) meetings of any class of members.
   (b) meetings of debentureholders.
   (c) meetings of any class of debentureholders.

8.0 REQUISITES FOR A VALID GENERAL MEETING OF MEMBERS

1. Proper Authority
2. Proper Notice
3. Proper Place
4. Proper Date
5. Proper Time
6. Proper Quorum
7. Proper Chairmanship
8. Proper Proxies
9. Proper Voting
10. Proper Adjournment
11. Proper Resolution
12. Proper Registration/Filing of Resolution
13. Proper Minutes

9.0 PROPER AUTHORITY

Explanation of Aforesaid Points in Details

Proper Authority to convene various types of meeting shall be as follows;

Case	*Proper Authority to convene meeting*
(a) ***Statutory Meeting***	Duly constituted Board of Directors is normally the proper authority. Neither the Managing director nor the secretary is empowered to convene such meeting unless authorised by the Board. The secretary or the managing director when calling the meeting must quote the authority of the board by adding the words 'By Order of the Board.'
(b) ***Annual General Meeting***	(i) Duly constituted Board of Directors where a company does not defaults in holding Annual General Meeting in accordance with Section 166, or (ii) Company Law Board where a company default in holding Annual General Meeting in accordance with Section 166 and an application is made by any member.
(c) ***Extraordinary General Meeting***	(i) Duly constituted Board of Directors whenever it thinks fit. (ii) One Director/two members of the company where number of directors in India is less than the quorum required for Board meeting. (Regulation 48) (iii) Duly constituted Board on deposit of requisition by requisite number of members under Section 169 (iv) Requisitionists if the Board did not proceed to convene the meeting 21 days from the date of deposit of the requisition or did not call a meeting within 45 days from the date of deposit of the requisition under Section 169. (v) Company Law Board on its own motion or on the application of a director or any member of the company where for any reason it is impracticable to call extraordinary general meeting of the company. [Section 186]

10.0 NOTICE [SECTIONS 171 TO 173 AND SECTION 53]

10.1 By whom Notice must be Given The notice must be given by the proper summoning authority which would normally be the Board of Directors. If however a notice has been issued without authority, the requisite authority may be given by ratification by the proper summoning authority before the meeting is held and notice may thus become good. [*Hooper* v. *Kerr, Stuart & Co*. (1900)]

10.2 Notice in Writing—Notice must be in writing as it is specifically provided in Section 171.

10.3 Length of the Notice [Section 171(1)] The length of the notice must be 21 clear days i.e. whilst computing the 21 days, the day of service of the notice and day of holding of the meeting are to be excluded. Each of the 21 days must be a full calendar day and not a part of the day.

Shorter Notice [Section 171(2)]

A general meeting may be called by giving a notice shorter than 21 clear days.

(a) ***In case of Annual General Meeting***	If the consent of *all members entitled to vote* at the meeting is obtained.
(b) ***In case of other general meeting of a company having share capital***	If the consent of members holding at least 95% of the *paid up share capital carrying voting rights* is obtained.
(c) ***In case of other general meeting of a company having no share capital***	If the consent of member *having at least 95% of the total voting power* is obtained.

Notes:

(i) Consent of members entitled to attend and vote at that meeting is required and not merely of members entitled to vote and present in person or proxy at that meeting. [*Nagappa (N.V.R) Chettiar* v. *Madras Race Club* (1949)]

Practical Illustration 9

Total No. of members of *X* Ltd. = 100

Total no. of members Present at AGM called by a shorter notice = 60

No. of members present who consented to shorter notice = 60

Although all members present have consented to short notice, it is not sufficient. The consent of total number of members entitled to vote i.e. 100 is required.

(ii) **When should such Consent be Obtained?**

The Act is silent on the point whether such consent should be obtained prior to or at or even subsequent to meeting concerned. In case of Self-help Private Industrial Estate (P) Ltd., it has been held that the subsequent convent obtained would validate the resolution passed without proper notice.

(iii) **How should such Consent be Obtained?**

The consent as to shorter notice should be obtained in writing in Form no. 22A.

(iv) **Can the Requirement as to Notice be Dispensed with?**

No, unless all the members are present at the meeting since " If you have all the shareholders present then all the requirements in connection with a company are complied with." [*Younger L.J. in Engineering Work* (1920)]

(v) The provision of Section 171 apply to Section 25 companies with the modification that a general meeting may be called by giving a notice in writing of at least 14 days.

10.4 Persons Entitled to Receive the Notice

The following persons are entitled to receive the notice:

(i) To every member of the company. [Section 172(2)(i)]

(ii) To the persons entitled to a share in consequence of the death or insolvency of a member. [Section 172(2)(ii)]

(iii) To a auditor or auditors of a company. [Section 172(2)(iii)]

Notes:

(i) In case of joint holders, notice is to be served on the senior or first named of joint holders.

(ii) Notice is to be sent to members who have given their addresses in India (Section 53). Hence notice need had not be given to members who are residents abroad.

(iii) The words 'every member' seems to suggest that notice must be given even to preference shareholders. The Department is of the view, the preference share holders have a right to attend the meeting but they may not be allowed to take part in the discussion in the meeting where the meeting does not discuss any matter in which such shareholders have any voting rights. [*Company News & Notes July* 16, 1964]

It may be noted that there is a statutory obligation to send notice to preference shareholders when their dividend is in arrears for more than a certain period [Section 87(2)(b)]. This obligation arises from the fact that preference shareholders whose dividends are in arrears are entitled to attend and vote at the meeting.

(iv) Beneficial owners of shares are not entitled to receive notice.

10.5 Effect of Accidental Omission or Non-Receipt of notice on Meeting

An accidental omission to give notice to, or the non-receipt of notice by any member or any other person to whom it should be given shall not invalidate the proceedings of the meeting. [Section 172(3)]

Notes:

(i) Omission to serve notice of meeting on a member on the mistaken ground that he is not a shareholder cannot be said to be an accidental omission. [*Musselwhite* v. *Musselwhite & Sons Ltd.*, (1962) 32 Comp. Cas 804]

(ii) 'Accidental omission' means that the omission must be not only designed but also not deliberate. [*Maharaja Export* v. *Apparels Exports Promotion Council* (1986) 60 Comp. Cas 353]

(iii) If a meeting is called without notice to a shareholder the omission not being accidental, it is invalid and proceedings therein are also invalid. [*Eastern Linkers (P) Ltd.* v. *Dina Nath Sodhi* (1984) (Delhi)]

10.6 Service of Notice [Section 53]

(i) A notice may be served by the company on any member either personally or by sending it by post to his registered address or if he has no registered address in India to the address in India given by him for the purpose of the giving of the notices to him. [Section 53(1)]

(ii) Where a notice is sent by post, service shall be deemed to be affected at the expiration of the 48 hours after the letter containing the same is posted. [Section 53(2)]

Practical Illustration 10

	Case I	Case II	Case III
Date of Meeting	30th Sep.	30th Sep.	30th Sep.
Date of sending notice by post	5th Sep.	6th Sep.	7th Sep.
No. of days from date of sending notice by Post to date of meeting	26	25	24
Less : Day of meeting	1	1	1
Less: Day of sending notice by post	1	1	1
Less: 2 days (i.e. equivalent to 48 hours) after date of posting	2	2	2
Number of clear days	22	21	20
Length of notice	Proper	Proper	Shorter

10.7 When is Notice Deemed to be Served?

Cases	*Notice shall be deemed to be duly served if . . .*
(i) ***In case no particular manner of service of notice has been requested by member.***	The notice is sent by properly addressing, prepaying, and posting to the registered address of the member.
(ii) ***In case particular manner of service has been requested by the member.***	The notice is sent in the manner requested by member.
(iii) ***In case a member who has no registered address in India and has not supplied to the company an address within India for giving notices to him.***	The notice is advertised in a newspaper circulating in the neighbourhood of the registered office of the company at least 21 clear days before the date of meeting. [Section 53] In this case notice is deemed to be served on the day on which advertisement appears in a newspaper.
(iv) ***In case of joint share holdings***	The notice is served on the joint holder whose name appears first in the register of members.

Notes:

(i) The presumption of deemed delivery cannot be raised when at the time of posting the post office was, within the knowledge of the company, on declared strike. [*Bredman* v. *Trinity Estate Plc*, (1989) BCLC 757 (Ch. D)]

(ii) Section 53 applies to all documents and not merely service of notice of meetings.

(iii) A person who is present and who votes at the meeting will not be entitled to challenge the resolution on the ground of an invalidity in the notice. [*Re, British Sugar Refining Co.* (1857) 3 K&J 408]

10.8 Contents of the Notice

Notice must be in writing and signed by a director or manager or the secretary or some other authorised offices of the company and specify the following:

(i) Company's full name and the address of its registered office. [Section 147(1)(c)]

(ii) The place date and hour of the meeting. [Section 172(1)]

(iii) The statement of the business to be transacted (Agenda). [Section 172(1)]

(iv) Where a resolution is to be passed as a special resolution, the intention to propose the resolution as such. [Section 189(2)(a)].

(v) In case of companies having share capital, the notice must also state with reasonable prominence that member entitled to attend and vote is entitled to appoint proxy to attend and vote instead of himself and proxy need not be a member. [Section 176(2)]

10.9 Explanatory Statement Required to be Annexed to Notice [Section 173]

An explanatory statement is required to be annexed to notice in case special business is to be transacted at the general meeting. Such statement shall include amongst other:

(a) The material fact concerning each item of business. [Section 173(2)]

A very minor defect arising out of strict non-conformity with provision contained in Section 173(2) might not render the resolution null and void. [*Joseph Michael* v. *Travancore Rubber & Tea Co. Ltd.*, (1986)]

(b) The nature of the concern or interest if any, therein of every director and manage. [Section 173(2)]

(c) If any item of the special to be transacted affect any other company then the extent of shareholding of every director and manager in that company in case it is at least 20% of the paid up share capital of the other company. [Proviso to Section 173(2)]

(d) The time and place where the document to be approved at the meeting can be inspected. [Section 173(3)]

10.10 Is it necessary to advertise explanatory statement in the newspaper in case a notice is advertised in the newspaper in case of case of a member who has no registered address in India and has not supplied to the company an address within India for giving notices to him?

No. It would be sufficient compliance if it is mentioned in the advertisement that the explanatory statements has been forwarded of the members. [Proviso to Section 172(2)]

10.11 Purpose of Sec 173

Section 173 is designed to secure that facts having a bearing on the issue on which the shareholders have to form their judgement, are brought to the notice of the shareholders so that they can exercise intelligent judgment.

11.0 PROPER PLACE

Proper place for holding various types of meetings shall be as follows:

Meeting	*Proper place for holding meeting*
(i) *Annual general Meeting*	An annual general meeting must be held either at the registered office of the company or at other some place within the city, town or village in which the registered office of the company is situated. [Section 166(2)] However an independent private company can fix the place for its annual general meeting and such a place need not be within the city, town or village in which the registered office of the company is situated.
(ii) *Annual general meeting adjourned due to lack of quorum*	At the same place where original meeting was held or at any other place as the board may determine. [Section 174(4)]
(iii) *Annual general meeting adjourned due to any other reasons other than lack of quorum*	As per Section 166(2) as applicable to original meeting.
(iv) *Any other meeting*	At any place as the board may determine since act is silent about it.

12.0 PROPER DATE

Proper date for holding various types of meetings shall be as follows:

Meeting	*Proper date for holding meeting . . .*
(i) *Annual General meeting*	Original Annual General Meeting must be held on a day which is not a public holiday. Public holiday "means a public holiday within the meaning of the Negotiable Instrument Act, 1881. [Section 2(38)] According to Negotiable Instrument Act the Public Holiday includes Sundays and any other day declared by the Central Government, by notification in the Official Gazette, to be a public holiday. If any day declared by the central Government as a public

(*Contd.*)

(*Contd.*)

	holiday after the notice calling the meeting has been issued, then such holiday shall not be deemed to be a public holiday in relation to such meeting. However 1st April and 30th September shall not be treated as public holiday for the purpose of Section 166.
(ii) ***Annual general meeting adjourned due to lack of quorum***	It may be held on any other day including public holiday as the board may determine since the act is silent about it.
(iii) ***Annual general meeting adjourned due to any other reasons other than lack of quorum***	Annual general meeting adjourned for any other reasons other than lack of quorum, must be held on a day other than public holiday.
(iv) ***Any other meeting***	It may be held on any other day including public holiday as the board may determine since the act is silent about it.

13.0 PROPER HOURS

The Department of Company Affairs has also clarified that there is no contravention of Section 166(2) if the adjourned annual general meeting comes to be accidentally held on a public holiday. [Department's Letter No. 8/16(1)/61-PR]

The proper time for holding various types of meetings are as follows:

Meeting	***Proper time for holding meeting . . .***
(i) ***Annual General meeting***	Annual General meeting must be called during **business hours** which means the normal working hours of a company.
(ii) ***Annual general meeting adjourned due to lack of quorum***	It may be called at a **time which may not fall within the business hours** as the board may determine since the act is silent on this point.
(iii) ***Annual general meeting adjourned due to any other reasons other than lack of quorum***	It must be called during **business hours** which means the normal working hours of a company.
(iv) ***General meeting other than Annual General meeting***	It may be called **at a time which may not fall within the business hours as** the board may determine since the act is silent on this point.

14.0 QUORUM (SECTION 174)

14.1 Meaning of Quorum

The term 'Quorum' means the minimum number of members that must be present in order to constitute a valid meeting and to transact business threat.

14.2 Quorum Required for General Meeting

Unless the articles provide for a larger number, quorum shall be:

Case	***Minimum Number***
In case of Public company	5 members personally present
In case of Private company	2 members personally present

(*Contd.*)

(*Contd.*)

In case of meeting adjourned due to lack of quorum	Members present **Notes:** (i) A single member present shall not constitute quorum at an adjourned meeting. (ii) Even 2 proxies present can constitute quorum at an adjourned meeting.
In case of meeting adjourned due to other reasons (i) *Public company* (ii) *Private company*	 5 members personally present 2 members personally present

In all of the above cases article may provide for the higher number for the purpose of constituting the quorum. But article cannot provide for the shorter number for the purpose of constituting quorum.

14.3 Who are/are not Considered as Members Personally Present

Following are considered as members personally present:

(i) a member of the company [Section 176]
(ii) Authorised representative of a body corporate. [Section 187(2)]
(iii) Representative of President/Governor of the state. [Section 187A]

Following are not considered as members personally present:

(i) Proxy appointed by the member. .
(ii) Proxy appointed by authorised representative of a body corporate/Representative of President/Governor.

14.4 Can Proxy be Counted for the Purpose for the Quorum?

Proxy can be counted for the purpose of the quorum in the following 3 cases:

(i) In case of the Annual general meeting convened, conducted and held by the Company Law Board. [Section 167]
(ii) In case of the General meeting other than Annual General meeting convened, conducted and held by the Company Law Board. [Section 186]
(iii) In case of the meeting adjourned due to lack of Quorum.

14.5 Can One Member Constitute Quorum?

One member can constitute quorum in the following 3 cases:

(i) In case of the Annual general meeting convened, conducted and held by the Company Law Board. [Section 167]
(ii) In case of the General meeting other than Annual General meeting convened, conducted and held by the Company Law Board. [Section 186]
(iii) In case of class meetings where a class of shares is held by one shareholder.

14.6 Consequences of Absence of Quorum

If the Quorum is not present within half an hour from the time appointed for holding of the meeting the meeting shall stand:

(i) Dissolved if it is called on the requisition of the member under Section 169 [Section 174(3)]
(ii) Adjourned to the same day in the next week at the same time and same place or to such other day, place and time as board may determine. [Section 174(4)]

But if in both 2 cases the articles of the company provide otherwise, then article shall be applied.

14.7 What will be Quorum if at Adjourned Meeting also Quorum is not Present [Section 174(5)]

If at adjourned meeting quorum is not present within half on hour from the time appointed for holding the meeting then members present shall form quorum unless articles provides otherwise. A single member shall not constitute quorum at an adjourned meeting.

14.8 When is Presence of the Quorum Required?

(i) According to the Regulation 49(1) of the Table A, the Quorum must be present at the time when the meeting proceed to business.

(ii) In the American Encyclopaedic Dictionary of Business, "A quorum must be present not only to begin meeting, but to transact business."

(iii) A reasonable conclusion can be drawn from the above statement that if during the meeting a number of members quits, leaving behind the members less than the number required to form quorum then meeting must be adjourned or as articles of the company provides for.

14.9 Effect of Failure of a Quorum

If no quorum is present, then there is no meeting and the proceedings are invalid *Re Romford Canal Co.,* (1883) 24 Ch. D 85]. However, acts done creating rights in favour of third parties at a meeting without a quorum being present would not affect the rights of such third parties, provided they had no notice of the irregularity [For example debentures issued at a meeting of directors where there was an insufficient quorum—*Re Romford Canal.*]

14.10 When is Quorum Immaterial?

If all the members are present, it is immaterial that the quorum required is more than the total number of members *(Re Express Engineering Works Ltd.*, (1920) Ch 466; *Re Oxted Motor Co. Ltd.* (1921) 3 KB 32]. If, for example, the articles of a private company provide that four members personally present shall be a quorum, and the number of members is reduced to three then the question of quorum will not arise when all the three members attend a meeting.

14.11 Cases where one Member can be Counted as more than one Member Personally Present

(i) In case where two or more bodies are represented by one person then each of the body corporate shall be deemed to be personally present by the individual representing it.

(ii) If individual attends the meeting in more than one capacity. For example in his individual capacity and as a representative of any body corporate. [*Neil McLeod & Sons, Petitioners* (1976)]

14.12 Joint Holders and Quorum

(i) In case of the joint holders any one of them may be counted for the purpose of the quorum.

(ii) Two joint holders are each member of the quorum and if they both are present in the meeting then they shall be counted as 2 members personally present. [(*Re Trans-Continental Hotel Ltd.*) & *Jarnail Singh* v. *Bakshi Singh*]

(iii) If the articles do not provide anything to the contrary, if appears that two or more joint holders when personally present can be counted as so many members for the purpose of forming a quorum.

14.13 Director Who is Not a Member

A director who is not the shareholder of the company cannot be counted for the purpose of the quorum neither he can propose or second a resolution. But by obtaining permission from the chairman he can speak on specific matters.

15.0 PROPER CHAIRMANSHIP [SECTION 175]

15.1 Appointment of Chairman

Section 175(1) provides that unless the article of a company provide otherwise, the members personally present at the meeting shall elect one of themselves to be the chairman thereof on a show of hands. Section 175(2) provides that if a poll is demanded on the election of the chairman (whether before/after the election of chairman on a show of hand) then it shall be taken forthwith and the person elected as chairman on show of hands shall exercise all the powers of chairman. If some other person is elected chairman as a result of poll he shall be the chairman for the rest of the meeting. [Section 175(3)]

15.2 Is it Necessary for a Chairman to be a Director?

No since according to Section 175(1) members shall elect one of themselves to be the chairman on a show of hands unless the Articles otherwise provides.

15.3 Is it Necessary for a Chairman to be a Member?

No since according to the Regulations of 50 and 51 director may be the chairman of general meeting and according to Section 270, director may not be required to obtain share qualification. Accordingly, the chairman of the general meeting could be a director who may not hold share in the company.

15.4 Voting Rights of a Chairman

Voting rights of a chairman are as follows:

Case	*Voting rights of chairman*
(i) *In case he is member of the company*	Chairman is entitled to exercise one vote as a member of a company and second/casting vote as a chairman in case of equality of votes (if articles provides) on a show of hands or a poll.
(ii) *In case he is not a member of the company*	As he is not a member chairman is entitled to exercise only second/casting vote as a chairman in case of equality of votes on a show of a hand or a poll.

15.5 What may Articles Provide Regarding the Appointment of Chairman?

Article may provide

(i) that the chairman of the Board shall preside as chairman at every general meeting of a company. [Regulation 50 of Table A]

(ii) that if no chairman is present or if the chairman is unwilling to act as the chairman of a meeting then the directors shall elect one of them to be the chairman of the meeting. [Regulation 51 of Table A]

(iii) Where no director is present within 15 minutes or where the director present are not willing to act as chairman, then the members shall elect one of themselves to be the chairman of the meeting. [Regulation 52]

16.0 PROXIES [SECTION 176]

16.1 Meaning of Proxy

A proxy may be defined as an instrument prescribed by the Act by which a member of a company appoints another person to attend a meeting and to vote on his behalf. This term is also used for the person so appointed.

16.2 Who Appoint a Proxy/More than One Proxy? [Section 176(1)]

Following person can appoint proxy:

(i) Every member who is entitled to attend and vote at a meeting of the company shall be entitled to appoint another person (whether a member or not) as his proxy to attend and vote instead of himself.

(ii) Member of company having no share capital is entitled to appoint proxy only if Article of Association so provide, a member of a private company having share capital is entitled to appoint more than one proxy if Articles so provide.

16.3 Is proxy is Bound to Vote According to the Directions of the Member Appointing Him?

The relationship between a member and his proxy is that of principal and agent. The proxy is bound to vote according to the directions of the member appointing him. [*Naryan* v. *Kaleshwara Mills Ltd.*, AIR (1952)]

16.4 What are the Rights of a Proxy?

Rights of a proxy are as follows:

(i) A proxy shall be entitled to vote in case of voting by poll even if articles does not provides so.

(ii) A proxy may demand for poll or joint demanding a poll unless the articles otherwise provide.

16.5 What are the Limitations of a Proxy?

(i) A proxy (if not member) shall not be entitled to speak at the meeting. [Section 176(1)]

(ii) A proxy shall not be entitled to vote in case of voting by show of hands unless Articles so provide. [Section 176(1)]

(iii) A proxy is not counted for the purpose of quorum except under Sections 167, 174 (5) and 186.

(iv) A proxy cannot also express his views in writing because it would tantamount to speech.

16.6 Statement Regarding Proxy in Notice [Section 176(2)]

In every notice calling a meeting of a company which has a share capital or the articles of which provides for voting by proxy at the meeting, there shall appear a statement that a "member entitled to attend and vote is entitled to appoint a proxy to attend and vote instead of himself and that a proxy need not be a member of the company."

In the contravention of the aforesaid provision every officer of the company who is in default is punishable with fine upto Rs 5,000.

16.7 Instrument Appointing Proxy

Instrument appointing Proxy must be:
(i) in writing
(ii) signed by the appointer/his attorney duly authorised in writing. If the appointer is body corporate, the instrument should be under its seal or be signed by an officer or an attorney authorised by its incomplete
(iii) properly stamped.

16.8 Form of Proxy [Section 176(6)]

In Schedule IX to the Act the following 2 forms are given:
(i) General Form
(ii) Form for affording member an opportunity of voting for or against a resolution.

An instrument appointing a proxy as set out in Schedule IX shall not be questioned on the ground that it fails to comply with any special requirement specified for such instrument by the articles.

16.9 Deposit of Proxy [Section 176(3)]

Where articles provide for a longer period than 48 hours before the time for holding meeting for depositing the proxy, then a period of 48 hours and not the longer period shall be considered for depositing the proxy. [Section 176(3)]

Since, the section speaks about the longer period and not the shorter period the company can provide for shorter period in its article.

Practical Illustration11

	Case				
	I	*II*	*III*	*IV*	*V*
Date of holding meeting	30/9/20X1	30/9/20X1	30/9/20X1	30/9/20X 1	30/9/20X1
Time of holding meeting	2 p.m.	2 p.m.	2 p.m.	2 p.m.	2 p.m.
Date of deposit of proxy	28/9/20X1	28/9/20X1	28/9/20X1	28/9/20X1	28/9/20X1
Time of deposit of proxy	2 p.m.	3 p.m.	2 p.m.	3 p.m.	4 p.m.
Hours before which Proxy is to be deposited as per articles	49 hours	49 hours	47 hours	47 hours	47 hours

Case I: Deposit of Proxy is valid because it is clear from the Act that if articles provide for a longer period than 48 hours then a period of 48 hours shall be considered.

Case II: Deposit of Proxy is not valid because statutory time limit of 48 hours provided by the Act has been expired.

Case III & Case IV: Deposit of proxy is valid because the time limit provided by the articles has not been expired.

Case V: Deposit of Proxy is not valid because the time limit provided by the articles has been expired.

There is nothing in law to exclude Sunday in the computation of the 48 hours and therefore a proxy delivered on Sunday for a meeting to be 48 hours later on Tuesday would be valid provided the receipt of the proxies at the time stated could be identified in some way. [*K.P. Chackochan* v. *Federal Bank* (1989)]

16.10 Deposit of Proxy at an Adjourned Meeting

Cases	Provision
(i) ***In case of Public company limited by shares if its articles are silent***	Proxies may be lodged even before adjourned meeting.
(ii) ***In case of other companies if their articles are silent***	Proxies cannot be lodged before adjourned meeting. Since adjournment is just a continuation meeting, 'it ought to be lodged within the stipulated time before the original meeting. [*Laren* v. *Thompson*, (1917) 2 Ch. 261]
(iii) ***'Where articles contain provision similar to Regulation 61 of Table A***	Proxies may be lodged even before adjourned meeting.
(iv) ***Where articles prohibit as such***	Proxies cannot be lodged before adjourned meeting.

16.11 Can a Person Give Proxies to a Different Person on Different Date to Different Persons?

Yes, he can do so but then the proxy whose date is subsequent to the date of other proxies will be accepted to the exclusion of other proxies.

16.12 Who can Appoint Proxy in Case of Joint Holdings?

Unless articles otherwise provides, in case of joint holdings, senior most joint holder (i.e. first named joint holder) sign the proxy.

16.13 Prohibition on Invitation by Company to Members [Section 176(4)]

If an invitation to member to appoint one or more person already specified in the invitation as proxies is sent, the every officer of the company who knowingly issues the invitation as aforesaid or willingly authorises or permits their issues shall be punishable with fine not exceeding Rs 10,000.

However, an officer shall not be punishable in case of issue of form of appointment naming the proxy or of a list of person willing to act as proxies provided:

(i) a request in writing is made by the member, and
(ii) the form/ list is available on request in writing to every member entitled to vote at the meeting by proxy.

16.14 Inspection of Proxy [Section 176(7)]

After giving 3 days' notice to the company, every member entitled to vote, may inspect during business hours the proxies lodged with the company during the period beginning 24 hours before the time fixed for commencement of the meeting and ending with the conclusion of the meeting.

16.15 Revocation of Proxy

A proxy can be revoked at any time and is said to be revoked if:

(i) When a written intimation of death or insanity of the principal or the revocation of the proxy or the transfer of shares is received by the company at its office before the commencement of meeting or adjourned meeting where articles are silent or contain provision similar to Regulation 63.

(ii) When a member having appointed a proxy, personally attends to vote at meeting. [*Cousins* v. *International Bricks Co. Ltd.* (1931)]

(iii) When a member having appointed a proxy, appoints another proxy at a later date. In this case the proxy appointed at later date will supersede the earlier proxies. [*Re Swadeshi Polytex Ltd.*, (1988)]

16.16 Lodging of Proxy at or before Taking Up Poll

Cases	*Provision*
(i) ***In case of Public company limited by shares if its articles are silent***	Proxies may be lodged at or before taking up poll.
(ii) ***In case of other companies if their articles are silent***	Proxies cannot be lodged at or before taking up poll. [*Shaw* v. *Tati Concession Ltd.* (1913)]
(iii) ***Where articles contain provision similar to Regulation 61***	Proxies may be lodged at or before taking up poll.
(iv) ***Where articles prohibit as such***	Proxies cannot be lodged at or before taking up poll.

16.17 Is Proxy Entitled to Put Question in Writing and Sending the Same to the Chairman?

Yes, a proxy is also entitled to put question in writing and sending the same to the chairman for answer since the Act is silent on this point.

16.18 Members of which Company are not Entitled to Appoint Proxy

Members of the company having no share capital cannot appoint proxy unless articles otherwise 'provides. [Proviso to Section 176(1)]

16.19 Members of which Company are not Entitled to Appoint more than One Proxy

In case of private company whether subsidiary of public company or not members cannot appoint more than one proxy unless articles otherwise provide. [Proviso to Section 176(1)]

19.20 Representations of Corporations at Meetings of Companies and of Creditors. [Section 187]

Where a company is a member of another company, it may attend the meeting of any other company through a representative. The representative must be appointed by a resolution of the board of directors or the other governing body. The person so appointed is entitled to exercise the same rights and powers (including the right to vote by proxy) on behalf of the company as the individual member of the company may exercise.

Where a company is a creditor of another company, it may attend the meeting of any other company through a representative. The representative must be appointed by a resolution of the board of directors or the other governing body.

A foreign company can also make the use of this provision or it may appoint a representative by means of power of attorney. [*CEPT* v. *Jeewanlal Ltd.*, (1951)]

In case of company which is in liquidation, the liquidator will be the governing body and may appoint where he is not himself able to be present, a representative. [*Hillman* v. *Crystal Bowl Amusement Ltd.*, (1973)]

16.21 Representation of the President and Governors in Meeting of Companies in which they are Members [Section 187A]

Where a president or Governor is a member of any company, then president or Governor as the case may be, may attend a meeting through representative appointed by the President or Governor. The person so appointed is entitled to exercise the same rights and powers (including the right to vote by proxy) on behalf of the president or governor as the individual member of the company may exercise.

17.0 PROPER VOTING

17.1 How shall a Resolution at a Meeting be Decided?

Section 177 provides that a resolution when put to vote at a meeting shall be decided by a show of hands unless a poll is demanded under Section 179.

The procedure generally followed is that a resolution is proposed either by a chairman or by any other member and is seconded by some other member or members. Chairman can also second a resolution if he has not proposed a resolution. Seconding is necessary if articles requires so otherwise it is not mandatory.

17.2 Voting by show of hands

(a) Who can Vote on Show by Hands?

The following persons can vote in case of voting by show of hands:

(i) Every member of a company. [Section 87]

(ii) First named member in case of Joint holder. [Regulation 57]

(iii) Authorised representative of a body corporate. [Section 187(2)]

(iv) Representative of President/Governor of the state. [Section 187A]

(v) Preference shareholders if resolution proposed is directly affecting them. [Section 87(2)]

Any resolution for winding up of the company or for the repayment or the reduction of preference share capital shall be deemed directly to affect the rights attached to the preference shares.

(vi) A cumulative preference shareholder in respect of every resolution if his dividend remains unpaid for an aggregate period of at least 2 years preceding the date of the meeting. [Section 87(2)(b)(i)]

(vii) A non-cumulative preference shareholder in respect of every resolution if his dividend remains unpaid for at least 2 years ending with the expiry of financial year immediately preceding the commencement of meeting or for an aggregate period of at least 3 years out of 6 years ending with the expiry of the financial year aforesaid. [Section 87(2)(b)(ii)]

(b) Who cannot vote in Case of Voting by Show of Hands?

Proxy shall not be entitled to vote in case of voting by show of hands unless the articles provides otherwise. [Section 176]

(c) What should be the Contents of the Minutes of the Minutes in Case of Voting by Show of Hands? [Section 178]

A declaration by the chairman to the effect that whether the resolution was carried or not, if carried whether unanimously or by majority, is required to be entered in the minute book and such entry shall be conclusive evidence of the fact.

It means, that it is not necessary to indicate in the minutes the number of persons who have voted in favour or against resolution.

It does not mean that shareholder cannot challenge the validity of the passing of the resolution in the court of law.

17.3 Voting by Poll

(a) **When may a Poll be Demanded? [Section 179(1)]**
A poll may be ordered either before or after the declaration of the resolution of a voting on a show of hands.

(b) **Who can Demand a Poll?**
A poll may be demanded by any of the following persons:
(i) Chairman on his own motion
(ii) in case of a public company having share capital, by any member or members present in person or by proxy and holding shares
(a) which carry at least 1/10th of the voting power, or
(b) on which at least Rs 50,000 has been paid up whichever is less.
(iii) In case of a private company, by at least 2 members present in person or by proxy and having right to vote where number of members personally present exceed 7 or by 1 where members personally present does not exceed 7.
(iv) in case any other company, by any member or members present in person or by proxy and having at least 1/10th of total voting power.

(c) **When and by Whom the Demand for Poll can be Withdrawn? [Section 179(2)]**
The demand for poll may be withdrawn at any time by the person or persons who made the demand.

(d) **What is Time for Taking Poll? [Section 180]**

Case	*Time Limit*
(i) ***A poll demanded on a resolution for the adjournment of the meeting or for the election of chairman.***	It must be taken immediately.
(ii) ***A poll demanded on other resolution.***	It must be taken within the expiry of 48 hours from the time the demand for poll was made.

(e) **Can the Poll be Continued on the Next Day?**
Yes. If a poll is not completed on the same day, it will be continued on the next day and the chairman shall not be entitled to close the poll.

(f) **Is it Necessary to have Poll for Each of Resolution Separately?**
Yes, where more than one resolution is to be passed.

(g) **Duties of Chairman to Appoint Scrutineers [Section 184]**
The chairman shall appoint two scrutineers to scrutinise the votes given on the poll and to report thereon to him. At least one of the two scrutineers shall be a member (not being an officer or an employee of the company) present at the meeting provided such a member is available and willing to be appointed.

(h) **Powers of Chairman Regarding poll [Sections 184 and 185]**
The chairman has the following power
(i) To remove the scrutineers and to fill up the vacancy arising from such removal any time before the result
(ii) To regulate the manner in which the poll should be conducted.

(i) **How can the Poll be Conducted?**
The poll may be taken by ballot/by show of hands.

(j) Nature of the Result of the Poll [Section 185]
The result of the poll shall be deemed to be the decision of the meeting on which the poll was taken.

(k) Is Proxy Entitled to Vote on Poll?
Yes, proxy is entitled to vote on poll. [Section 176]

(l) Can a Proxy Demand for Poll ?
Yes, since proxy is entitled to vote on a poll, he is also entitled to demand for poll.

(m) Voting Rights in Case of Voting by Show of Hands
Each member personally present shall be entitled to one vote on show of hands irrespective of his shareholding.

Note: A proxy is not entitled to vote on show of hands unless authorised by the articles.

(n) Voting rights in case of voting by polls

Case	***Voting Rights***
(i) ***Voting rights of Equity Shareholders***	In the same proportion as the paid up capital in respect of equity shares bears to the total paid up equity capital of the company.
(ii) ***Voting rights of Preference Shareholders***	In the same proportion as the paid up capital in respect of preference shares bears to the total paid up equity capital of the company.
(iii) ***Voting rights of Joint Shareholders***	First named shareholder shall be entitled to vote.

Practical Illustration 12

1000 Equity shares of Rs 10 each Rs 8 called and paid up Rs 8,000
500 Preference shares of Rs 10 each Rs 8 called and paid up Rs 4,000
Total Called and Paid up Share Capital Rs 12,000

Additional Information:
100 Equity shares of Rs 10 each Rs 8 paid up hold by Mr. *X*
50 Preference shares of Rs 10 each Rs 8 paid up hold by Mr. *Y*
Determine the voting rights of Mr. *X* and Mr. *Y*.

Answer
Voting Rights of Mr. *X* = (800/8000) *100 = 10%
Voting Rights of Mr. *Y* = (400/8000) *100 = 5%

(o) Right to Vote on Every Resolution Placed before the Company
(i) Every member of a company. [Section 87]
(ii) First named member in case of Joint holder. [Regulation 57]
(iii) Authorised representative of a body corporate. [Section 187(2)]
(iv) Representative of President/Governor of the state. [Section 187A]
(v) A cumulative preference shareholder if his dividend remains unpaid for an aggregate period of at least 2 years preceding the date of the meeting. [Section 87(2)(b)(i)]
(vi) A non-cumulative preference shareholder if his dividend remains unpaid for at least 2 years ending with the expiry of financial year immediately preceding the commencement of meeting or for an aggregate period of at least 3 years out of 6 years ending with the expiry of the financial year aforesaid. [Section 87(2)(b)(ii)]

(p) Right of Preference Shareholder to Vote [Section 87(2)]
(i) A preference shareholder shall have a right to vote only on resolution placed before the company which directly affects the rights attached to the preference shares.

(ii) Any resolution for winding up of the company or for the repayment or the reduction of preference share capital shall be deemed directly to affect the rights attached to the preference shares.

(q) Restriction on Exercise of voting rights [Sections 181 and 182]

(i) On the ground of non-payment of calls or other sum presently payable in regard to which the company has exercise any right is valid. [Section 181]

(ii) On any other ground, is not valid. [Section 182]

(r) Can a Member Use His Votes Differently? [Section 183]

A member can use his vote differently (some votes in favour or against the same resolution) in case of voting by poll.

18.0 PASSING OF RESOLUTION BY POSTAL BALLOT [SECTION 192A]

18.1 Power of a Company to Pass a Resolution by Postal Ballot

Section 192A permits a company to pass a resolution by postal ballot.

18.2 Duties of a Company in Case of Passing of Resolution by Postal Ballot

Where a company decides to pass any resolution by postal ballot—

(a) It must send a notice to all members along with a draft resolution stating the reasons therefor. [Section 192A(1)]

(b) The notice must request the members to send their assent or dissent in writing on a postal ballot within 30 days from the date of the posting of the letter. [Section 192A(2)]

(c) The notice must be sent by a registered letter or by any other method as prescribed by the Central Government. [Section 192A(3)]

(d) A postage pre-paid envelope along with the notice must also be sent to all the members to receive their assent or dissent. [Section 192A(3)]

(e) A resolution shall be deemed to have been duly passed at a general meeting if the resolution is assented to by a requisite majority of members by mean of postal ballot. [Section 192A(4)]

(f) Any person who defaces or destroys the ballot paper or declaration of the identity of the member shall be punishable with imprisonment upto 6 months or with fine or with both. [Section 192(A)(5)]

Meaning of Postal Ballot—"Postal Ballot" includes voting by shareholders by postal or electronic mode instead of voting personally by presenting for transacting businesses in a general meeting of the company.

Meaning of Requisite Majority—"Requisite Majority" with regard to special resolution means votes cast in favour of the business is three times more than the votes cast against, with regard to ordinary resolution, votes cast in favour is more than the votes cast against.

18.3 Penalty for Contravention [Section 192A(6)]

The company and its every offices in default shall be punishable with fine upto Rs 5,00,000 in respect of each such default if any of the provisions of Section 192A is not complied with.

18.4 Businesses in which the Resolutions May be Passed Through Postal Ballot

(a) alteration in the object clause of memorandum;

(b) alteration of articles of associations in relation to deletion or insertion of provisions defining private company;

(c) buy-back of own shares by the company under Sub-section (1) of Section 77A;
(d) issue of shares with differential voting rights as to voting or dividend or otherwise under Sub-clause (ii) of Clause (a) of Section 86;
(e) change in place of registered office out side local limits of any city, town or village as specified in Sub-section (2) of Section 146;
(f) sale of whole or substantially the whole of undertaking of a company as specified under Sub-clause (a) of Sub-section (1) of Section 293;
(g) giving loans or extending guarantee or providing security in excess of the limit prescribed under Sub-section (1) of Section 372A;
(h) election of a director under Sub-section (1) of Section 252;
(i) power to compromise or make arrangements with creditors and members as specified under Sub-section (2) of Section 391;
(j) variation in the rights attached to a class of shares or debentures or other securities as specified under Section 106.

18.5 Procedure to be Followed for Conducting Business through Postal Ballot

(a) The company may make a note below the notice of general meeting for under-standing of members that the transactions(s) at serial number requires consent of shareholders through postal ballot;
(b) The board of directors shall appoint one scrutinizer, who is not in employment of the company, may be a retired judge or any person of repute who, in the opinion of the board can conduct the postal ballot voting process in a fair and transparent manner;
(c) The scrutinizer will be in position for 35 days (excluding holidays) from the date of issue of notice for annual general meeting. He is to submit his final report on or before the said period.
(d) The scrutinizer will be willing to be appointed and he is available at the registered office of the company for the purpose of ascertaining the requisite majority;
(e) The scrutinizer shall maintain a register to record the consent or otherwise received, including electronic media, mentioning the particulars of name, address, folio number, number of shares, nominal value of shares, whether the shares have voting, differential voting or non-voting rights and the scrutinizer shall also maintain record for postal ballot which are received in defaced or mutilated form. The postal ballot and all other papers relating to postal ballot will be under the sate custody of the scrutinizer till the chairman considers, approves and signs the minutes of the meeting. Thereafter, the scrutinizer shall return the ballot papers and other related papers/register to the company so as to preserve such ballot papers and other related papers/register safely till the resolution is given effect to;
(f) Consent or otherwise relating to issue mentioned in notice for annual general meeting received after 35 days from the date of issue will be strictly treated as if the reply from the member has not been received.

18.6 Penalty for Default

If default is made in following this procedure, fine of Rs 50,000 can be levied for each default.

19.0 ORDINARY BUSINESS AND SPECIAL BUSINESS [SECTION 173]

19.1 Ordinary business

The following four busineses to be transacted at Annual General meeting shall be considered as ordinary business:

(i) Consideration of accounts, balance sheet and the report of Board of Directors and auditors.
(ii) Declaration of Dividend.
(iii) Appointment of Directors in the place of those retiring.
(iv) Appointment of, and fixing of the remuneration of the auditors.

19.2 Special Business

(a) All businesses except the following four businesses to be transacted at AGM shall deemed to be special business.
   (i) Consideration of accounts, balance sheet and the report of Board of Directors and auditors.
   (ii) Declaration of Dividend.
   (iii) Appointment of Directors in the place of those retiring.
   (iv) Appointment of, and fixing of the remuneration of the auditors.

(b) All businesses to be transacted at any other meeting shall be deemed to be special business.

19.3 Explanatory Statement [Section 173(2) and (3)]

Where any special business is to be transacted at the meeting, an Explanatory Statement is required to be annexed to the notice. Such statement shall include amongst other:
(a) All material facts concerning each item of business.
(b) The nature of the concern or interest if any, therein of every director and manager.
(c) If any item of the special business affects any other company, then the extent of shareholding of every director and manager in that company in case their share holding interest is at least 20% of the paid up share capital of the other company.
(d) The time when and place where the document to be approved at the meeting can be inspected.

Note: If the notice convening the meeting states no particulars or insufficient particulars as to the special business to be transacted threat, the meeting would be deemed to have been convened irregularly. [*Jain* v. *Kalinga Tubes* (1965)]

20.0 RESOLUTION

20.1 Meaning

Resolution is a formal proposal put to the meeting for approval.

20.2 Kinds

Basically there are two kinds of resolutions—ordinary and special.

20.3 Ordinary Resolution [Section 189(1)]

A resolution shall be an ordinary resolution when—
(a) the notice of general meeting required under the Act has been duly given,
(b) the votes cast including the casting vote if any of the chairman (whether on show of hand or on a poll as the case may be) exceed the votes if any cast against the resolution.

Practical Illustration 13

Total number of members	300
Total number of members present at meeting	210
Total votes cast	200
Total votes cast in favour of the resolution	101
Total votes cast against the resolution	99

Solution:

In this case the ordinary resolution will be said to have been passed since votes in favour (i.e. 101) exceeds votes cast against (i.e. 99)

20.4 Matters Requiring only Ordinary Resolution

Subject to the articles, an ordinary resolution is sufficient, for *inter alia* any of the following matters:

(a) To authorise an issue of shares at a discount [Section 79];
(b) To increase the share capital if authorised by the articles, or otherwise, alter the share capital apart from its reduction [Sections 94, 100];
(c) To appoint auditors [Section 224(1)]; but in the case of a company in which not less than 25 per cent of the subscribed share capital is held, whether singly or in any combination, by a public financial institution or a Government company or Central or any State Government, or a nationalised bank or an insurance company carrying a general insurance business, the appointment of auditors requires a special resolution [Section 224A];
(d) To appoint directors;
(e) To adopt annual accounts;
(f) To declare dividends;
(g) To wind up voluntarily when the period, if any, fixed for the duration of the company by the articles has expired, or the event, if any, has occurred, on the occurrence of which the articles provided that the company is to be dissolved [Section 484(1)];
(h) To appoint liquidators in a members 'voluntary winding-up and to fix their remuneration [Section 490];
(i) To register an unlimited company as a limited company (Section 32); and generally to do all things for which a special resolution is not specifically required either by the Act or the company's articles.

20.5 Special Resolution [Section 189(2)]

A resolution shall be an ordinary resolution when—

(a) the notice of general meeting required under the Act has been duly given,
(b) the votes cast including the casting vote if any of the chairman (whether on show of hand or on a poll as the case may be) are at least 3 times the number of votes if any cast against the resolution.
(c) the intention to propose the resolution as a special resolution has been duly specified in the notice calling the general meeting or other intimation given to the members.

Practical Illustration 14

Total numbers of members	300
Total numbers of members present at meeting	210
Total votes cast	200
Total votes cast in favour of the resolution	120
Total votes cast against the resolution	40
Total invalid votes	40

Soluton:

In this case the special resolution will be said to have been passed since the number of votes cast in favour (i.e. 120) are 3 times the number of votes cast against (i.e. 40)

20.6 Matters Requiring Special Resolution

The Act requires that the following matters, *inter alia,* have to be resolved by the company, by a special resolution:

1. To alter any provision contained in the memorandum which could lawfully have been contained in the articles instead of the memorandum [Section 16];
2. To alter the objects or the place of registered office of a company (Section 17);
3. To change the name of the company [Section 21];
4. To alter the articles of association [Section 31];
5. To create a reserve liability, that is, to determine that a portion of the uncalled capital shall not be capable of being called up, except in the event of a winding up (Section 99);
6. To reduce the share capital [Section 100];
7. To move the company's registered office within the same State but outside the local limits of the city, town or village where such office is situated [Section 146(2)];
8. To commence any new business which is not germane to the business the company is carrying on currently, though covered by the objects clause of the memorandum [Section 149(2A)];
9. To pay interest on shares out of capital [Section 208];
10. To appoint auditors, if not less than 25 per cent of the company's subscribed capital is held, whether singly or in any combination, by the Central or any State Government, Government companies, financial institutions, nationalised banks, etc. (Section 224A);
11. To support an application to the Central Government to appoint inspectors to investigate the affairs of the company [Section 237];
12. To appoint sole selling agents, if the company's paid-up capital is Rs 50 lakh or more [Section 294AA(3)];
13. To authorise the payment of remuneration to non-executive directors by way of commission on the basis of a percentage of the net profits, in the case of public company or a private company which is a subsidiary of a public company [Section 309(4)];
14. To authorise directors, etc. to hold office or place of profit under the company [Section 314];
15. To alter the memorandum where the articles permit, to make unlimited the liability of director (Section 323);
16. Investment exceeding the limits prescribed in Section 372A.
17. To have the company wound up by the court [Section 433(a)];
18. To wind up voluntarily for any reason not otherwise provided for by the section (Section 484).
19. To authorise the liquidator to transfer or sell the assets of the company, which is proposed to be, or is in the course of being wound up voluntarily, to another company in exchange for shares [Sections 494 and 507];
20. To authorise the liquidator in a members' voluntary winding up to exercise the powers given by Clauses (a) to (d) Section 457(1) to a liquidator in a winding up by the Court [Section 512(1)(a)]
21. To sanction the exercise by the liquidator in volunteer winding up of powers mention in Section 546;
22. To direct the disposal of books and papers of the company in a members, voluntary winding up [Section 550(3)(a)];
23. To adopt *Table A* in Schedule I in the case of registration of a company under Part IX of the Act [Section 578(3)(a)];
24. To alter the form of constitution of a company registered under Part IX of the Act [Section 579(1)].

In addition to the requirements of the Act, a company's own articles may prescribe for special resolution where the Act requires only an ordinary resolution.

21.0 SPECIAL NOTICE [SECTION 190]

21.1 Length of Special Notice

Where, by any provision contained in the Act or in the Articles, Special Notice is required of any resolution, notice of the intention to move the resolution is given to the company at least 14 clear days (exclusive of days on which notice is served or deemed to be served and the day meeting is to be held) before the meeting at which it is to be moved. [Section 190(1)]

21.2 Duty of Company After Receipt of Special Notice

The company immediately after receipt of the notice must give notice of any such resolution to its members in the same manner as it gives notice of meeting or if that is not practicable, give the notice thereof either by advertisement in a newspaper having an appropriate circulation or in any other mode allowed by Articles at least 7 days before the meeting. [Section 190(2)]

21.3 Resolutions for which Special Notice is Required Under the Act

(i) To provide that a retiring auditor shall not be appointed. [Section 225]

(ii) To appoint an auditor other than retiring one. [Section 225]

(iii) To appoint a director other than retiring one. [Section 257]

(iv) To remove a director before expiry of time of the term. [Section 284(2)]

(v) To appoint another director in place of removed director. [Section 284(2)]

(vi) To appoint certain person who cannot be appointed in the ordinary course as director provided for in Section 261. [Section 261(2)]

The articles of the company may add additional matter in respect of which Special Notice is required.

22.0 CIRCULATION OF MEMBERS' RESOLUTION [SECTION 188]

22.1. Who can make a Requisition for Moving Resolution at AGM or for Circulation of Statement with Regard to any Proposed Resolution or Business to be dealt with at any General Meeting? [Section 188(2)]

The following members can make a requisition for moving resolution at AGM or for circulation of statement with regard to any proposed resolution or business to be dealt with at any general meeting:

(a) members having at least 5% voting power or

(b) at least 100 members having right to vote who hold shares on which at least Rs 1 lakh has been paid up.

22.2. Duty of Company after Receipt of Requisition [Section 188(1)]

The company on receipt of the written requisition must—

(a) give notice to members entitled to have notice of meeting of any resolution which is intended to be moved at AGM.

(b) circulate to members entitled to have notice of meeting any statement of not more than 1,000 words with regard to any proposed resolution or business to be dealt with at any general meeting

22.3 Service of Notice of Intended Resolution or Circulation of Statement [Section 188(3)]

The notice of intended resolution or circulation of statement must be served by serving a copy of resolution of statement in the same manner and at the same time as the notice of the meeting or where it is not practicable as soon as practicable thereafter.

22.4 When Company not Bound to Give the Notice or Circulate Statement? [Section 188(4)]

A company shall not be bound to give the notice of any resolution or to circulate any statement unless—

(a) a copy of the requisition signed by the requisitionists is deposited at the registered office of the company—
  (i) at least 6 weeks before the meeting in case of requisition requiring notice of resolution.
  (ii) at least 2 weeks before the meeting in case of any other requisition.

(b) a sum reasonably sufficient to meet the company's expenses in giving effect to the requisition has been deposited or tendered with the requisition.

Note: If after a copy of requisition requiring notice of a resolutions has been deposited at the registered office of the co. an AGM called for a date six weeks or less after the copy has been deposited, then the copy although not deposit at time shall be deemed to be deposited properly.

22.5 Other Cases where the Company is not Bound to Circulate Statement [Section 188(5) and (6)]

A company shall not be bound to circulate any statement in the following two cases:

(i) If on the application of the company or any other aggrieved person, the Company Law Tribunal is satisfied that the right is being abused to secure needless publicity for defamatory matter; and

(ii) If it is a banking company and in the opinion of its board of directors, the circulation will injure the interest of the company.

22.6 Effect of Accidental Omission to Serve the Notice [Section 188(7)]

Any accidental omission to serve notice upon one or more members will not invalidate the proceedings.

22.7 Penalty for Default [Section 188(8)]

Every officer of the company who is in default shall be punishable with fine upto Rs 50,000.

23.0 REGISTRATION OF CERTAIN RESOLUTIONS AND AGREEMENTS [SECTION 192(4)]

23.1 What is Required to be Filed?

The following resolutions/agreements are required to be filed with the registrar:

(a) Special resolution not passed by all the members.

(b) Special resolution passed by all the members.

(c) Ordinary resolution passed by all members.

(d) A resolution of the Board or an agreement executed by a company relating to the appointment, reappointment, renewal of the appointment or variation of the terms of managing directors.

(e) Ordinary resolution passed by the company conferring power under Section 293 upon its directors:
   (i) to sell or dispose the whole or any part of the company's undertaking, or
   (ii) to borrow money beyond the limits of the paid up capital and free reserves of the company;
   (iii) to contribute the charities beyond Rs 50,000 or 5% of profit.

(f) Resolution regarding voluntary winding up of the company under Section 484(1).

(g) Resolution regarding appointment of Sole selling Agent u/s 294 or 294AA

(h) Copies of the terms and conditions of appointment of sole selling agents under section 294 or a sole selling agent or other person under Section 294AA.

23.2 When to be Filed? [Section 192(1)]

The above resolution/agreements duly certified under the signature of an officer of the company, are required to be filed in Form 23 within 30 days after the passing of resolution or making of an agreement, as the case may be in the office of the Registrar.

23.3 Duty of Company Regarding Annexing of a Copy of Resolution and a Copy of Agreement [Section 192(2) and (3)]

Where the articles have been registered, the following are required to be embodied in or annexed to every copy of articles issued after the passing of the resolution or the making of an agreement:

(i) A copy of every agreement referred to in Section 192(1).

(ii) A copy of every resolution referred to in Section 192(1) which has the effect of altering the Articles.

However, Section 40 provides that copies of all agreements referred to under Section 192 shall be annexed to every copy of the memorandum and Articles issued after the date of alterations.

Where Articles have not been registered, a printed copy of every resolution and agreement shall be forwarded to any member on his request on payment of Re 1.

23.4 Penalties for Default [Section 192(5) and (6)]

(i) For default in filing with registrar—The company and every officer at default shall be punishable with fine of Rs 200 for every day during which default continues.

(ii) For default in annexing or forwarding a copy of resolution and copy of agreement—The company and every officer at default shall be punishable with fine of Rs 100 for each copy.

24.0 MINUTES [SECTIONS 193 TO 197]

24.1 Meaning of Minute

Minute may be defined as the written record of proceedings at a meeting including decision arrived at such meeting.

24.2 Types of Minutes

Minutes are of two kinds:

(a) Minutes of narration which record simple statements of happening which do not require any formal resolution. For example "The minutes of the previous Executive committee Meeting held on 10th August 20X1 were read, approved and signed by the chairman as a correct record."

(b) Minutes of resolutions record the formal decisions of the meeting which require passing of a resolution.

24.3 Distinction between Minutes and Reports

Minutes are the records of what was done at meeting but reports are the records of what was said for or against a particular proposition. Unlike the minutes, reports do not have the same legal significance.

Minutes signed by the chairman, although not conclusive, is *prima facie* evidence of the proceedings thereat and decision recorded therein until the contrary is proved.

24.4 Recording [Section 193(1)]

Every company must prepare minutes of all proceedings of every general meeting or Board meeting or Committee of the Board and such minutes must be recorded in the books kept for this purpose within 30 days from the conclusion of every such meeting and such book must have page consecutively numbered.

24.5 Contents of Minutes [Section 193(2), (3), (4), (5)]

(i) The minutes of each meeting shall contain a fair and correct summary of the proceedings thereat and the appointment of the officers made thereat.

(ii) The minutes of board shall also **contain**:

(a) the names of the directors present, and

(b) in case of each resolution passed at the meeting names of the directors, if any, dissenting from or not concurring with the resolution.

The minute shall **not contain** any matter which in the opinion of the chairman of the meeting—

(a) is or could reasonably be regarded as defamatory

(b) is irrelevant or immaterial to the proceedings;

(c) is detrimental to the interests of the company.

The chairman shall exercise an absolute discretion with regard to the inclusion or non-inclusion of any matter in the minutes on the grounds mentioned above.

24.6 Signature on Minute Book [Section 193(1A)]

Each page of every such minute book should be initialled or signed and the last page of record of the proceeding of each meeting in such book shall be dated and signed:

(a) in the case of minutes of proceedings of a meetings of the Board or of committee thereof, by the chairman of said meeting or the chairman of the succeeding meeting;

(b) in the case of the minutes of proceedings of a general meeting by the chairman of the same meeting within the period of 30 days of the conclusion of the meeting or in the event of the death of or inability of that chairman within that period, by a director duly authorised by the board for the purpose.

Notes:

(i) Since there is no prohibition, such a resolution is passed within thirty days so that there is time for the director to sign the minutes within the said period.

(ii) Time gap between the preparation and signing of the minutes of general meeting could be of 30 days.

(iii) Time gap between the preparation and signing of the minutes of Board could be more than 3 months e.g. in case the 1st Board meeting is held on 1st January and 2nd Board meeting is held on 30th June.

24.7 Maintenance of Minutes [Section 193(1B)]

The minutes in no case, shall be attached by pasting or otherwise to the minute books kept for this purpose. The Central Government has classified that entering of minutes in bound books by a chemical process which does not amount to attachment to any book by pasting or otherwise is permissible provided on the mechanical impression of the minutes, the original signature of the chairman is given on each page.

The department of company affairs has expressed the view that in certain exceptional cases i.e. in the case of large companies where the minutes of the meeting runs into great lengths, minutes may be kept in a loose leaf binder provided:

(a) the pages are duly typed and serially numbered;
(b) the loose leaves must be kept in proper lock for safe custody.
(c) the loose leaves are bound up at a reasonable interval not exceeding 6 months; and
(d) prior commission of the Company Law Tribunal has been obtained.

24.8 Confirmation of Minutes

The term 'confirmation' means verification. In true technical sense, the decision already taken does not require any ratification or confirmation.

There is no provision in Act which requires the minutes of the Board or general meeting to be read or confirmed at the subsequent meeting but in practice minutes of the Board meeting are read at the next board meeting and request by the chairman is made to the directors present whether they have any comments on the minutes of the previous Board meeting or general meeting which have circulated to them. Normally the minutes covering the confirmation of the minutes of the previous board meeting is usually worded as follows:

"Minutes of the last Board meeting held on...which were circulated to the directors were read, approved and signed by the chairman as correct record".

24.9 Penalty [Section 193(6)]

If default is made in complying with aforesaid provision company and every officer of the company who is in default shall punishable with fine which may extend to Rs 500.

24.10 Minutes as Evidence [Section 194]

The minutes of meeting kept in accordance with the provision of Section 193 shall be evidence of the proceedings thereon.

24.11 Presumption [Section 195]

Where the minutes have been duly drawn in accordance with the provision of Section 193, then until the contrary is proved the meeting shall be deemed to have been duly called and held and all the proceedings thereat shall be deemed to duly taken place and in particular all appointments of directors and liquidators made at the meeting shall be deemed to be valid.

24.12 Inspection of Minutes [Section 196]

(i) The minutes of proceedings of any general meeting of the company shall be:
   (a) kept at the registered office, and
   (b) be open during business hour for inspection by member for at least two hours a day without charge subject to such reasonable restrictions as may be imposed by articles.

(ii) Every member is entitled to inspect the minutes and to be furnished with a copy of the minutes of the general meeting within 7 days from the date of his request to the company on payment of Re 1 for every hundred words or fractional part thereof required to be copied. [Section 196(2)]

(iii) However, these rights are not available to the member in respect of minutes of Board meetings. But directors, Auditors and investigator appointed by the Central Government are entitled to inspect the minutes of Board and committees thereof.

24.13 Default Regarding Refusal of Inspection/Not Furnishing a Copy of Minute. [Section 196(3) and (4)]

In case of default regarding refusal of inspection/not furnishing a copy of minute:

(a) The company and every officer of the company who is in default shall be punishable with fine not exceeding Rs 5,000 in respect of each.

(b) The Company Law Board may direct the immediate inspection of the minutes or delivery of the copy of minutes.

24.14 Publication [Section 197]

(a) No document purporting to be a report of the proceeding of any general meeting of the company shall be circulated or advertised at the expense of the company unless it includes matters required by Section 193 to be contained in the minutes of the proceedings of such meetings.

(b) In case of contravention of aforesaid provision, the company and its every officer in default shall be punishable with fine which upto Rs 5,000. It is to be noted that no penalty is attracted when the publication/circulation does not purport to be proceedings of the meeting.

(c) Where any reports of general meetings are published at the expense of the company, all matters required to by Section 193 to be included in the minutes of the proceedings of the meeting, are to be included in publication.

Appendix I – Summarised Table Showing the various Provisions Applicable to Various Meetings

	Basis of Comparison	*Statutory Meeting*	*Annual General Meeting*	*Extra Ordinary General meeting*	*Board of Directors Meeting*
1.	**Persuant to section**	Section 165	Section 166 to 168	Section 169	Section 285 to 290
2.	**Companies required to hold**	Public limited company having share capital	Every Company	No Company (Optional)	Every Company
3.	**When is to be held**	After expiry of 1 month but before expiry of 6 Months from the date of certificate to commence business.	**First AGM**— Within 18 months of incorporation & within 9 months (a) of end of financial year. **Subsequent** — Within 6 months of the end of financial year but within 15 months of previous AGM. It must be held in each calender year. **Note:** The period of Financial year must not exceed 15 months but may extend to 18 months with special permission of the Registrar.	(a) **By B.O.D. on its own Motion [Reg. 48 of Table A]** (b) **By B.O.D. on Requisition:** Convey within 21 days & call within 45 days from the date of deposit of requisition by members. (c) **By Requisitionsts:** Within 3 months if B.O.D. did not convey within 21 days & did not call within 45 days from the date of deposit of requisition.	Once every 3 calander months & atleast 4 meetings during a calender year.
4.	**Who can call**	Duly Constituted Board	Duly Constituted Board/Central Govt u/s 167 on application of any member if a default is made in holding AGM	Duly Consituted Board/ Requistionists/Tribunal u/s 186	As per A/A
5.	**Notice [Sec. 171 to 173]**	Atleast 21 clear days' notice to all members and auditors	At least 21 clear days' notice to all members and auditors	Same as in case of SM	To Every Director whether or not in India or interested directors

6. Can shorter Notice be given?	With consent of members holding **at least 95%** paid up capital/ voting power obtained prior to or at or even subsequent to meeting.	With consent of **all** members entitled to vote.	Same as in case of Statutory Meeting	—
7. Documents with Notice	Statutory Report, Admission Card, Proxy Form	Audited, A/cs, Balance Sheet and Auditor's Report, Directors' Report Proxy Form, Admission Card Explanatory Statement (if special business to be transacted)	Explanatory Statement, Proxy Form, Admission Card	(i) In case of matters covered covered by Sec. 316,372, 386- Draft Resolution (ii) In other cases, as per A/A
8. Hour, days & place of meeting	Any time, any day & at any place since the Act is silent on this point.	During Business Hours. Day Other than Public Holiday, Regd Office or other place within the city, town or village in which RO is situated. [Sec. 166(2)]	Same as in case of Statutory Meeting	—
9. Adjournment – *Hour, Day &* Place **- Quorum**	To same day in the next week at the same time and place or to such other day and at such other time and place as the Board may determine if the quorum is not present within **half an hour** from the time appointed. Members present shall form the quorum.	(a) To **same day** (even on Public Holiday) at the same **time and place if** AGM is **adjourned due to lack of quorum** (b) **To any day other than public holiday if adjourned due to any other reason**	• Adjorn if meeting has not been called on requisition of members. • Meeting shall stand dissolved if quorum is not present within half an hour from time appoin-ted and it is called on requisition of members.	Day other than Public Holiday
10. Consequences of default notice.	**Penalty:** for any default us/165 fine upto Rs 5,000 for every officer in default.	For any default u/s 166 or 167 Fine upto Rs 50,000 & Rs 2,500 per day for continuing default for **company and every officer** in default	--	Fine upto Rs 1000 for every officer for default in issuing

	Other Consequence: U/s 433—The Tribunal may also order for compulsory winding up if default is made in deliverying Statutory Report or in holding Statutory Meeting	—	—	—
11. Minimum Quorum [Sec. 174] **1. At Original Meeting** **2. At meeting adjourned due to lack of quorum** **3. At meeting adjourned due to other reasons**	5 Members Personally present Members present Personally or by proxy. 5 members personally present	**1. At Original Meeting** (a) **In case of AGM called by Central Govt.** **One** member present personally or by proxy (b) **In case of other AGM — Public Co : 5** Members Personally present **Other Cos : 2** members personally present **2. Same point as in case of SM** **3. Same point as in (1)(b) above**	**In case of EGM called by Tribunal** one member present personally **In case of class meeting**—Even one shareholder can constitute quorum if that class consists of only one member.	1/3 of total no. of directors (excluding interested director) or two which ever is higher.
12. Proxies [Sec 176]	(a) Members of public co. having share capital are entitled to appoint more than one proxy even **if A/A** does not provide so. (b) Members of public company having **no** share **share capital** are entitled to appoint proxy only if A/A so provides	(a) Members of **public co.** having share capital are entitled to appoint more than one proxy even if A/A does not provide so. (b) Members of **pvt. co.** having capital are entitled to appoint more than one proxy if A/A provides. (c) Members of company having no share capital are entitled to appoint **proxy** only if A/A so provides	Same as in case of AGM	Proxy can not be appointed.
13. Chairman	Unless the articles provide otherwise & poll is demanded. Chairman is to be elected by show of hands.	Same	Same	Same

14. Voting (177 to 185) **1. by Show of hand**	**1.** (a) Each member has **one** vote by show of hands. (b) Proxy may vote by show of hands if A/A so provides (c) Proxy (if not member) has no right to speak unless A/A otherwise provide.	Same	Same	Each director has one vote. Chairman has casting vote if allowed by A/A **1. In case of items covered by Sec.316(2), 372(5) & 386(2)** — unanimous consent **2. In other cases**—majority
2. by Poll	**2.** Voting rights as per A/A & Sec 86 & 89.			
15. Ordinary/Special Business which can be transacted	Special Business	Ordinary as well as Special Business	Special Business	—
16. Ordinary/Special Resolution which can be passed	**Ordinary:** By simple majority of vote. **Special:** By 3/4th majority	Ordinary & Special Resolution	Ordinary & Special Resolution	– Resolution at Board's meeting – Resolution by Circulation
17. Special Remark (if any)	(a) Statutory Report can be sent in Form **22** at notice shorter than of atleast 21 clear days' if **so agreed** by all **members.** (b) Members may discuss any matter relating to the formation of company or arising out of special resolution whether previous notice has been given or not but nc resolution may be passed unless notice is given in accordance with provisions of Act.	—	If default is made in calling the meeting by the Board, then (i) The requisitionists shall be entitled to claim all reasonable expenses incurred for conveining a meeting from the company (ii) The company shall be entitled to retain such sum from the fees or other remuneration due to directors who were in default.	—

Appendix II : Summarised Table showing Proper Place, Proper Date, Proper Hours and Quorum for Various Meetings

S. No.	*Proper Place*	*Proper Date*	*Proper Hours*	*Quorum*
1. Original AGM	At Registered Office or at some other place within the city, town or village in which the registered office is situated. **Note:** An Independent Pvt. Co. can fix any place.	On any day other than Public Holiday.	During Business Hours	1. **Called by Central Govt. —** One member present personally or by proxy **Other AGM —** **Public Co.:** 5 Members personally present **Pvt. Co.:** 2 Members personally present
2. AGM adjourned due to lack of Quorum	At same place where original AGM was held or at any other place as the Board may determine.	On any day (including public holiday) as the board may determine	At any time (whether or not falling within business hours) as the board may determine.	2. Members present personally or by proxy
3. AGM adjourned due to any other reason	As original AGM	As original AGM	As original AGM	3. As original AGM
4. Any other General Meeting	At any place as the board may determine	As AGM adjourned due to lack of quorum	As AGM adjourned due to lack of quorum.	4. **EGM called by Tribunal**—one member personally present **Other GM —** As original other AGM.

EXERCISES

SHORT ANSWER TYPE QUESTIONS

1. (a) "AGM may be held on Public Holiday". Comment
   (b) "AGM may be held on a place other than registered office". Comment
   (c) "AGM may be held at a time outside business hours". Comment
2. (a) Can proxy be counted for the purposes of quorum?
   (b) Can one member constitute quorum?
   (c) State the consequences of absence of quorum.
3. (a) "Chairman should be a director". Comment.
   (b) "Chairman should be a member". Comment.
4. Who can demand a poll?
5. Distinguish between:
   (a) Ordinary Business and Special Business.
   (b) Ordinary Resolution and Special Resolution
6. List five matters requiring the
   (a) Ordinary Resolution
   (b) Special Resolution
   (c) Special Notice
7. Write short notes on the following:
   (a) Statutory Report
   (b) Quorum
   (c) Proxy
   (d) Explanatory Statement
   (e) Ordinary and Special Business
   (f) Ordinary and Special Resolution
   (g) Special Notice
8. (a) Are all the provisions of Section 171 to 186 applicable to all companies?
   (b) Is provision of Section 174(1) relating to quorum applicable to a private company which is not a subsidiary company?
   (c) Is provision of Section 182 relating to restriction on exercise of voting right application to a private company which is not a subsidiary company?
   (d) Can an independent private company make special provisions in its Articles in respect of any of the matters covered by Section 171 to 186?
   (e) If the Articles of an independent private company are silent, shall the provision of Section 182 apply to it?

LONG ANSWER TYPE QUESTIONS

1. (a) Name the Companies required to hold Statutory Meeting.
   (b) When is this meeting to be held?
   (c) State the provisions relating to Statutory Report.
   (d) State the consequences of default in holding statutory meeting.
2. (a) When is AGM to be held?

(b) State the consequences of default in holding AGM

3. (a) Who can call Extra-ordinary Meeting.
   (b) State provisions relating to requisition for Extra-ordinary Meeting.
   (c) When can Company Law Tribunal call Extra-ordinary Meeting?
4. State provisions relating to Class Meetings.
5. (a) What should be the length of notice?
   (b) Can a general meeting be called by giving a shorter notice?
   (c) Who are entitled to receive notice of general meetings?
   (d) State the provisions relating to service of notice.
   (e) State the contents of notice of general meeting.
6. (a) State the rights and limitations of proxy.
   (b) State the provisions relating to deposit of proxy.
   (c) State the provisions relating to revocation of proxy.
7. (a) List the businesses in which the resolution may be passed through postal ballot?
   (b) State the procedure to be followed for conducting business through postal ballot.
8. State the provisions relating to the registration of certain resolution and agreements.
9. State the provisions relating to recording, contents, signature and maintenance of minutes.

CHAPTER 13

Winding Up

1.0 MEANING OF WINDING UP

According to Prof. Gower, ***"The liquidation or winding up (the two terms are used indiscriminately) of a company is the process whereby its life is ended and its property is administered for the benefit of its creditors and members. An administrator, called liquidator, is appointed and he takes control of the company, collects its assets, pays its debts and finally distributes any surplus among the members in accordance with their rights."***

2.0 MODES OF WINDING UP

A company may be wound up in any of the following modes:

1. Compulsory Winding up by the Tribunal, or
2. Voluntary Winding up, or
   (a) Members' Voluntary Winding Up
   (b) Creditors' Voluatary Winding Up
3. Winding up subject to the Supervision of the Court.

3.0 COMPULSORY WINDING UP BY TRIBUNAL [SEC. 433]

The Tribunal may order for compulsory winding up on any of the following **nine** grounds:

3.1 Special Resolution

The tribunal may order for compulsory winding up of a company if the company has passed a special resolution to that effect. However, the tribunal may refuse to order winding up if the winding up is likely to be against public interest.

3.2 Default in Delivering the Statutory Report or Holding Statutory Meeting u/s 165

The Tribunal may order for compulsory winding up of a company if a default is made —

(a) in delivering the Statutory Report to the Registrar, or
(b) in holding the Statutory Meeting

However, the tribunal may instead order the company to —

(i) deliver the Statutory Report to the Registrar
(ii) hold the Statutory Meeting.

3.3 Non-commencement/Suspension of Business

The Tribunal may order for compulsory winding up of a company if the company has —

(a) not commenced business within 1 year of its incorporation, *or*
(b) suspended its entire business for at least 1 year.

However, the Tribunal may refuse to order winding up if —

(i) the suspension is not of the entire business,

(ii) the suspension is satisfactorily explained,

(iii) the majority of shareholders oppose the winding up.

3.4 Reduction of Membership below the Statutory Minimum

The Tribunal may order for the compulsory winding up of a company if the numbers of member of a company is reduced in the case of a public company below 7 and in case of a private company below 2.

3.5 Inability to Pay Debts

The Tribunal may order for the compulsory winding up of the company if the company is unable to pay its debts. A company shall be deemed to be unable to pay its debts —

(a) If a creditor to whom the company is indebted a sum exceeding Rs 500 has served upon the company a notice requiring the company to pay the sum due and the company has for 3 weeks thereafter neglected to pay or otherwise satisfy him. For computing the period of 3 weeks the days on which the demand notice is despatched, the day of service should be excluded. Instead of making a winding up order, the Tribunal may direct the company to furnish security.

(b) If execution or other process issued on a decree or order of any Tribunal in favour of a creditor of the company is returned unsatisfied in whole or in part, or

(c) where the Tribunal is satisfied that the company is unable to pay its debts. If its existing and probable assets are insufficient to meet the existing liabilities, it would then be deemed to be unable to pay its debts.

However, the Tribunal may not order the winding up if the debt is bonafide disputed by the company.

3.6 Just and Equitable Grounds

The Tribunal may order for compulsory winding up of the company on just and equitable grounds. Some of the instances under which the Tribunal has ordered winding up on the just and equitable grounds are as follows:

(a.) **Where there is Deadlock in the Management** — In ***Re. Yenidje Tabacco Co. Ltd. (1916),*** the Court ordered for winding up since the company was having two directors having equal voting rights and these directors became so hostile that they were not talking to each other except through their secretories.

However, in ***V. Seethiahar v. Venkatasubbiah (1949)*** it was held that a mere difference of opinion or mere incompatibility of good relations between the two groups of directors would not constitute deadlock and, therefore, will not attract winding up.

(b.) **Where the Substractum of the company has disappeared** — To determine whether the substratum of the company has diasppeared, following tests were laid down in ***Re Kaithal Cotton and General Mills Co. Ltd. (1961).***

(i) Whether the subject matter of the company is gone; or

(ii) Whether the object for which the company was incorporated had substantially failed; or

(iii) Whether the company can carry on business otherwise than at a loss; or

(iv) Whether the existing and probable assets are insufficient to meet the existing liabilities.

In ***Re German Date Coffee Company's case,*** a company was formed with the primary object of manufacturing coffee from dates under a patent to be sanctioned by the German Government. Such patent was never granted. The Court ordered the company to be wound up since its main object had failed to materialise.

(c.) **Where the business cannot be carried on except at Loss —** In ***Re Factage Parisien, Ltd. (1867),*** a company carried on business at a loss and paid its debts by making new calls on the members. The company was ordered to be wound up. But the court will not be justified in making a winding-up order merely on the ground that the company has made losses, and it was likely to make further losses. ***[Re. Shah Steamship Navigation Co. (910)]***

(d.) **Where the company was formed for fraudulent purposes —** In ***Re T. E. Brinsmead & Sons (1897),*** T.E. Brinsmead and his two sons, who were the employees of a firm called Johan Brinsmead & Sons, formed a company under the name of T.E. Brinsmead & Sons to carry business similar to that of John Brinsmead & Sons. The Court ordered the company to be wound up since it had been formed for fraudulent purpose.

(e.) **Where majority exercise Oppression towards Minority —** In Sabapothy Rao v. Sabapathi Press Ltd, (1925) the directors were able to exercise a dominating influence on the management of the company and the managing director managed to outvote the minority and retain the profits of the business between the members of the family. It was also complained that the shareholders neither received a copy of the balance sheet nor was the auditor's report read at the general meeting and that dividends were not regularly paid and the rate was diminishing, the Court held it to be fit case for winding up.

(f.) **Where there is only a Bubble Company —** A company having no real business or property is termed as a 'bubble company'. Since such a company will never have resources to commence business it may be ordered to be wound up **[Re London and Country Coal Co., (1807)]**

(g.) **Where Right to Prticipate in the Management is Denied to any Director —** In ***Re Davis and Coltelt Ltd. (1935),*** where one member holding half the shares was denied by the other the right to participate in the company's business, the Court passed the winding up order.

(h.) **Where it is necessary in Public Interest —** In ***Re Walter L Jacob & Co. Ltd., 1989,*** where a company maintained no proper records, pretended to be an investment adviser though it was only a share vending company which suggested to invest in the shares of companies whose shares were not often traded, the Court ordered winding up in public interest.

3.7 Default in Filing with the Registrar

If the company has made a default in filing with the Registrar its Balance Sheet and Profit and Loss Account or Annual Return for any 5 consecutive financial years;

3.8 Act against Sovereignty and Integrity of India

If the company has acted against the interests of the sovereignty and integrity of India, the security of the State, friendly relations with foreign States, public order, decency or morality; The Tribunal shall make an order for the winding up on application made by the Central Government or a State Government.

3.9 Circumstances specified u/s 424G

If the Tribunal is of the opinion that the company should be wound up under the circumstances specified in section 424G:

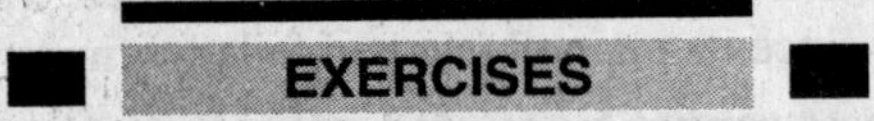

EXERCISES

1. State the circumstances under which the Tribunal may order for the compulsory winding up of a company.
2. State the circumstances under which the Tribunal may order for the compulsory winding up of a company on just and equitable grounds.

EMERGING ISSUES IN COMPANY LAW

1. Producer Companies
2. Corporate Governance

CHAPTER

14 Producer Companies

1.0 DEFINITIONS

1.1 Producer Company

Producer Company means a body corporate having objects or activities specified u/s 581B; and registered as Producer Company under The Companies Act.

1.2 Producer

Producer means any person engaged in any activity connected with or relatable to any primary produce.

1.3 Producer Institution

Producer Institution means:

(a) a Producer Company; *or*

(b) any other institution having only producers or Producer Companies as its Members whether incorporated or not having any of the objects specified u/s 581B and which agrees to make use of services of Producer Companies.

1.4 Primary Produce

Primary Producer means:

(a) produce of farmers, arising from–

- agriculture (including animal husbandry, horticulture, floriculture, pisciculture, viticulture, forestry, forest products, re-vegetation, bee raising and farming plantation products); or
- from any other primary activity or service.

(b) produce of persons engaged in handloom, handicraft and other cottage industries.

(c) any product resulting from any of the above activities, including by products of such products

(d) any product resulting from an ancillary activity that would assist or promote any of the aforesaid activities

(e) any activity which is intended to increase the production of anything referred to in sub-clauses (a) to (d) or improve the quality thereof.

1.5 Patronage

Patronage means the use of services offered by the Producer Company to its Members by participation in its business activities

1.6 Patronage Bonus

Patronage Bonus means payment made by a Producer Company out of its surplus income to the Members in proportion to their respective patronage.

1.7 Withheld Price

Withheld price means part of the price due and payable to any Member for goods supplied to the Producer company.

1.8 Limited Return

Limited return means the maximum dividend as may be specified by the articles.

1.9 Member

Member means a person or Producer institution (whether incorporated or not) admitted as a Member of a Producer Company and who retains the qualifications necessary for continuance as a member

1.10 Active Member

Active Member means a Member who fulfils the quantum and period of patronage as may be required by the articles.

2.0 OBJECTS OF A PRODUCER COMPANY [SEC 581 B]

The objects of a Producer Company are:

(a) Production, harvesting, procurement, grading, pooling, handling, marketing, selling, export of ***primary produce of Members***.

(b) ***Processing the*** produce of Members (*i.e.*, preserving, drying, distilling, brewing, vinting, canning and packaging of produce of Members).

(c) Manufacture, sale or supply of ***machinery, equipment or consumables*** to its Members.

(d) Providing ***education*** on the mutual assistance principles to its Members.

(e) Rendering ***services*** – technical, consultancy, training, research and development.

(f) Generation, transmission and distribution of ***power, revitalisation*** of land and water resources.

(g) ***Insurance of producers or their primary produce***.

(h) ***Welfare measures*** or facilities for the benefit of Members

(i) ***Promoting mutuality*** and mutual assistance.

(j) Any other activity, ***ancillary or incidental*** to any of the activities referred to in above clauses.

(k) ***Financing*** of procurement, processing, marketing or other activities specified in above clauses (*i.e.*, extending credit facilities or any other financial services to its Members)

3.0 FORMATION OF A PRODUCER COMPANY AND ITS REGISTRATION

3.1 Who can make the application?

The application for registration as a Producer Company shall be made by —

(a) 10 or more individuals, being producers; *or*

(b) 2 or more producer institutions; *or*

(c) a combination of above.

3.2 Enclosure to application

Following documents must be attached with the application:

(a) Memorandum

(b) Articles duly signed by the subscriber to the memorandum.

3.3 Application to whom

The application shall be made to the Registrar of the State where registered office of Producer Company is proposed to be situated.

3.4 Conditions for incorporation

(a) **Objects**—The object clause of the memorandum must contain all or any of the matters specified u/s 581B.

(b) **Nature of company—**The Producer Company shall be a company limited by shares.

(c) **Compliance**—The proposed Producer Company shall comply with all the provisions of Part IX-A of the Act.

3.5 Issue of certificate of incorporation

(a) **Conditions for issue of certificate**— If the Registrar is satisfied that the Producer Company has compiled with all the requirements of Act in respect of registration and matters precedent and incidental thereto, he shall—

(i) register the memorandum, articles and other documents; and

(ii) issue the certificate of incorporation.

(b) **Time limit for issue of certificate**— The Registrar must issue the certificate of incorporation *within 30 days* of the receipt of the documents required for registration.

3.6 Reimbursement of promotional expenses

(a) Payment to whom— The producer company may reimburse the promotional expenses to Promoters.

(b) Nature of payment

- All the direct costs associated with the promotion and registration of the Producer Company may be reimbursed by the Producer Company after its formation.
- Such payment may be by way of registration fees, legal fees, printing of memorandum and articles, or any other lawful expenses.

(c) Approval of Members at General Meeting—Such payment made by the Producer Company shall be subject to the approval in the first GM.

3.7 Effects of incorporation

(a) On registration, the Producer Company shall become a body corporate

(b) All the provisions of the Act shall apply to a Producer Company as if it is a private limited company. However, a Producer Company is neither a private company in terms of Sec. 3(1)(iii), nor a public company in terms of Sec. 3(1)(iv) of the Act.

(c) A Producer Company shall not, under any circumstance whatsoever, become or be deemed to become a public limited company.

4.0 MANAGEMENT OF A PRODUCER COMPANY

4.1 Number of Directors [Sec. 581O]

(a) **Minimum**—The minimum no. of directors required is 5.

(b) **Maximum**—The maximum limit on directors required is **15.**

(c) **Where Producer Company is formed by conversion**—The Producer Company may continue to have more than 15 directors for a period of 1 year if it is formed by way of conversion of an ISCS into a producer company.

4.2 Appointment of Directors [Sec. 581P]

(a) Time limit for election of directors

(i) The directors shall be elected ***within 90 days*** from the date of registration of the Producer Company.

(ii) If a Producer Company is formed by conversion, the election of directors shall be conducted ***within 1 year.***

(b) Tenure of office

(i) The tenure of office of every director shall be specified in the articles.

(ii) The tenure shall be—

(a) Minimum—1 year

(b) Maximum—5 years.

(c) Appointing Authority

The directors shall be elected or appointed by the Members in the Annual General Meeting.

(d) Retirement of Directors

(i) The directors shall retire in accordance with the articles of the company.

(ii) A retiring director shall be eligible for re-appointment.

(e) Additional Directors

(i) The Board may co-opt one or more expert directors or additional directors.

(ii) These directors shall not exceed 1/5th of the total number of directors.

4.3 Meetings of Board and Quorum [Sec. 581V]

(a) Minimum number of Board Meetings

(i) At least 4 **Board Meetings** must held in each calendar year.

(ii) At least 1 **Board Meeting** must be held in every quarter.

(b) Notice of Board Meeting

(i) Notice of every **Board Meeting** shall be given in writing.

(ii) The notice shall be given to every director for the time being in India, and at his usual address in India to every other director.

(c) Duty to give notice of Board Meeting

It shall be the duty of Chief Executive to give notice of all **Board Meetings.**

(d) Length of notice

(i) The notice of every **Board Meeting** shall be given by the Chief Executive *at least 7 days* before the date of **Board Meeting.**

(ii) If a **Board Meeting** is called at a shorter notice, the reasons thereof shall be recorded in writing by the Board.

(e) Quorum for Board Meeting

The quorum for a Board Meeting shall be higher of —

(i) 1/3rd of the total strength; *or*

(ii) 3 directors.

(f) Sitting fees

(i) The directors may be paid such fees and allowances for attending Board Meeting, as may be decided by the Members in General Meeting.

(ii) Sitting fees can also be paid to additional or expert directors.

4.4 Secretary of Producer Company [Sec. 581X]

(a) **Mandatory Appointment**—Every Producer Company having an average annual turnover exceeding Rs. 5 crores in each of 3 consecutive financial years shall have a whole-time secretary.

(b) **Qualifications of Secretary**—Only a member of ICSI can be appointed as secretary.

(c) **Penalty**—Failure to appoint a secretary shall be punishable with fine upto Rs. 500 for every day during which the default continues.

However, it shall be a defence to prove that—

(i) all reasonable efforts were made to appoint a whole-time secretary; *or*

(ii) the financial position of the company was such that it was beyond its capacity to engage a whole-time secretary.

5.0 CANCELLATION OF REGISTRATION OF A PRODUCER COMPANY [SEC 581 ZP]

5.1 Circumstances in which registration can be cancelled

The Registrar has the power to pass an order cancellation the registration of a Producer Company in the following cases:

(i) Where a Producer Company fails to commence business *within 1 year* of its registration

(ii) Where a Producer Company ceases to transact business with the Members.

(iii) Where the Registrar is satisfied that the Producer Company is no longer carrying on any of its objects specified u/s 581B.

5.2 Conditions for making an order of cancellation

(i) The Registrar shall give a reasonable opportunity of being heard to the Producer Company.

(ii) A copy of show cause notice shall also be given to all the directors of the producer company.

5.3 Appeal against order of cancellation

(i) **Who can appeal?—Any Member** of the Producer Company who is aggrieved by order of cancellation of registration of the Producer Company may file an appeal.

(ii) **Appeal with whom**—The appeal shall be filed with **Company Law Board**.

(iii) **Time limit for filing appeal**—The appeal shall be filed ***within 60 days*** of order of Registrar cancelling the registration shall not take effect until the appeal is disposed of.

(iv) **Effect of filling appeal**—The order of cancellation of registration shall not take effect until the appeal is disposed of.

EXERCISES

SHORT ANSWER TYPE QUESTIONS

1. What is 'Producer Company'?
2. Who is 'Producer'?
3. State any four objects of a Producer Company.
4. Who can make the application for registration as a Producer Company?
5. State the basic conditions for incorporation of Producer Company.
6. Is a Producer Company a private Company or a Public Company?
7. State the minimum number of directors of a producer company.
8. State the maximum number of directors of a producer company.
9. State the time limit for election of directors of a producer company.
10. State the tenure of office of a director of a Producer Company.
11. How many expert directors or additional directors can be appointed in case of a Producer Company?
12. How many Board Meetings of a Producer Company must be held?
13. State the quorum for a Board Meeting of a Producer Company.
14. State the circumstances in which the registration of a producer company may be cancelled.

LONG ANSWER TYPE QUESTIONS

1. Define the following terms under the Companies Act, 1956:

   (a) Producer Company
   (b) Producer
   (c) Producer Institution
   (d) Primary Produce
   (e) Patronage
   (f) Patronage Bonus
   (g) Withheld Price
   (h) Limited return
   (i) Member
   (j) Active Member

2. (c) What is Producer Company?
   (d) What are the objects of a producer company?
3. Briefly explain the provision relating to the formation of a Producer Company.
4. Briefly explain the provisions relating to the management of a Producer Company.
5. Briefly explain the provisions relating to the cancellation of registration of a Producer Company.

CHAPTER

15 Corporate Governance

1.0 MEANING OF CORPORATE GOVERNANCE

1.1 Corporate Governance deals with the manner in which companies are directed and controlled by the Board of Directors in order to create stakeholder value by appropriately crafting the corporate strategy that creates tomorrow's organization.

1.2 Corporate Goverance refers to the conduct of business in accordance with the stakeholders' desires, which primarily means to create wealth for the stakeholders, but at the same time conforming to the laws, rules and regulations established by the society. The stakeholders include, besides the share holders, other participants in the corporation such as board of directors, managers, employees, workers, customers, vendors, lenders, dealers, regulators, society and even the government.

1.3 Corporate Governance is governance with the highest standards of professionalism, integrity, accountability, fairness, transparency, social responsiveness and business ethics.

1.4 Good Corporate Governance, is a critical doctrine to the global economic system, enabling the business to not only effectively and efficiently achieve its corporate objectives but also provides it the structure and methodology to sustain its survival in globally competitive environment.

1.5 The recent happenings in the corporate world leading to financial scams, battles for corporate takeovers, accounting scandals, have questioned the legitimacy of the manner in which the Directors work in the interest of shareholders. Across the globe, the laws have been made and rules have been modified so as to make the accountability of the Directors transparent and to ensure that Directors work not in their own interest but work in the interest of the shareholders, without sacrificing the interest of other stakeholders. In the arena of accounting, the core of corporate governance relates to designing and putting in place disclosures, monitoring, oversight, and corrective system that ensures alignment of objectives of managers and other stakeholders. To this end Securities and Exchange Board of India has caused the amendment of Listing Agreement where by Clause 49 was inserted to ensure certain disclosures on the part of listed companies with respect to corporate governance.

2.0 IMPORTANCE OF CORPORATE GOVERNANCE

2.1 Professionalism

It promotes adherence to the highest standards of **Professionalism.**

2.2 Integrity

It promotes adherence to the highest standards of **Integrity** and thereby ensures integrity in financial reports.

2.3 Accountability

It promotes adherence to the highest standards of **Accountability.**

2.4 Fairness

It promotes adherence to the highest standards of **Fairness.**

2.5 Transparency

It promotes adherence to the highest standards of **Transparency.** It emphasises the adoption of transparent procedures and practices by the Board.

2.6 Social Responsiveness.

It promotes adherence to the highest standards of **Social Responsiveness.**

2.7 Business Ethics

It promotes adherence to the highest standards of **Business Ethics and Code of Conduct.**

2.8 Investors' Confidence

It strengthens Investors' confidence by making provision for adequate number of Non-executive and Independent directors on the Board to look after the interests and well-being of all the shareholders.

2.9 Globally Compatibility

It prepares the Corporates to be globally compatable by promoting adherence to the Corporate Governance practices with global standards.

3.0 REQUIREMENTS OF CLAUSE 49 OF LISTING AGREEMENT

Clause 49 of Listing Agreement contains following two types of requirements:

Mandatory Requirements	*Non-mandatory Requirements*
1. Board of Directors	1. The Board
2. Audit Committee	2. Remuneration Committee
3. Subsidiary Companies	3. Shareholder Rights
4. Disclosures	4. Audit Qualifications
5. CEO/CFO Certification	5. Training of Board Members
6. Report on Corporate Governance	6. Machanism for evaluating non-executive Board Members
7. Compliance Certificate	7. Whistle Blower Policy

MANDATORY REQUIREMENTS OF CLAUSE 49 OF LISTING AGREEMENT

4.0 BOARD OF DIRECTORS

4.1 Composition of Board

1. **At least 50% Non-executive Directors**—The Board of directors of the company shall have an optimum combination of executive and non-executive directors with atleast 50% of the board of directors comprising of non-executive directors.
2. **At least 1/3rd or 1/2 Independent Directors**—Where the Chairman of the Board is a non-executive director, at least one-third of the Board should comprise of independent directors and in case he is an executive director, at least half of the Board should comprise of independent directors.
3. **Meaning of Independent Director**—'Independent director' means a non-executive director of the company who:
   (a) apart from receiving director's remuneration, does not have any material pecuniary relationships or transactions with the company, its promoters, its directors, its senior management or its holding company, its subsidiaries and associates which may affect independence of the director;
   (b) is not related to promoters or persons occupying management positions at the board level or at one level below the board;
   (c) has not been an executive of the company in the immediately preceding three financial years;
   (d) is not a partner or an executive or was not partner or an executive during the preceding three years, of any of the following:
      i) the statutory audit firm or the internal audit firm that is associated with the company, and
      ii) the legal firm(s) and consulting firm(s) that have a material association with the company.
   (e) is not a material supplier, service provider or customer or a lessor or lessee of the company, which may affect independence of the director; and
   (f) is not a substantial shareholder of the company i.e. owning atleast 2 % of the block of voting shares.

Meaning of Associate, Senior Management and Relative

(a) **Associate** shall mean a company which is an "associate" as defined in Accounting Standard (AS) 23, "Accounting for Investments in Associates in Consolidated Financial Statements", issued by the Institute of Chartered Accountants of India.

(b) **"Senior management"** shall mean personnel of the company who are members of its core management team excluding Board of Directors. Normally, this would comprise all members of management one level below the executive directors, including all functional heads.

(c) **"Relative"** shall mean "relative" as defined in section 2(41) and section 6 read with Schedule IA of the Companies Act, 1956.

4. **Nominee Directors**—Nominee directors appointed by an institution which has invested in or lent to the company shall be deemed to be independent directors.

Meaning of Institution—"Institution' for this purpose means a public financial institution as defined in Section 4A of the Companies Act, 1956 or a "corresponding new bank" as defined in section 2(d) of the Banking Companies (Acquisition and Transfer of Undertakings) Act, 1970 or the Banking Companies (Acquisition and Transfer of Undertakings) Act, 1980 [both Acts]."

4.2 Non executive directors' compensation and disclosures

1. **Fixed by Board and require Approval of Shareholders.**

   All fees (excluding sitting fees)/compensation, if any paid to non-executive directors, including independent directors, shall be fixed by the Board of Directors and shall require previous approval of shareholders in general meeting.
2. The shareholders' resolution shall specify the limits for the maximum number of stock options that can be granted to non-executive directors, including independent directors, in any financial year and in aggregate.

4.3 Other provisions as to Board and Committees

1. **Minimum No. of Board Meetings**

   The board shall meet at least four times a year,
2. **Maximum Time Gap between Two Board Meetings**—

   The maximum time gap between any two Board Meetings must not be exceed 4 months.
3. **Minimum information to Board**—The minimum information to be made available to the board is given in **Annexure– I A.**

INFORMATION TO BE PLACED BEFORE BOARD OF DIRECTORS (AS PER ANNEXURE–IA)

1. Annual operating plans and budgets and any updates.
2. Capital budgets and any updates.
3. Quarterly results for the company and its operating divisions or business segments.
4. Minutes of meetings of audit committee and other committees of the board.
5. The information on recruitment and remuneration of senior officers just below the board level, including appointment or removal of Chief Financial Officer and the Company Secretary.
6. Show cause, demand, prosecution notices and penalty notices which are materially important
7. Fatal or serious accidents, dangerous occurrences, any material effluent or pollution problems.
8. Any material default in financial obligations to and by the company, or substantial nonpayment for goods sold by the company.
9. Any issue, which involves possible public or product liability claims of substantial nature, including any judgement or order which, may have passed strictures on the conduct of the company or taken an adverse view regarding another enterprise that can have negative implications on the company.
10. Details of any joint venture or collaboration agreement.

11. Transactions that involve substantial payment towards goodwill, brand equity, or intellectual property.
12. Significant labour problems and their proposed solutions. Any significant development in Human Resources/ Industrial Relations front like signing of wage agreement, implementation of Voluntary Retirement Scheme etc.
13. Sale of material nature, of investments, subsidiaries, assets, which is not in normal course of business.
14. Quarterly details of foreign exchange exposures and the steps taken by management to limit the risks of adverse exchange rate movement, if material.
15. Non-compliance of any regulatory, statutory or listing requirements and shareholders service such as non-payment of dividend, delay in share transfer etc.

4. **Maximum limit of Membership/Chairmanship of Commitees**—A director shall not be a member in more than 10 committees or act as Chairman of more than 5 committees across all companies in which he is a director.
5. **Duty of Director to inform about Committee Positions**—Furthermore it should be a mandatory annual requirement for every director to inform the company about the committee positions he occupies in other companies and notify changes as and when they take place.
   (a) **Companies included in the limit of Committees**—For the purpose of considering the limit of the committees on which a director can serve, all public limited companies, whether listed or not, shall be included.
   (b) **Companies excluded in the limit of Committees**—All other companies including private limited companies, foreign companies and companies under Section 25 of the Companies Act shall be excluded.
   (c) Chairmanship/membership of the Audit Committee and the Shareholders' Grievance Committee alone shall be considered.
6. **Periodic Review of Compliance Reports**— The Board shall periodically review compliance reports of all laws applicable to the company, prepared by the company as well as steps taken by the company to rectify instances of non-compliances.

4.4 Code of Conduct

1. The Board shall lay down a code of conduct for all Board members and senior management of the company.
2. The code of conduct shall be posted on the website of the company.
3. All Board members and senior management personnel shall affirm compliance with the code on an annual basis.
4. The Annual Report of the company shall contain a declaration to this effect signed by the CEO.

Explanation: For this purpose, the term "senior management" shall mean personnel of the company who are members of its core management team excluding Board of Directors.. Normally, this would comprise all members of management one level below the executive directors, including all functional heads.

5.0 AUDIT COMMITTEE

5.1 Qualified and Independent Audit Committee

1. A qualified and independent audit committee shall be set up, giving the terms of reference.
2. **Minimum No. of Directors as Member**—The audit committee shall have minimum **3** directors as members.
3. **Minumim No. of Independent Directors**—Two-thirds of the members of audit committee shall be independent directors.
4. **Financially Literate**—All members of audit committee shall be financially literate
5. **At least one Accounting or Finance Expert**—At least one member shall have accounting or related financial management expertise.
   (a) The term **"financially literate"** means the ability to read and understand basic financial statements i.e. balance sheet, profit and loss account, and statement of cash flows.
   (b) A member will be considered to have accounting or related financial management expertise if he or she possesses experience in finance or accounting, or requisite professional certification in accounting, or any other comparable experience or background which results in the individual's financial sophistication, including being or having been a chief executive officer, chief financial officer or other senior officer with financial oversight responsibilities.
6. **Who will be the Chairman**—The Chairman of the Audit Committee shall be an independent director;
7. **Who will be answer Shareholders' Queries**—The Chairman of the Audit Committee shall be present at Annual General Meeting to answer shareholder queries;
8. **Invitees**—The audit committee may invite such of the executives, as it considers appropriate (and particularly the head of the finance function) to be present at the meetings of the committee, but on occasions it may also meet without the presence of any executives of the company. The finance director, head of internal audit and a representative of the statutory auditor may be present as invitees for the meetings of the audit committee;
9. **Secretary**—The Company Secretary shall act as the secretary to the committee.

5.2 Meeting of Audit Committee

1. **Minimum No. of Meetings**—The audit committee should meet at least 4 times in a year.
2. **Maximum Time Gap between two meetings**—The maximum gap betwee any two meetings of audit committee must not exceed 4 months.
3. **Quorum**—The quorum shall be either two members or one third of the members of the audit committee whichever is greater, but there should be a minimum of two independent members present.

5.3 Powers of Audit Committee

The audit committee shall have powers, which should include the following:

1. To investigate any activity within its terms of reference.
2. To seek information from any employee.
3. To obtain outside legal or other professional advice.
4. To secure attendance of outsiders with relevant expertise, if it considers necessary.

5.4 Role of Audit Committee

The role of the audit committee shall include the following:

1. Oversight of the company's financial reporting process and the disclosure of its financial information to ensure that the financial statement is correct, sufficient and credible.

2. Recommending to the Board, the appointment, re-appointment and, if required, the replacement or removal of the statutory auditor and the fixation of audit fees.
3. Approval of payment to statutory auditors for any other services rendered by the statutory auditors.
4. Reviewing, with the management, the annual financial statements before submission to the board for approval, with particular reference to:
   (a.) Matters required to be included in the Director's Responsibility Statement to be included in the Board's report in terms of clause (2AA) of section 217 of the Companies Act, 1956
   (b.) Changes, if any, in accounting policies and practices and reasons for the same
   (c.) Major accounting entries involving estimates based on the exercise of judgment by management
   (d.) Significant adjustments made in the financial statements arising out of audit findings
   (e.) Compliance with listing and other legal requirements relating to financial statements
   (f.) Disclosure of any related party transactions
   (g.) Qualifications in the draft audit report.
5. Reviewing, with the management, the quarterly financial statements before submission to the board for approval
6. Reviewing, with the management, performance of statutory and internal auditors, adequacy of the internal control systems.
7. Reviewing the adequacy of internal audit function, if any, including the structure of the internal audit department, staffing and seniority of the official heading the department, reporting structure coverage and frequency of internal audit.
8. Discussion with internal auditors any significant findings and follow up there on.
9. Reviewing the findings of any internal investigations by the internal auditors into matters where there is suspected fraud or irregularity or a failure of internal control systems of a material nature and reporting the matter to the board.
10. Discussion with statutory auditors before the audit commences, about the nature and scope of audit as well as post-audit discussion to ascertain any area of concern.
11. To look into the reasons for substantial defaults in the payment to the depositors, debenture holders, shareholders (in case of non payment of declared dividends) and creditors.
12. To review the functioning of the Whistle Blower mechanism, in case the same is existing.
13. Carrying out any other function as is mentioned in the terms of reference of the Audit Committee.

Explanation (i): The term "related party transactions" shall have the same meaning as contained in the Accounting Standard 18, Related Party Transactions, issued by The Institute of Chartered Accountants of India.

Explanation (ii): If the company has set up an audit committee pursuant to provision of the Companies Act, the said audit committee shall have such additional functions / features as is contained in this clause.

5.5 Review of information by Audit Committee

The Audit Committee shall mandatorily review the following information:

1. Management discussion and analysis of financial condition and results of operations;

2. Statement of significant related party transactions (as defined by the audit committee), submitted by management;
3. Management letters / letters of internal control weaknesses issued by the statutory auditors;
4. Internal audit reports relating to internal control weaknesses; and
5. The appointment, removal and terms of remuneration of the Chief internal auditor shall be subject to review by the Audit Committee

6.0 SUBSIDIARY COMPANIES

6.1 At least one independent director on the Board of Directors of the holding company shall be a director on the Board of Directors of a material non listed Indian subsidiary company.

6.2 The Audit Committee of the listed holding company shall also review the financial statements, in particular, the investments made by the unlisted subsidiary company.

6.3 The minutes of the Board meetings of the unlisted subsidiary company shall be placed at the Board meeting of the listed holding company. The management should periodically bring to the attention of the Board of Directors of the listed holding company, a statement of all significant transactions and arrangements entered into by the unlisted subsidiary company.

Explanation 1: The term "material non-listed Indian subsidiary" shall mean an unlisted subsidiary, incorporated in India, whose turnover or net worth (i.e. paid up capital and free reserves) exceeds 20% of the consolidated turnover or net worth respectively, of the listed holding company and its subsidiaries in the immediately preceding accounting year.

Explanation 2: The term "significant transaction or arrangement" shall mean any individual transaction or arrangement that exceeds or is likely to exceed 10% of the total revenues or total expenses or total assets or total liabilities, as the case may be, of the material unlisted subsidiary for the immediately preceding accounting year.

Explanation 3: Where a listed holding company has a listed subsidiary which is itself a holding company, the above provisions shall apply to the listed subsidiary insofar as its subsidiaries are concerned.

7.0 DISCLOSURES

7.1 Basis of related party transactions

1. A statement in summary form of transactions with related parties in the ordinary course of business shall be placed periodically before the audit committee.
2. Details of m aterial individual transactions with related parties which are not in the normal course of business shall be placed before the audit committee.
3. Details of material individual transactions with related parties or others, which are not on an arm's length basis should be placed before the audit committee, together with Management's justification for the same..

7.2 Disclosure of Accounting Treatment different from that prescribed in AS

Where in the preparation of financial statements, a treatment different from that prescribed in an Accounting Standard has been followed, the fact shall be disclosed in the financial statements, together with the management's explanation as to why it believes such alternative treatment is more representative of the true and fair view of the underlying business transaction in the Corporate Governance Report.

7.3 Board Disclosures – Risk management

The company shall lay down procedures to inform Board members about the risk assessment and minimization procedures. These procedures shall be periodically reviewed to ensure that executive management controls risk through means of a properly defined framework.

7.4 About Uses/Applications of Proceeds from Public Issues, Rights Issues, Preferential Issues etc.

When money is raised through an issue (public issues, rights issues, preferential issues etc.), it shall disclose to the Audit Committee, the uses / applications of funds by major category (capital expenditure, sales and marketing, working capital, etc), on a quarterly basis as a part of their quarterly declaration of financial results. Further, on an annual basis, the company shall prepare a statement of funds utilized for purposes other than those stated in the offer document/prospectus/notice and place it before the audit committee. Such disclosure shall be made only till such time that the full money raised through the issue has been fully spent. This statement shall be certified by the statutory auditors of the company. The audit committee shall make appropriate recommendations to the Board to take up steps in this matter.

7.5 Remuneration of Directors

1. All pecuniary relationship or transactions of the non-executive directors vis-à-vis the company shall be disclosed in the Annual Report.
2. Further the following disclosures on the remuneration of directors shall be made in the section on the corporate governance of the Annual Report:
   (a) All elements of remuneration package of individual directors summarized under major groups, such as salary, benefits, bonuses, stock options, pension etc.
   (b) Details of fixed component and performance linked incentives, along with the performance criteria.
   (c) Service contracts, notice period, severance fees.
   (d) Stock option details, if any – and whether issued at a discount as well as the period over which accrued and over which exercisable.
3. The company shall publish its criteria of making payments to non-executive directors in its annual report. Alternatively, this may be put up on the company's website and reference drawn thereto in the annual report.
4. The company shall disclose the number of shares and convertible instruments held by non-executive directors in the annual report.
5. Non-executive directors shall be required to disclose their shareholding (both own or held by / for other persons on a beneficial basis) in the listed company in which they are proposed to be appointed as directors, prior to their appointment. These details should be disclosed in the notice to the general meeting called for appointment of such director

7.6 Management

1. As part of the directors' report or as an addition thereto, a Management Discussion and Analysis report should form part of the Annual Report to the shareholders. This Management Discussion

& Analysis should include discussion on the following matters within the limits set by the company's competitive position:

i. Industry structure and developments.
ii. Opportunities and Threats.
iii. Segment–wise or product-wise performance.
iv. Outlook
v. Risks and concerns.
vi. Internal control systems and their adequacy.
vii. Discussion on financial performance with respect to operational performance.
viii. Material developments in Human Resources / Industrial Relations front, including number of people employed.

2. Senior management shall make disclosures to the board relating to all material financial and commercial transactions, where they have personal interest, that may have a potential conflict with the interest of the company at large (for e.g. dealing in company shares, commercial dealings with bodies, which have shareholding of management and their relatives etc.)

Explanation: For this purpose, the term "senior management" shall mean personnel of the company who are members of its. core management team excluding the Board of Directors). This would also include all members of management one level below the executive directors including all functional heads.

7.7 Shareholders

1. In case of the appointment of a new director or re-appointment of a director the shareholders must be provided with the following information:
   (a) A brief resume of the director;
   (b) Nature of his expertise in specific functional areas;
   (c) Names of companies in which the person also holds the directorship and the membership of Committees of the Board; and
   (d) Shareholding of non-executive directors as stated in Clause 49 (IV) (E) (v) above
2. Quarterly results and presentations made by the company to analysts shall be put on company's web-site, or shall be sent in such a form so as to enable the stock exchange on which the company is listed to put it on its own web-site.
3. A board committee under the chairmanship of a non-executive director shall be formed to specifically look into the redressal of shareholder and investors complaints like transfer of shares, non-receipt of balance sheet, non-receipt of declared dividends etc. This Committee shall be designated as 'Shareholders/Investors Grievance Committee'.
4. To expedite the process of share transfers, the Board of the company shall delegate the power of share transfer to an officer or a committee or to the registrar and share transfer agents. The delegated authority shall attend to share transfer formalities at least once in a fortnight.

8.0 CEO/CFO CERTIFICATION

The CEO, i.e. the Managing Director or Manager appointed in terms of the Companies Act, 1956 and the CFO i.e. the whole-time Finance Director or any other person heading the finance function discharging that function shall certify to the Board that:

(a) They have reviewed financial statements and the cash flow statement for the year and that to the best of their knowledge and belief :

(i) these statements do not contain any materially untrue statement or omit any material fact or contain statements that might be misleading;

(ii) these statements together present a true and fair view of the company's affairs and are in compliance with existing accounting standards, applicable laws and regulations.

(b) There are, to the best of their knowledge and belief, no transactions entered into by the company during the year which are fraudulent, illegal or violative of the company's code of conduct.

(c) They accept responsibility for establishing and maintaining internal controls and that they have evaluated the effectiveness of the internal control systems of the company and they have disclosed to the auditors and the Audit Committee, deficiencies in the design or operation of internal controls, if any, of which they are aware and the steps they have taken or propose to take to rectify these deficiencies.

(d) They have indicated to the auditors and the Audit committee

(i) significant changes in internal control during the year;

(ii) significant changes in accounting policies during the year and that the same have been disclosed in the notes to the financial statements; and

(iii) instances of significant fraud of which they have become aware and the involvement therein, if any, of the management or an employee having a significant role in the company's internal control system

9.0 REPORT ON CORPORATE GOVERNANCE

9.1 There shall be a separate section on Corporate Governance in the Annual Reports of company, with a detailed compliance report on Corporate Governance.

9.2 Non-compliance of any mandatory requirement of this clause with reasons thereof and the extent to which the non-mandatory requirements have been adopted should be specifically highlighted. The suggested list of items to be included in this report is given in **Annexure- I C** and list of non-mandatory requirements is given in **Annexure – I D.**

SUGGESTED LIST OF ITEMS TO BE INCLUDED IN THE REPORT ON CORPORATE GOVERNANCE IN THE ANNUAL REPORT OF COMPANIES [AS PER ANNEXURE IC]

1. *Philosphy on Governance*	i. A brief statement on company's philosophy on code of governance.
2. *Board of Directors:*	i. Composition and category of directors, for example, promoter, executive, non-executive, independent non-executive, nominee director, which institution represented as lender or as equity investor. ii. Attendance of each director at the Board meetings and the last AGM.

	iii. Number of other Boards or Board Committees in which he/she is a member or Chairperson. iv. Number of Board meetings held, dates on which held.
3. ***Audit Committee:***	i. Brief description of terms of reference ii. Composition, name of members and Chairperson iii. Meetings and attendance during the year
4. ***Remuneration Committee:***	i. Brief description of terms of reference ii. Composition, name of members and Chairperson iii. Attendance during the year iv. Remuneration policy v. Details of remuneration to all the directors, as per format in main report.
5. ***Shareholders Committee:***	i. Name of non-executive director heading the committee ii. Name and designation of compliance officer iii. Number of shareholders' complaints received so far iv. Number not solved to the satisfaction of shareholders v. Number of pending complaints
6. ***General Body meetings:***	i. Location and time, where last three AGMs held. ii. Whether any special resolutions passed in the previous 3 AGMs iii. Whether any special resolution passed last year through postal ballot – details of voting pattern iv. Person who conducted the postal ballot exercise v. Whether any special resolution is proposed to be conducted through postal ballot vi. Procedure for postal ballot
7. ***Disclosures:***	i. Disclosures on materially significant related party transactions that may have potential conflict with the interests of company at large. ii. Details of non-compliance by the company, penalties, strictures imposed on the company by Stock Exchange or SEBI or any statutory authority, on any matter related to capital markets, during the last three years. iii. Whistle Blower policy and affirmation that no personnel has been denied access to the audit committee. iv. Details of compliance with mandatory requirements and adoption of the nonmandatory requirements of this clause

8. *Means of communication.*	i. Quarterly results ii. Newspapers wherein results normally published iii. Any website, where displayed iv. Whether it also displays official news releases; and v. The presentations made to institutional investors or to the analysts.
9. *General Shareholder information:*	i. AGM : Date, time and venue ii. Financial year iii. Date of Book closure iv. Dividend Payment Date v. Listing on Stock Exchanges vi. Stock Code vii. Market Price Data : High., Low during each month in last financial year viii. Performance in comparison to broad-based indices such as BSE Sensex, CRISIL index etc. ix. Registrar and Transfer Agents x. Share Transfer System xi. Distribution of shareholding xii. Dematerialization of shares and liquidity xiii. Outstanding GDRs/ADRs/Warrants or any Convertible instruments, conversion date and likely impact on equity xiv. Plant Locations xv. Address for correspondence

NON-MANDATORY REQUIREMENTS [AS PER ANNEXURE I D]

(1) *The Board*	(i) A non-executive Chairman may be entitled to maintain a Chairman's office at the company's expense and also allowed reimbursement of expenses incurred in performance of his duties. (ii) Independent Directors may have a tenure not exceeding, in the aggregate, a period of nine years, on the Board of a company.
(2) *Remuneration Committee*	(i) The board may set up a remuneration committee to determine on their behalf and on behalf of the shareholders with agreed terms of reference, the company's policy on specific remuneration packages for executive directors including pension rights and any compensation payment.

	(ii) To avoid conflicts of interest, the remuneration committee, which would determine the remuneration packages of the executive directors may comprise of at least three directors, all of whom should be non-executive directors, the Chairman of committee being an independent director. (iii) All the members of the remuneration committee could be present at the meeting. (iv) The Chairman of the remuneration committee could be present at the Annual General Meeting, to answer the shareholder queries. However, it would be up to the Chairman to decide who should answer the queries.
(3) ***Shareholder Rights***	A half-yearly declaration of financial performance including summary of the significant events in last six-months, may be sent to each household of shareholders.
(4) ***Audit Qualifications***	Company may move towards a regime of unqualified financial statements.
(5) ***Training of Board Members***	A company may train its Board members in the business model of the company as well as the risk profile of the business parameters of the company, their responsibilities as directors, and the best ways to discharge them.
(6) ***Mechanism for evaluating non-executive Board Members***	The performance evaluation of non-executive directors could be done by a peer group comprising the entire Board of Directors, excluding the director being evaluated; and Peer Group evaluation could be the mechanism to determine whether to extend / continue the terms of appointment of non-executive directors.
(7) ***Whistle Blower Policy***	The company may establish a mechanism for employees to report to the management concerns about unethical behaviour, actual or suspected fraud or violation of the company's code of conduct or ethics policy. This mechanism could also provide for adequate safeguards against victimization of employees who avail of the mechanism and also provide for direct access to the Chairman of the Audit committee in exceptional cases. Once established, the existence of the mechanism may be appropriately communicated within the organization.

9.3 Quaterly Compliance Report—The companies shall submit a quarterly compliance report to the stock exchanges within 15 days from the close of quarter as per the format given in **Annexure I B**. The report shall be signed either by the Compliance Officer or the Chief Executive Officer of the company.

FORMAT OF QUARTERLY COMPLIANCE REPORT ON CORPORATE GOVERNANCE

Name of the Company: ....

Quarter ending on: ....

Particulars	*Clause of Listing agreement*	*Compliance Status Yes/No*	*Remarks*
I. Board of Directors	49 I		
(A) Composition of Board	49(IA)		
(B) Non-executive Directors' compensation & disclosures	49 (IB)		
(C) Other provisions as to Board and Committees	49 (IC)		
(D) Code of Conduct	49 (ID)		
II. Audit Committee	49 (II)		
(A) Qualified & Independent Audit Committee	49 (IIA)		
(B) Meeting of Audit Committee	49 (IIB)		
(C) Powers of Audit Committee	49 (IIC)		
(D) Role of Audit Committee	49 II(D)		
(E) Review of Information by Audit Committee	49 (IIE)		
III. Subsidiary Companies	49 (III)		
IV. Disclosures	49 (IV)		
(A) Basis of related party transactions	49 (IV A)		
(B) Disclosures of Accounting Treatment	49 (IV B)		
(C) Proceeds from public issues, rights issues, preferential issues etc.	49 (IV C)		
(D) Remuneration of Directors	49 (IV D)		
(E) Board Disclosure Risk Management	49 (IV E)		
(F) Shareholders	49 (IV F)		
V. CEO/CFO Certification	49 (V)		
VI. Report on Corporate Governance	49 (VI)		
VII. Compliance Certificate	49 (VII)		

Notes:

(1) *The details under each head shall be provided to incorporate all the information required as per the provisions of the Clause 49 of the Listing Agreement.*

(2) *In the column No.3, compliance or non-compliance may be indicated by Yes/No/N.A.. For example, if the Board has been composed in accordance with the Clause 49 I of the Listing Agreement, "Yes" may be indicated. Similarly, in case the company has no related party transactions, the words "N.A." may be indicated against 49 (IV A).*

(3) *In the remarks column, reasons for non-compliance may be indicated, for example, in case of requirement related to circulation of information to the shareholders, which would be done only in the AGM/EGM, it might be indicated in the "Remarks" column as – "will be complied with at the AGM". Similarly, in respect of matters which can be complied with only where the situation arises, for example, "Report on Corporate Governance" is to be a part of Annual Report only, the words "will be complied in the next Annual Report" may be indicated.*

10.0 COMPLIANCE CERTIFICATE

10.1 Compliance Certificate

The company shall obtain a certificate from either the auditors or practicing company secretaries regarding compliance of conditions of corporate governance as stipulated in this clause and annex the certificate with the directors' report, which is sent annually to all the shareholders of the company.

10.2 Filing of compliance certificate with Stock Exchanges

The same certificate shall also be sent to the Stock Exchanges along with the annual report filed by the company.

10.3 The non-mandatory requirements given in **Annexure – I D** may be implemented as per the discretion of the company.

10.4 However, the disclosures of the compliance with mandatory requirements and adoption (and compliance) / non-adoption of the non-mandatory requirements shall be made in the section on corporate governance of the Annual Report.

EXERCISES

SHORT ANSWER TYPE QUESTIONS

1. What is Corporate Governance? State its importance.
2. State the mandatory requirements of clause 49 of the Listing Agreement.
3. State the Non-mandatory requirements of clause 49 of the Listing Agreement.
4. Write short notes on the following:
   (a) Corporate Governance
   (b) Mandatory Requirements of clause 49 of Listing Agreement
   (c) Non-Mandatory Requirements of clause 49 of Listing Agreement
   (d) Independent Directors
   (e) Audit Committee
5. Give the format of quarterly compliance report on Corporate Governance.

SECTION B

Compensation LAWS

16. The Employees' State Insurance Act, 1948
17. The Workmen's Compensation Act, 1923

CHAPTER

16

The Employees' State Insurance Act, 1948

1.0 INTRODUCTION

The Employees' State Insurance Act, 1948 is *an Act to provide for certain benefits to employees in case of sickness, maternity and employment injury and make provision for certain other matters in relation thereto.*

2.0 WHAT IS THE TERRITORY TO WHICH THE ACT APPLIES? [SEC 1 (2)]

The Employees' State Insurance Act, 1948 extends to the whole of India.

3.0 WHEN THE ACT CAME INTO FORCE. [SEC 1 (3)]

It shall come into force on such date or dates as the Central Government may, by notification in the Official Gazette, appoint, and different dates may be appointed for different provisions of this Act and for different States or for different parts thereof.

4.0 FACTORIES TO WHICH THE ACT APPLIES. [SEC 1 (4)]

It shall apply, in the first instance, to all factories (including factories belonging to the Government) other than seasonal factories:

Provided that nothing contained in this sub-section shall apply to a factory or establishment belonging to or under the control of the Government whose employees are otherwise in receipt of benefits substantially similar or superior to the benefits provided under this Act.

5.0 POWER OF APPROPRIATE GOVERNMENT TO EXTEND THE PROVISIONS TO ANOTHER FACTORY. [SEC 1 (5)]

The appropriate Government may, in consultation with the corporation and where the appropriate Government is a State Government, with the approval of the Central Government, after giving 6 months' notice of its intention of so doing by notification in the Official Gazette, extend the provisions of this Act or any of them, to any other establishment or class of establishments, industrial, commercial, agricultural or otherwise:

Provided that where the provisions of this Act have been brought into force in any part of a State, the said provisions shall stand extended to any such establishment or class of establishments within that part if the provisions have already been extended to similar establishment or class of establishment in another part of that State.

6.0 CONTINUOUS APPLICATION OF THE ACT. [SEC 1 (6)]

A factory or an establishment to which this Act applies shall continue to be governed therein at any time falls below the limit specified by or under this Act or the manufacturing process therein ceases to be carried on with the aid of power.

Notes:

(i) Once the Act has become applicable to a factory or an establishment, its application will be continuous. [*Kuriacone* v. *Employees' State Insurance Corporation,* (1988) 2 CLR 301 (Ker).]

(ii) Regional office which carries on the administration and supervises the business of selling of goods in various branches and sales emporiums is a shop. [*Employees' State Insurance Corporation* v. *The Tamil Nadu Handloom Weavers Co-op. Society Ltd.,* (1990) 60 FLR 305 (AP)].

(iii) The premises of an advertising agency is a "shop" [*Employees' State Insurance Corporation* v. *R.K. Swamy,* 1994 LLR 51 (SC).]

(iv) The word 'shop' has acquired an expanded meaning. Where in a premises any economic activity is carried on leading to sale or purchase that premises will have to be held a 'shop' for the purpose of the Act even though there is no actual giving or taking of goods in such premises. If the business carried on in a premises results in having some nexus with the purchase or sale of goods is sufficient to be 'shop' for the purpose of the Act. [*Southern Agencies, Rajamundry* v. *Andhra Pradesh Employees' State Insurance Corporation,* AIR 2000 SC 3718.]

7.0 DEFINITIONS OF SOME TERMS USED IN THE ACT. [SEC 2]

7.1 "Contribution" [Sec 2 (4)]

Contribution means the sum of money payable to the corporation by the principal employer in respect of an employee and includes any amount payable by *or* on behalf of the employee in accordance with the provisions of the Act.

7.2 "Dependent" [Sec 2 (6A)]

Dependent means any of the following relatives of a deceased insured person, namely:

1. a widow, a minor legitimate or adopted son, an unmarried legitimate or adopted daughter.
2. a widowed mother
3. if wholly dependent on the earnings of the insured person at the time of his death, a legitimate or adopted son or daughter who has attained the age of 18 years and is infirm;
4. if wholly or in part dependent on the earnings of the insured person at the time of his death,—
   (a) a parent other than a widowed mother,
   (b) a minor illegitimate son, an unmarried illegitimate daughter or a daughter legitimate or adopted or illegitimate if married and a minor or if widowed and a minor,
   (c) a minor brother or an unmarried sister or a widowed sister if a minor,
   (d) a widowed daughter-in-law,
   (e) a minor child of a pre-deceased son,
   (f) a minor child of a pre-deceased daughter where no parent of the child is alive, or
   (g) a paternal grand-parent if no parent of the insured person is alive.

7.3 "Employment Injury" [Sec 2 (8)]

It means a personal injury to an employee caused by accident or an occupational disease arising out of and in the course of his employment, being an insurable employment, whether the accident occurs or the occupational disease is contracted within or outside the territorial limits of India.

The essentials of an Employment Injury are:

(1) The injury must be ***personal*** to an employee.

(2) The injury must be **caused by** an (i) **accident** (ii) **occupational disease.**

(3) The injury must arise ***out of and in the course of employment.***

(4) The employment must be **insurable.**

It is immaterial whether accident occurs or the occupational disease is contracted within or outside the territorial limits of India.

Personal Injury is a very wide term. It does not only mean physical or bodily injury but any other kind of injury affecting the capacity of the workman. It includes physical, mental, phychological or an injury by mental shock.

Arising out of and in the course of employment. This expression *'arising out of'* suggests some sort of casual connection between employment and the injury caused to a workman as result of accident. In other words, it is pointer of cause and origin of the accident. The other half *'arising in the course of'* refers to time and place of accident which means that the accident must have taken place during the currency of employment.

7.4 Factory [2 (12)]

"Factory" means any premises including the precincts thereof—

(a) whereon **at least 10** persons are employed or were employed for wages on any day of the preceding 12 months, and in any part of which a manufacturing process is being carried on **with the aid of power** or is ordinarily so carried on, or

(b) whereon **at least 20** persons are employed or were employed for wages on any day of the preceding 12 months, and in any part of which a manufacturing process is being carried on **without the aid of power** or is ordinarily so carried on.

But does not include a mine subject to the operation of the Mines Act, 1952 or a railway running shed;

7.5 Manufacturing Process [Sec 2 (14AA)]

"Manufacturing Process" shall have the meaning assigned to it in the Factories Act, 1948.

7.6 Permanent Partial Disablement [Sec 2 (15 A)]

"Permanent Partial Disablement" means such disablement of a permanent nature, as reduces the earning capacity of an employee in every employment which he was capable of undertaking at the time of the accident resulting in the disablement:

Provided that every injury specified in Part II of the Second Schedule shall be deemed to result in permanent partial disablement;

The **essentials of permanent partial disablement** are:

(1) The disablement must be of a **permanent nature.**

(2) The disablement must **reduce the earning capacity** of the employee.

(3) **Reduction of earning capacity** must be **in every employment** which he was undertaking at the time of accident resulting in the disablement.

(4) Every injury specified in **Part II of the Second Schedule** shall be deemed to result in permanent partial disablement.

7.7 Permanent Total Disablement [Sec 2 (15B)]

"Permanent Total Disablement" means such disablement of a permanent nature as incapacitates an employee for all work which he was capable of performing at the accident in such disablement:

Provided that permanent total disablement shall be deemed to result from every injury specified in Part I of the Second Schedule or from any combination of injuries specified in Part II thereof where the aggregate percentage of the loss of earning capacity, as specified in the said Part II against those injuries, amounts to 100% or more.

The **essentials of permanent total disablement** are:

(1) The disablement must be of a **permanent nature.**

(2) The disablement must be of such nature which renders the workmen incapable for all work which he was capable of performing at the time of accident.

(3) Every injury, given in **Part I of Schedule II**, shall be deemed to result in total disablement.

(4) It shall be deemed to be the result of any combination of injuries specified in Part II of Second Schedule when the aggregate percentage of loss of earning amounts to 100%.

7.8 Principal Employer [Sec 2 (17)]

"Principal employer" means—

(i) in a factory, the owner or occupier of the factory and includes the managing agent of such owner or occupier, and where a person has been named as the manager of the factory under the Factories Act, 1948, the person so named;

(ii) in any establishment under the control of any department of any Government in India, the authority appointed by such Government in this behalf or where no authority is so appointed the head of the Department;

(iii) in any other establishment, any person responsible for the supervision and control of the establishment.

7.9 Temporary Disablement [Sec 2 (21)]

"Temporary Disablement" means a condition resulting from an employment injury which requires medical treatment and renders an employee, as a result of such injury, temporarily incapable of doing the work which he was doing prior to or at the time of injury.

7.10 Wages [Sec 2 (22)]

"Wages" means all remuneration paid or payable in cash to an employee, if the terms of the contract of employment, express or implied, were fulfilled and includes any payment to an employee in respect of any period of authorized leave, lock-out, strike which is not illegal or lay-off and other additional remuneration, if any, paid at intervals not exceeding 2 months, **but does not include—**

(a) any contribution paid by the employer to any pension fund or provident fund, or under this Act;

(b) any travelling allowance or the value of travelling concession;
(c) any sum paid to the person employed to defray special expenses entailed on him by the nature of his employment; or
(d) any gratuity payable on discharge;

8.0 EMPLOYEES' STATE INSURANCE CORPORATION [SEC 3]

8.1 Who can Establish Employees' State Insurance Corporation [Sec 3 (1)]

With effect from 1.10.1948 the Central Government has established for the administration of the scheme of Employees' State Insurance in accordance with the provisions of this Act a Corporation to be known as the Employees' State Insurance Corporation.

8.2 Nature of ESI Corporation [Sec 3 (2)]

The Corporation shall be a body corporate by the name of Employees' State Insurance Corporation having perpetual succession and a common seal and shall by the said name sue and be sued.

8.3 Constitution of Corporation [Sec 3 (4)]

The Corporation shall consist of the following members, namely:—
(a) a Chairman to be appointed by the Central Government;
(b) a Vice-Chairman to be appointed by the Central Government;
(c) not more than 5 persons to be appointed by the Central Government;
(d) one person each, representing each of the States in which this Act is in force to be appointed by the State Government concerned;
(e) one person to be appointed by the Central Government to represent the Union territories;
(f) 10 persons representing employees to be appointed by the Central Government in consultation with such organisations of employees as may be recognised for the purpose by the Central Government;
(g) 10 Persons representing employees to be appointed by the Central Government in consultation with such organisations of employees as may be recognised for the purpose by the Central Government;
(h) 2 persons representing the medical profession to be appointed by the Central Government in consultation with such organisations of medical practitioners as may be recognised for the purpose by the Central Government;
(i) 3 persons members of Parliament of whom 2 shall be members of the House of the People (Lok Sabha) and one shall be a member of the Council of States (Rajya Sabha) elected respectively by the members of the House of the People and the members of the Council of States; and
(j) the Director General of the Corporation, *ex officio.*

8.4 Term of Office of Members of Corporation [Sec 5 & 6]

(a) The term of office of members of the Corporation, other than the members referred to in clauses (a), (b), (c), (d) and (e) of section 4 and the *ex officio* member, shall be 4 years commencing from the date on which their appointment or election is notified:
(b) a member of the Corporation shall, continue to hold office until the appointment or election of his successor is notified.

(c) The members of the Corporation referred to in clauses (a), (b), (c), (d) and (e) of section 4 shall hold office during the pleasure of the Government appointing them.

(d) An outgoing member of the Corporation, the Standing Committee, or the Medical Benefit Council shall be eligible for re-appointment or re-election as the case may be.

8.5 Authentication of orders, decisions, etc. [Sec 7]

All orders and decisions of the Corporation shall be authenticated by the signature of the Director General of the Corporation and all other instruments issued by the Corporation shall be authenticated by the signature of the Director General or such other officer of the Corporation as may be authorised by him.

9.0 STANDING COMMITTEE [SEC 8 AND 9]

9.1 Constitution of Standing Committee [Sec 8]

A standing Committee of the Corporation shall be constituted from among its members, consisting of—

(a) a Chairman, appointed by the Central Government;

(b) 3 members of the Corporation, appointed by the Central Government;

(c) 3 members of the Corporation representing such 3 State Governments thereon as the Central Government may, by notification in the Official Gazette, specify from time to time;

(d) 8 members elected by the Corporation as follows:—

(i) 3 members from among the members of the Corporation representing employers;

(ii) 3 members from among the members of the Corporation representing employees;

(iii) 1 member from among the members of the Corporation representing the medical profession; and

(iv) 1 member from among the members of the Corporation elected by Parliament;

(e) the Director General of the Corporation, *ex officio*.

9.2 Term of Office of Members of Standing Committee. [Sec 9]

(a) the term of office of a member of the Standing Committee, other than a member referred to in clause (a) or 3[clause (b) or clause (bb)] of section 8, shall be 2 years from the date on which his election is notified:

(b) a member of the Standing Committee shall continue to hold office until the election of his successor is notified:

(c) a member of the Standing Committee shall cease to hold office when he ceases to be a member of the Corporation.

(d) a member of the Standing Committee referred to in clause (a) or clause (b) or clause (bb)] of section 8 shall hold office during the pleasure of the Central Government.

10.0 MEDICAL BENEFIT COUNCIL [SEC 10]

10.1 Constitution of Mediacal Benefit Council [Sec 10 (1)]

The Central Government shall constitute a Medical Benefit Council consisting of—

(a) the Director General, Health Services *ex officio,* as Chairman;

(b) a Deputy Director General, Health Services, to be appointed by the Central Government;

(c) the Medical Commissioner of the Corporation, *ex officio*;

(d) 1 member each representing each of the States (other than Union territories) in which this Act is in force to be appointed by the State Government concerned;

(e) 3 members representing employers to be appointed by the Central Government in consultation with such organisations of employers as may be recognised for the purpose by the Central Government;

(f) 3 members representing employees to be appointed by the Central Government in consultation with such organisations of employees as may be recognised for the purpose by the Central Government; and

(g) 3 members, of whom at least 1 shall be a woman, representing the medical profession, to be appointed by the Central Government in consultation with such organisations of medical practitioners as may be recognised for the purpose by the Central Government.

10.2 Term of Office of a Member of the Medical Benefit Council [Sec 10(2)]

(a) The term of office of a member of the Medical Benefit Council, other than a member reffered to in any of the clauses (a) to (d) of Sub-section (1), shall be 4 years from the date on which his appointment is notified:

(b) A member of the Medical Benefit Council, shall, notwithstanding the expiry of the said period of 4 years continue to hold office until the appointment of his successor is notified.

(c) A member of the Medical Benefit Council referred to in clauses (b) and (d) of sub-section (1) shall hold office during the pleasure of the Government appointing him.

11.0 RESIGNATION OF MEMBERSHIP [SEC 11]

A member of the Corporation, the Standing Committee or the Medical Benefit Council may resign his office by notice in writing to the Central Government and his seat shall fall vacant on the acceptance of the resignation by that Government.

12.0 CESSATION OF MEMBERSHIP. [SEC 12]

12.1 A member of the Corporation, the Standing Committee or the Medical Benefit Council shall cease to be a member of the body if he fails to attend 3 consecutive meetings thereof:

12.2 The Corporation, the Standing Committee or the Medical Benefit Council, as the case may be, may, subject to rules made by the Central Government in this behalf, restore him to membership.

12.3 Where in the opinion of the Central Government any person appointed or elected to represent employers, employees or the medical profession or the Corporation, the Standing Committee or the Medical Benefit Council, as the case may be, has ceased to represent such employers, employees or the medical profession, he Central Government may, by notification in the Official Gazatte declare that with effect from such date as may be specified therein such person shall cease to be a member of the Corporation, the Standing Committee or the Medical Benefit Council, as the case may be.

12.4 A person referred to in clause (i) of Section 4 shall cease to be a member of the Corporation, when he ceases to be a Member of Parliament.

13.0 DISQUALIFICATION FOR BEING A MEMBER. [SEC 13]

A person shall be disqualified for being chosen as or for the Corporation, the Standing Committee or the Medical Benefit Council—

(a) if he is declared to be of unsound mind by a competent court; or

(b) if he is an undischarged insolvent; or

(c) if he has directly or indirectly by himself or by his partner any interest in a subsisting contract with, or any work being done for, the Corporation except as a medical practitioner or as a shareholder (not being a Director) of a company; or

(e) if before or after the commencement of this Act, he has been convicted of an offence involving moral turpitude.

14.0 FILLING OF VACANCIES. [SEC 14]

14.1 Vacancies in the office of appointed or elected members of the Corporation, the Standing Committee and the Medical Benefit Council shall be filled by appointment or election, as the case may be.

14.2 A member of the Corporation, the Standing Committee or the Medical Benefit Council appointed or elected to fill a casual vacancy shall hold office only so long as the member in whose place he is appointed or elected would have been entitled to hold office if the vacancy had not occurred.

15.0 FEES AND ALLOWANCES OF MEMBER [SEC 15]

Members of the Corporation, the Standing Committee and the Medical Benefit Council shall receive such fees and allowances as may from time to time be prescribed by the Central Government.

16.0 POWERS OF THE STANDING COMMITTEE [SEC 18]

16.1 Subject to the general superintendent and control of the Corporation, the Standing Committee shall administer the affairs of the Corporation and may exercise any of the powers and perform any of the functions of the Corporation.

16.2 The Standing Committee shall submit for the consideration and decision of the Corporation all such cases and matters as may be specified in the regulation made in this behalf.

16.3 The Standing Committee may, in its discretion, submit any other case or matter for the decision of the Corporation.

17.0 CORPORATION'S POWER TO PROMOTE MEASURES FOR HEALTH, ETC., OF INSURED PERSON [SEC 19]

The Corporation may, in addition to the scheme of benefits specified in this Act, promote measures for the improvement of the health and welfare of insured persons and for the rehabilitation and re-employment of insured persons who have been disabled or injured and may incur in respect of such measure expenditure from the funds of the Corporation within such limits as may be prescribed by the Central Government.

18.0 MEETINGS OF CORPORATION, STANDING COMMITTEE AND MEDICAL BENEFIT COUNCIL. [SEC 20]

Subject to any rules made under this Act, the Corporation, the Standing Committee and the Medical Benefit Council shall meet at such times and places and shall observe such rules or procedure in regard to transaction of business at their meetings as may be specified in the regulations made in this behalf.

19.0 SUPERSESSION OF THE CORPORATION AND STANDING COMMITTEE [SEC 21]

19.1 If in the opinion of the Central Government, the Corporation or the Standing Committee persistently makes default in performing the duties imposed on it by or under this Act or abuses its powers, that Government may, by notification in the official Gazatte, supersede the Corporation, or in the case of the Standing Committee, supersede in consultation with the Consultation with the Corporation, the Standing Committee:

Provided that before issuing a notification under this sub-section the Central Government shall give a reasonable opportunity to the Corporation or the Standing Committee, as the case may be, to show cause why it should not be supercede and shall consider the explanations and objections, if any, of the Corporation or the Standing Committee, as the case may be.

19.2 Upon the publication of a notification under sub-section (1) superseding the Corporation or the Standing Committee, al the members of the Corporation or the Standing Committee, as the case may be shall, as from the date of such publication, be deemed to have vacated their offices.

19.3 When the Standing Committee has been superseded, a new Standing Committee shall be immediately constituted in accordance with section 8.

19.4 **When the Corporation has been superceded, the Central Government may**

(a) immediately appoint or cause to be appointed or elected new members to the Corporation in accordance with section 4 and may constitute a new Standing Committee under section 8;

(b) in its discretion, appoint such agency, for such period as it may think fit, to exercise the powers and perform the functions of the Corporation and such agency shall be competent to exercise all the powers and perform all the functions of the Corporation.

19.5 The Central Government shall cause a full report of any action taken under this section and the circumstances leading to such action to be laid before parliament at the earliest opportunity and in any case not later than 3 months from the date of the notification superceding the Corporation or the Standing Committee, as the case may be.

20.0 DUTIES OF MEDICAL BENEFIT COUNCIL. [SEC 22]

The Medical Benefit Council shall—

(a) advise the Corporation and the Standing Committee on matters relating to the administration of medical benefit, the certification for purposes of the grant of benefits and other connected matter;

(b) have such powers and duties of investigation as may be prescribed in relation to complaints against medical practitioners in connection with medical treatment and attendance; and
(c) perform such other duties in connection with medical treatment and attendance as may be specified in the regulations.

21.0 ACTS OF CORPORATION, ETC., NOT INVALID BY REASON OF DEFECT IN CONSTITUTION ETC. [SEC 24]

No act of the Corporation, the Standing Committee or the Medical Benefits Council shall be deemed to be invalid by reason of any defect in the constitution of the Corporation, the Standing Committee or the Medical Benefit Council, or on the ground that any member thereof was not entitled to hold or continue in office by reason of any disqualification or of any irregularity in his appointment or election, or by reason of such act having been done during the period of any vacancy in the office of any member of the Corporation, the Standing Committee or the Medical Benefit Council.

22.0 REGIONAL BOARDS, LOCAL COMMITTEES, REGIONAL AND LOCAL MEDICAL BENEFIT COUNCILS. [SEC 25]

The Corporation may appoint Regional Boards, Local Committees and Regional and Local Medical Benefit Councils in such areas and in such manner, and delegate to them such powers and functions, as may be provided by the regulations.

23.0 PROVISIONS RELATING TO CONTRIBUTIONS. [SEC 39]

23.1 Composition [Sec 39 (1)]

The contribution payable under this Act in respect of an employee shall comprise contribution payable by the employer (hereinafter referred to as the employer's contribution) and contribution payable by the employee (hereinafter referred to as the employee's contribution) and shall be paid to the Corporation.

23.2 The Rate of Contribution [Sec 15]

The Contribution shall be paid at such rates as may be prescribed by the Central Government:

Provided that the rates so prescribed shall not be more than the rates, which were in force immediately before the commencement of the Employees' State Insurance (Amendment) Act, 1989.

23.3 Wage Period [Sec 39 (3) & (4)]

(a) The wage period in relation to an employee shall be the unit in respect of which all contributions shall be payable under this Act.
(b) The contribution payable in respect of each wage period shall ordinarily fall due on the last day of the wage period, and where an employee is employed for part of the wage period, or is employed under two or more employers during the same wage period, the contributions shall fall due on such days as may be specified in the regulations.

23.4 Interest for delayed payment [Sec 39 (5)]

(a) If any contribution payable under this Act is not paid by the principal employer on the date on which such contribution has become due, he shall be liable to pay simple interest at the rate of 12% p.a. or at such higher rate as may be specified in the regulations till the date of its actual payment provided that higher interest specified in the regulations shall not exceed the lending rate of interest charged by any scheduled bank.

(b) Any interest recoverable under clause (a) may be recovered as an arrear of land revenue or under section 45C to section 45I.

23.5 Principal employer to pay contribution in the first instance. [Sec 40]

(a) The principal employer shall pay in respect of every employee, whether directly employed by him or by or through an immediate employer, both the employer's contribution and the employee's contribution.

(b) The principal employer shall, in the case of an employee directly employed by him (not being an exempted employee), be entitled to recover from the employee the employee's contribution by deducation from his wages and not otherwise:

Provided that no such education shall be made from any wages other than such as relate to the period or part of the period in respect of which the contribution is payable, or in excess of the sum representing the employee's contribution for the period.

(c) Neither the principal employer nor the immediate employer shall be entitled to deduct the employer's contribution from any wages payable to an employee or otherwise to recover it from him.

(d) Any sum deducted by the principal employers from wages under this Act shall be deemed to have been entrusted to him by the employee for the purpose of paying the contribution in respect of which it was deducted.

(e) The principal employer shall bear the expenses of remitting the contribution of the Corporation.

23.6 Recovery of contribution from immediate employer. [Sec 41]

(a) A principal employer, who has paid contribution in respect of an employee employed by or through an immediate employer,shall be entitled to recover the amount of the contribution so paid (that is to say the employer's contribution, as well as the employee's contribution, if any) from the immediate employer, either by deduction from any amount payable to him by the principal employer under any contract or as a debt payable by the immediate employer.

(b) The immediate employer shall maintain a register of employees employed by or through him as provided in the regulations and submit the same to the principal employer before the settlement of any amount payable.

(c) The immerdiate employer shall be entitled to recover the employee's contribution from the employee employed by or through him by deducation from wages and not otherwise,

23.7 General provisions as to payment of contributions

(a) No employee's contribution shall be payable by or on behalf of an employee whose average daily wages are below during a wage period are below such wages as may be prescribed by the Central Government:

Explanation— The average daily wages of an employee shall be calculated in such manner as may be prescribed by the Central Government.

(b) Contribution (both the employer's contribution and the employee's contribution) shall be payable by the principal employer' for each wage period, in respect of the whole or part of which wages are payable to the employee and not otherwise.

23.8 Method of payment of contribution—Subject to the provisions of this Act, the Corporation may make regulations for any matter relating or incidental to the payment and collection of contributions payable under this Act and without prejudice to the generally of the foregoing power such regulations may provide for—

a. the manner and the time of payment of contributions;
b. the payment of contributions by means of adhesive or other stamps affixed to or impressed upon books, cards or otherwise and regulating the manner, times and conditions, in at and under which, such stamps are to be affixed or impressed;
c. the date of which evidence of contributions have been paid is to be received by the Corporation;
d. the entry in or upon books or cards of particulars of contributions paid and benefits distributed in the case of the insured persons to whom such books or cards relate; and
e. the issue, sale, custody, production, inspection and delivery of books or cards and the replacement of books or cards which have been lost, destroyed or defaced.

23.9 Employers to furnish returns and maintain registers in certain cases. [Sec 44]

(a) Every principal and immediate employer shall submit to the Corporation or to such officer of the Corporation as it may direct such returns in such form and containing such particulars relating to persons employed by him or to any factory or establishment in respect of which he is the principal or immediate employer as may be specified in regulations made in this behalf.

(b) Where in respect of any factory or establishment the Corporation has reason to believe that a return should have been submitted under sub-section (1) but has not been so submitted, the Corporation may require any person in charge of the factory or establishment to furnish such particulars as it may consider necessary for the purpose of enabling the Corporation to decide whether the factory or establishment is a factory or establishment to which Act applies.

(c) Every principal and immediate employer shall maintain such register or records in respect of his factory or establishment as may be required by regulations made in this behalf.

24.0 RECOVERY OF CONTRIBUTIONS [SEC 45 B, 45 C, 45 D]

24.1 Any contribution payable under this Act may be recovered as an arear of land revenue. [Sec 45 B]

24.2 Issue of Certificate to the Recovery Office [Sec 45 C]

(a) Where any amount is in arrears under this Act, the authoried officer may issue, to the Recovery Officer, a certificate under his signature specifying the amount of arrears and the Recovery Officer, on receipt of such certificate, shall proceed to recover the amount specified therein from the factory or establishment or, as the case may be, the principal or immediate employer by one or more of the modes mentioned below:

(i) Attachment and sale of the movable or immovable property of the factory or establishment or, as the case may be, the principal, or immediate employer;

(ii) Arrest of the employer and his detention in prison;

(iii) Appointing a receiver for the management of the movable or immovable properties of the factory or establishment or, as the case may be, the employer:

Provided that the attachment and sale of any property under this section shall first be effected against the properties of the factory or establishment and where such attachment and sale is insufficient for recovering the whole of the amount of arrears specified in the certificate, the Recovery Officer may take such proceedings against the property of the employer for recovery of the whole or any part of such arrears.

(b) The authorized officer may issue a certificate under sub-section (1) notwithstanding that proceedings for recovery of the arrears by any other mode have been taken.

24.3 Recovery Officer to whom certificate is to be forwarded. [Sec 45 D]

(a) The authorized officer may forward the certificate referred to in section 45C to the Recovery Officer within whose jurisdiction the employer—

(i) carries on his business or profession or within whose jurisdiction the principal place of his factory or establishment is situate; or

(ii) resides or any movable or immovable property of the factory or establishment or the principal or immediate employer is situate.

(b) Where a factory or an establishment or the principal or immediate employer has property within the jurisdiction of more than one Recovery Officers and the Recovery Officer to whom a certificate is sent by the authorized officer—

(i) is not able to recover the entire amount by the sale of the property movable or immovable, within his jurisdiction; or

(ii) is of the opinion that, for the purpose of expediting or securing the recovery of the whole or any part of the amount, it is necessary so to do,

he may send the certificate or, where only a part of the amount is to be recovered, a copy of the certificate certified in the manner prescribed by the Central Government and specifying the amount to be recovered to the Recovery Officer within whose jurisdiction the factory or establishment or the principal or immediate employer has property or the employer resides, and thereupon that Recovery Officer shall also proceed to recover the amount due under this section as if the certificate or the copy thereof had been the certificate sent to him by the authorized officer.

25.0 BENEFITS [SEC 46]

25.1 Who are entitled to the Benefits under the ESI Act, 1948?

1. Insured Person
2. Dependants of Insured Person
3. In case of funeral expenses, the eldest surviving member of the family of an insured person or any other person who actually incurs such expenses where the insured person did not have a family pr was not living with his family at the time of his death.

25.2 Six Benefits

1. Sickness Benefit

(a) Sickness must by certified by a duly appointed medical practitioner or any other person possessing such qualifications and experience as corporation may specify.

(b) Contributions must have been payable for at least 78 days or half the number of days available for working in such contribution period (in case of a person who becomes an employee for the first time and for whom a shorter contribution period of less than 156 days is available) during the corresponding contribution period.

(c) Benefit for the first 2 days of sickness will not be available unless the spell of sickness reoccurs within 15 days.

(d) Sickness benefits shall not be paid to any person for more than 91 all days in any two consecutive benefit periods.

(e) Sickness benefits will be available at the standard benefit rate specified in Rule 54.

2. Maternity Benefits

(a) The woman must be insured.

(b) The woman must be certified to eligible by prescribed authority.

(c) The contributions must have been payable for at least 70 days in the immediately preceding 2 consecutive contribution periods.

(d) The daily rate of maternity benefits shall be equal to twice the 'Standard Benefit Rate specified in Rule 54 or Rs 20 whichever is higher.

3. Disablement Benefit

(a) Disablement must be as a result of employment injury sustained as an employee.

(b) The insured person must be certified to be eligible by the prescribed authority.

(c) The payment for temporary disablement shall be made if temporary disablement remains for at least 3 days (excluding the day of accident).

(d) The payment for permanent disablement shall be made for limited period (if disablement assessed provisionally) or for life (if assessed finally).

(e) The daily rate of disablement shall be 40% more than the standard benefit rate specified in Rule 54.

4. Dependent's Benefits

(a) The Death of an insured person must be as a result of an employment injury sustained as an employee.

(b) Dependent's benefits shall be payable to his widow, children and widowed mother at an amount equivalent to 3/5 or 2/5th and 2/5 of the full rate.

(c) In case the deceased person does not leave a widow or legitimate or adopted child a widowed mother, dependent's benefits shall be available to other dependents.

(d) If there are more than one other dependents, the amount payable shall be equally divided between them.

(e) The daily rate of dependent's benefit shall be 40% more than the Standard Benefit Rate as specified in Rule 54.

5. Medical Benefits

(a) An insured person or a member of his family (where such medical benefit is extended to his family) where condition requires medical treatment and attendance is entitled to receive medical benefit.

(b) Medical treatment may be given in the following form:

(i) out patient treatment; or

(ii) attendance in a hospital, dispensary, clinic or other injuries; or

(iii) by visits to the home of injured person; or

(iv) treatment as patient in a hospital or other institution.

6. Funeral Expenses

Payment to the eldest surviving member of the family of an insured person who has died, towards the expenditure on the funeral of the deceased insured person, or, where the insured person did not have a family or was not living with his family at the time of his death, to the person who actually incurs the expenditure on the funeral of the deceased insured person.

Provided that the amount of such payment shall not exceed 6[such amount as may be prescribed by the Central Government] and the claim for such payment shall be made within three months of the death of the insured person or within such extended period as the Corporation or any officer or authority authorised by it in this behalf may allow.

25.2 Presumption as to accident arising in course in employment— For the purposes of this Act, an accident arising in the course of an insured person's employment shall be presumed, in the absence of evidence to the contrary, also to have arisen out of that employment.

Note: Accident arisen out of employment is to be presumed and no other evidence is required [*Harjinder Kaur v. Employees' State Insurance Corporation,* (1987) 55 FLR 772 (P&H)].

25.3 Can an insured person claim sickness benefits and disablement benefits for temporary disablement simultaneously, under the ESI Act, 1948?

Section 65 of Employee's State Insurance Act, 1948, deals with benefits not to be combined. As per Section 65(1)(b), an insured person shall not be entitled to receive for the same period, both the sickness benefit and the disablement benefit for temporary disablement. Section 65(2) of Employees' State Insurance Act, 1948, provides that where a person is entitled to more than one of the benefits mentioned in sub section (1), he shall be entitled to choose the benefit he wants to receive.

25.4 Can an Insured employee claims medical benefit for himself and his spouse after retirement from service on superannuation?

Yes, he and his spouse are entitled to receive medical benefit after his retirement on superannuation if he had been insured for at least 5 years and pays a contribution at the prescribed rate in lumpsum for 1 year at a time in advance. [Rule 61 of Employees' State Insurance (Central) Rules, 1950].

26.0 ADJUDICATION OF DISPUTE AND CLAIMS [SEC 74]

26.1 Constitution of Employees' Insurance Court—

(a) The State Government shall, by notification in the Official Gazette, constitute an Employees' Insurance Court for such local area as may be specified in the notification.

(b) The Court shall consist of such number of Judges as the State Government may think fit.

(c) Any person who is or has been a judicial officer or is a legal practitioner of five years' standing shall be qualified to be a Judge of the Employees' Insurance Court.

(d) The State Government may appoint the same Court for two or more local areas or two or more Courts for the same local area.

(e) Where more than one Court has been appointed for the same local area, the State Government may by general or special order regulate the distribution of business between them.

Note: An employee insured under this Act cannot claim 'compensation' under the Workmen's Corporation Act; [*Abad Fisheries* v. *Commissioner for Workmen's Compensation,* (1985) 50 FLR 512.]

27.0 MATTERS TO BE DECIDED BY EMPLOYEES' INSURANCE COURT [SEC 75]

(a) If any question or dispute arises as to—

(i) whether any person is an employee within the meaning of this Act or whether he is liable to pay the employee's contribution, or

(ii) the rate of wages or average daily wages of an employee for the purposes of this Act, or

(iii) the rate of contribution payable by a principal employer in respect of any employee, or

(iv) the person who is or was the principal employer in respect of any employee, or

(v) the right of any person to any benefit and as to the amount and duration thereof, or

(vi) any direction issued by the Corporation under section 55A on a review of any payment of dependants' benefit, or

(vii) any other matter which is in dispute between a principal employer and the Corporation, or between a principal employer and an immediate employer or between a person and the Corporation or between an employee and a principal or immediate employer, in respect of any contribution or benefit or other dues payable or recoverable under this Act, or any other matter required to be or which may be decided by the Employees' Insurance Court under this Act,

such question or dispute subject to the provisions of sub-section (2A)] shall be decided by the Employees' Insurance Court in accordance with the provisions of this Act.

(b) Subject to the provisions of sub-section (2A), the following claims shall be decided by the Employees' Insurance Court, namely:—

(a) claim for the recovery of contributions from the principal employer;

(b) claim by a principal employer to recover contributions from any immediate employer;

(c) claim against a principal employer under section 68;

(d) claim under section 70 for the recovery of the value or amount of the benefits received by a person when he is not lawfully entitled thereto; and

(f) any claim for the recovery of any benefit admissible under this Act.

(c) If in any proceedings before the Employees' Insurance Court a disablement question arises and the decision of a Medical Board or a Medical Appeal Tribunal has not been obtained on the same and the decision of such question is necessary for the determination of the claim or question before the Employees' Insurance Court, that Court shall direct the Corporation to have the question decided by this Act and shall thereafter proceed with the determination of the claim or question before it in accordance with the decision of the Medical Board or the Medical Appeal Tribunal, as the case may be, except where an appeal has been filed before the Employees' Insurance Court under section 54A (2) in which case the Employees' Insurance Court may itself determine all the issues arising before it.

(d) No matter which is in dispute between a principal employer and the Corporation in respect of any contribution or any other dues shall be raised by the principal employer in the Employees' Insurance Court unless he has deposited with the Court 50% of the amount due from him as claimed by the Corporation:

Provided that the Court may, for reasons to be recorded in writing, waive or reduce the amount to be deposited under this sub-section.

(e) No Civil Court shall have jurisdiction to decide or deal with any question or dispute as aforesaid on any liability which by or under this Act is to be decided by Medical Board, or by a Medical Appeal Tribunal or by the Employees' Insurance Court.

28.0 REFERENCE TO HIGH COURT [SEC 81]

An Employees' Insurance Court may submit any question of law for the decision of the High Court and if it does so shall decide the question pending before it in accordance with such decision.

29.0 APPEAL [SEC 82]

29.1 Save as expressly provided in this section, no appeal shall lie from an order of an Employees' Insurance Court.

29.2 An appeal shall lie to the High Court from an order of an Employees' Insurance Court if it involves a substantial question of law.

29.3 The period of limitation for an appeal under this section shall be 60 days.

29.4 The provisions of sections 5 and 12 of the Limitation Act, 1963 shall apply to appeals under this section.

30.0 STAY OF PAYMENT PENDING APPEAL

Where the Corporation has presented an appeal against an order of the Employees' Insurance Court, that Court may, and if so directed by the High Court, shall, pending the decision of the appeal, withhold the payment of any sum directed to be paid by the order appealed against.

EXERCISES

SHORT ANSWER TYPE QUESTIONS

1. Write short notes on the following under the Employees' State Insurance Act, 1948:
   (a) Employment Injury
   (b) Factory
   (c) Manufacturing Process
   (d) Permanent Partial Disablement
   (e) Permanent Total Disablement
   (f) Temporary Disablement
   (g) Wages
   (h) Employees' State Insurance Corporation
   (i) Standing Committee
   (j) Medical Benefit Council
   (k) Wage Period
   (l) Contribution
   (m) Sickness Benefit
   (n) Maternity Benefit
   (o) Disablement Benefit
   (p) Dependent's Benefit

(q) Medical Benefit
(r) Funeral Expenses

2. Explain the terms 'Permanent Partial Disablement, Permanent Total Disablement' and Disablement Benefit under the ESI Act, 1948.
3. Explain the conditions which must be observed by the recipient of disablement benefits under the Employees' Statement Insurance Act, 1948.
4. State the provisions of the ESI Act, 1948 for the payment of medical benefit.
5. Can an insured person claim sickness benefit and disablement benefits for temporary disablement simultaneously, under the ESI Act, 1948.
6. Can an insured person claim medical benefit for himself and his spouse after retirement from service on super annuation?

LONG ANSWER TYPE QUESTIONS

1. State the provisions relating to various benefits available to an employee under the ESI Act, 1948.
2. (a) State how the Medical Benefit Council has been constituted under the Employees' State Insurance Act 1948.

   (b) What are the powers and duties of the Medical Benefit Council?
3. State briefly the constitution of the Employees' State Insurance Corporation. What is the duration of the term of office of its members? Is an outgoing member eligible for re-nomination or re-election?
4. State the constitution of the Standing Committee under the Employees' State Insurance Act, 1948. What is the duration of the term of office of its members?

CHAPTER

17

The Workmen's Compensation Act, 1923

1.0 INTRODUCTION

The Workmen's Compensation Act is an Act which provides for the payment by certain classes of employers to their workmen of compensation for injury by accident.

It is well-settled that the Act is a piece of social security and welfare legislation. Its dominant purpose is to protect the workman and, therefore, the provisions of the Act should not be interpreted too narrowly so as to debar the workman from compensation which the Parliament thought they ought to have. The intention of the Legislature was to make the employer an insurer of the workman responsible against the loss caused by the injuries or death, which ought to have happened, while the workman was engaged in his work. *[Sunita Devi* v. *Autar Singh,*(2004) 104 FJR 1007 (Jhar).]

2.0 WHAT IS THE TERRITORY TO WHICH THE ACT APPLIES?

It extends to the whole of India.

3.0 WHEN THE ACT CAME INTO FORCE.

It came into force on the first day of July, 1924.

4.0 DEFINITION OF SOME TERMS USED IN THE ACT.

4.1 Dependent [Sec2 (1) (d)]

"Dependant" means any of the following relatives of deceased workman, namely:—

(i) a widow, a minor legitimate or adopted son, an unmarried legitimate or adopted daughter or a widowed mother; and

(ii) if wholly dependant on the earnings of the workman at the time of his death, a son or a daughter who has attained the age of 18 years and who is infirm;

(iii) if wholly or in part dependant on the earnings of the workman at the time of his death,—

(a) a widower,

(b) a parent other than a widowed mother,

(c) a minor illegitimate son, an unmarried illegitimate daughter or a daughter (legitimate or illegitimate or adopted) if married and a minor or if widowed and a minor,

(d) a minor brother or an unmarried sister or a widowed sister if a minor,

(e) a widowed daughter-in-law,

(f) a minor child of a pre-deceased son,

(g) a minor child of a pre-deceased daughter where no parent of the child is alive, or

(h) a paternal grandparent if no parent of the workman is alive;

Explanation.— For the purposes of sub-clause (ii) and items (f) and (g) of sub-clause (iii) references to a son, daughter or child include an adopted son, daughter or child respectively.

4.2 Employer [Sec 2 (1) (e)]

"Employer" includes–

(a) any body of persons whether incorporated or not

(b) any managing agent of an employer

(c) the legal representative of a deceased employer, and,

(d) any person to whom the services of a workman are temporarily lent or let on hire by the person with whom the workman has entered into a contract of service or apprenticeship,

4.3 Partial Disablement [Sec 2 (1) (g)]

Partial Disablement can be of Permanent or Temporary Nature:

(a) **Temporary Partial Disablement** This disablement is one which reduces the earning capacity of workman in that particular employment in which he was engaged at the time of accident, resulting in such disablement; and

(b) **Permanent Partial Disablement** This disablement is one which reduces the earning capacity of a workman in every employment which he was capable of undertaking at that time.. It is provided that every injury specified in Part II of Schedule I shall be deemed to result in permanent partial disablement. The percentage of loss of earning capacity is specified in respect of various injuries.

The distinction between the two types of disablement depends on whether an injury results in the reduction in earning capacity in all the employments which the workman was capable of doing or in that particular employment in which he was engaged at the time of injury.

4.4 Total Disablement [Sec 2(1)(l)]

(a) "Total Disablement" means such disablement, whether of a temporary or permanent nature, which incapacitates a workman for all work which he was capable of performing at the time of the accident resulting in such disablement:

(b) Permanent total disablement shall be deemed to result from every injury specified in Part I of Schedule I or from any combination of injuries specified in Part II thereof where the aggregate percentage of the loss of earning capacity, as specified in the said Part II against those injuries, amounts to at least 100%.

Part I of Schedule I provides for injuries resulting in total disablement and Part II of Schedule I provides for injuries which result in partial disablement. However, in case of more than one injury specified in Part II, if the total percentage of all injuries sustained comes to 100% or more it would be total disablement. But difficulty arises in the case of injuries which are not covered under the Schedule. In such cases the question whether the disablement is partial or total will depend upon the circumstances of each case.

4.5 Workman [Sec 2 (1) (n)]

"Workman" means any person who is—

(i) a railway servant as defined in Railways Act, 1989 not permanently employed in any administrative, district or sub-divisional office of a railway and not employed in any such capacity as is specified in Schedule II, or

(ii) (a) a master, seaman or other member of the crew of a ship,
(b) a captain or other member of the crew of an aircraft,
(c) a person recruited as driver, helper, mechanic, cleaner or in any other capacity in connection with a motor vehicle,
(d) a person recruited for work abroad by a company, and who is employed outside India in any such capacity as is specified in Schedule II and the ship, aircraft or motor vehicle, or company, as the case may be, is registered in India, or;

(iii) employed in any such capacity as is specified in Schedule II, whether the contract of employment was made before or after the passing of this Act and whether such contract is expressed or implied, oral or in writing; but does not include any person working in the capacity of a member of the Armed Force of the Union and any reference to a workman who has been injured shall, where the workman is dead, include a reference to his dependants or any of them.

Notes:

(i) **Conditions for treating a person as workman**
From the definition of 'workman' given a section 2 (1) (n) of the Act, it is clear that for not treating a person as workman, two conditions are required to be proved namely that his employment is of casual nature and he is not employed for the purpose of employee's trade or business and the onus is on the employer to prove these conditions. [*Mangala Ben* v. *Dalip Motwani,* 1998 LLR 656.]

(ii) Salesman in arrack shop is a workman. [*Mathew Joseph* v. *Johay Sunny,* 1995 LLR 390 (Ker).]

(iii) Workman does not include his heirs and legal representatives [*Sumuben* v. *Patel Industries,* 1994 LLR 338 (Guj).]

5.0 WHEN DOES THE EMPLOYER'S LIABILITY FOR COMPENSATION ARISE [SEC 3 (1)]

If personal injury is caused to a workman by accident arising out of and in the course of his employment, his employer shall be liable to pay compensation in accordance with the provisions of the Chapter II

Thus, in order to attract Sec 3 (1), the following two conditions must be fulfilled:

1. **Personal Injury by an Accident**— Personal injury must have been caused to the workman by an accident, and;

   Personal injury The words "personal injury" have a connotation wider than bodily injury. They include any physiological injury e.g. nervous shock or insanity as a result of witnessing a terrible accident. Thus "personal injury" includes phychological and physiological injury as well.

   Accident 'Accident' is not defined in the Act. But, in a series of decisions, it has been interpreted to mean "an unlooked for mishap or untoward event which was not expected or designed."

   In other words, an accident means an unexpected and undesigned occurrance of mishap or untoward event.

   If a person becomes insane as a result of an accident and in such cases commits suicide, the death is the result of the accident and in such cases compensation is awarded. A series of tiny accidents each producing some unidentifiable result operating cumulatively to produce the final condition of injury constitute together an accident.

2. **Accident arising out of and in the course of employment.**—The accident must have arisen out of and in the course of employment.

Accident arising out of an employment The words 'arising out of employment' imply that the accident must be done to an employment. There must be a casual connection between accidental personal injury, and employment. Employment must be distinctive and proximate cause of the personal injury and an accident *(Bhagubhai v. Central Railway).* An accident is said to arise out of employment when the risk or hazard is incidental to an employment and the injured workman was performing some duty imposed upon him by his contract of service *(Lancashire & Yorkshire Railway v. Highway).* The burden of proving that the accident arose out of an employment is upon the workman. Further, the facts and circumstances of each case will have to be examined.

The following conditions must be satisfied to prove that an accident arose out of an employment:

(i) Personal injury must have resulted from some risk inherent in an employment when an accident occurred *(Munshi & Co. v. Yashwant Tukaram Tall).*

(ii) At the time of an injury, the workman must have been engaged in the business of an employer. If he was doing something for his personal benefit or outside the scope of his duties, he is not entitled to compensation.

Accident in the course of an employment The words 'in the course of an employment' emphasise the time of an accidental injury. An accident is said to occur 'in the course of an employment' when a workman is engaged in doing something which is directly or indirectly imposed on him by his employer. It may be said to cover the whole of the time of a workman in carrying out the duties required by him as incidental to his contract of service. In case a workman suffers from an accident during transit on work undertaken on behalf of his employer but out of his ordinary place of work an accident is said to occur in the course of employment. *For example* a workman was to repair railway clocks at various stations was stabled in a railway compartment while he was in transit and it was held that the death was due to an accident arising in the course of an employment.

6.0 CIRCUMSTANCES UNDER WHICH EMPLOYER SHALL NOT BE LIABLE TO PAY COMPENSATION OR DEFENCES AVAILABLE TO AN EMPLOYER [PROVISIO TO SEC 3 (1)]

The employer shall not be liable—

(a) in respect of any injury which does not result in the total or partial disablement of the workman for a period exceeding 30 days;

(b) in respect of any injury, which had not resulted in death or permanent total disablement caused by an accident which is directly attributable to—

(i) the workman having been under the influence of drink or drugs, or

(ii) the wilful disobedience of the workman to an order expressly given, or to a rule expressly framed, for the purpose of securing the safety of workmen, or

(iii) the wilful removal or disregard by the workman of any safety guard or other device which he knew to have been provided for the purpose of securing the safety of workman.

7.0 WHEN SHALL THE CONTRACTING OF THE DISEASE BE DEEMED TO BE AN INJURY BY ACCIDENT? [SEC 3(2)]

The contracting of the disease shall be deemed to be an injury by accident within the meaning of this section and, unless the contrary is provided, the accident shall be deemed to have arisen out of, and in the course of, the employment in the following **three cases:**

7.1 If a workman employed in any employment specified in Part A of Schedule III contracts any disease specified therein as an occupational disease peculiar to that employment.

7.2 If a workman, whilst in the service of an employer in whose service he has been employed for a continuous period of at least 6 months (which period shall not include a period of service under any other employer in the same kind of employment) in any employment specified in Part B of Schedule III, contracts any disease specified therein as an occupational disease peculiar to that employment,

7.3 If a workman whilst in the service of one or more employers in any employment specified in Part C of Schedule III for such continuous period as the Central Government may specify in respect of each such employment, contracts any disease specified therein as an occupational disease peculiar to that employment

Notes:

(i) In order to attract section 3 (1) of the Act, following three conditions must be fulfilled:—

(a) personal injury;

(b) accident; and

(c) arising out of and in the course of employment; [*Kalayni P. v. Divisional Manager, Southern Railway (Personal Branch), Divisional Office, Madras,* 2004 LLR 207 (Mad HC): 2004 I LLJ 49.]

(ii) It is no doubt true that in order to succeed in an application for getting compensation under section 3 of the Act the following points are required to be established:—

(a) that the accident must arise out of and in the course of the workman's employment;

(b) there must be casual connection between the injury and the accident and the work done in the course of the employment;

(c) the workman has to say that while doing a part of his duty or incidental thereto it has resulted into an accident.

It is necessary that the workman must be actually working at the time of the injury or the accident. Therefore, the three factors, that there must be injury, which must be caused in an accident, it must be caused in the course of and out of the employment must be established; [*Branch Manager, New India Assurance Co. Ltd.* v. *Siddappa, Major,* 2004 LLR 731 (Kant HC).]

(iii) **Meaning of the expression "arising out of employment"**

(a)The expression "arising out of employment" means that there must be casual relationship between the accident and the employment. If the accident has occurred on account of the risk which is an incident of employment, it has to be held that the accident has arisen out of the employment; [*Oriental Insurance Co. Ltd.* v. *Nanguli Singh,* 1995 LLJ (Orissa) HC ORS (298).]

(b) The words "out of employment" is not limited to mere nature of the employment, but it (arising out of employment) applies to its nature, its conditions and obligations and its incidents. An accident which occurs on account of a risk, which is an incident of employment, then the claim for compensation can succeed provided the workman has not exposed himself to an added peril by his own imprudent act; *Executive Engineer 19th Div. R.C.P., Bikaner v. Heeraram, 1982* (44) FLR 179 Raj: 1980 Raj LW 412.

8.0 HOW IS AMOUNT OF COMPENSATION CALCULATED? [SEC 4 (I)]

Subject to the provisions of this Act, the amount of compensation shall be as follows:—

(a) Where death results from the injury	An amount equal to 50% of the monthly wages of the deceased workman multiplied by the relevant factor; or Rs 80,000 whichever is more
(b) Where permanent total disablement results from the injury	An amount equal to 60% of the monthly wages of the injured workman multiplied by the relevant factor or Rs 90,000 which is more. (i) **Meaning of "relevant factor" in relation to a workman**—The factor specified in the second column of Schedule IV against the entry in the first column of that Schedule specifying the number of years which are the same as the completed years of the age of the workman on his last birthday immediately preceding the date on which the compensation fell due. (ii) Where the monthly wages of a workman exceed Rs 4,000 his monthly wages of a workman for the purposes of clauses (a) and clause (b) shall be deemed to be Rs 4,000 only;
(c) Where permanent partial disablement results from the injury	(i) In the case of an injury specified in Part II of Schedule I, such percentage of the compensation which would have been payable in the case of permanent total disablement as is specified therein as being the percentage of the loss of earning capacity caused by that injury; and (ii) In the case of an injury not specified in Schedule I, such percentage of the compensation payable in the case of permanent total disablement as is proportionate to the loss of earning capacity (as assessed by the qualified medical practitioner) permanently caused by the injury; *Explanation I*— Where more injuries than one are caused by the same accident, the amount of compensation payable under this head shall be aggregated but not so in any case as to exceed the amount which would have been payable if permanent total disablement had disablement had resulted from the injuries.

	Explanation II— In assessing the loss of earning capacity for the purpose of sub-clause (ii), the qualified medical practitioner shall have due regard to the percentages of loss of earning capacity in relation to different injuries in Schedule I;
(d) Where temporary disablement whether total or partial results from the injury	a half monthly payment of the sum equivalent to 25% of monthly wages of the workman, to be paid in accordance with the provisions of Sec 4 (2)

8.1 When shall half monthly payment be payable?

The half-monthly payment be payable on the 16th day—

(i) from the date of disablement where such disablement lasts for a period of at least 28 days

(ii) after the expiry of a waiting period of 3 days from the date of disablement where such disablement lasts for a period of less than 28 days; and thereafter half-monthly during the disablement or during a period of five years, whichever period is shorter:

Provided that—

(a) there shall be deducted from any lump sum or half-monthly payments to which the workman is entitled the amount of any payment or allowance which the workman has received from the employer by way of compensation during the period of disablement prior to the receipt of such lump sum or of the first half-monthly payment, as the case may; and

(b) no half-monthly payment shall in any case exceed the amount, if any by which half the amount of the monthly wages of the workman before the accident exceeds half the amount of such wages which he is earning after the accident.

Explanation— Any payment or allowance which the workman has received from the employer towards his medical treatment shall not be deemed to be a payment or allowance received by him by way of compensation within the meaning of clause (a) of the proviso.

On the ceasing of the disablement before the date on which any half-monthly payment falls due there shall be payable in respect of that half-month a sum proportionate to the duration of the disablement in that half-month.

8.2 Deposit of Rs 2,500 in case of Death

If the injury of the workman results in his death, the employer shall, in addition to the compensation deposit with the Commissioner a sum of Rs 2,500 for payment of the same to the eldest surviving dependant of the workman towards the expenditure of the funeral of such workman or where the workman did not have a dependant or was not living with his dependant at the time of his death to the person who actually incurred such expenditure.

9.0 PAYMENT OF COMPENSATION [SEC 4A]

9.1 When is the Compensation to be paid? [Sec 4A(1) & (2)]

(1) Compensation under section 4 shall be paid as soon as it falls due.

(2) In cases where the employer does not accept the liability for compensation to the extent claimed, he shall be bound to make provisional payment based on the extent of liabiliy which he accepts, and such payment shall be deposited with the Commissioner or made to the workman, as the case may be, without prejudice to the right of the workman to make any further claim.

9.2 What is the penalty for default?

Where any employer is in default in paying the compensation due under this Act within 1 month from the date it fell due, the Commissioner shall—

(a) direct that the employer shall, in addition to the amount of the arrears, pay simple interest thereon at the rate of 12% per annum or at such higher rate not exceeding the maximum of the lending rates of any scheduled bank as may be specified by the Central Government, by notification in the Official Gazette, on the amount due; and

(b) if, in his opinion, there is no justification for the delay, direct that the employer shall, in addition to the amount of the arrears, and interest thereon pay a further sum not exceeding 50% of such amount by way of penalty:

Provided that an order for the payment of penalty shall not be passed under clause (b) without giving a reasonable opportunity to the employer to show cause why it should not be passed.

9.3 To whom interest and penalty payable [Sec 4A (3A)]

The interest and the penalty shall be paid to the workman or his dependant, as the case may be.

10.0 PROVISIONS RELATING TO PRINCIPAL'S LIABILITY TO PAY COMPENSATION IN CASE OF CONTRACTING [SEC 12].

10.1 Where any person (hereinafter in this section referred to as the principal) in the course of or for the purposes of his trade or business contracts with any other person (hereinafter in this section referred to as the contractor for the execution by or under the contractor of the whole or any part of any work which is ordinarily part of the trade of business of the principal, the principal shall be liable to pay to any workman employed in the execution of the work any compensation which he would have been liable to pay if that workman had been immediately employer by him; and where compensation is claimed from the principal, this Act shall apply as if references to the principal were substituted for references to the employer except that the amount of compensation shall be calculated with reference to the wages of the workman under the employer by whom he is immediately employed.

10.2 Where the principal is liable to pay compensation under this section, he shall be entitled to be indemnified by the contractor, or any other person from whom the workman could have recovered compensation and where a contractor who is himself a principal is liable to pay compensation or to indemnify a principal under this section he shall be entitled to be indemnified by any person standing to him in the relation of a conductor from whom the workman could have recovered compensation, and all questions as to the right to and the amount of any such indemnity shall, in default of agreement, be settled by the Commissioner.

10.3 Nothing shall prevent a workman from recovering compensation from the contractor instead of the principal.

10.4 This section shall not apply in any case where the accident occurred elsewhere that on, in or about the premises on which the principal has undertaken or usually undertakes, as the case may be, to execute the work or which are otherwise under his control or management.

11.0 REFERENCE TO COMMISSIONERS [SEC 19]

11.1 If any question arises in any proceedings under this Act as to the liability of any person to pay compensation (including any question as to whether a person injured is or is not a workman) or as to the amount or duration of compensation (including any question as to the nature or extent of disablement), the question shall, in default of agreement, be settled by a Commissioner.

11.2 No Civil Court shall have jurisdiction to settle, decide or deal with any question which is by or under this Act required to be settled, decided or dealt with by a Commissioner or to enforce any liability incurred under this Act.

11.3 Appointment of Commissioners

(1) The State Government may, by notification in the Official Gazette, appoint any person to be a Commissioner for Workmen's Compensation for such area as may be specified in the notification.

(2) Where more than one Commissioner has been appointed for any area, the State Government may, by general or special order, regulate the distribution of business between them.

(3) Any Commissioner may, for the purpose of deciding any matter referred to him for decision under this Act, choose one or more persons possessing special knowledge of any matter relevant to the matter under inquiry to assist him in holding the inquiry.

(4) Every Commissioner shall be deemed to be a public servant within the meaning of the Indian Penal Code.

11.4 **Venue of proceedings and transfer—** Where any matter under this Act is to be done by or before a Commissioner, the same shall, subject to the provisions of this Act and to any rules made here under, be done by or before the Commissioner for the area in which—

(a) the accident took place which resulted in the injury; or

(b) the workman or in case of his death, the dependant claiming the compensation ordinarily resides; or

(c) the employer has his registered office.

12.0 PROCEDURE FOR FILING APPLICATION BEFORE COMMISSIONER [SEC 22]

12.1 Where an accident occurs in respect of which liability to pay compensation under this Act arises, a claim for such compensation may, subject to the provisions of this Act, be made before the Commissioner.

12.2 No application for the settlement of any matter by Commissioner other than an application by a dependant or dependants for compensation, shall be made unless and until some question has arisen between the parties in connection therewith which they have been unable to settle by agreement.

12.3 **Prescribed Form, Fees and Contents:** An application to a Commissioner may be made in such form and shall be accompanied by such fee, if any, as may be prescribed, and shall contain, in addition to any particulars which may be prescribed, the following particulars namely:—

(a) a concise statement of the circumstances in which the application is made and the relief or order which the applicant claims;
(b) in the case of a claim for compensation against an employer, the date of service of notice of the accident on the employer, and if such notice has not been served or has not been served in due time, the reason for such omission;
(c) the names and addresses of the parties; and
(d) except in the case of an application by dependants for compensation a concise statement of the matters on which agreements has and those on which has not been come to.

12.4 If the applicant is illiterate or for any other reason is unable to furnish the required information in writing, the application shall, if the applicant so desires, be prepared under the direction of the Commissioner.

13.0 POWER OF COMMISSIONER [SEC 22A & SEC 23]

13.1 Power of Commissioner to require further deposit in cases of fatal accident [Sec 22A (1)]: Where any sum has been deposited by an employer as compensation payable in respect of a workman whose injury has resulted in death, and in the opinion of the Commissioner such sum is sufficient, the Commissioner may, be notice in writing stating his reasons, call upon the employer to show cause why he should not make a further deposit within such time as may be stated in the notice.

13.2 Power to make an Award [Sec 22 A (2)]. If the employer fails to show cause to the satisfaction of the Commissioner, the Commissioner may make an award determining the total amount payable, and requiring the employer to deposit the deficiency.

13.3 Power of a Civil Court [Sec 23] The Commissioner shall have all the powers of a Civil Court under the Code of Civil Procedure, 1908 for the purpose of taking evidence on oath (which such Commissioner is hereby empowered to impose) and of enforcing the attendance of witnesses and compelling the production of documents and material objects, and the Commissioner shall be deemed to be a Civil Court for all the purposes of the Code of Criminal Procedure 1973.

PRACTICAL PROBLEMS

Problem 1

There was an agreement between the employer of a colliery and the railway authorities that the workmen of the colliery might use a specified train at a reduced fare. The fare was deducted from the wages of the workmen. There were other routes which the workmen could use. While boarding the train, a coolier was injured. Could he recover compensation for the injuries sustained by him?

Solution:

The workmen can recover compensation for the injuries sustained by him as arising during the course of his employment. To fall within the expression "arising during the course of employment", the workman at the time of accident must have been employed in the performance of his duties. The accident must have taken place at or about the place where he was performing his duties. The second is that the injury must be within the reasonable limits to a definite place, time or cause. It is also that the concept of duty is not limited to the period of time. The workman actually commences his work at the time he downs his tools, provided there is a nexus between the time and place of the accident and the employment and if the person or workman at a particular time and place was so related to the

conclusion that he was working within the scope of employment. Thus, the accident having occurred in the course of the employment. In the present problem the time and place of the accident were arising out and in the course of employment and therefore, the employer is liable.

Problem 2

A workman working in a shed was injured by the fall of a wall which was not the property of his employer or under his employees control. Is the employer liable to pay compensation?

Solution:

In the present problem, the employer is liable for compensation, because the injury arose out of and in the course of employment, no mater whether the wall belongs to him or someone else. Section 3(1) of the Workmen's Compensation Act, 1923 provides that an employer shall be liable to pay compensation of a personal injury caused to a workman by accident arising out of and in the course of his employment.

Problem 3

Discuss the nature of disablement:

(i) A miner was blind in the right eye as a result of an accident, but was physically fit to do his former job. Inspite of all his efforts he failed to secure a job as a miner or quarry-man.

(ii) A personal injury was caused to a carpenter in the course of employment and his left arm above the elbow had to be amputated.

Solution:

(i) The disablement is deemed to be a total permanent disablement and the miner will be awarded compensation on the basis of total disablement. It was held in *Tonnoch v. Brownside Coal Co. Ltd.,* that if, after a partial permanent disablement, a workman becomes physically fit to resume his former employment and earns his former wage, but fails to secure a job because of such disablement, he will be deemed to be totally disabled and will get compensation on the basis of total disablement.

(ii) In this case, the disablement is total. In *Pratap Narain Singh Deo v. Srinivas Sahata,* the Supreme Court held that where personal injury was caused to a carpenter in the course of employment and his left hand above the elbow had to be amputated, the disablement was total and not partial, since a carpenter cannot work with one hand.

Problem 4

***F*, a permanent security guard of *XYZ & Co*., was returning home after his duty was over. Within the factory premises, another employee, *G*. abused him and in the fight, *F* was killed. Explain whether *F*'s widow is entitled to compensation under the Workmen's Compensation Act, 1923. Will it make any difference if *F* was killed outside the factory by a felow employee before reaching his home after the duty hours?**

Solution:

F*'s widow is entitled to Compensation under Section 3 of the Workmen's Compensation Act, 1923 *(Naima Bibi v. Lodhne Colliery Ltd.)

In *R.S. Moodere & Co. v. Mst. Bhanwari,* it was held that if a workman dies due to an accident arising out of and in the course of employment, it cannot be pleaded that death was due to any of exceptions like influence of drugs alcohol, or willfully disobeying orders or disregard of any instructions of safety guards, etc.

Proximity of place to that of employment is important. A gate comes within the definition of premises *(Daudhiben Dharmase v. New Jehangir Vakil Mills Co. Ltd. Bhavnagar)*. But not a public road far off from factory. Each case has to be decided on the relevance of the facts involved.

Problem 5

Answer with reasons and with the help of case laws, whether the claim for Workmen's Compensation could be obtained in the following:

(i) A workman who was employed as an electrician had to go from a heating room to a cooling plant to perform his duties. He was attacked by pneumonia and died after a short illness.

(ii) A workman, while on his way to factory for work in a state transport bus, dies in a road accident.

Solution:

(i) According to Section 3 of the Workmen's Compensation Act, 1923, an employer becomes liable if the personal injury is caused to the workman by an accident arising out of and in the course of employment. Injury is not confined to physical or mental injury. In the *Indian News Chronicle Ltd. v. Mrs. Lazarus,* the facts of which are similar to that of the given problem, it was held that the death of the workman contracting pneumonia was due to personal injury which was an accident that arose out of employment and hence the employer was held liable to pay compensation. In view of this decision, the heir of the workman may succeed in claiming compensation.

(ii) In the given problem, the employer may not be liable to pay compensation. It was decided in the case of *Saurashtra Salt Mfg. Co. v. Bai Velu Raja,* the theory of notional extension of employment cannot be extended to the place of accident and therefore the accident could not be said to have occurring during the course of employment. In this case, the workman died in a boat accident while returning home from his work palace. Taking into account this case decision, the claim for compensation may not succeed against the employer.

EXERCISES

SHORT ANSWER TYPE QUESTIONS

1. Define the following under the Workman's Compensation Act, 1923:

   (a) Dependent, (b) Employer
   (c) Partial Disablement (d) Total Disablement

2. Distinguish between Partial and Total Disablement.
3. When does the employer's liability for compensation arise?

LONG ANSWER TYPE QUESTIONS

1. Explain the expression 'accident arising out of and in the course of employment' as used in Sec 3 of the Workmen's Compensation Act, 1923.
2. State the circumstances under which employer shall not be liable to pay compensation.
3. When shall the contracting of the disease be deemed to be an injury by accident?
4. How is the amount of compensation calculated?
5. When is the compensation to be paid? What is the penalty for default?
6. Explain the provisions relating to principal's liability to pay compensation in case of contracting.
7. What are the defences available to an employer against a claim for compensation made by a workman under the Workman's Compensation Act, 1923?

APPENDIX

I Important Distinctions

DISTINGUISH BETWEEN THE FOLLOWING:

1. Body Corporate and Company.
2. Company limited by shares and company limited by Guarantee.
3. Private Company and Public Company.
4. Preliminary Contracts and Provisional Contracts.
5. Memorandum of Association and Articles of Association.
6. Shelf Prospectus and Red-herring Prospectus.
7. Demartialisation and Rematerialisation of Shares.
8. Brokerage and Underwriting.
9. Calls-in-arrears and Calls-in-advance.
10. Share Certificate and Share Warrant.
11. Transfer and Transmission of Shares.
12. Forfeiture and Surrender of Shares.
13. Lien on Shares and Forfeiture of Shares.
14. Authorised Capital and Issued Capital.
15. Reserve Capital and Capital Reserve.
16. Share and Stock.
17. An Equity Share and a Preference Share.
18. Reduction of Share Capital and Diminution of Share Capital.
19. Member and Shareholder.
20. Interim Dividend and Final Dividend.
21. Bonus Shares and Right Shares.
22. Ordinary Business and Special Business.
23. Ordinary Resolution and Special Resolution.
24. Independent Director and Alternate Director.
25. Additional Director and Alternate Director.

APPENDIX II

Important Short Notes

WRITE SHORT NOTES ON THE FOLLOWING:

1. One man company
2. Common Seal and Perpetual Succession
3. Lifting of Corporate Veil
4. Licensed Company u/s 25
5. Government Company
6. Holding and Subsidiary Company
7. Public Financial Institutions
8. Illegal Association u/s 11
9. Legal Position and Remuneration of Promoters
10. Liability of Promoters for Preliminary Contracts
11. Provisional Contracts
12. Doctrine of Ultra Vires
13. Doctrine of Constructive Notice
14. Doctrine of Indoor Management/Rule in Turquand Case
15. Restrictions on Alteration of Articles
16. Rule of Golden Legacy
17. Misleading Prospectus
18. Deemed Prospectus
19. Shelf Prospectus
20. Abridged Prospectus
21. Red-herring Prospectus
22. Statement in lieu of Prospectus
23. Expert in Prospectus
24. Book Building
25. Dematerialisation of Shares
26. Irregular Allotment
27. Return of Allotment
28. Requisites of a valid call on shares
29. Sweat Equity Shares
30. Buy-back of Shares
31. Right Shares
32. Certificate of Transfer
33. Lien on Share
34. Reduction of Share Capital

35. Position of Minor and firm as member in a company
36. Unpaid/Unclaimed Dividend
37. Investor Education and Protection Fund
38. Payment of Interest out of Capital
39. Revolation of declared Dividend
40. Appointment of Directors by Board
41. Limit on No. of Directorships
42. Alternative Director
43. Additional Director
44. Statutory Meeting
45. Annual General Meeting
46. Extra Ordinary Meeting
47. Statutory Report
48. Notice in case of an Annual General Meeting
49. Resolution requiring Special Notice
50. Explanatory Statement
51. Quorum and Proxy
52. Consequences of default in holding Statutory Meeting and Annual General Meeting
53. Postal Ballot
54. Grounds for Compulsory Winding up by Tribunal
55. Just and Equitable Grounds for Winding up by Tribunal
56. Corporate Governance
57. Independent Directors
58. Audit Committee
59. Meaning and Formation of Producer Company
60. Permanent Partial Disablement and Permanent Total Disablement under the ESI Act, 1948.
61. Disablement Benefit under the ESI Act, 1948.
62. Medical Benefit under the ESI Act, 1948.
63. Benefits under the ESI Act, 1948.
64. Partial and Total Disablement under the Workman's Compensation Act, 1923.
65. Employer's liability for Compensation under the Workmen's Compensation Act, 1923.
66. 'Accident arising out of and in the course of employment.'

Special Revisional Test Paper

1. (a) What is meant by Lifting the Corporate Veil? State any three circumstances under which the veil of a company can be lifted by the Court.
   (b) "A limited company can be formed without the word 'limited' as the last word of its name" Comment.
   (c) What is meant by Guarantee Company? State the similarities and dissimilarities between a Guarantee company and a company having Share Capital.
   (d) Define Private Company and Holding & Subsidiary Company.
   (e) State the procedure for conversion of a public company into a private company.
   (f) State the procedure for conversion of a private company into a public company.
   (g) Distinguish between Preliminary Contracts and Provision Contracts.
   (h) Define 'Public Financial Institutions' u/s 4A.
   (i) "A subsidiary company can be member of its holding company." Comment.
2. (a) State the purposes for which 'Object Clause' can be altered.
   (b) Briefly state the procedure to alter Object Clause and Name Clause.
   (c) Briefly state the procedure to alter Registered Office—
   (i) Within the same state,
   (ii) from one state to another state
   (d) Briefly explain the Doctrine of Constructive Notice. State the exception to this doctrine. Also state the exceptions to the exception to the Doctrine of Construction Notice.
   (e) Briefly explain the Doctrine of Ultravires. State the consequences of ultravires acts.
   (f) Briefly state the limitations relating to alteration of Articles of Association of company.
3. (a) Define the following terms under the Companies Act, 1956:
   (i) Prospectus, (ii) Public, (iii) Shelf Prospectus, (iv) Red-herring Prospectus, (v) Apridged Prospectus, (vi) Deemed Prospectus, (viii) Misleading prospectus, (viii) Statement in lieu of Prospectus
   (b) What is misleading prospectus? State the remedies available against a company to a subscriber on the faith of misleading prospectus.
   (c) Who is an expert? When is an expert not liable for the mis-statement in the prospectus.
4. (a) State the meaning of 'Sweat Equity Shares' and the conditions for the issue of such shares.
   (b) State the source of funds that can be utilized by the company for purchasing its own shares and the requirements to be compiled with before and after the shares are so purchased.
   (c) State the meaning and effects of Irregular Allotment.
   (d) Briefly state the conditions and procedure for the forfeiture of shares.

(e) Distinguish between the following:
(i) Transfer and Transmission of Shares
(ii) Forfeiture and Surrender of Shares
(iii) Share Certificate and Share Warrant
(iv) Diminution of Capital and Reduction of Capital.
(f) State the procedure for the reduction of share capital.
(g) State the conditions for the payment of underwriting commission.

5. (a) Distinguish between Members and Shareholders.
(b) State the position of the following with regard to membership in a company:
(i) Minor (ii) An insolvent (iii) Partnership Firm

6. (a) State the provisions relating to declaration and payment of dividend.
(b) State the provisions relating to establishment of an 'Investors Education and Protection Fund.'
(c) 'Interest can be paid out of capital'. Comment.
(d) State SEBI Guidelines as to issue of Bonus Shares.

7. (a) How are the first directors appointed?
(b) How are directors appointed by the Board?
(c) State the qualification and disqualification of a director of a company.
(d) Distinguish between Additional Directors and Alternate Directors.

8. (a) Explain the provisions relating to holding of Statutory Meeting/Annual General Meeting/Extra Ordinary Meeting.
(b) State any four matters which require:
(i) Ordinary Resolution (ii) Special Resolution (iii) Special Notice
(c) State the provisions relating to Notice, Quorum and Proxy of General Meeting of Members.
(d) State the procedure for transacting business of the General Meeting through Postal Ballot.

9. (a) State the circumstances under which the Tribunal can order for the compulsory winding up of a company.
(b) State the circumstances under which the Tribunal can order for the compulsory winding up of a company on just and equitable grounds.

10. Write short notes on the following:
(a) Corporate Governance (b) Audit Committee
(c) Producer Company (d) Independent Directors

11. (a) Explain the terms 'Permanent Partial Disablement, Permanent Total Disablement' and Disablement Benefit under the ESI Act, 1948.
(b) Explain the conditions which must be observed by the recipient of disablement benefits under the Employees' Statement Insurance Act, 1948.
(c) State the provisions of the ESI Act, 1948 for the payment of medical benefit.
(d) State the provisions relating to various benefits available to an employee under the ESI Act, 1948.

12. (a) Define the following under the Workmen's Compensation Act, 1923:
(a) Dependent, (b) Employer
(c) Partial Disablement (d) Total Disablement
(b) Distinguish between Partial and Total Disablement.
(c) When does the employer's liability for compensation arise?
(d) Explain the expression 'accident arising out of and in the course of employment' as used in Sec 3 of the Workmen's Compensation Act, 1923.
(e) What are the defences available to an employer against a claim for compensation made by a workman under the Workmen's Compensation Act, 1923?

(e) Distinguish between the following:
(i) Transfer and Transmission of Shares
(ii) Forfeiture and Surrender of Shares
(iii) Share Certificate and Share Warrant
(iv) Diminution of Capital and Reduction of Capital
(f) State the procedure for the reduction of share capital.
(g) State the conditions for the payment of underwriting commission.

5. (a) Distinguish between Members and Shareholders.
(b) State the position of the following with regard to membership in a company:
(i) Minor (ii) An insolvent (iii) Partnership Firm

6. (a) State the provisions relating to declaration and payment of dividend.
(b) State the provisions relating to establishment of an Investors Education and Protection Fund.
(c) Interest can be paid out of capital. Comment.
(d) State SEBI Guidelines as to issue of Bonus Shares.

7. (a) How are the first directors appointed?
(b) How are directors appointed by the Board?
(c) State the qualification and disqualification of a director of a company.
(d) Distinguish between Additional Directors and Alternate Directors.

8. (a) Explain the provisions relating to holding of Statutory Meeting/Annual General Meeting/Extra Ordinary Meeting.
(b) State any four matters which require:
(i) Ordinary Resolution (ii) Special Resolution (iii) Special Notice
(c) State the provisions relating to Notice, Quorum and Proxy of General Meeting of Members.
(d) State the procedure for transacting business of the General Meeting through Postal Ballot.

9. (a) State the circumstances under which the Tribunal can order for the compulsory winding up of a company.
(b) State the circumstances under which the Tribunal can order for the compulsory winding up of a company on just and equitable grounds.

10. Write short notes on the following:
(a) Corporate Governance (b) Audit Committee
(c) Producer Company (d) Independent Directors

11. (a) Explain the terms Permanent Partial Disablement, Permanent Total Disablement and Disablement Benefit under the ESI Act, 1948.
(b) Explain the conditions which must be observed by the recipient of disablement benefits under the Employees State Insurance Act, 1948.
(c) State the provisions of the ESI Act, 1948 for the payment of medical benefit.
(d) State the provisions relating to various benefits available to an employee under the ESI Act, 1948.

12. (a) Define the following under the Workmen's Compensation Act, 1923:
(a) Dependent (b) Employer
(c) Partial Disablement (d) Total Disablement
(b) Distinguish between Partial and Total Disablement.
(c) When does the employer's liability for compensation arise?
(d) Explain the expression 'accident arising out of and in the course of employment' as used in Sec. 3 of the Workmen's Compensation Act, 1923.
(e) What are the defences available to an employer against a claim for compensation made by a workman under the Workmen's Compensation Act, 1923?